Era3 of humanity:

Shape Paradise or Slip into Hell

Aviel Verbruggen

Published by Mayfly Books. Available in paperback
and free online at www.mayflybooks.org in 2025.

ISBN (Print)   978-1-906948-78-8
ISBN (PDF)   978-1-906948-79-5

Cover art work by Jess Parker who retains the image copyright.

may f l y

Era3 of humanity:

Shape Paradise or Slip into Hell

Aviel Verbruggen

Preface

This book explores the intertwined issues of climate change, energy, oil geopolitics, neoliberalism, human behaviour, and community governance, which are responsible for the grim conflicts and calamitous impacts that abound today.

Several authors[1] on climate change report facts and forecasts in *apocalyptic phrasing*, as actuated by St. John the Divine in the *Book of Revelation*. St. John's[2] intent was to encourage the emerging, yet dispersed and unsure Christian communities, to overcome numerous threats in striving for a blessed future. The victory over evil required three main achievements: the disciples had to adopt and maintain a steadfast and alert moral disposition[3], the deceiving narratives by fraudulent antichrists had to be revealed and rejected, and liberation implied the destruction of *Babylon*, a secret reference to the satanic forces of the Roman Empire. St. John, exiled to the island of Patmos, was a rebellious prophet during the persecution of Christian followers by Rome.

Two millennia later, humankind faces similar challenges: profound socio-economic inequalities paired with aggressive exploitation of people and nature foreshadowing ecological collapse; public discourse larded with flawed narratives and *delusive truths*[4]; the reliance on *Big Money* and manipulative power, activating conflicts and wars, while eroding the living conditions of the majority. The steadfast and alert face enormous tasks and dangers to beat the monsters of neoliberalism.

This interdisciplinary book adopts the device of *Let's go and see*[5]. It holds stern analyses and disquieting confrontations with mainstream economic thinking and its fallout in the mainstream media. The confrontations open perspectives about necessary, possible, and desirable actions to dismantle major threats and reveal paths to a peaceful future. To preserve focus and reasonable size, the book skips apocalyptic descriptions of physical phenomena and deleterious impacts of climate change[6] and other woes. They are documented in numerous publications. How human beings suffer from climate change impacts is visible daily on TV and other media[7].

Part I of the book recalls and unveils material-societal truths about energy – renewable, atomic, hydrogen, and fossil. The first chapter tells us what energy really is. Full attention to energy is necessary because it is impossible to develop a meaningful strategy for climate change without addressing the central role of energy. Covering the world of energy is not just techno-economics. Immediately, one faces Big Money, lobbyism, discursive power with delusive truths, ... realities of the present world.

Part II addresses politics and money in its functions of exchange vehicle, debt and credit, savings and accumulation, exploitation and extortion. Neoliberalism is defined by three substantive attributes and three main pillars. For the analysis, some basic terms and concepts of economics are introduced. Neoclassical economics and their recipes are debunked as delusions, favoured and broadcast by dominating neoliberal narratives. This reveals several deceptions that impede the realisation of the ready and available solutions for the myriad crises. Searching for proper ways to address the energy, climate and societal problems is invigorating.

Part III explores how to make Our Common Future of Sustainable Development. Transformation of energy systems is an economically beneficial and prerequisite component in addressing the climate crisis and ending neoliberalism. The building of democratic communities is helped by all sciences, techno-economic and human-social-political disciplines. After processing and clarifying several elements substantiating the analysis and propositions, I sought to formulate a consistent strategy for designing and walking paths of transformation. However, standard strategic planning is too constrained in scope to develop the required novel insights and suggestions. Therefore, the book is completed not by a standard chapter, but by an essay in thinking out-of-the-box.

My life path has been erratic and appealing, stimulated by a dynamic balance of fortunes and adversities. This book is written during years of exile, silenced by the neoliberal media, eclipsed by neoclassical economists and by complacent politicians and bureaucrats. Thanks to my opponents, I had the time and distance to observe the slip into hell caused by the neoliberal regime, and to discover the narrow path to escape the collapse of climate and humanity.

Contents

Dedication

An invention is reinvented until invented at the right time[8], *and Ideas are revisited until they are proclaimed at the right time.* This book leans on the work of numerous persons whose published results, engagement, or interaction have contributed to my personal formation and academic work. Naming all those who influenced my ideas and activities would fill pages and still be incomplete. Referencing via endnotes provides information about important sources for writing the book.

Let me dedicate the work to my companion activists of Extinction Rebellion, Scientist Rebellion, Youth for Climate, grassroots initiatives and communities, independent critical media, NGOs and initiatives against war and genocide, and so many pioneers already constructing exemplary projects and communities. I hope they accept a major suggestion of this book: stop wasting time and effort spent on *asking and pressing neoliberal regime leaders* to bring solutions to the climate and societal crises they occasion. Transformation comes from resolve and action by ordinary people from the grassroots, bottom-up, with inevitable destruction of neoliberalism. Destroy neoliberalism before it destroys you and hope for a human future for your children and grandchildren.

About the author

Aviel Verbruggen (born 1949) is Emeritus Professor at the University of Antwerp, Belgium. Engaged in 50 years of interdisciplinary research, covering engineering thermodynamics, electric power generation with Combined Heat & Power and on-site independent production units as contenders of centralised, vertically integrated incumbents, he graduated (Ma, PhD) in applied quantitative economics, later adding political economy. As project leader of the Flemish State-of-the-Environment reports, he has in-depth knowledge of environmental issues, particularly climate change. From 1998 to 2014, he contributed to IPCC-Working Group III.

Motto: *"Prefer to speak true words receiving blame, above deceiving advice in soliciting praise."*

The site www.avielverbruggen.be holds a repository of publications and lectures.

Glossary

This glossary describes known and novel terms (in italic, specific to this book).

Big Money: The group of people and organisations, financial and industrial corporations that command large fortunes; they are the founders and beneficiaries of neoliberalism

Business-as-Usual (BaU): Continuation of practices, thinking, expectations, planning, etc., without disruptive change. BaU is not a standstill. Part of BaU is autonomous technological, social, economic, and cultural innovation. Absent are disruptive, transformative changes[9].

Captive customers: Electricity consumers buy their power from the grid on the terms of an access contract without owning practical means to exert pressure on the supplier by generating their own power. Captive customers are being cheated by monopoly prices.

Delusive truth: Stealth and fake narrative. Construct a counterfeit of a truth, such as a law of physics, a mathematical theory, or an observed fact. Delusive because materialising the truth is impossible or nonsensical. An example is Archimedes' *I lift the Earth with a fulcrum and a lever*. Undeniable truths are the levers of physics and practice. The plain delusion of lifting the Earth is easy to recognise and innocuous because no resources have been wasted on it. Desperate delusive truths are atomic power [chapter 3], the hydrogen energy economy [chapter 4], and the EU Emissions Trading System [chapter 8].

Fringe price is a surrogate for **marginal cost price**. A fringe price is linked to the edge of an economic activity, while not reflecting its entirety. Some fringe prices are proxies of marginal cost prices; many are deliberate falsifications, deceiving the citizenry. Section 7.3 explains fringe pricing in detail, with examples in sections 7.4 and 8.6.

Marginal cost price: In a competitive market, demand for and supply of a good or service are equilibrated at a price equal to the short-run marginal cost of the aggregated supply by numerous producers. The pursued equilibrium engenders the highest welfare, as the sum of consumers' benefits and producers' profits. This theoretical ideal is rarely observed in practice.

Masterminding of public policy processes is the neoliberal substitute for *capturing regulations* established by autonomous public authorities. For Big Money, masterminding is the most effective and efficient, without divulgence and responsibility. Neoliberal think tanks, academics, officials, media, and politicians conceive, shape and defend neoliberal recipes according to the agenda of corporations and big money. Masterminding is illustrated in section 2.7 and chapter 8.

Neoliberalism: The socio-political regime that has grown out of liberalism since the 1970s and was politically adopted by Margaret Thatcher (1979–1990) in the UK and Ronald Reagan (1981–1988) in the US. The attributes and pillars of neoliberalism are described in chapter 6, section 6.2.

Political economy *is the study of rational decisions in a context of political and economic institutions*[10]. *Rational decisions* refer to economic actors maximising utility and profit. The context of institutions is *political*. Practising political economy faces icebergs with one-tenth visible and decisive parts beneath the waterline. Political economy bridges the gap between economics and political science. It was standard economics from Adam Smith in 1776 to the last quarter of the 19th century, when neoclassical theory took over, and evolved into academic time-spending, distant from the real world.

Super profits are revenues without effort, called **rents** by the World Bank. Chapter 5 reveals the billions of US dollars of super profits captured by petrostates, speculators, and oil & gas corporations since 1970. The European electricity corporations cashed in on super profits in the EU ETS, and during the gas price crisis in 2022, were paid mainly by their captive customers. Profits without effort typically occur when firms wield oligopoly or monopoly power.

Sustainable Development (SD): In the jungle of terms around sustainable, the book uses Sustainable Development and SD to refer exclusively to the description (definition) of the World Commission on Environment and Development in *Our Common Future* (WCED, 1986, chapters 1 and 2).

Abbreviations and Acronyms

Abbreviation/ Acronym	Statement
C	Chemical symbol for carbon.
CAP & TRADE	Economic instrument for reducing emissions, effluents, and waste. Public authorities put a cap on the total quantity of emissions and the regulated actors can trade the emissions permits they own or need.
CBA	Cost-Benefit Analysis to assess whether projects or proposed projects are beneficial. Costs should include private expenses and public loss and damage. Benefits are material and non-material returns for the community.
CC	Climate change.
CCS	Carbon Capture & Storage of carbon dioxide. Now, this is often extended to CCUS, where U stands for the **use** of some captured carbon.
CHP	Combined Heat & Power, also known as Cogeneration. Thermal electricity generation units equipped to deliver heat above ambient temperature.
CO_2; CO_2-eq	Carbon dioxide, the main greenhouse gas, is mainly produced by combustion of fossil fuels. Carbon dioxide equivalent is a measure of the greenhouse effect of non-CO_2 greenhouse gases.
COP	Conference of the Parties of the UNFCCC. In 1995, the first conference (COP1) took place in Berlin. Afterwards, it has taken place annually, such as COP3 in Kyoto (1997), COP15 in Copenhagen (2009), COP21 in Paris (2015).
EEX; EPEX	European Energy Exchange (Leipzig) is a trading platform for energy and related products; EPEX is the European Power Exchange, a subsidiary of EEX. EEX also provides a platform for speculative trading in ETS permits.
EPA	Environmental Protection Agency, usually refers to the US environmental administration established in 1970.
ETS	Emissions Trading System = system of trading greenhouse gas emissions permits. One permit = 1000 kg CO_2-eq emissions.
EU ETS	European Union Emissions Trading Scheme / System.
GCC	Gulf Cooperation Council. A council for consultation between the Arab oil & gas states around the Arabian/Persian Gulf. Saudi Arabia, United Arab Emirates, Qatar, Oman, Kuwait, Bahrain.
GHG	Greenhouse Gases. IPCC focuses on six gases: carbon dioxide CO_2, methane CH_4, nitrous oxide N_2O, and three fluor F gases. The non-CO_2 gases' radiative forcing is the variable to obtain their CO_2-eq value.
H/H_2	Hydrogen atom/molecule.
IAEA	International Atomic Energy Agency (IAEA). Established in 1957 to promote atomic nuclear energy and monitor the proliferation of atomic weapons, and headquartered in Vienna.
IEA	International Energy Agency (IEA). Established in 1975 by the OECD (Organisation for Economic Cooperation and Development), and based in Paris. Member countries of the OECD and the IEA are rich countries.
IGOP	Independent Generator of Own Power, a more precise name than Prosumer (contraction of Producer-Consumer), and Independent Power Producer (IPP).
IMF	International Monetary Fund. Established as part of the Bretton Woods Agreement (1944) on a post-war monetary framework centred around the US dollar.

IPCC	Intergovernmental Panel on Climate Change (climate panel), established in 1988. It has three working groups (WG1, WG2, WG3) differentiated by their contents, as well as the quality of the reports delivered.
IRENA	International Renewable Energy Agency. Founded in 2009, headquartered in Abu Dhabi.
LNG	Liquid Natural Gas. Natural gas is liquefied at by cooling to -162°C at close to atmospheric pressure.
MSR	Market Stability Reserve, a mechanism added to the EU ETS in 2019 to manage the quantity of surplus permits.
NATO	North Atlantic Treaty Organisation.
NGO	Non-Governmental Organisation (of any kind, with any objectives).
NPT	Non-Proliferation Treaty, or the treaty to prevent the proliferation of nuclear weapons. IAEA should monitor compliance with this treaty.
O/O_2	Oxygen atom/molecule.
OPEC and OPEC+	Organisation of the Petroleum Exporting Countries. Consists of two groups of countries, to agree on quantities of oil & gas supplies.
OSCE	Organisation for Security and Cooperation in Europe.
PEM	Proton Exchange Membrane fuel cell/electrolysis.
PV	Photovoltaic: a process by which a current of light (photons) is converted into an electric current.
RE	Renewable Energy / Electricity.
R/P	R/P = Reserves / Production of oil in a given year = # of years the oil sector is prepared to supply to the global market, and published annually by BP.
SMR	Small Modular Reactors (for nuclear power plants).
SO_2	Sulphur dioxide is a gas produced mainly during the combustion of coal and crude oil containing sulphur. The precipitation of SO_2 and H_2SO_4 (sulphuric acid) on buildings and crops is known as 'acid rain'.
SRMC	Short Run Marginal Cost: the *avoidable* cost of the last produced unit by an aggregate of supply sources. Avoidable cost is primarily the variable cost; in electricity generation, it is mainly the fuel cost.
UK	United Kingdom (of Great Britain and Northern Ireland).
UNDP	The United Nations Development Programme, which publishes annual Human Development Reports.
UNESCO	United Nations Educational, Scientific and Cultural Organisation.
UNFCCC	United Nations Framework Convention on Climate Change: a framework agreement on tackling climate change agreed in 1992 at the World Summit in Rio de Janeiro (see also COP).
US	United States (of America).
W, kW, MW, MWe	W, abbreviation of Watt (= Joule/second), being the unit of power in energy and electricity. kW = 1,000 W, MW = 1,000,000 W = 1,000 kW, MWe is a symbol to indicate electrical power.
WB	World Bank, a bank that emerged from the Bretton Woods accord of 1944 (like the IMF).
Wh, kWh, MWh	Wh = (Joule/s) x 3600s = 3,600 Joules = an amount of energy; kWh = 3,600,000 Joules (3.6 Mega Joules) MWh = 3,600,000,000 Joules (3.6 Giga Joules)

List of figures

Introduction

The introduction introduces major themes and crosscutting aspects of the book. By treating these upstream, repetitive overlaps are avoided.

1. Global political challenge #1: Climate Change

Climate change, driven by global warming, is the foremost global challenge, exacerbating other major calamities on Earth[11]. The primary global policy goals are to limit *the increase in the global average temperature to well below 2°C above pre-industrial levels*, and pursue efforts *to limit the temperature increase to 1.5°C*. In 2009, the largest countries' political heads defined and adopted these goals at COP15 in Copenhagen. It took six years before the Paris COP21 reaffirmed the goals.

Atmospheric warming is determined by the concentration of greenhouse gases (GHGs). The concentration indicates the thickness of the GHG blanket around the globe. The thicker the blanket, the higher the temperature will rise. The steadily increasing concentration is due to annual gigatons of GHG emissions caused by human activities.

Figure 1 shows the trends in GHG emissions and the atmospheric GHG concentration over the past few decades. Since 1970, four pauses in the annual emissions of GHGs have been observed: in the mid-1970s due to the oil price increase; at the beginning of the 1980s due to advancing energy efficiency; around 2008 due to the global financial crisis; and in 2020 due to the COVID-19 lockdowns. Despite these pauses, the trend remains upward due to *business-as-usual* production and consumption[12] activities. GHG emissions can decrease, even to very low levels, when the global population engages in the necessary mitigation actions.

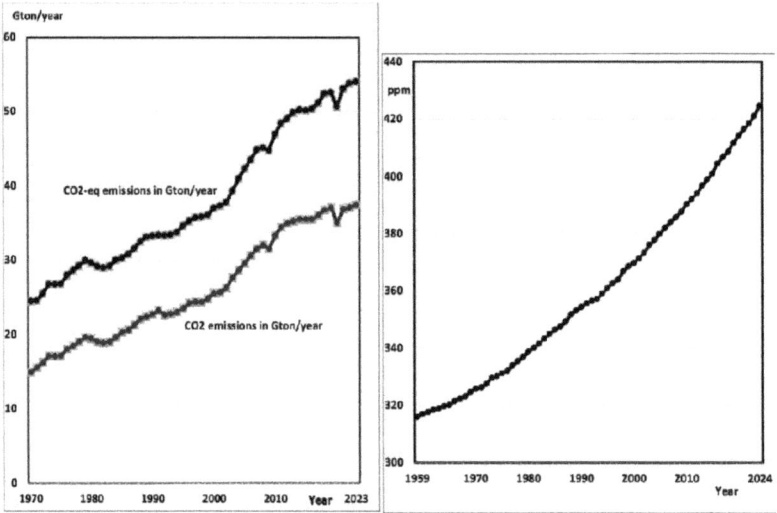

Figure 1: Rising greenhouse gas emissions and concentration reflect failing climate policies (data source: Statista.com)

While emissions can be halted at any time, the accumulated concentration in the atmosphere cannot decrease in the coming centuries. The maximum result of a zero GHG emissions scenario is a stationary concentration. The concentration level and the ensuing damage caused to ecosystems, environmental amenities, and human habitats are *irreversible for centuries*. Despite its crucial importance, *irreversibility* is often poorly understood[13] and overlooked by policymakers. In addition to irreversibility, the delayed and feedforward effects of increased GHG concentrations make climate change an utterly precarious problem. This all loads a heavy responsibility on past, present and future policymakers related to energy and climate.

The curves in figure 1 underscore the *ineffectiveness of policies and political actions* up to 2025 in halting the rise of GHG concentration in the atmosphere. Despite the commissioning of hundreds of atomic power plants during the 1960s to 1980s, numerous reports from the

IPCC and UN agencies, and a series of international summits, high-level meetings, COPs, complicated emissions trading mechanisms, etc. from the 1990s to the 2020s, the steep climb in ppm concentration has not been curbed. This uncurbed trend explains the unpredictable, shocking temperatures and weather irregularities worldwide, worsening yearly. Although all people observe and experience these changes firsthand, the gaps between *talk & walk, know & act* remain significantly large[14].

GHG emissions are mostly linked to the direct or indirect use of fossil fuels and biofuels. Fuel use is unevenly spread globally, with wealthy and industrialising nations using the lion's share of fossil fuels. The effects of climate change are also globally uneven, with vulnerable nations suffering the most damaging impacts.

The global nature of climate change was formally acknowledged in 1992 at the Rio Summit[15]. However, the accompanying top-down policies largely failed and continue to do so, overshadowing the needed multi-level and polycentric governance[16] approaches, with a solid basis for community governance.

This observation warns that uniform solutions are ineffective in addressing highly heterogeneous realities. Developing community and polycentric governance requires a deep dive into institutional design and human behaviour, with full attention to context-specific factors and effects[17]. The intricacies of actual governance are further discussed in part III.

2. Context factors framing the book's analyses
Figure 2 shows a context description wherein societal transformations take place. The description enlarges the *Actors-Ideas-Interests-Institutions* framework familiar to social scientists[18]. MIGRANTS are explicitly added among the usual Actors. Techno-economic factors are included. *Infrastructures* refer to the world of things, abundantly available in the Global North, but too scarce in the global South. Crucial is the *Substratum of energy and technology*, on which every society is built[19]. Energy and technology are precursors and drivers of societal transformations, and an indispensable, major component of

effective climate policy.

ACTORS are categorised into two groups: the 500 million EU Actors and the 7,500 million non-EU Actors. A significant portion of this book focuses on Europe. The 7,500 million non-EU global citizens are a reminder that proposals and actions without global solutions fall short in addressing climate issues. The inclusion of MIGRANTS signals potential shifts in the 500/7,500 ratio. If solutions do not come to people where they live, people will seek them elsewhere[20]. Migration is more closely tied to energy and climate policy in the Global North than is usually mentioned. Actors pursue their goals by building, managing and enduring a multitude of *Ideas, Interests, Institutions*, and *Infrastructures* intertwined with a *Substrate of Energy & Technology*.

IDEAS influence and determine people's thoughts and motivations, from which attitudes and actions follow. Ideas in the form of Myths, Narratives, Ideologies, and Paradigms greatly influence and legitimise the actions and positions of certain groups of actors. Donella Meadows[21] argues that new systems arise from the mindset or paradigm, being the real influential leverage point. Manipulated Ideas, Symbols and Language can create flawed thinking patterns and blinding beliefs in people's minds. From the 1980s to the present, Myths, Discourse and Ideology of neoliberalism define the dominant paradigm. In industrial countries, most people have been caught up in the dogma of unlimited economic growth. The wielding of power by the super-rich and giant corporations is shrouded in myths and rhetoric of *free markets* and *democratic* regimes. In reality, oligopoly and monopoly power of the big corporations have marginalised the true free market and forced it to the fringes of economic activity. Small-scale economic activities with direct citizen supervision preclude the unfair power games of neoliberalism. To what extent can one consider regimes democratic when Big Money determines the election of professional politicians? The US, the world's largest so-called democracy, is a salient example. Meanwhile, institutions that support neoliberalism continue to expand and strengthen[22].

INTERESTS refer to various manifestations. The dominance of financial-economic power is central to Money, especially *Big Money*.

The giant projects and investments driven by Big Money interests extend beyond the financial statements of corporations. Often, they cause negative impacts on the environment and society, such as pollution, damage to flora, fauna and human health, and the overall destruction of life-support systems. Climate change is now an obvious example. Private interests pass on the harmful effects to the people, communities and future generations.

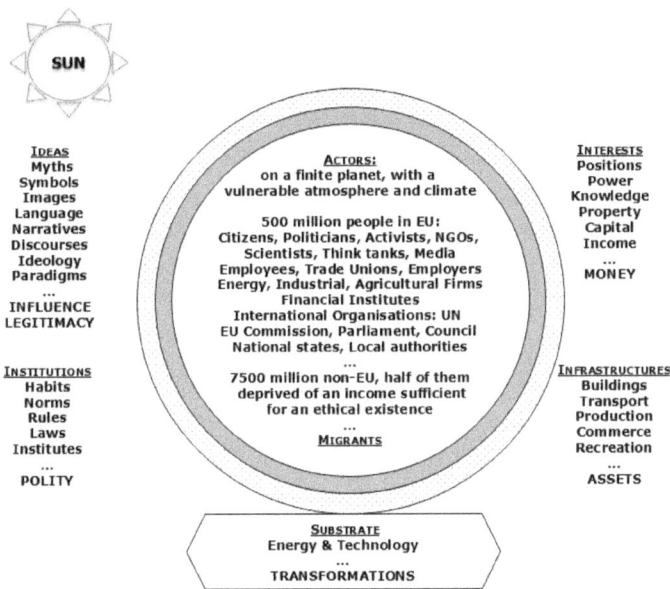

```
        SUN

IDEAS                    ACTORS:                    INTERESTS
Myths              on a finite planet, with a       Positions
Symbols          vulnerable atmosphere and climate  Power
Images                                               Knowledge
Language           500 million people in EU:         Property
Narratives    Citizens, Politicians, Activists, NGOs, Capital
Discourses        Scientists, Think tanks, Media     Income
Ideology      Employees, Trade Unions, Employers      ...
Paradigms    Energy, Industrial, Agricultural Firms   MONEY
  ...                Financial Institutes
INFLUENCE      International Organisations: UN
LEGITIMACY   EU Commission, Parliament, Council
               National states, Local authorities
INSTITUTIONS              ...                      INFRASTRUCTURES
Habits           7500 million non-EU, half of them   Buildings
Norms            deprived of an income sufficient    Transport
Rules              for an ethical existence          Production
Laws                       ...                       Commerce
Institutes              MIGRANTS                      Recreation
  ...                                                   ...
POLITY                                               ASSETS

                       SUBSTRATE
                  Energy & Technology
                        ...
                  TRANSFORMATIONS
```

Figure 2: Overview of context FACTORS wherein ACTORS function when addressing Climate Change

INSTITUTIONS are the social fabric through which people interact with each other in a civilised manner. They enable the realisation and protection of the common good, including a high and well-distributed prosperity. Many institutions are inherited from generation to generation. They are customs, shared norms, unwritten rules of respect, reciprocity, and benevolence. These unwritten institutions are the foundation of trust for formal institutions. Political institutions enact rules and laws, providing the legal, administrative, communicative, social, economic, and scientific structures that shape modern societies and enhance the quality of life.

INFRASTRUCTURES are the tangible real estate upon which societies function and prosper. Drastic and urgent change is often hindered by large and long-lived structures that are partly publicly owned and partly owned by private companies. When governments consider removing certain privately owned infrastructures, discussions about *stranded investments* often arise, requiring governments to provide reimbursement. Compensation is sometimes a negotiated amount of money, but mostly legally enforced[23]. Transforming energy systems to avoid climate collapse necessitates the removal of significant portions of outdated infrastructure. Continuing to invest in outdated infrastructure such as thermal power plants, LNG terminals, and oil tankers poses a significant obstacle to achieving zero carbon emissions.

In figure 2, *Energy & Technology* are assigned the place and role of substrate on which the myriad activities of Actors thrive. Several chapters address the essential role of Energy & Technology, extending the study beyond technical aspects to highlight their connections with social factors such as Actors, Interests, Ideas and Institutions.

Figure 2 helps draw attention to factors other than one's speciality. Research is often set up to address infrastructure issues. For example, research on mobility for people and transport of goods will deal with vehicles, roads, tracks, waterways, etc. To obtain socially useful results and recommendations, the researchers should also consider the broader context of Ideas, Interests, Institutions, Energy & Technology.

3. Disciplinary perspectives and analyses

The new world is a polycentric, multi-nodal, multi-sector, multi-level, multi-actor, multi-logic, multi-media, multi-practice place characterised by complexity, dynamism, uncertainty and ambiguity in which a wide range of actors are engaged in public value creation and do so in shifting configurations[24]. This staggered description is hard to digest, yet leaves an impression of the kind of world in which climate change is happening, and wherein drastic reductions of GHG emissions are due.

How can *scientists* effectively tackle the immense societal problems?

First and foremost, they can do so through valid scientific research and advice that is fact-based, transparent and practically useful. The diversity and scale of problems call for coherent and comprehensive investigations across nearly all scientific disciplines, interconnected as cross-, multi-, inter- or trans-disciplinary research. In such a *broad* scope, problems are approached from multiple angles, and different methods are integrated to fully synthesise *deep* knowledge. Ideally, this would involve *broad & deep* multidisciplinary work. However, this is cumbersome and takes many years, especially in the social sciences. In most real-life situations, a choice between *broad & shallow* versus *deep & narrow* approaches is imposed by lack of time, funds, or available expertise.

Both shallow multi-disciplinarity and deep mono-disciplinarity fall short in addressing the challenges raised by climate change and the required policies. Academics tend to see their discipline as central or overarching. For example, neoclassical economists impose their uniform recipes in top-down climate politics, like global carbon emission permit trading[25] or a harmonised global carbon tax, without considering the broader, multifaceted context.

A single author evidently cannot sufficiently master the intricacies of many scientific disciplines; hence, I had to make choices. First, I prioritise *deep* analysis without overly focusing on any discipline. Where necessary for the coherence of the argumentation, I incorporate insights from multiple fields. Second, the analyses are grounded in *facts, transparency,* and *practical relevance.* Third, I adopt a *spearhead* approach prioritising climate change as the foremost global challenge, which societally necessitates the substantial and rapid reduction of GHG emissions. Fourth, the focus is on *energy & technology* as key topics, given that over 80% of GHG emissions are linked to the use of energy in fossil and biofuels.

In part I of the book, the essential disciplines include physics, engineering, neoclassical economics, political economy, and political philosophy. Parts II and III explore the future of societal functioning, drawing on a broad range of social sciences, such as philosophy, political science, sociology, and psychology. Incorporating social sciences literature strengthens the book's argumentation, without claiming to offer exhaustive depth in any of the visited fields.overall, the book bridges three major knowledge fields of primary importance for understanding climate change and climate policy: energy & technology, economics & political economy, and some highlights from human & socio-political sciences. The interdisciplinary approach ensures a broader perspective, incorporating diverse insights and viewpoints, reducing the risk of confinement to a single discipline. The outcome resembles a laminated bundling of several disciplines rather than an integrated multi-disciplinary construction.

The book's content is consistently marked by themes of polity, policies and politics. However, it does not delve deeply into political science[26]. Political tension and conflict are woven throughout the analyses by intentionally avoiding the use of 'we' and 'our' language. Such inclusive terminology is confusing and apolitical, masking the conflicting interests among different groups within society. A rough but useful societal classification[27] distinguishes the 90% ordinary people from the 10% rich group. The heterogeneous familiar people range from the dispossessed half of humankind to the gradually more well-off workers whose livelihoods depend on their continuous hard work. At the wealthy top, about 9% of this group consists of highly paid, technically skilled professionals and courtiers who serve the interests of the 1% super-rich. This 10% rich group continue to enrich themselves at the expense of the ordinary people. They cause an outsized share of the GHG emissions and damage the climate and biodiversity. This group is unlikely to initiate or support the transformations needed to maintain a hospitable planet Earth.

The numerous initiatives and publications begging the responsible technocrats and organisations to change their minds and handling of the situation is a *waste of time and effort*. This statement follows from observing that the energy, technology and societal transformations for escaping climate collapse require revolutionary U-turns, and that real disruptive turns result from bottom-up grassroots actions[28]. Most bottom-up actions emerge suddenly, erratically, and unpredictably, when the underground societal magma, energised by inequality and social conflicts, erupts. Such eruptions and their aftermath do not obey desk designs of academics and officials, nor the commands of the incumbent political and economic power holders in the globalised neoliberal regimes. In light of the coming thunderstorms and turmoil, what positions will the rich, educated class take? Likely, a vast majority of the rich group simply serve the vested powers against people's interests and emerging bottom-up initiatives. A minority is concerned with and supportive of the transformative forces and actions.

Most academic literature on climate change addresses the *What & Why* questions, detailing the present and expected perilous state of nature and society. The mainstream literature and media do not reveal the *failure* of mainstream climate policies and politics, while they cause the continuing rise of GHG emissions. Absolutely frightening is the naive belief that Green Deal business-as-usual is capable of addressing climate change. Such a belief causes the curves in figure 1 to continue to rise. Explicating the failures and severely criticising present business and political practices and plans are necessary tasks, not a cynical pleasure. Investigation is due to how the super-rich maintain their privileges and interests, and how subservient intellectuals are instrumental in this maintenance. As a follow-up, attention should go to *Who* and *How* to end the business-as-usual. My vision is clear: without a complete transformation in energy use and the accompanying shifts in human activities and lifestyles, the Earth's mild climate and civilisation will face severe disruption. The necessary U-turns must happen now.

This book aims to shed light on the obstacles and opportunities faced by grassroots movements in the Global North and South. The necessary research, investigation and unravelling of delusive truths were tedious work. Yet, clear insight delivers hopeful findings: when neoliberalism crumbles, the dawn of a new era of human civilisation—era3—presents a path toward a more equitable and ethical way of life, offering the majority better opportunities and quality of life.

4. Intended readership

The book targets the attention of the many concerned citizens seeking more clarity about *who blocks* the available measures needed to address the ongoing ecological and societal crises, and *how* blockages can be removed. I have strived to compose a book that is *accessible, novel, scientific, and robust.*

Accessible: by means of clear language, avoiding technical jargon. Headlines and results come first, with extensive argumentation relegated to source documents. The formality of academic publishing is omitted. No references to published work or footnotes are inserted in the text; only superscript numbers point to endnotes. Each chapter starts by clarifying the contents of its sections, and ends with a reminder list of a few takeaways.

Novel: by means of disruptive analysis, findings, propositions, and perspectives, based on cross-disciplinary research. Revealing the major causes of the growing chaos and outlining the essential characteristics of humans' future in era3, may surprise many readers. It is important to be open-minded to inconvenient facts, novel ideas and propositions. Novel concepts are briefly described in the Glossary.

Scientific: by basing the statements and conclusions on performed research, publications, and experienced activities and processes. Readers curious for detail beyond the text may explore the endnote hints. Endnotes refer to a bibliography at the end of the book. Some also include brief information notes.

Robust policy analysis requests *comprehensiveness, coherence and specificity. Comprehensiveness* acknowledges the global scope of energy & climate policy, affecting all human activities, values, ideas, interests, institutions, and infrastructures [figure 2]. However, attempting to cover everything mostly results in a mess of generalities. The book skips the mess by focusing on the principal axes of societal functioning and spearheading policies. *Coherence* is achieved through respect for nested polycentric and multilevel institutions[29]. The granularity of institutions depends on the *diversity* of issues, actors, causes and solutions they address. A proper handling of heterogeneity means its decomposition into workable homogeneous parts, as many as required to obtain an appropriate degree of *specificity*, i.e., the application of the right approaches for particular problems. This seems complicated as decomposition is a complicated task[30]. The role of *small-scale, bottom-up* renewable electricity generated *locally* from sunlight, wind, water, and geothermal sources is an example of appropriate specificity because it includes the distinction from large-scale, corporate-owned installations.

Debunking official fictions paves the way for *drastic and urgent*[31] transformation, the only path to slowing down climate change and escaping irreversible collapse. While today's still dominant neoliberalism imprints on people that *there is no alternative to neoliberalism*[32], the physical reality is that *only alternative solutions*[33] are possible. Moreover, the alternative solutions are available, applicable and affordable. They may create the substrate and setting of joyful living for the many on Earth. Revealing analysis and refreshed insight about the state of the world will invigorate you.

Part I
On Energy & Money

Without energy, life on earth is impossible. Take away energy, and all life disappears. Everyone is familiar with energy in different ways. Those who feel a bit sick will say *I have no energy*. Or those who exercise will eat more to have enough energy. When fuel and electricity bills go up drastically, common people's attention to energy multiplies.

Energy and related technologies have played a most crucial role since the start of human civilisation, and will do so forever. The technologies are first-order transformers in quitting unsustainable fossil and atomic fuelled energy supplies. Drastic reductions in emissions of the GHGs carbon dioxide, methane and nitrous oxide are necessary. With fossil fuel use alone accounting for over 80% of the global GHG emissions, decisions on energy are vital for the survival of human civilisation. This blunt fact is known by everyone implied in climate affairs. Also known is that the energy sector stands as the foundation of industrial activity, commanding significant investments, employment, and profits. Annual super profits from fossil fuels amount to thousands of billions of US dollars[1], fuelling powerful incumbent interests that resist necessary change and transformations.

Given the predominant role of fossil fuels in causing climate change, energy experts outlined the only remaining feasible path for humanity, as follows:

- keep fossil fuels in the ground;
- enhance energy conservation and energy efficiency in

using commercial energy;

- deliver nearly all energy services through electricity;
- ensure all electricity obtained from light, wind, water, or geothermal currents, with bioenergy reserved for fuel applications[2].

This outlined path was once shaky when renewable electricity was expensive. Today, this path is solid and robust: possible, desirable for the majority of humanity, necessary and sufficient to bring GHG emissions down. Energy experts are enthusiastic about this path because of the central role of electricity, being clean, versatile, top-quality energy, and for the first time in history: cheap, with confidence to stay cheap and become cheaper by technological progress. Economics for the public good, for sustainable development at the global scale, cannot include fossil and atomic fuels given their inferiority to renewable electricity.

The triptych *Renewable Energy (RE), Nuclear Power (NP), Carbon Capture & Storage (CCS)* is adopted by IPCC Working Group III[3] as standard policy approach. The juxtaposition presents the three uneven options as equivalent and compatible solutions. However, this discourse negates the big differences in contributions and the mutual technical and sustainability conflicts. The triptych is a discourse curtain for protecting business-as-usual practices.

Eliminating thermal power generation, with its associated fuel cycle sources and waste flabs could reduce annual global CO_2 emissions by approximately 18 billion tonnes, or half of the energy sector related CO_2 emissions. The elimination is also financially advantageous due to the low costs of wind and solar power. The nowadays ca. 95 million tonnes hydrogen per year for industrial applications in petroleum refineries, manufacturing of fertilisers, and for steel, is obtained from fossil fuels, with concurrent GHG emissions of more than 1 billion tonnes. These emissions will be mitigated by degrowth in the three major consuming sectors. The residual demand for hydrogen could be fabricated with renewable electricity.

Part I consists of five chapters, briefly introduced here.

Chapter 1: Energy: an ever-present but unknown companion

When asking people what energy is, you will likely hear about various modes of energy or its uses. Chapter 1 introduces the scientific definition in such a way that the reader is familiarised with energy. Energy is omnipresent. There is no life without energy. All energy of value for humans is manufactured by the Sun and the Earth, without sending invoices. At the source, energy is a free good. Yet humans have transformed many of nature's free energy packages into economic commodities by installing a variety of property rights systems. All human activities require energy. Every activity wants a given quantity of the applicable type, at the right time, in the right place. There are three main sources of energy: renewable flows and stocks, fossil fuels, and uranium. There are various choices of sources and uses of energy, requesting appliances for conversions, transmission, storage, ... and the intermediate role of secondary energy as power and heat. Electricity has since the 1880s been gaining more prominence because of its quality, and since 2018 is the cheapest type of commercial energy when derived from the free sources of wind and sunlight. The chapter equips the reader with solid insights with which to enter the fascinating world of energy.

Chapter 2: Renewable energy: wonderful opportunities for all on Earth

Figure 5 sketches the history of human civilisation based on energy supplies. Era1 until around 1800 was based on RE sources. Era2 of fossil fuels and uranium causes huge gaseous litter and waste with irreversible deleterious impacts. For survival, Era3 will be entirely based on RE sources, attuning the planet's modern technologies to the laws of the Sun. In the 1970s, grassroots communities in Germany and Denmark started the development of small-scale RE technology for local use. Since 2018, electricity generated from sunlight and wind currents outcompetes all other options. Photovoltaics (PV) and wind turbines continue to improve and their kWh price continues to decrease. In 2025, PV supplies affordable electricity to everyone, including developing countries. Now, people and communities can own the supply of energy, the most crucial socio-technical sector in every society. The RE development path since the 1970s has been bumpy as a result of neoliberal interests' tactics, aligning with Schopenhauer's three stages: ridiculing, opposing, conquering by accepting as being self-evident. Salient examples are: blocking the access of Independent Generators of Own Power to the electric grid; disrupting the best RE support mechanisms; in 2014, organising a coup against the small-scale RE generators to obtain priority for large-scale RE.

Chapter 3: The delusive truth of atomic energy

Atomic energy in practice is a *delusive truth* fabricated on Einstein's equation $E = mc^2$. Atomic weapons are the motive for subsidy flows to atomic energy. The International Atomic Energy Agency's sneaky activity in IPCC's Working Group 3 avoids independent assessment of atomic energy, while maintaining the flawed "RE, NP, CCS" triptych in framing climate policy. Propaganda disguises the reality for shaping complacent public passivity, to debunk by facts and scientific arguments. The 85 year history of atomic power has reminded us of its failures, irreversible waste, proliferation of atom technology, production and transmission incompatibilities with renewable electricity from sunlight and wind. The 1950s to 1980s claim of uranium as a substitute for fossil fuels was void. Both are expensive when external costs and risks are included. In 2007, Saatchi & Saatchi as *Merchants of Doubt* conceived the campaign to confuse the general public and politicians. The campaign was successful, but unfortunate for the future of mankind.

Figure 6 clarifies why atomic fission and fusion have no future. The atom fuel cycles need enormous *source and sink flabs*. Private investors eschew investing in atomic power plants. In order to avoid atomic power's disastrous perils in the pipeline, it should be phased out sooner rather than later.

Chapter 4: The delusive truth of the hydrogen energy economy

The delusive truth of the hydrogen energy economy is based on carbon-free combustion of hydrogen molecules H2. In 2022, the industry utilized 95Mt hydrogen worldwide as a *chemical substance* for ammonia fertilisers, refining petroleum, oxygen steel and explosive matter. Practically all hydrogen is derived from fossil fuels, causing more than 1Gt GHG emissions. In 2003, oil industry familiar US-president Bush launched the H2 hype, joined by EC-president Prodi. The EC's 2020 hydrogen strategy is Eurocentric advertising without considering facts, proposing neo-colonial megalomaniacal projects in Global South countries. Quasi-free use of renewable electricity and affordable CCS are assumed. In 2005, the IPCC assessed CCS as technically feasible, with energy and financial efficiency problematic. As of now, no commercial CCS has succeeded.

The hydrogen economy is a delusion by H2's inherent characteristics: phase changing parameters, flammability, embrittlement, warming potential of leaked hydrogen, most hydrogen needs manufacturing. Transport and storage are technically exigent and financially prohibitive. Circumventing the problems by making synthetic fuels continues the hydrocarbon economy. The *announced* HYRASIA megaproject of 11Mt ammonia in Kazakhstan is 550 times the size of a realised project in Norway. By wasting human and material capital, the hydrogen hype disrupts the transformation to renewable electricity to serve direct energy needs.

Chapter 5: Fossil fuels: geopolitics for excessive super profits

Staggering super-profits on oil & gas sales are cashed by petrostates, transnational corporates, traders and speculators. From 1970 to 2020, they amounted to 52,544bn in US$-value-year 2020, on average 1,030bn per year. The yearly amounts fluctuate between 92bn in 1970 and 2,696bn in 2011, when NATO invaded Libya. Extreme super-profits coincide with sanctions, embargoes and wars against Western-hostile petrostates like Iran, Iraq, Libya, Venezuela, and Russia. The prevailing media narrative explains super-profits by *depleting* oil & gas resources, causing *struggles* to capture the *scarce* oil & gas remnants. In reality, the oil & gas resources in the Earth's crust are too abundant. Wars create *artificial scarcity* via embargoes on oil & gas exports by petrostates labelled as *enemies*. Enemies are countries with their own nationalistic views and practices, challenging the US world hegemony. The war in Ukraine and related embargoes also created artificial scarcity, and super-profits are expected to exceed previous maxima. The super-profits harm the non-petrostates: the poor countries and wealthy areas like Europe, Japan, South Korea, Taiwan, and industrialising countries like China and India. In these countries, low-income families suffer most. The competitivity of energy intensive industries in Europe and the Far East declines as a result of the higher energy prices.

Chapter 1
Energy: an ever-present but unknown companion

Energy is an inexhaustible topic, continually revealing surprises and new insights, even for those with a lifetime of professional involvement in the field[4]. So, as a reader, don't be discouraged if you can't follow every issue to its root. To debunk the widespread flawed discourses, perseverance in learning is a must, particularly in the realm of energy. It is worth exploring *energy* to know better this ever-present, yet largely unknown, companion.

Energy is already a fascinating technical subject, but its social, economic, and political significance makes it even more compelling. Energy is indispensable for all life on Earth, providing the substrate and nourishment on which human life thrives. The forms of society that humans develop and maintain depend largely on the types of energy and related technologies available for use. In chapter 2, there is a description of human civilisation in three eras, each determined by the types of energy and technology used.

This chapter holds four sections:
Section 1.1 deals with the essential attributes of energy. The definition of energy needs a few axioms sufficient to explain all energy phenomena. Using energy is degrading its availability or quality. Energy is present as stocks and as flows. Utilising energy is combining a source and a technique, except in the case of direct use, such as for example daylight.

Section 1.2 is an overview of the various free energy sources the sun and Earth offer humanity as flows and stocks. People paying high bills for energy supplied by corporates is due mainly to three factors.

Section 1.3 describes the four ways to obtain energy useful for mankind. Section 1.4 is an overview of energy demand and supply in the present industrialised societies. The numerous human activities all need the right quantity of the proper type of energy at the right moment and place. The supply is mainly forthcoming from three major sources of energy: renewables, fossil fuels, and uranium.

1.1 What is energy?

It's a bit sad to read and talk about the subject of energy, and to answer *Hmm, I don't know* when asked *What is energy, anyway?* You don't want to experience that. So, this question certainly deserves an answer, but it is impossible to give a simple, direct answer. To truly understand, one needs to take a few steps.

First, energy is omnipresent and manifest in many different forms. People are familiar with light, motion, heat, and more. A closer look reveals that energy undergoes myriad forms of change. Some of the changes occur spontaneously in nature, such as the transformation of wind energy into waves. Today, humans set up many conversions. For example, igniting and burning the chemical energy in fuel generates heat. And in car or aircraft engines, part of the heat is converted into mechanical energy and kinetic energy to obtain mobility.

Understanding energy is not a straightforward task. It is not something that can be easily grasped for a simple examination. Even science grapples with some aspects of the energy puzzle, posing questions like *What explains gravity?* Nonetheless, all humans deal daily with gravity and it plays a prominent role in our solar system and the universe.

Second, because energy does not reveal itself in a straightforward manner, a detour is needed. By attentively observing the phenomena caused by energy in all forms of life and motion on Earth and beyond, scientists discovered the properties of energy step by step. They have retained the smallest number of properties sufficient to explain all experienced and observed energy phenomena. Those three properties are:

1. Energy is everywhere, nothing exists without energy.

2. In the study of energy phenomena, a *system* is delineated as a separate segment from its environment. Studying energy involves examining the interactions of energy within the *system* itself and the *system's* surrounding environment. The second property of energy is: energy in the *whole system* is the sum of the energy in its constituent parts.

3. The total quantity of energy/mass remains constant. One cannot create or dissipate energy/mass. This property applies to the universe. It also applies to individual systems when completely isolated from their environment.

Einstein demonstrated the conversion of mass into energy with the equation $E = mc^2$, where E is energy, m is mass, c is the speed of light. This is why mass is mentioned alongside energy in property 3. But for now, let this not be a concern until chapter 3, which deals with atomic energy.

Just a language tip: *consuming* energy is impossible because the amount of energy remains constant. Instead say: *use energy*. You can, however, consume certain forms of energy like petrol, gas, electricity by converting it into other forms of energy such as motion power, heat, light. While this may not be a major concern, using precise language demonstrates an understanding of energy concepts.

Third, attention should also be paid to the quality of different forms of energy. Not all forms of energy are equally useful to humans. The measure of usefulness lies in the ability of an energy form to be converted into other desirable forms. For instance, electricity stands out as a top-quality form of energy due to its convertibility into practically all desirable forms of power, light, and heat. Electricity is versatile and doesn't produce direct emissions; it is truly remarkable that the cheapest available energy on Earth is renewable electricity from sunlight and wind.

In contrast, the quality of heat depends on its temperature. Heat at a very high temperature is of high quality. Heat at ambient temperature is of very low quality and is often referred to as *waste heat* or *waste energy*. This ambient heat is freely available when you open the door, in any amount you wish, though not necessarily at a temperature you desire. However, ambient heat cannot be converted into another useful form of energy without an additional input of energy.

Using a package of energy to obtain services, such as mobility, heat, or light, inevitably degrades the quality of the quantity of energy used[5]. As a consequence, the quantity of energy can be used either only once or in a cascade of decreasing quality of its service. For example: a high-temperature industrial process uses fresh fuel such as natural gas. The waste heat from the process is usually released directly into the environment. But sometimes the waste heat is captured for space heating, providing a second service before being released. High-quality *energy recycling* is not feasible. However, a heat pump[6] can tap low-temperature heat from the environment and deliver it indoors at a higher temperature than the ambient temperature. But this process requires the use of electricity, the top-quality form of energy.

The properties of energy and of its quality are explained by physical laws. These laws are not just imperative but also essential for a well-organised and efficient use of energy in its diverse forms. Applying the laws properly is pivotal for serving various human needs, including timely travel, comfortable living spaces, food storage, communication via telephone, internet, and TV, among other aspects of daily life. There is more on energy uses in section 1.4, but first a few words about the different forms of energy. The omnipresent unique energy manifests itself in many forms, and people all over the world has given energy many different names.

Energy is present in dispersed and concentrated *stocks*—for example, the widespread presence of heat in the Earth's atmosphere. Solar radiation continuously replenishes this stock, and the Earth radiates heat back to the universe. The natural greenhouse effect maintains the heat balance between the sun's replenishing and Earth's radiating, which keeps Earth's temperatures within comfortable limits. However, excessive burning of fossil fuels leads to the accumulation of greenhouse gases in the atmosphere, destabilising the heat balance and causing a rise in Earth's temperatures[7].

Concentrated stocks of energy such as petroleum fields, natural gas reserves, and coal veins remain dormant until people extract them. Mining turns energy stocks into usable *energy flows* suitable in many ways for diverse applications. Energy flows make our machines and appliances work to help us in labour tasks, travel and comfort needs.

Effective utilisation of energy always requires an *energy source* and, in most cases[8] a *technique* to convert the energy source into usable forms for wanted applications. Energy is only useful when it is available in the right form, quantity, place, and time—these four factors must align. Achieving such alignment requires vigilant monitoring and management of energy flows, especially when energy wastage is no longer tolerated. Wasteful practices were common in rich countries until recently, and they persist among the wealthiest individuals in both rich and poor countries up until today.

As an example of commercial energy, observe the route of natural gas imported by ships. After cleaning at the source, natural gas is converted into its liquid state (LNG) by cooling it to -162°C, allowing large amounts to be shipped. The loaded ships then sail to LNG terminals in importing countries. Further steps include the storage of liquefied gas, regasification, pumping through transport and distribution pipelines, ultimately delivering natural gas to businesses and buildings. When it's time to cook, households take the appropriate amount of gas from the gas network.

For the future, another way is using sunlight as a source, with photovoltaic (PV) panels on the roof providing electricity. In this case, the cooking range to prepare meals would be electric. However, because the Sun doesn't always provide enough energy to meet people's needs at a given location, additional techniques are required. These might include drawing electricity from a home battery or from the grid, importing electricity from locations with excess renewable electricity.

Properly designed energy systems are tiered according to the needs of end-users, ranging from households and businesses to local, supra-local and international facilities for provision and exchange of energy. Public authorities at local, national, and international levels share the responsibility to co-develop sustainable, affordable, and secure energy systems.

1.2 Free energy sources serving people

Figure 3 illustrates the sources of energy used by people, with the Sun taking the central role alongside Earth. Without the Sun, life on Earth would quickly wither away. Daylight, crop growth, the water cycle, wind, or ventilation – all provided by the Sun, and all for free. Inside the Sun, mass is constantly being converted into heat according to Einstein's $E = mc^2$ equation. This keeps the Sun radiating in all directions. The Earth, at a safe distance from the Sun, receives about one billionth of the solar radiation. Of the solar energy penetrating the atmosphere, just over half reaches the Earth's surface.

The Sun provides us with light during the day, longer and more in summer than in winter in the Northern Hemisphere. Sunlight is free. Since the 1960s, photovoltaic (PV) solar cells have been in production, initially to power spacecraft. After 2000, people began to install PV panels on the roofs of houses and other buildings, transforming free sunlight into electricity. By 2025, installed solar cells are able to convert about 21 percent of the received sunlight energy into electricity, with newer tested designs achieving an impressive 28 percent efficiency. After 2000, the cost of electricity from solar cells has dropped incredibly fast. Together with onshore wind turbines, they now provide the cheapest kWh of electricity ever, and the cost reductions in solar technology are far from over[9].

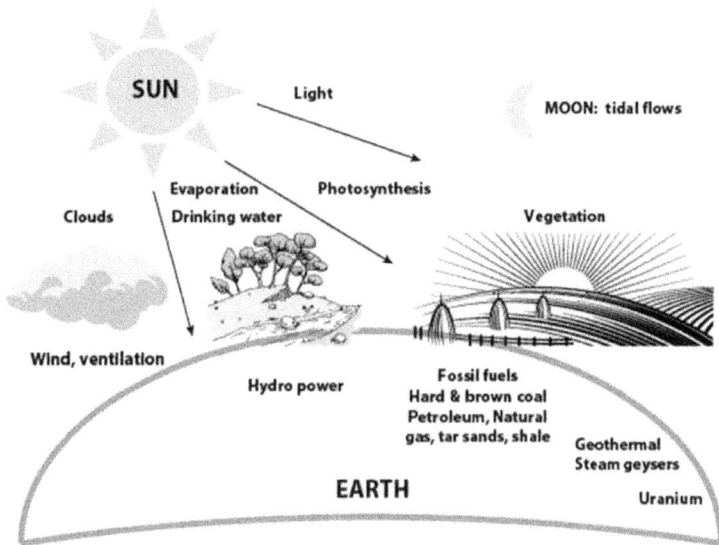

Figure 3: The Sun and Earth are the sources of free energy

For millions of years, crops have used sunlight to grow and flourish through the process of photosynthesis. Typically, plants convert less than 2 percent of the received sunlight energy into biomass. Millions of years ago, in many parts of planet Earth, plant and animal material became buried and, and over time, transformed into fossil fuels. This process can be typified as natural Carbon Capture & Storage (CCS)[10]; it decreased the CO_2 concentration in the atmosphere, while the availability of oxygen (O_2) was raised.

Coal was formed as plant material underwent compression for millions of years, deep underground in a warm environment. Coal is composed of 92-98 percent carbon atoms (C). Petroleum contains 85 percent carbon atoms (C) and 10 percent hydrogen atoms (H). Natural gas is mainly methane, with one carbon and four hydrogen atoms (CH_4). Raw natural gas also contains traces of ethane (C_2H_6), and of propane (C_3H_8). This shows that carbon is the main element of fossil fuels, so when it is burned, a lot of carbon dioxide CO_2 is produced. CO_2 is the most common greenhouse gas, the biggest contributor to the greenhouse effect, and stays in the atmosphere for 100 years or more on average before breaking down into other molecules.

The Sun's radiant energy and heat play a pivotal role in the water cycle by evaporating water from oceans, seas, lakes, rivers, and also moisture from crops. This water vapour forms clouds that fall as snow and rain in different places on Earth. These precipitation patterns create pressure differences that drive wind currents. Water and snow also fall on the high-altitude parts of continents. In mountainous regions, water collected in lakes at higher altitude can serve as a source for rivers, and act as reservoirs, enabling the production of hydropower.

Besides the Sun, there are some other, albeit minor, sources of energy. The ebb and flow of ocean tides represent a form of hydropower, created by the gravitational force of the Moon acting on the Earth as it rotates daily. Coastal locations with suitable conditions may harness this energy. One such example is the 240 MWe tidal power station at the mouth of the river Rance, near Saint-Malo in Brittany[11].

Extracting geothermal heat is quite expensive in places where the heat is deep in the Earth's crust and temperatures are moderate. In places where steam constantly gushes out of the Earth in large quantities and at high temperatures, geothermal heat becomes a viable option for electricity generation. Such power plants have been built in volcanic regions of Iceland, California, Italy, Kenya, and more. Heat pumps for space heating often take heat from a nearby underground area.

Uranium is the raw material for enriched isotopes in atomic fission, converting mass into energy. Atomic energy is discussed further in chapter 3.

All energy sources in the atmosphere and on Earth are *freely available*, thanks to the cooperation between the Sun and Earth for billions of years. The manufacturing cost of nature's energy, used by humans, is zero, because neither the Sun nor Earth send invoices. The phrase *the Sun rises for free* captures this idea well. Even the wind that brings in fresh air, the rain and snow from which rivers rise, it is all for free. Trees, shrubs, plants, herbs, and flowers, exist without human intervention, as do the reserves of coal, petroleum and natural gas in the Earth's crust. These free stockpiles of energy, too, were manufactured by the Sun and Earth.

Nature is generous, but some people are greedy. While energy sources are inherently free, the energy bills faced by individuals, households, and institutions are high — sometimes prohibitively high. Why is that? There are three factors, each of which explains to some degree the difference between the abundance of free energy flows and high energy bills experienced by people.

The first factor is a human-made institution, namely the establishment and enforcement of particular *property rights*. Here the distinction between free energy flows and energy resources is important. Sunlight, rain and wind are completely free of property rights. Water can be free under some circumstances. For fossil fuel reserves, full property rights are granted to the owner of the land or sea surface under which the reserves are located. Typically, nation-states are the primary owners, deciding whether to transfer ownership – wholly, partially, or not at all – to private entities owning land above the stockpiles. Everyone is now used to the fact that the underground wealth, created by the Sun and Earth over millions of years, has been nationalised by nations and privatised by private owners. The reason is obvious: it provides wealth with little effort, aside from the occasional need to defend this property from intruders. Money is made from these resources, and fuel consumers ultimately bear the cost.

The second factor is economic. Harvesting free energy flows and depleting free energy stocks requires the *deployment of economic resources*, such as labour, technology, equipment and sometimes large amounts of energy to power them. Consider the example of liquefying natural gas, shipping it, storing it, and delivering it to homes. These resources also need to be paid for by the end users who ultimately benefit from the energy's use value. Until 2018, the costs of harnessing light and wind to generate electricity were quite high. However, since then, the cheapest kWh in the history of electricity is coming from harvested light and wind, and the costs continue to fall. In contrast, extracting fossil fuels remains expensive, and only giant corporates can capitalise on economies of scale for these projects.

The third factor driving up energy bills is the *high rents or super profits* in particular on the extraction, treatment and sale of oil and gas. Large corporates leverage their financial and political power to secure oligopolistic or monopolistic positions, enabling them to generate significant super profits at the expense of end-users. This was particularly evident again in 2022, when such practices led to an excessive rise in energy bills. This issue is further detailed in chapter 5.

1.3 In what ways do people obtain useful energy?

Useful energy is defined here as energy used for the benefit of people pursuing a good life and happiness for themselves and others. Excluded from this definition is the large quantity of energy spent on the global military apparatus[12] and its operations. This includes military exercises, training programmes of fighter pilots and tank drivers, clandestine operations, actual wars, occupation of foreign lands, and distant military bases. Ending these barbaric practices would preserve substantial amounts of fossil fuels in the ground and represent a big step towards a better world in all aspects. In the 21st century, the powerful and rich countries continue to squander humanity's future by escalating conflicts and war, as seen in Iraq, Syria, Libya, Ukraine, and, most recently, Iran. Without energy, everything comes to a halt. Without fossil fuels, the ferocity of wars and crimes would be significantly smaller.

The *four ways or methods* to obtain useful energy are:

1. Direct use of natural energy from the environment
2. Harnessing the human body as a small energy factory
3. Harvesting energy in the close proximity to people and communities for own use
4. Buying energy from industries specialised in coal, petroleum, natural gas, uranium extraction, processing, and commercialisation

The traditional energy reports from the International Energy Agency (IEA) and national ministries of economy, as well as the traditional media, until recently focused on the fourth item in the above list — industrial-scale extraction, processing, and commercialisation of energy resources. Even today, most of their publications are still devoted to it. But outside the circles of influence and power of the established industries, profit-driven markets and media, there is growing interest in the first three methods of obtaining energy. These approaches are increasingly seen as essential tools for addressing the climate crisis (part III). The following is a brief exploration of the four ways or methods.

Method 1

Adapting to local environments and effortless use of the benefits of natural energy resources. This involves harnessing energy directly from natural sources like daylight and ventilation from wind, or gathering food from nature, such as nuts, berries, grains, and fish. The Earth's gravity can be used to transport water[13]. These methods have no harmful side effects such as waste or emissions of pollutants and greenhouse gases. They require minimal technology, if any, to achieve desired results. The key is to understand the potential of these natural energy flows and think creatively and forwardly about how to apply them for personal benefit.

This is important both when constructing new buildings and when renovating them. Passive design elements are crucial in this respect. For example, optimising the orientation of façades and roofs to maximise the utilisation of sunlight and solar heat, using overhanging eaves and adjustable sun blinds for control. Also, the provision of underground cellars or basements can be used to store drinks, food or even to house a freezer. Sufficient and high-quality thermal insulation of roofs, walls and floors reduces the need for heating in winter and ensures adequate cooling with natural night ventilation in summer. If these passive solutions are not devised before construction, they often cannot be introduced afterwards. However, when successfully applied, residents obtain high comfort by incorporating what nature provides for free.

Method 2

The human body operates as an energy factory, requiring regular food to maintain mental and physical health and to perform a variety of daily tasks. These tasks include modes of transport such as walking or biking, as well as practical activities like cooking, cleaning, gardening, and more. Additionally, the human body engages in mental and cultural tasks such as reading, writing, drawing, or playing musical instruments. Although the energy services provided by the human body may be modest in scale, they are remarkably versatile. With a healthy body and common sense, individuals can efficiently perform a wide range of diverse and sometimes complicated tasks without significant effort.

In its essence, this requires little or no technology, unless the extensions of our actions are considered. For example, preparing a plot of land for planting can be done with simple tools like a spade and rake, or with more advanced equipment such as a tractor with a plough and harrow. Using basic tools requires more physical effort from the human body compared to operating a tractor. But the extended chains, the tractors, consume fuels, thus placing them in the fourth method of energy use. During the era dominated by fossil fuels and atomic power, the role of the human body in energy use has been overshadowed. Recently, resistance to this phenomenon has been growing, especially among young people, demanding more space for walking and cycling, in the meantime enhancing the quality of life. In many cities and towns, a big push has already been made, but this is only the beginning of claiming living space by and for the people.

Method 3

Harvesting heat and electricity in the close environment, from natural energy flows. This method mainly involves the purchase and use of photovoltaic solar panels to generate electricity for local use. Since electricity is a non-storable current, the mismatch between moments of production and use creates a bottleneck. In many situations, aiming for *full self-supply* is not practical, and the best choice is to cooperate within local communities through local smart grids. In this approach, communities can invest in nearby wind turbines, potentially partnering with experienced cooperatives for larger-scale projects. In addition to electricity, rooftops can be equipped to harvest solar heat for domestic hot water supply. This is typically abundant in summer months, sufficient in most months of spring and autumn, but absent during winter in the Northern Hemisphere. Local production of one's own electricity is a key factor for a successful revolution of existing energy systems. All possibilities are available for this path to be widely realised and to make the problematic fourth method of obtaining energy largely or completely obsolete.

Method 4

Companies, typically multinational corporates, mine and process energy resources to sell energy as a commercial product. In both industrialised and developing countries, the energy sector stands as the largest investor, wielding significant power and influence in political and economic spheres, backed by substantial financial resources, which are secured via monopoly rents or super profits [chapter 5].

Significant investments are channelled into many techniques and activities within the business chains of commercial energy companies, with three successive links. It starts with extracting primary energy from coalmines, oil and gas wells, both onshore and offshore. The second link is transporting, storing and processing of mined energy into secondary energy suitable for use by appliances in buildings, industrial facilities and transport vehicles. The third link is the supply of final energy for utilisation, as explained at the end of section 1.1. This includes delivering the appropriate amount of energy in the appropriate form, in the required place, at the right time. This can include heat, ventilation, and cooling for buildings, power for industries, buildings, and vehicles. Development, construction, and operation of the many techniques and devices lead to high expenses. These expenses are included in the financial statements of the multinational energy corporations.

What is not accounted for are the staggeringly high external[14] costs caused by the fourth method of obtaining energy, based on fossil fuels and atomic power. One of the most pressing costs is the damage caused by atmospheric pollution and climate change. There are extensive environmental reports on depletion, pollution, destruction of the environment and nature at global, regional and national levels. They describe various themes such as acidification, habitat fragmentation, habitat destruction, biodiversity loss, dispersion of hazardous substances, and more. In most themes, the method of using energy from fossil fuels emerges as the *most harmful cause*. In a fair economy, those causing external costs should bear the financial burden. However, this is not the case for the daunting costs imposed by the fossil energy sector. Given that the irreversible destruction of the climate and other global ecosystems threatens all forms of life on Earth, phasing out the fourth method of using energy is urgent. Only the elements serving Method 3, which focus on local and sustainable energy solutions, remain beneficial.

1.4 Energy supply and demand

Figure 4 is an outline of energy supply and demand in societies today. All activities undertaken by people require energy. Daily operations span across households, services, agriculture, industry, commerce, cultural institutions, educational facilities, transportation of people and goods, and more. Each of these activities demands specific forms and quantities of energy, available in the right place and at the right time.

The forms of energy services are also numerous and diverse, such as light, heat, cooling, and power. To provide energy services, there are three important[15] human-useable energy sources. The first is the direct and indirect flows from the Sun, with biomass and biofuels as derivatives, as indicated by the horizontal arrow at the bottom of figure 4. Second, there are fossil fuel reserves. Third, uranium and thorium can be converted into fissile uranium. The three sources are shown in the lower half of figure 4, with the central position occupied by electricity, not being an energy source[16]. Electricity is an energy carrier, a current generated from other energy flows, including natural flows such as sunlight, wind, water, geothermal, or manufactured flows such as high-pressure steam or pressurised combustion gases. Since safe electricity cannot be provided directly by nature, it must be generated by human action.

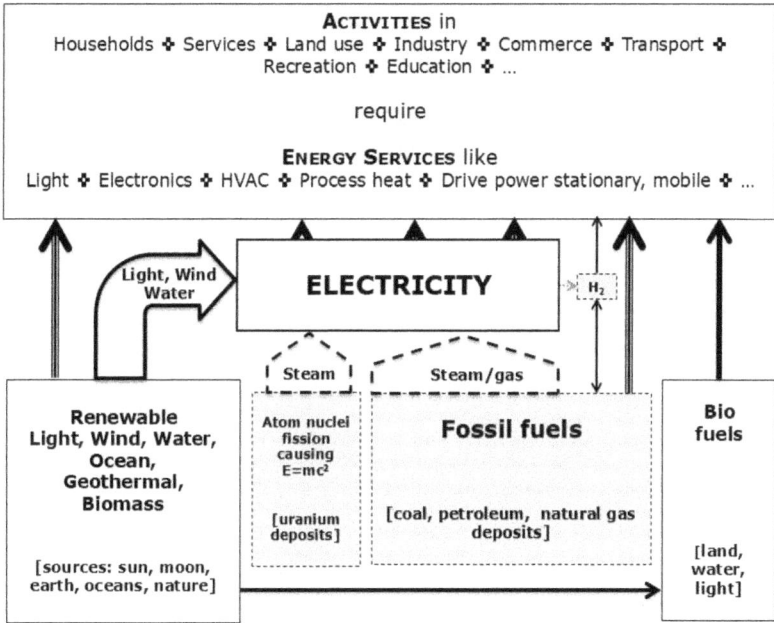

Figure 4: Human Activities Need Energy Services. Energy sources are renewable streams and biofuels, fossil fuels and uranium stocks.

Next to electricity in figure 4 is a small box mentioning H2 or hydrogen. Hydrogen, abundant in the universe, is not readily available on Earth in significant quantities. Hydrogen is manufactured, mostly from natural gas or petroleum products or from water via electrolysis. It is mainly used as a feedstock in industry. Those derivatives require equipment and energy inputs, and storing and transporting hydrogen are problematic technically and financially. Hydrogen may eventually play a modest role after electricity. Hydrogen as a path for continuing the use of fossil fuels is the wrong track. However, a hydrogen hype is evolving with support from the incumbent fossil fuel multinationals [chapter 4].

The numerous and diverse activities of the rich part of the world's population rely heavily on elaborate energy systems that have become deeply embedded in society. From the 18th century onwards, these systems have increasingly been fuelled by fossil fuels, which are mined and pumped from the Earth in large quantities[17]. In 2023, use of fossil fuels produced 37.4 billion tonnes of CO_2 emissions out of a total of 40.6 billion tonnes[18], clearly the biggest cause of the rising GHG concentration in the atmosphere [figure 1]. Because of climate change alone, fossil fuels are non-negotiable and must remain in the ground. Whether atomic power is a worthwhile part of future energy supply is discussed in chapter 3. The role of steam and gas streams to generate electricity is overdue and is best reduced now. Continuing to extend the life of existing fossil fuel or nuclear plants and making reckless investments in new ones is a counterproductive approach.

It is up to the diverse forms of renewable energy to meet the world's energy needs moving forward. In that daunting task at the supply side, a look back at the demand side is needed. What energy is needed for what valuable activities? How much energy is needed for an activity if energy waste is eliminated? Which of the activities that lavishly use and waste commercial energy and materials today are still justifiable in a future sustainable world on a global scale? Inevitably, energy conservation and energy efficiency are two key allies in the transformation of energy systems.

A reminder
- Without energy, humans can do nothing, anywhere, ever. Energy exists everywhere and always.
- You can neither make nor recycle energy. Constantly fresh sources are needed.
- The Sun and Earth generously provide free resources in the form of energy flows and energy reserves from stockpiles.

- Intelligent application of energy resources requires intelligence, technology, investment, management and a sound evaluation of the energy needs in an ethical world.
- Fossil fuel and atomic energy systems have brought the world to the present situation. For a sustainable future, renewable energy systems are necessary, possible and desirable.

Chapter 2
Renewable energy: wonderful opportunities for all on Earth

The title mentions salient attributes of the discussed topic. Energy is *renewable* when sourced from the unstoppable working of the Sun. Benefiting from this energy opens wonderful *opportunities* for living on Earth. Because the Sun cannot be privatized, *all people on Earth* can benefit from it, more so when they can valorise the various opportunities. When not all people of the world have access to low-carbon energy, climate change remains unsolvable.

Up to the 18th century, all energy used by people came from solar energy and its derivatives such as wind and water currents, plants and trees. Industrialisation fed by stocks of fossil fuels has been the fundament for immoral wealth and power accumulation by a minority of the world's population. After two centuries of growth, immense production and consumption agglomerates have changed the face of the Earth[1]. Biodiversity is jeopardised, natural and human habitats menaced, and life-support systems endangered[2]. State-of-the-environment reports on *driving forces, pressures, state,* and *impact and responses* provide extensive and detailed information[3] about the harm caused by human modes of living. Fossil fuels play a problematic role in every sector and activity, direct or indirect. Without renewable energy fully substituting for fossil fuels, the responses are futile.

The chapter consists of seven sections:

Section 2.1 sketches a vision on human energy use over thousands of years to the present day. Three eras are distinguished [figure 5].

The pivotal period between era2 and era3 is now. The passage involves huge restructuring, with pushing and pulling by numerous interest groups. Deployment of the promising era3 implies an entire transformation of energy systems and a revolution of the modes of living of rich people.

Section 2.2 recapitulates the perplexing meaning of solar energy. It is a sufficient source for all energy needs on Earth. Humankind has turned its back on the Sun for two centuries, and is on the brink of self-destruction. There is a narrow path to attune the planet's modern technology to the laws of the Sun.

Section 2.3 lends the results of colleague Ruggero Schleicher-Tappeser to show that there is a technology attuned to the Sun: photovoltaics (PV). Now PV is fully available and affordable, even in developing countries. No other technology can supply electricity, the best quality in the energy world, so cheaply to everyone. What neoliberalism denounces as impossible makes photovoltaics possible.

Section 2.4 takes a look at the incumbent electricity sector in the neoliberal regime. Some of the detail may at first glance look unimportant for the future, given this sector is in line for a full shake up. However, it will not leave the scene due to demands by naive activists. The section ends with a warning. The incumbent giant electricity companies have a history of defending their monopoly against intruders, being prosumers, Independent Generators of Own Power (IGOP). Their weapon was to prohibit grid access for independent producers, or to make the terms of access incredibly opaque and uneven, stripping the profit of IGOP projects. In essence, the attitude and actions of the giant electricity companies have not changed: they will defend their stronghold, with money extracted mainly from captive customers.

Section 2.5 is a brief summary of how in 1975, the peaceful community of Wyhl on the Southern Rhine resisted the full phalanx of the German nuclear power sector to prohibit the construction of an atomic reactor in their forest. The people of Wyhl and nearby villages and cities such as Freiburg im Breisgau are the initiators of renewable energy development in Europe. They wanted to create real sustainable alternatives and pushed renovation in renewable energy. Freiburg Eco-Institute and the Fraunhofer Institute for Solar Energy Systems proceeded with the innovation track, in times when the German government and the power corporates scoffed at the initiators and inventors.

Section 2.6 explains the conflict between the European Commission (EC) and a group of Member States led by Germany about the policy for supporting the development of renewable energy technology. The EC desired the creation of an artificial market in tradable green permits, as it was blinded by the neoclassical and neoliberal discourse of *markets solve the problems*. The few experiments with such markets failed disastrously, with the bill footed by captive electricity customers. The German instrument supported the separate renewable technologies at the proper pace with adjusted support to create a growing demand for the technologies. It created successful innovation and decreasing costs of renewable electricity.

Section 2.7 tells the story of the coup in 2014 organised by the Magritte group of European energy corporates to conquer a market for their large-scale renewable energy projects, pushing aside the sustainable projects by small-scale grassroots, community-based deployment. While the grassroots initiated, innovated, and developed solar and wind electricity generators, the corporates were up until 2008 ordering large-scale coal plants in Europe! When they woke up around 2010 to 2012 to the fact that bottom-up development was ready to take over, they started to plan the coup. In April 2014, EC commissioner Joaquín Almunia was the willing channel to adapt the state aid guidelines in favour of large-scale projects. He also stated that small-scale renewables had received enough support, while in October 2014 he granted the 35-year subsidy scheme for atomic power plants at the UK's Hinkley Point C. If you look for Merchants of Hypocrisy, they are available.

2.1 Three eras in humanity's energy use

The history of carbon use by mankind dates back to the development of agriculture, approximately ten thousand years ago[4]. Control of fire and expanding agricultural practices have increasingly utilised carbon to harness useful energy. Renewable energy sources, which originate from the Sun—directly as light and heat and indirectly as wind and water—greatly exceed annual carbon use. They open the window to the future and provide insight into the three eras of energy use by humans.

Figure 5 shows the three eras of energy use. The path begins in prehistory, before the onset of human civilisation, around 11,700 years before the Western time scale started 2025 years ago. The first 13,500 years of human civilisation, which saw its most rapid growth in China, was a period of increasingly inventive use of renewable energy flowing in nature, such as light, wind, heat, and water.

After 1800, the trajectory of inventive progress was disrupted by a surge of predatory exploitation of fossil fuel reserves in the Earth's crust. After 1950 the energy sector expanded by the scary use of uranium to obtain weapons grade plutonium from atomic power plants. At the dawn of the second millennium of the Western epoch, the third era is emerging, propelled by society-wide technological innovations. Technologies that harvest electricity from ambient energy flows have surfed on many innovations. They have become a part of it, providing electricity at the lowest costs ever seen, while having minimal environmental impact and avoiding greenhouse gas emissions. Era3 beckons.

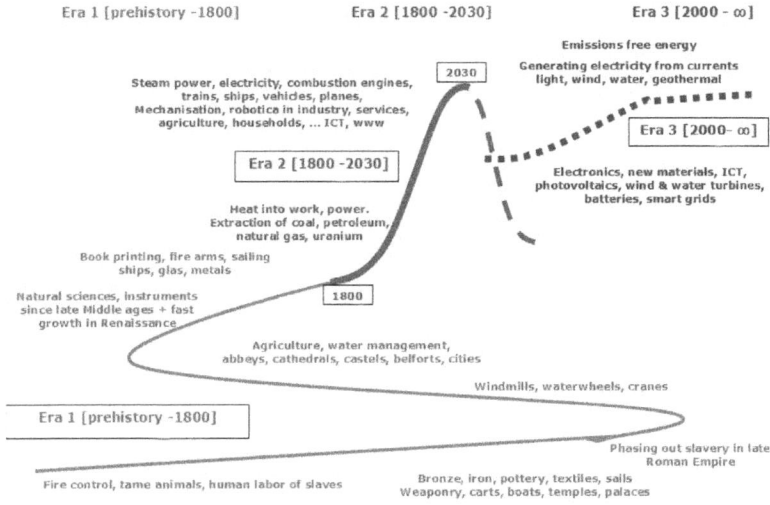

| Era 1 [prehistory -1800] | Era 2 [1800 -2030] | Era 3 [2000 - ∞] |

Emissions free energy

Generating electricity from currents
light, wind, water, geothermal

Steam power, electricity, combustion engines,
trains, ships, vehicles, planes,
Mechanisation, robotica in industry, services,
agriculture, households, ... ICT, www

2030

Era 3 [2000- ∞]

Era 2 [1800 -2030]

Electronics, new materials, ICT,
photovoltaics, wind & water turbines,
batteries, smart grids

Heat into work, power.
Extraction of coal, petroleum,
natural gas, uranium

Book printing, fire arms, sailing
ships, glas, metals

Natural sciences, instruments
since late Middle ages + fast
growth in Renaissance

1800

Agriculture, water management,
abbeys, cathedrals, castels, belforts, cities

Windmills, waterwheels, cranes

Era 1 [prehistory -1800]

Phasing out slavery in late
Roman Empire

Fire control, tame animals, human labor of slaves

Bronze, iron, pottery, textiles, sails
Weaponry, carts, boats, temples, palaces

Figure 5: Three eras of human civilisation built on different energy-technology substrates; era3 is emerging

Era1: slow drawing out: from primitive to inventive use of renewable energy

To explore the earliest years of the human species, you cannot simply order tickets online. Instead, you must navigate through the conflicting views of the scientific community and the romanticised fantasies of bestselling authors[5], who weave narratives that resonate with their contemporaries.

How the *naked* ape, humans, struggled to become ruler of the Earth is also a result of the art or the cunning of taming animals and fire. Consider, for example, the animal kingdom. The tamed wolf, later called dog, is a real success story. Dogs not only kept watch, allowing humans to sleep peacefully, but also helped in hunting by scavenging and driving prey to hunters, making hunting less laborious. Similar, tamed donkeys, horses, camels and oxen for labour and mobility, proved to be many times stronger and faster than the naked ape. Don't forget sheep, goats, poultry. They provide milk, meat, eggs, wool, and yarn. Humans have also coerced their own kind into slavery, imposing varying degrees of dependency and restrictions on movement. This subjugation of fellow humans showed significant variations in the extent of control and loss of freedom for the unfortunate.

Then there is the taming of natural phenomena, with fire being a prime example. The use of fire provided security by deterring dangerous predators and enemies. With torches, candles and oil lamps, fire gave light. Cooking, roasting and frying transformed food preparation and improved health. Fire also played a crucial role in crafting, such as baking jars, pots, bowls and stones, and melting ores to forge bronze and iron weapons, tools, utensils and artifacts. It also allowed hot baths for hygiene and relaxation, and for dyeing textile fibres and threads for clothing, fabrics and carpets.

There was a gradual development of new and improved techniques to use muscle power, fire and force from nature more effectively and efficiently. Think of looms, levers, knives, axes, saws, and pulleys, all allowing force to be used more effectively. Wheels and vehicles obtained better results from traction power. Ovens, grates, and hearths enabled more efficient use of fire. Sails, water wheels and windmills were helpful in harvesting power from natural energy flows.

Improved agricultural techniques continually increased yields by effectively utilising sunlight for photosynthesis, soils and water currents, benefiting humankind day after day across planet Earth.

The many examples show how energy use is a combination of, on the one hand, an energy source and, on the other, a technique to obtain from the source the appropriate amount of energy, in the desired form, at the appropriate time and place.

The civilisations that have developed in many places still arouse our amazement and admiration. To this day, artworks and buildings testify to the cultural and social flourishing of civilisations on all continents[6]. For instance, China is the country where an administrative system first developed 6,000 years ago. Structured societies emerged on surplus food production in naturally rich agricultural areas. In most of these societies, power, wealth and prestige were concentrated in the hands of small groups. The structure of governance and arrangement was usually pyramidal. In contrast, some smaller city-states developed democratic structures where citizens delegated power to administrators who acted within the rules of law. However, women and slaves, the majority of the population, were officially excluded from activities in political functioning.

Early civilisations also produced inspiring thinkers. In Iran, about 1,300 years[7] before the beginning of the Western calendar, Zarathustra described life as being defined by four main elements: soil, air, water, and fire. He taught that these essential elements of life should not be polluted by people under any circumstances, not even by burying or burning deceased peers. Therefore, his followers have built towers, on which the deceased persons were laid down, so that predatory birds removed the flesh, and the remaining bones were no longer a source of pollution. The towers of silence can still be visited in Yazd, Iran. Later influential thinkers were Confucius in China, Buddha in the Indian subcontinent, the Greek philosophers, the Jewish prophets in the Levant, with later Christian and Islamic prominences.

The lives and thoughts of early thinkers significantly shaped history. For instance, Christianity played a role in recognising the universal right to life of every human being, even if that human being was enslaved in the Roman Empire. The Roman eagle as a symbol of military superpower was supplanted by the cross[8]. The cross was the torture device on which disobedient, rebellious slaves were crucified until death. During this reversal of symbols, sweeping socio-economic and political transformations took place. Despite all wisdom, divine frameworks and widespread preaching, Heaven did not come to Earth. Wealth and possession of the 1 percent were significant, in the hands of landlords, military commanders, weapon manufacturers, mandarins, courtiers, high priests, and the like. The elites managed to maintain power and wealth through a monopoly on knowledge, indoctrinating obedience through sermons from pulpits. They controlled networks and communication channels through couriers and later carrier pigeons.

From around 1500, the spread of printed books and texts began to undermine the established monopoly on knowledge. The last 300 years of era1 were stormy, with Europe emerging as a tumultuous and aggressive continent. Colonisation of the world began with the continental coasts from Africa to India, Latin America, ... respecting neither peoples, cultures, nor borders, nor showing mercy.

The colonisation efforts were significantly aided by the development of sailing ships and gunpowder-based firearms[9], leveraging advances in what could be termed energy technology applied for military ends. Until the end of the 18th century, renewable energy sources were predominantly used, with innovations in water wheels, windmills, sailing ships, carriages, lifting tools, and the introduction of blast furnaces powered by charcoal.

During this time, alchemy's interest in nature and its materials was paralleled by significant advancements in mathematics, astronomy, chemistry, and physics. These sciences flourished, providing humans with tools and insights that greatly increased their power—power that was often used for domination and exploitation, not only of one's own people but also of other cultures and peoples. This unrestrained exploitation extended to the Earth, soil, water, air, and all forms of life within them. With this exploitative mindset towards nature and fellow human beings, some Western European countries entered the dawn of era2, in the years 1750 to 1800.

Era2: Predatory eruption: fossil fuels take over

Energy in its various forms is a subject of study by natural sciences. In the second half of the 18th century, English scientists discovered steam power. By heating water to create steam, they unlocked a new source of power, leading to the development of thermodynamics. The insight that energy transfer occurs in either ordered forms of work or chaotic heat[10] was gained after trial and error in research and experiment.

In 1824, French engineer Carnot formulated the basic principles of heat-to-work conversion, later translated into practical formulas by Maxwell. They improved the designs of power-out-of-heat machinery.

Later, Joule, Kelvin and Clausius formulated the specific *laws of thermodynamics*. The first main law is the conservation of energy. The second main law concerns the decreasing availability of heat energy depending on its temperature.

During the 19th century, scientists like Franklin, Volta, Coulomb, Ørsted, Ampère, and Faraday explored the phenomena of electricity and magnetism. This led to the invention of devices such as the dynamo and alternator, which convert the mechanical energy of a rotating shaft into electricity. Keeping the shaft spinning is done with turbines powered by energy from steam or from falling and pressurised water. Initially, most steam was produced by burning coal, oil and natural gas. From the 1950s, atomic fission reactors also began providing steam for electricity generation, with the share in global electricity generation by atomic plants reaching a peak of 17.5 percent in 1996, dropping to 9.8 percent by 2021[11].

In the 1880s, the delivery of electricity from power generation stations to customers started in cities like New York, London, Berlin and Paris: the beginning of an industrial success story, with a profound impact on societies in which electricity permeates. On the one hand, steam disappears as the direct source for providing power to various applications, being replaced by electricity. On the other hand, steam as an energy flow feeding power plants increases exponentially after World War 2. In recent years, thermal electricity production has resulted in 14.4 billion tonnes of CO_2 emissions annually, or 40 percent of the ca.36 billion tonnes of energy-related CO_2 emissions[12]. Add to this another 10 percent, and possibly more, caused by the large quantity and size of auxiliary installations necessary for fuel supply and waste removal, all inherent to thermal power generation plants. To stop half or more of the 36 billion tonnes of direct energy-related CO_2 emissions, it would suffice to shut down fossil fired thermal power generation plants, including their associated source and waste flabs.

In the 1880s petroleum extraction also started, later followed by an expansion of the range of refined products. In the 20th century, the availability of petrol fuels has changed the face of all countries, especially those undertaking reckless industrialisation. Storage, transportation, and use of petrol fuels is technically easy. This has allowed the various economic activities to be established everywhere. Automobility and other means of transport like ships, aeroplanes and tractors, allowed the connection of remote places where people live, work, study, shop, play sports, etc. Addiction to fossil fuels is widespread. Change in energy use is now hindered by existing infrastructures that are still expanding, such as roads and airports. Automobility remains prevalent due to habits formed from past decisions, such as living far from city and village centres. Moreover, multinational oil and gas companies have accumulated enormous wealth and influence [chapter 5]. They consider their own profits and power more important than a liveable atmosphere and mild climate, and prepare for an expanded use of fossil fuels.

The downside of the wild use of fossil fuels is a future of an unliveable planet. The usage either causes or exacerbates virtually all significant environmental issues, such as climate change, photochemical air pollution, dispersion of hazardous substances, acidification, fragmentation of open space, noise pollution, water and soil contamination, and more. The scope of damage from these impacts exceeds human comprehension, especially when it comes to *irreversible* loss of the clean atmosphere, the mild climate, and other vital ecosystems. Moreover, pillage driven by fossil fuels destroys not only natural heritage, but also cultural heritage. For example, military invasions and wars such as those carried out by NATO countries in Iraq and Libya have also destroyed highly valuable cultural assets. The big military apparatuses can only function by means of a massive supply of oil fuels and products.

Era3: Turn to sustainability (2000- ∞ infinity)

The world must get rid of fossil fuels and atomic power generation. This is a condition of survival for the human species on Earth. This transformation presents an enormous challenge, but it is feasible due to human ingenuity and the decisive actions of some countries, their politicians, and citizens, who have pioneered significant technological advances. By 2018, the reversal is irrevocable, as photovoltaic cells and wind turbines began generating the cheapest electricity in history. Moreover, these technologies are constantly improving so that electricity harvested from sunlight and wind currents is becoming cheaper and cheaper. Harvesting electricity from sunlight and wind currents is remarkably simple, compared to electricity generation from fossil fuels or uranium. Devices such as PV panels or wind turbines are installed where natural flows of sunlight or wind can pass by. Part of these natural flows is generating electricity and the other part of the flows stays in nature. Hence there is no fuel cycle, no cooling water circuits, no source flabs, and no waste flabs needed in order to obtain electric power.

These are structural, fundamental developments. They surf on numerous technological innovations with no end in sight. They have become part of the innovations, and are now providing electric power at the lowest cost ever since electricity generation began in 1880.

The natural currents of light and wind are variable, and largely diffuse. So radically different energy systems are necessary compared to those prevailing in era2. Everything is in place for successful energy transformations. Hesitation is no longer an option. The incredulous eyes of students hearing for the first time about living on 100% renewable energy are brightened with the following suggestion. *'Think for a moment of the great river basins of the world: Amazon, Congo, Ganges, Mekong, Mississippi, Nile, Yangtze, Volga, ...Where do these thousands of cubic metres of water per second at the mouths of these streams come from? Yes, from the drops of rain, snow and hail lifted by the Sun and blown to land by the wind. Many drops together achieve a big result.*

Nature is generous to humans, if they understand their place in natural systems, and act accordingly.

2.2 Recapitulating the perplexing meaning of solar energy

Where to begin, when you wish to write about a perplexing reality that permanently decides about the life and future of all human beings on Earth? No wonder that many earlier civilizations have venerated the Sun as their main God. The depiction of the Sun in figure 2 informs that the businesses of all Actors on Earth depend on the services delivered by the Sun, a fact formally developed in figure 3. In the history of mankind's energy provision [figure 5], daily solar currents in the troposphere and inherited underground reserves mark the Sun's omnipresent and dominant role. Unlike ancient civilizations worshipping the Sun as the source of all life, the Ancient East, Middle-East, and Mediterranean peoples created belief systems around the human mind and soul. The heavenly projections ranged from mythological theatres (Greek-Roman, Hindu), over monotheism (Jewish, Christian, Islam), to spiritual reflection (Buddhism).

Parallel to worshipping the God in Heaven, many people on Earth were captivated by pursuing wealth accumulation. The golden calf during Moses' Exodus, King Midas of Phrygia, and Rome's Crassus are testimony to the widespread practice. Philosophers like Aristotle, spiritual masters and prophets, and hermits resisted the power of wealth accumulation as the chief goal in a human's life. Nonetheless, towards the end of the European Middle Ages, trade and mercenary armies increased the weight of money, exacerbated by Spain's plundering of silver and gold in Latin America. By means of mercantilism, a new class of wealthy citizens emerged, eager to increase their possessions.

In the late 18th century and beyond, steam power pushed industrialisation based on coal. Capitalism was born, with the nose towards the ground searching for coal and materials, and the back to the Sun[13]. The mode of living changed by adopting as a directing principle *on the command of human will,* as a substitute for *smart adaptation to nature's offers.*

Nature was no longer a generous partner, but became the object for exploitation, veiled by the delusive discourse of exploitation being a divine mission[14]. Colonialism, capitalism, hegemony, warmongering, extractive economics, lack of responsibility and of liability for the spillover effects of industrialising and its preferred technologies, have been inherently interrelated since the dawn of capitalism and up to present-day neoliberalism.

Greed is the predominant trait of human beings, and greed being excellent for economic growth is an entrenched belief after two centuries of stunning expansion. The enormous quantity and variety of goods and services is also a result of astonishing progress in science and technology. The latter are mostly presented as being neutral; something like a knife you may use either to cut vegetables or to kill a living being. Such neutrality is an easy escape for scientists to negate their own duties and responsibilities, with pernicious consequences. Let us think over the following case, directly connected to the use of fossil fuels and climate change.

Thermodynamics is the scientific fundament of fossil fuel use. In 1824, Sadi Carnot clearly stated the basic laws of energy/mass conservation and the deteriorating quality of burning coal. The mass equality of *high quality IN = low quality OUT* was known to be valid for every combustion process. Had scientists' attention been on mass flows out, Arrhenius' description in 1896 of the greenhouse effect would have been widely accepted, already at the end of the 19th century. In human-nature centred societies, the use of fossil fuels would then have been drastically limited.

In the 1960s and 1970s, the destructive impact on nature caused by the industrialised living mode began to receive attention. In 1966, Boulding published *The Economics of the Spaceship Earth*, a vision of an Earth thriving exclusively on energy from the Sun[15]. From 1993 to 2001, Scheer developed this vision in *A Solar Manifesto*, concluding with: *The challenge is to attune the planet's modern technology to the laws of the Sun.*

2.3 Photovoltaics make possible what neoliberalism denounces as impossible

The technological history[16] of photovoltaics starts with quantum theory, formulated between 1926 and 1928, which emerged after decades of research on the phenomena of radiation that could not be explained by classical physics. The theory had an impact on all sciences dealing with very small structures, measured not in metres but in nanometres[17].

The first practical application of quantum theory was the atomic bomb, which showed the enormous energy coming from a small amount of mass (E = m.c²); one of the far-reaching implications of the new scientific discoveries. Technology at the atomic level has such a bad reputation due to the societal choices to develop it foremost for bombs. The civil application to cook water with it had evolved from being a world saviour, to being a very contested activity, due to its links with the military, and due to accidents and the insolvable problem of radioactive waste with a lifespan of millennia [chapter 3].

Of much higher relevance are the many peaceful applications that the knowledge of quantum physics could generate. The rapid advancement of microelectronics and computer technology was mainly driven by the huge new commercial opportunities they created. Computer technology is based on the discovery of semiconductors: the transistor was invented in 1947, the microprocessor in 1971, which then enabled software development largely independent of the hardware, all the way to artificial intelligence. For that, however, solid-state physics first had to learn how to manufacture, harness and nanostructure extremely pure semiconductor crystals. Today, it is possible to fit 100 billion transistors on a single chip.

At the atomic and molecular level, the use of elementary processes allows for the compression and acceleration of these processes and offers an undreamt of variety of connections that are not feasible at the macro level. These microscopic innovations have directly influenced the development and efficiency of photovoltaic technology.

Ruggero Schleicher-Tappeser, an expert in sustainable energy, identifies four key nanoscience-based technology clusters that are accelerating the energy transition at an unprecedented pace. For a long time, these technologies were neglected because the energy industry resisted structural changes. However, they have now passed a *point of no return*, not only technically but also economically, which is driving their implementation ever faster. The four nanoscience innovations driving the energy transformation are:

1. The conversion of radiation to electricity, i.e. photovoltaics (PV). Due to dramatic cost reductions, PV has now overtaken all other methods of power generation. As its costs continue to fall, photovoltaics will become the dominant energy source of the future. However, it has a handicap: generation depends on sunshine, requiring supplementary technologies and practices to respect the reliability standards of various end-uses of electricity.

2. Power electronics, closely related to signal electronics, allowing remote digital process control, without human or mechanical mediation. It significantly enhances the flexibility of the energy system, facilitating the integration of variable solar and wind power in electricity grids.

3. Advanced batteries. Only a detailed understanding of ion intercalation in crystal structures and systematic research on new materials enable the development of batteries that are more cost-effective, powerful and lightweight. Decreasing costs and increasing reliability make their use in power grids more and more interesting to improve grid utilisation, security of supply and integration of solar power. The rapidly developing field of physical-chemical electricity storage is vast and promises further breakthroughs.

4. The conversion of electricity to radiation. Some are already familiar, such as light-emitting diodes (LED), lasers, and microwaves. They are transforming lighting, material processing, process heat and photochemistry, with substantial gains in energy efficiency.

These four areas of innovation have overcome crucial economic and technical hurdles after long resistance from established industries. The call to keep all technology options open is often a sign of helplessness or shameless patronage politics. A better understanding of technological lock-ins and deliberate disruptions becomes a prerequisite for democracy. For this, political economy is a helpful discipline.

2.4 The vested electricity generation sector under neoliberalism

With electricity becoming the *predominant* energy supply for most human activities, good knowledge about its societal context helps in navigating around the cliffs on the transformative path. A major cliff is the sector of vested companies, also called utilities, which were and still are supplying electric current to most households, services, industries, etc.

From pure monopoly power to mixed market structures

The electricity sector is most interesting, given that electricity is becoming the main carrier of energy to be used in the coming years [figure 4]. Ever since the start of commercial electricity sales in the 1880s, the expansion of the sector has continued globally.

An important physical-technical property of electricity supply is the scale at which activities are put into practice. Can it be done in a household (like cooking a meal), or is a large plant needed (for example, for casting steel). A scale is optimal when goods and services are delivered at the least social costs.

When industrialisation took off, *economies of scale* supported the building of always larger production plants by giant companies. In the world of energy, small-scale power supplies by means of water and wind mills were replaced by engines driven by steam, and later electricity. The electricity sector evolved within a century (1880 to 1980) from kilowatt power generation plants to Megawatt and Gigawatt dam-hydro, coal-fired and atomic power stations. By neglecting payment for external costs, the generation expenses declined due to improved technologies and larger scale. On the drawing tables of engineer-designers, the curves show declining prices for generated kWh when the plant capacity increases. However, in practice, plants larger than the optimal scale show *diseconomies of scale*, with product prices increasing. This is seemingly the case in contemporary atomic power plant construction.

The incumbent model is the one grown in industrialised countries, stacking the three major supply activities in a vertical pile: power *generation*, *transmission* over high-voltage grids, and *distribution* via medium- and low-voltage networks. The activities were mostly organised by a single company as a *vertically integrated monopoly*. The monopoly rights were assigned to a country, a state or another geographically *demarcated area*, because transmission and distribution of electricity are natural monopolies. When a single supplier is a cheaper solution than two or more suppliers, the monopoly status is called natural. This is the case in power transmission via wires, where the price per transmitted kWh declines the more delivery occurs via a *single* wire.[18] Public ownership of the grids is also natural, yet some grids were in the hands of private companies connected to their ownership of the generation plants.

Public authorities needed for regulating power businesses

Monopolies, public or private, natural or arranged, show a strong tendency to build administrative strongholds. They acquire monopoly profits (also called *rents*) by charging prices much higher than their costs. They can charge such excessive prices especially to *captive customers* who depend on grid power and lack alternatives for obtaining power[19]. To suppress monopolistic practices, supervision by public regulatory authorities is warranted.

In the US, state Public Utility Commissions regulate electricity and other monopoly sectors. The positive outcome of regulation for the captive consumers will be minor when *captured regulation*[20] occurs. Regulation is captured when the regulators follow the discourse, proposals, and interests of the monopolies. This is stimulated by the technocracy populating governmental energy departments being educated in the same colleges as the technocracy of the power companies. It augments mutual understanding and thinking in similar frames. Sometimes soft bribing and enforcing may happen in exclusive clubs or restaurants. The monopolies' budgets for public and media relations are lavish. Salaries and working conditions of the companies' staff are excellent to exuberant, minimising defection by engaged staff.

In Europe, several nations with public monopolies did not install specific regulators, assuming that the board of the public company would automatically serve the public interest. It was often unclear whether the government controlled the electricity monopoly, or vice versa, as was likely in the case of EDF (Électricité de France). More subtle was the Belgian private electricity sector, which developed and maintained a *self-regulation* system, *masterminding* the ideas and actions of most politicians from the local to the national level.[21] Masterminding strategy and tactics are also very observable in the EU's climate policy [chapter 8].

Neoliberalism reshuffles the cards

In the first breakthrough of neoliberalism in the 1980s and 1990s, the privatisation and deregulation of state-owned industries and public services were crucial pillars. IMF and the World Bank advocated, if not imposed, the agenda of privatisation and deregulation globally. Salient efforts were directed towards the electricity services in the US and Europe. In the UK, the Central Electricity Generation Board was Thatcher's primary economic objective, linked to the dismantling of coal mining. After the privatisation of the UK's electricity assets, the City of London was eager to extend the practice to the European continent. One of the main targets were the hundreds of city companies[22] in Germany.

The European utilities viewed the new models for the electric power sector unevenly, from favouring, to lukewarm acceptance, to hostile rejection.

Nevertheless, at the end of 1996 an EU Directive[23] concerning *common rules for the internal market in electricity* was adopted, but unevenly implemented by the Member States. The promise was that free markets and competition would substitute old-style regulation of fossilised monopolies. Such ideological slogans are mostly a deception. Electric current is different from storable batch delivery. Electricity generation and transmission must respect strict technical rules *second-by-second, all year round*. Expert operators continuously monitor crucial parameters and take measures to synchronise the generation facilities and balance the grids. Soon it became evident that the planned market would fail if not designed, monitored and enforced by superior regulators. However, these were not available when the neoliberal storms from the US and UK landed on the European continent. The *market* label was pasted on a bureaucratically concocted structure, which opened the doors for big finance.

The conditions for establishing functional competitive markets are demanding. *Competition* requires a *level playing field* for all market parties. Hence, significant efforts in *harmonisation* across the heterogeneous power generation systems in the Member States were needed. A prerequisite for installing effective harmonisation is high *transparency* of the electricity systems and the financial flows across their major activities. A sufficient level of transparency requires *separating*[24] the three main activities of generation, transmission, and distribution. Once fully separated, a specific regulation per activity is recommended because of their different natures and purposes. In generating electricity, competition among private producers opens opportunities[25] for higher efficiency and for Independent Generators of Own Power (IGOP), now mostly named *prosumers*. However, transmission and distribution as natural monopolies remained public companies, now regulated by more arm's length politics.

Warning

The incumbent giant electricity companies have a history of defending their monopoly against intruders, being IGOP. Their weapon was to prohibit grid access for independent producers, or to make the terms of access incredibly opaque and uneven, stripping the profit of IGOP projects. At the time, the IGOP were mostly CHP units of a few tens of MW of electricity; electricity from wind turbines was paltry and from photovoltaics non-existent.

In essence, the attitude and actions of the giant electricity companies have not changed: they will defend their stronghold, mainly with money extracted form captive customers. This requires many millions of captive customers, which implies the preclusion of millions of customers becoming IGOP organised in communities via local smart grids. IGOP communities are a spearhead component of escaping climate collapse and dethroning neoliberal big money. PV is a small-scale technology, best applied at the place of use. It is a household technology. Wind is also best harvested in a decentralised way on land, yet on a MW-scale with sufficient axis height. It is a community, cooperative technology.

Giant energy corporates have been and are masterminding energy and climate politics to protect their business model. They obtained and still obtain the support of neoclassical, neoliberal economists whose minds are troubled by the fetish of free markets and perfect competition. In the following section, two important cases of discreditable policymaking in RE history are documented. They are instructive for everyone engaged in the movement to escape climate collapse.

2.5 Unexpected initiators of renewable energy development in Europe

Three main actor groups are identified in the whirlpool of RE development in Europe over the last 50 years: *grassroots*, *politics*, and *corporates*. There is insufficient room to provide a comprehensive description of the groups' composition and actions. All three groups are heterogeneous, hard to demarcate, and variable over the considered timespan. Around the main groups, other important actors have had a significant impact, such as Chinese low-cost producers initiating PV-panel price cuts in 2008. The order of introducing the three groups represents their historic and future importance for RE.

Grassroots

Includes the independent, socially driven, maverick characters that reacted to the nascent environmental concerns and oil price crises of the 1970s, with a strong focus on renewable energy, energy conservation and efficiency. They were active people from diverse backgrounds, such as artists, students, teachers, academics, politicians, entrepreneurs, physicians, engineers, etc. The main motivations were love and care for nature, critique of the military and civil use of atomic power, and striving for communal political democracy with high self-reliance.

Politics

Here, the focus is on the European Commission (EC). The EC has a variety of Directorates with many officials and technocrats in the service of the European Union. The EU grew out of the European Coal and Steel Community founded in 1951. The Directorate Energy of the EC has been pursuing a communal energy policy. Policy integrations are only partly feasible, because the Member States maintained final authority on energy matters, similarly to taxation. The EC has to submit its draft policy documents to the European Parliament and Council, leading to a negotiation process concerning the submitted texts. Via the Council, the Member State officials and technocrats weigh in on the negotiation and final outcomes.

The split in authority results in compromises, and in deceptive language. For example, the word *tax* is like a red rag to a bull, hence the EC invents other words to cover up policies actually implying taxation of households [chapter 8]. By means of Member States holding authority in the matters of energy and taxation, the EC was not able to fully impose her neoclassical, neoliberal recipes on the Member States. Nevertheless, the significant budget of the EC allowed the build-up of an extensive bureaucracy, supported by consultants and research programmes. The EC produced in the domain of energy and climate several Directives with significant impact on the Member States' policy space. The impact is visible in the reallocation of lobbyism budgets of corporates from the national capitals to Brussels, where most European Institutes are headquartered.

Corporates

The largest industrial corporates in the world are active in energy. BP, Chevron, Exxon, Shell, Total and others are oil and gas transnational companies. Their names come back in chapter 5, revealing the huge super profits made on oil and gas. The focus here is on electric power corporates active in Europe. Over the study period many have changed names, merged, metamorphosed, disappeared. Some were less affected by the turmoil of the previous decades. For example: the public corporates EDF, France; RWE, Germany; Vattenfall, Sweden. New names were E.ON now Uniper (former Preussen Elektra); ENGIE (former Suez, Electrabel, Gaz de France). Several power corporates have split their power generation assets into two types: *obsolete* includes fossil and uranium fuelled plants, and *future* for the investments in renewable electricity generation. Section 2.5 gives some insight into how the electricity generation corporates function.

The Wyhl-Freiburg rebellion starting in 1975

In 1975, the small peaceful community of Wyhl on the banks of the Upper Rhine in Southern Germany rebelled against the Berlin-made plans to build an atomic power plant in their pristine forest. The Wyhl-Freiburg grassroots protest community initiated a range of initiatives most influential for the development of RE in Germany[26]. The grassroots opposition to atomic power, and the desire to find alternatives to it, help explain how RE developed from the bottom up in a country where top-down policymaking is the norm, and in a region whose political leadership was tied particularly strongly to the atomic energy industry.

The Wyhl protesters were scientifically and technologically forward looking. Its participants helped to debunk the myth of neutral expertise and to expose the economic and political interests behind the pro-nuclear coalition. They also created their own sources of expertise and scientific institutions, which gave a home to experts critical for atomic power. The community was a catalyst for the local development of solar technologies and sustainable business practices. These dovetailed with the larger-scale solar pioneering efforts of the Fraunhofer Institute for Solar Energy Systems and the connected Freiburg Eco-Institute innovators with like-minded people and organisations at the national and international levels. Neither the German federal government nor the traditional utilities showed much interest in this. Few believed there would be much of a market for RE technologies.

Grassroots communities also fostered social innovation, by supporting a new societal model based on decentralised, small-scale, ecologically sustainable production and community-based democratic decision making. This model poses a direct challenge to the centralised corporatist one.

There are several reasons for the success and impact of the Wyhl-Freiburg grassroots rebellion. Salient among those are the creativity, openness, and honesty of the community itself versus the vanity, secrecy, and deception of the atomic power interests. From the 1960s up until the Chernobyl disaster in 1986, atomic power interests and their followers believed in their own technological and economic superiority. The present generation of atomic power advocates has learned that hubris is a bad advisor, and in their fight to keep the option on board, their tactics have been reversed [chapter 3].

When big money, adhering to the neoliberal ideology, observes dangerous initiatives arising, it will nip them in the bud. If it is too late to smother the upcoming initiative at its origin, big money will capture it and deform it for its own use. Such a capture happened with the sustainability discourse, when in 1987 the World Commission on Environment and Development published a worldview opposite to neoliberalism. It also happened with climate policymaking, when the UNFCCC became operational in 1994, and the COPs had to launch measures for its implementation. Another clear case was the coup in 2014 by Europe's energy corporates on the deployment of RE. Brief reports about the two energy and climate dossiers follow next, and there is more concerning this in later chapters.

2.6 The incredible history of the EU's policy of supporting RE development

In the 1990s, discussions began about which policies were suitable to abate global warming. Given that economic activities cause the bulk of the GHG emissions, economists' views are influential. They narrowed the frame to financial incentives for mitigating the GHG emissions.

In light of the Rio Summit in 1992, the EC Climate Directorate advised imposing an energy-carbon tax of 1 EUR[27] per ton of CO_2 emitted, adding the same amount in subsequent years to arrive at a tax of 10 EUR per ton by the end of the decade. The European energy and industrial companies rejected the tax proposal. In 1997, at COP3 in Kyoto, global trading in carbon emission permits was imposed by the US delegation. The EU reluctantly accepted carbon trading to keep the US on board. One year later, the EC made a U-turn on carbon trading and became its zealous defender [chapter 8].

On energy matters, the EC Energy Directorate was most occupied with launching Europe's internal electricity and gas markets in 1996 and 1997. These concocted markets performed far less well than announced, and the Energy Directorate had to add more specific Directives, including one concerning the development of renewable energy technologies. The question was: *how* should this development be promoted? An intense debate about answering this question unfolded.

The debate was between *market advocates* and *practice realists*. The market advocates were neoclassical economists, the EC, and energy and industrial corporates. The practice realists were grassroots communities, entrepreneurs, enlightened politicians, supported by knowledge centres such as Fraunhofer, Freiburg Eco-institute and Wuppertal Institute, political scientists and a few engineering economists.

The debate was largely dominated by the substantial financial backing of the market advocates. They championed the theoretical superiority of artificial markets. The practice realists proposed technological and market development at a proper pace for every diverse renewable technology.

In 1999, the EC imagined a European artificial market for green certificates. The EC proposed to impose a *pan-European system of tradable green certificates* (TGC) for renewable electricity on the then fifteen EU Member States. The EC lauded such a certificates market as possessing superior qualities: similar talk to that around the Emissions Trading Scheme [chapter 8].

A number of preparations had to be made to launch the TGC instrument. First, a group of technologies was accepted as generators of renewable electricity, such as wind turbines, small hydropower turbines, PV panels, biomass combustion for power generation, and others. Similarly, some parts of household waste incineration, imported palm oil, and the likes were also labelled as renewable. For one MWh (1000 kWh) of electricity produced by one of the listed sources and techniques, the producer received one *green certificate*. The total volume of green certificates allocated by the EU Commission would correspond to the pursued market share of green electricity in the total of consumed electricity.

The *artificial demand* for green certificates would be created by requiring *all electricity vendors* in a region or member state to surrender green certificates annually for a regulatorily prescribed percentage of their electricity sales in the previous year.

With supply of certificates by green electricity producers and demand for certificates by electricity sellers to end-users, a market would simply emerge with further trade in green certificates. At least, this was neatly written as such on paper. Flanders, and the other Belgian regions of Wallonia and Brussels, have adopted this theoretical idea; an experience that its proponents and experimenting politicians at the time now prefer to remain silent about[28].

Germany rejected the EC proposal of an EU-wide green certificate market, and most Member States supported Germany. The EC failed in imposing its market utopia. After some bickering, each Member State was given the freedom to choose how they would encourage renewable power development. This was essentially a choice between two systems: the EC's proposal for a TGC limited to their own borders, or Germany's approach of providing differentiated and regularly adjusted direct support for every individual renewable technology, a practice already in place in Germany since 1990 and set to continue.

Flanders and the failed tradable green certificate experiment

Flanders adopted the TGC idea. This was to the delight of groups of beneficiaries at the expense of the captive electricity customers who saw the bill reflected in their electricity bills. The failing TGC siphoned hundreds of millions of euros from less well-off households to richer households, investors and electricity corporates[29]. It did not bring an iota of technological innovation; most of the money went to dubious projects like burning biomass in old coal-fired power stations. Such activities are a technological *race to the bottom*. The experiment teaches us that heterogeneous technologies and activities cannot be captured by a uniform approach[30]. The uniform approach allowed the power companies to rake in hundreds of millions in super profits with outdated technology and biomass with a dubious sustainability record.

The German-Danish-Spanish success story

In some EU countries, grassroots movements, energy communities, local governments, and knowledge centres such as those described in section 2.5 closely monitored energy policy developments. In the 1980s, they were concerned about wasting the penultimate opportunity to implement effective energy and environmental policies in a timely manner. They remained actively committed to energy conservation, energy efficiency and renewable energy as the way forward. These movements were strongest in Denmark[31] and Germany, with active professional politicians also on board[32].

The Chernobyl atomic power plant catastrophe in April 1986 was a major blow to the political zeal for atomic power. The desire to develop renewable energy technology with innovation support was strong. The mechanism of support was the deployment of a market for each specific technology, with its own history and potential. Annually, the amount of support for new projects was adjusted according to the technological progress made. This is how Germany did it, as well as Denmark, Austria and Spain. The technologies of photovoltaics and wind turbines were developed to industrial scale by Germany, Denmark and Spain. Imagine if the EC could have prevented this by imposing its fictitious

TGC system as an obligation! The world would today be in a much worse state than the already poor condition one can observe. The EC market-oriented policies played a discreditable role.

The Renewable Energy Directive of 2001 included an obligation to evaluate the two applied systems. The evaluation report had to be ready by the year 2005 at the latest. The studies were carried out at the initiative and expense of the EC. Scientific reports confirmed the success of the *German approach*, highlighting the need for diverse and adaptable policies to achieve swift and cost-effective results. Moreover, the evidence of the failure of an artificial certificate trading system was presented with clear facts and figures.

The conflict between the EC and Germany, joined by other Member States leading in renewable energy, took place during the years 1998 to 2002. These are the years when the EU ETS was fabricated. Hence, the TGC experiments were a suitable testing ground to evaluate *artificial markets* as a policy instrument. Important lessons could be learned from the disastrous experiences in TGC, *before the launch of the EU ETS*. The market-worshipping EC turned out to be blind and deaf. The construction of the utopia of GHG emissions trading continued. The EC officials looked the other way. They knew but did not want to know. In legal terms, this attitude is called *guilty of negligence*.

2.7 The 2014 coup by Europe's energy corporates

The insight is growing that renewable electricity will be the major supplier of carbon-free energy in the future. Still there is discussion about *bottom-up* versus *top-down* approaches and *small-scale* versus *large-scale* production. In electricity generation, these dichotomies manifest as *grassroots bottom-up small-scale production* versus *corporate top-down large-scale production*. The opposing poles may cooperate to attain the least costs. In 2024 however, corporates still dominate over grassroots.

The business model of the corporates relies on large-scale generation, which flows into the electric transmission grid from the top, to consumers who pay obediently for the electricity supplied. In the period 2008 to 2020, major European electricity corporates rubberstamped, built, and opened new coal-fired power plants, including in the Netherlands and Germany. Around 2010, the corporates became aware that their coal plant investments were wrong. They recognised the need for changing their generation assets to plants exploiting renewable energy sources. To maintain the core of their business model, the plants have to be large-scale. They also wanted to maintain control over data and knowledge to make a profit from power transactions.

The corporates concentrated their money and lobbying power at the EC for a coup. On March 19, 2014, under the aegis of the Magritte lobby group, a press conference was organised in Brussels[33]. The CEOs of major European energy companies issued a *call for government and state heads to implement immediate and drastic measures to safeguard Europe's energy future.* They presented the politicians with nine recommendations, and three proposals (rather commandments): *1) Preference for mature renewables in the regular market; 2) Priority to the utilisation of existing competitive power capacity rather than subsidising new constructions; 3) Restore the ETS as a flagship climate and energy policy.*

The Magritte CEOs are keen to maintain their oligopoly power, with a revenue model that can finance their inertia and incorrect decisions in previous years. The ETS fulfils a significant role in this, but the *explicit* designation of the ETS as a third commandment is remarkable. It is indirect evidence that the ETS serves industry interests. Or will companies advocate for public policies that impose additional responsibilities and duties on themselves?

In 2014, to align with the preferences of these CEOs and facilitate their shift towards renewable energy, European Commissioner Joaquín Almunia revised the state aid rules[34]. Large-scale renewable projects have since been favoured over small-scale ones. This is an example of how lobbyism and political weakness go hand in hand. The renewable energy transformation has been placed in the hands of companies with the biggest CO_2 emissions. The renewable energy future model lost a major battle in 2014[35]. The coup had an effect: the growth of small-scale bottom-up generation of renewable electricity was choked.

Why did the big energy companies make this power grab? Clearly, because the grassroots driven small-scale renewable energy developed rapidly and could take over more and more of the electricity supply, being a result of far-sighted policies of Germany and Denmark. These policies developed a suitable mechanism to finance both technology and market development. An important element of success was respect for the *diversity* of technologies and local conditions. Wind turbines and PV panels appeared everywhere and gave oxygen to their technological development, through the creativity, commitment, and efforts of grassroots movements. The European corporates in power generation—the coal plant builders—hijacked the results of these movements, with the support of the EU Commission.

A reminder

- Specific technology promoting policies in Germany, Denmark, and Spain developed wind turbines, PV cells, and other renewable electricity technology.
- All market-based policies advocated and tried by the EU Commission failed, a forthright showcase being the infamous *tradable green certificate experiments.*
- Wind turbines and PV panels are since 2018 producing the cheapest electricity in history, since electricity generation started in the 1880s.
- In 2014, major European energy conglomerates carried out a coup to gain priority and subsidies for their large-scale renewable energy projects, hindering the grassroots pioneers' attempts to deploy small-scale bottom-up installations and solutions.

Chapter 3
The delusive truth of atomic energy

Atomic[1] energy is the second item of the triptych[2] discourse for mitigating GHG emissions. It is an apparently permanent, deep-rooted and globally spread delusive truth of the highest order. Honestly contributing to a case of social importance starts by exploring its history. *Why*, *how* and *where* did the case originate? *What* has it accomplished so far, for better and for worse? The short history of atomic energy is overloaded with important facts and political interventions. In the societal debate on atomic energy, proponents seem unaware of the past. In any case, they do not use the facts in their advice for continuing the daredevil atomic perils. Without a profound evaluation of the past, projections for the future lack solid foundations and are merely wishful thinking or delusion to advance their proponents' own ideology or interests. The stories about atomic energy have degenerated into mere propaganda, masterminded by the International Atomic Energy Agency, the Nuclear Forum with Saatchi & Saatchi support, and boosted by the neoliberal *breakthrough* clan.

The chapter consists of seven sections:

Section 3.1 presents a selection of salient facts that characterise the 85 year long history of experiments and projects to obtain the energy—for evil and for good—from fission and fusion of atoms.

Section 3.2 shows atomic energy in practice as a delusive truth fabricated around Einstein's popular equation $E = mc^2$.

Section 3.3 sheds light on the uniqueness, role and activities of the International Atomic Energy Agency (IAEA). The IAEA's sneaky activity in Working Group 3 of the IPCC climate panel is a silenced public secret.

Section 3.4 reveals the lies of the atomic industry about *announced* successes over the past 70 years. In all cases, the huge promises turned out to be false and more than once the source of technical, economic, and social disasters. This is why private investors are no longer putting their own money into new atomic power plants[3].

Section 3.5 tells how Saatchi & Saatchi as *Merchants of doubt*[4] set up in 2007 the campaign for the Nuclear Forum to confuse the general public and politicians. This campaign was successful for the image of atomic power, but unfortunate for the future of mankind.

Section 3.6 provides a clarification on why atomic energy, from atomic fission or fusion, has no future. Figure 6 shows the enormous source and sink flabs related to the atom fuel cycles and massive cooling needs.

Section 3.7 concludes on what to decide now about atomic power. Fully opposite to the neoliberal *Breakthrough* and *Build nuclear Now* campaigns, the advice is to phase out and finish atomic power generation. To avoid the disastrous atomic perils in the pipeline, it should be phased out sooner rather than later.

3.1 Salient facts from the 70-year history of atomic power[5]

This brief overview of the history of atomic energy presents several milestones, shedding light on the atomic domain, and perhaps prompting the reader's own exploration of the facts. Beyond the endnotes, it is recommended to use Wikipedia as a source of factual information on the milestones.

The military cradle

Atomic energy originated after the development of atomic weapons. In 1941, the US launched the Manhattan Project for this purpose. In 1942, Enrico Fermi[6] and his collaborators at the University of Chicago achieved the first chain reaction by splitting atomic nuclei. In 1944, the US Hanford research centre supplied plutonium suitable for bombs. The culmination of these efforts occurred in August 1945 when the US dropped the uranium bomb *Little Boy* on Hiroshima and the plutonium bomb *Fat Man* on Nagasaki.

After World War 2, several nations, including the Soviet Union, the UK and France, commenced the construction of uranium-based reactors, readily allowing the extraction of plutonium. Atomic bomb possession proliferated rapidly: the Soviet Union acquired them in 1949, the UK in 1952, France in 1960 and China in 1964. The US Nautilus submarine in 1954 and the Soviet Lenin icebreaker in 1955 were the first ships powered by atomic energy. In 1951, an experimental breeder reactor[7] generated atomic electricity for the first time.

Atoms for Peace, and for less noble intentions

In December 1953, President Eisenhower proclaimed the *Atoms for Peace* initiative at the UN General Assembly. The US expressed its willingness to provide technology, fuel, assistance and installations to third countries for peaceful purposes. However, the concept of *controlled access* to atomic technology eventually degenerated into unchecked proliferation, imprudently opening doors to weapons development, as soon occurred in Israel and India. The knowledge of atomic physics and the techniques for handling uranium and its derivative isotopes in experimental reactors provided fissile material for the production of atomic weapons[8]. Besides, the US Atomic Energy Act authorised *private companies* to own atomic facilities. The US Atomic Energy Commission provided the money for Research and Development, such as for prototypes of the Fermi-1 breeder reactor, the Hallam gas-cooled reactor, and the Bonus boiling water reactor.

In the 1950s, atomic power was acclaimed as the safe and cheap way to an energy paradise. Academics announced that atomic energy would satisfy all the world's energy needs once and for all, hence making the use of fossil fuels obsolete. Governments, officials, industry, science, media and most of the population shared the belief that atomic energy would soon be ready to provide massive, cheap electricity. The ATOMIUM[9] in Brussels was the main attraction at the 1958 World's Fair, and is an enduring symbol of the *zeitgeist in the 1950s*. However, royal court objections at that time prevented the construction of the third Belgian research reactor BR3 with 11MWe capacity in the vicinity of the ATOMIUM and the royal palace in Laken, Brussels.

Breeder reactors for unlimited amounts of electricity!?

In the 1960s, the designs of breeder reactors fuelled the wildest expectations and bold promises, claiming to generate *enough electricity to meet any reasonable energy budget for many millions of years*. It was then announced that fusion would be operationally available by the year 2000. In the economic energy models of the 1970s, breeder reactors and fusion assumed the role of *backstop technology*. The atomic energy backstop, as envisioned in the publications of atomic scholars and of theoretical economists, held the promise of providing unlimited energy forever[10].

Despite 60 years and US$100 billion spent on research, development and demonstration, all breeder reactors in Western countries have been closed. The Fermi-1 *partial meltdown* in 1966 cooled enthusiasm in the US. In 1985, Germany, Belgium and the Netherlands abandoned their almost ready-to-start breeder reactor in Kalkar, Germany[11], after spending EUR4.1 billion of taxpayers' money. Both the UK and Japan have also terminated their breeder reactor programmes. France did likewise in 2019, concluding its operations with the 233 MWe research reactor Phénix, which ran from 1973 to 2004. In the 1980s a construction budget of US$10 billion was spent on France's 1200 MWe commercial breeder reactor Superphénix, which operated from 1986 to 1996. During those 11 years, barely 7.5TWh of electricity was generated[12]. Superphénix failed technically and financially.

India, Russia, and China are reportedly still spending money on breeder reactors, but information about them is sparse. For example, a Chinese breeder reactor was reported to have operated for 26 hours in 2011. Afterwards, there is no more information available about this reactor. Fast forward to 2024, and the great hope among proponents for reviving atomic power lies in small breeder reactors that are promised to be operational *soon*. Belgium is investing in a lead-cooled fast neutron—a new name for breeder—research reactor, requiring progressively more time and budget, and desperately inviting other countries to join this experimental atomic gamble [section 3.4].

Atomic energy technology is fully researched

The 1950s and 1960s witnessed intensive research across the entire range of atomic reactors and fuel cycles, exploring fast neutron breeder reactors, atomic fission in a bath of boiling water or pressurised hot water, gas-cooled reactors, and graphite reactors akin to the one that exploded at Chernobyl in 1986. Research also extended to designs on nuclear fusion. Practically all public energy research funds were allocated to atomic technology during this period. This exclusivity in focus and spending fits the beliefs of the time that atomic power would fulfil humankind's energy demand forever.

The borderline between civilian and military targets was and often remains unclear. In atomic research, military targets usually take centre stage. On 5 December 2022, the Livermore laboratory at the University of Berkeley in the US achieved controlled fusion of atomic nuclei. Notably, this experiment was in the service of US atomic armament[13].

Atomic technology is known from top to bottom, left to right, one might even say chipped to the bone. Several industrial countries, such as the UK, Germany, and Sweden, developed their own reactor types. Most countries later bought pressurised water or boiling water reactors from US companies Westinghouse and General Electric.

Atomic energy expands and stalls

The 1973 oil price crisis served as a tailwind for the ordering of hundreds of atomic power plants. Several European countries built large reactors ranging from 900 MWe to 1300 MWe, experiencing limited overruns in budget and construction time. Many of these plants also achieved the expected performance, such as in Belgium, Germany, Finland, Sweden and Switzerland. France has been praised for building 56 atomic power plants in series. The talk is that this happened at low cost, but French atomic accounts are not transparent. The intertwining of the state-owned monopoly EDF with state coffers and military activities is acknowledged, but the specific links and money flows remain obscure.

Despite Germany's technological reputation, it nevertheless struggled with atomic power. For instance, the Niederaichbach power plant supplied electricity equivalent to 18 days of full capacity for a year and a half of operation, and was finally shut down in July 1974. Similarly, the Mülheim-Kärlich power plant operated occasionally during 13 months and was shut down in September 1988.

A number of countries, including Norway, Denmark and New Zealand, have thoughtfully rejected atomic power. After a referendum in 1978, Austria did not start up the completed atomic power plant in Zwentendorf near Vienna and decommissioned it.

Globally, the majority of the ordered atomic plants ended in failure. In the US, motherland of atomic technology, electricity companies started cancelling their ordered reactors from 1974 onwards. Less than half of the 197 reactors in the order books have been commissioned for power generation. After 1978, only two projects with two reactors each were initiated in the US. One of them, VC Summer in South Carolina, was stopped in 2017 after billions of US dollars in losses.

For the other project, Vogtle in Georgia, estimated construction costs of two 1117 MWe units went from US$14 billion in 2009 to US$36.8 billion in 2023. In July 2023, one unit started commercial operation, with the second starting in April 2024.

Most affected by the atomic failures were countries in the Global South, enticed by the IAEA into the atomic adventure. They experienced a severe financial aftermath. Some reactors under construction were left as scrap after decades of work and billions of dollars in expenditure. Others continued the agony since the 1970s at the expense of small-scale electricity users or taxpayers.

Among the four new 1600 MWe giant reactors in Europe, the one in Finland (Olkiluoto) has been operating since April 2023. Its construction began in 2005. Out of the 12 billion euros in construction costs, the French state, acting as the problematic builder of the Finnish project, is paying a substantial 9 billion euros itself! In

France, the completion of Flamanville has been delayed repeatedly due to technical problems with the reactor vessel, and in 2024, an experimental start-up was beginning. For the Finnish and French atomic plants, the building time is way overdue and the cost three to four times the original budget.

The construction of the two reactors at Hinkley Point C (UK) started in March 2017. By May 2022, the building cost had been increased by 50 percent to £25–26 billion. Interestingly, these cost overruns are of no concern to atomic energy adepts. The UK Conservative government has granted an assured power purchase price of £92.5 per MWh for the Hinkley reactors, guaranteed for 35 years from start-up, with the purchase price indexed. In October 2014, EU commissioner Joaquín Almunia authorised this *exuberant* subsidy scheme, while ending support for grassroots renewable energy projects [section 2.7].

Accidents happen

Fatal accidents have marked the history of atomic endeavours, starting early with two incidents during the Manhattan Project. The subsequent timeline unfolds as a series of ruinous events, some of which are highlighted here. In 1952, a nuclear meltdown in Canada's Chalk River occurred. In 1957, a fire broke out at Windscale in the UK during the reprocessing of high-level radioactive waste, and an explosion occurred at Mayak in the Soviet Union. The accidents persisted over the years, including an atomic meltdown in 1961 at Idaho Falls, US, in 1966 a partial meltdown at the Fermi-1 breeder reactor in Michigan, US, and in 1975 a fire at Browns Ferry power plant, US. Atomic meltdowns struck Leningrad in 1975 and Beloyarsk in 1977, both in the Soviet Union. In 1979, a partial meltdown occurred at Three Mile Island, Pennsylvania, US. In April 1986, a failed experiment in a reactor of Chernobyl, Ukraine, caused a catastrophe. Due to its overshadowing impact, the accident at the German thorium high-temperature reactor on 4 May 1986, received minimal public attention. The 300 MWe plant, operational since 1983, was permanently shut down in 1989. This information is worth knowing for those advocating thorium or high-temperature reactors as future technologies.

On 11 March 2011, the cores of three reactors at Japan's Fukushima atomic power plant melted: one with a capacity of 460 MWe and two with a capacity of 784 MWe[14]. This resulted in the release of large quantities of radioactive substances into the surrounding area and the Pacific Ocean. The clean-up of the radioactivity pollution will take decades. The expenditure associated with it has been rising over time, and is now estimated at US$500–750 billion. As a result of such expenses, Japan's 30-year nuclear power programme has proven unprofitable. In addition, there are huge unpaid costs for the tens of thousands who have lost their habitat. Japanese taxpayers are charged for clean-up and waste disposal costs. The impacts on nature on land and in the Pacific Ocean are profound. At present, the atomic power interests wish to loosen the safety standards to lower the bills of the clean-up by dumping radioactive contaminated waste water into the Pacific.

After this brief summary of some salient facts, an obvious question would be: *Why not simply abandon the failed and failing technology and phase it out?* While the question is valid, the answers by vested powers are elusive, due to the prevailing delusions engendered by the atomic interest community.

3.2 Atomic energy is a showcase of delusive truth

The truth aspect related to atomic energy

Quantum physics is the foundation of the truth aspect of atomic fission and fusion. Quantum physics is a fundamental advancement from ordinary physics. Some youngsters are fascinated by the wonders of science, including my own granddaughter Marwa, who proudly refers to the first female Nobel laureate Marie Curie. She was awarded the Nobel Prize in physics in 1903 along with her husband. In 1911, she received the Nobel Prize in chemistry for her groundbreaking discovery of radium and polonium. In 1906, Einstein published the famous equation $E = mc^2$. This formula is a blockbuster for its simplicity and dizzying significance. A small amount of mass m holds massive amounts of energy E. The formula made and makes the minds of many people spin. Marie Curie's work on radioactivity and Albert Einstein's theory of relativity, collectively with other scientists[15], laid the foundations for the understanding and practical application of atomic processes, occurring in atomic bombs and in controlled reactions in a reactor to obtain heat.

In the first decades of the 20th century, scientists collaborated across national borders to advance knowledge in atomic physics and explore its possible practical implications. However, the rise of Fascism in Italy and Nazism in Germany strained these partnerships, especially with World War 2 looming on the horizon. By 1941, the US military recognised the potential of quantum physics in developing atomic weapons, leading to test explosions in New Mexico. In August 1945, atomic bombs were dropped on Hiroshima and Nagasaki. Whether this was a responsible act of war is still up for debate.

The terrible consequences of these bombings intensified the reflections of ethically concerned scientists, including Einstein and colleagues. In response, they took a notable step in 1948, by founding the *Bulletin of the Atomic Scientists*[16] to amplify an independent scientific voice on atomic weapons and atomic energy. The Bulletin provides insight and analysis from scientists, particularly atomic physicists. Access to the bulletin is open, offering a wealth of in-depth information on atomic issues.

Another noteworthy initiative by independent scientists is the annual publication of the *World Nuclear Industry Status Report*[17], also freely accessible. It contains factual information on the ups and downs of all atomic power plants standing worldwide, with in-depth coverage of countries with a significant number of such plants, and of topical issues. By strictly adhering to facts and avoiding speculative narratives about the future of the sector, the authors offer excellent information for a sober view of the past and present.

Interestingly, many newcomers to the field of atomic energy appear to ignore these valuable sources of information. The reason behind this oversight can be surmised: facts and knowledge do not fit the delusive truth and propaganda about atomic energy constructed by fraudsters[18] who put their short-term interests above the safe future of the world's population.

Misleading atomic story since 1953

The *Atoms for Peace* programme was ambiguous and misleading from the beginning. In the 1950s, large US private companies such as Westinghouse, General Electric, and Babcock & Wilcox, showed interest in designing and building atomic power plants, foreseeing substantial future profits. Other industrial countries such as Belgium, Canada, Germany, France, the Soviet Union, the UK, and Sweden, also set course to develop and apply atomic technology. The US, aiming to assert its precedence and dominance, sought to control the international market through cooperation, licensing, and stimulating demand in countries with limited technological capacity. *Atoms for profit* would have been a more accurate slogan than *Atoms for peace*, albeit too clear an exposure of the true intentions of the US.

3.3 The International Atomic Energy Agency (IAEA)

The establishment of the IAEA in July 1957 marked a significant development. The IAEA is an intergovernmental agency, its members being contributing UN states which join it voluntarily. As of 2022, IAEA operates with a full-time equivalent staff of 1377 persons, including 914 in general services. Its total budget was €668 million, with €396 million allocated for regular operational activities, and an additional €117 million for Technical Cooperation. IAEA is a well-mediated organisation with significant autonomy.

The IAEA's mission is clearly stated in its statutes, Article 2: *The Agency shall seek to accelerate and enlarge the contribution of atomic energy to peace, health and prosperity throughout the world. It shall ensure, so far as it is able, that assistance provided by it or at its request or under its supervision or control is not used in such a way as to further any military purpose.*

The goal and mandate of the IAEA is the promotion of atomic energy worldwide, including in poor countries where industrial capability for atomic energy is lacking. In addition, the IAEA should *so far as it is able* prevent the proliferation of atomic weapons. However, the five recognised atomic weapons states, primarily the US and the Soviet Union, accumulated massive atomic weapons arsenals. Subsequently, further proliferation of atomic weapons occurred.

The NPT[19], an international treaty on the non-proliferation of atomic weapons, came into force in March 1970, and now has 191 participating countries. Nevertheless, the NPT did not stop the proliferation of atomic weapons. Indeed, supervision of the implementation of the NPT was assigned to the IAEA, an organisation that also promotes atomic energy. It is bad practice to assign incompatible tasks to one organisation.

The inherent conflict between promoting a technology and regulating the same technology poses a significant challenge, particularly in the realm of atomic matters where such incompatibility is comparable to playing with fire. Control over possession and proliferation of nuclear weapons is substandard. The examples of Israel, not a party to the NPT, and of North Korea, which became party to the NPT in 1985 and left in 2003, illustrate this. Geopolitical agendas exert influence over the control exercised by IAEA. While Israel's atomic weapons are tolerated, Iran's atomic activities undergo the most stringent restrictions and controls, and were bombed by Israel and the US in June 2025. Moreover, the IAEA has no influence on US and Russian nuclear arsenals. A UN organisation is needed to better protect humanity from the threat of atomic weapons. A thoroughly reformed IAEA, divested of tasks, budgets and staff related to the promotion of atomic energy could be the solution. The resources thus freed could be redirected toward enhancing control over weapons and managing atomic waste. This would end the ambiguous position and activities of the IAEA.

IAEA: spider in the web of atomic propaganda today

The IAEA's formal status as an intergovernmental organisation under the auspices of the UN is similar to that of the IPCC. Such status ensures contacts, privileged access, and influence at the highest echelons of global policy. IAEA makes ample use of this status to infiltrate global climate policy cenacles, in order to position atomic power as a valid mitigation option. IAEA therefore desires to be present in the IPCC and at the COP meetings of the UNFCCC.

The 2015 Paris climate agreement stands out for its vagueness, notably avoiding explicit mention of terms such as *fossil fuel, oil, gas, and coal*. Apart from confirming the 2009 Copenhagen agreement on the 2°C warming limit, with a target of 1.5°C, and US$100 billion in support for developing countries from the year 2020 onwards, there is nothing concrete to read in the agreement. Nothing? No, Article 16§8 contains one other concrete element: it provides for IAEA's right to be present at the upcoming annual climate COPs. Amidst the presence of fossil fuel lobbyists already infiltrated in the COPs, the IAEA as atomic energy lobbyist is explicitly named as a participant.

IAEA has contributed to diluting the revolutionary essence of Sustainable Development. In a 2008 report[20], IAEA bestowed the label *sustainable* upon atomic energy – a classification that defies imagination. According to IAEA, sustainability in the context of atomic energy corresponds to mainstream thinking and practices regarding electricity supply. This includes *information to the public that complies with best international practice* in the construction of power plants. For environmental protection, it is enough to have *lower impacts compared to existing plants*. As for the insoluble waste problem, IAEA considers *limiting waste generation to the practical minimum*, and *managing waste in a way that does not impose unnecessary burdens on future generations* to be sufficient and adequate measures.

IAEA relies on its own sector's best practices as evidence enough to claim that atomic energy meets the criteria of Sustainable Development for *Our Common Future*[21].

However, the agency appears resistant to consider external criteria and examples that could contribute to a more robust sustainability assessment[22]. Ethical issues associated with atomic energy, such as the care and aftercare for uranium miners and the local populations in mining areas, are mostly marginalised. In case of catastrophes such as Chernobyl and Fukushima, there are inadequate compensations for those displaced from their familiar habitat. The use of atomic power inherently perpetuates inequality for future generations. To obtain bulk electricity during a few decades for the richest part of today's generations, a serious problem of atomic waste is passed on to all future generations. This negates elementary ethical thinking and moral standards.

The promises of the 1950s and 1960s that a solution to the atomic waste issues would soon be found, have still not been fulfilled and will forever be unfulfilled. Precautionary measures are deficient. Risks are being passed on to the people of today, of tomorrow and to all future generations. Also, the activity of atomic energy and its catastrophic impacts cannot be insured[23]. It is an irresponsible act of public policy to license high-risk industrial activities that the major reinsuring companies of the world refuse to insure.

IAEA infiltrates IPCC Working Group 3

A pinnacle of IAEA infiltration is the role played in the IPCC Working Group 3 (WG3), particularly observable in the 2014, 2018, and 2022 reports of WG3[24]. In framing the role of atomic power in the realm of climate policy, the IAEA juggles two conflicting objectives.

One objective is to *conceal the facts and problems* associated with atomic power. For this objective, IAEA strives to prevent IPCC reports publishing a complete and accurate representation and assessment of the literature from independent scientists on atomic power. The second objective is to *leverage the IPCC label* to portray atomic energy as a fully-fledged low-carbon option. Achieving both objectives together requires quite some balancing and manoeuvring – skills that the IAEA has honed through its ambiguous role in terms of promotion and control of atomic energy.

Objective one is highly problematic for the IPCC, as it directly contradicts the IPCC's essential mission[25]. IPCC's core mission is delivering comprehensive reviews of the available knowledge, requesting the assessment of all peer-reviewed literature, and to *clearly identify disparate views for which there is significant scientific or technical support, together with the relevant arguments.* The IAEA scam undermines the essence of the IPCC mission, as evident in the almost exclusive use of IAEA documents and those of related organisations, such as the OECD's Nuclear Energy Agency. From the literature, mostly pro-nuclear energy articles are cited, with a few critical authors in the bibliography cited incorrectly[26]. All independent literature that is based on the facts of atomic power and on solid evaluation methods is negated.

Moreover, comprehensive and substantiated critical comments on the IPCC draft texts about atomic energy through the formal scientific review process delivered to the IPCC secretariat are not responded to[27]. This non-fulfilment of regular practice is also completely against the IPCC working rules. Reviewing comments and replies in a transparent, objective way is core practice in science.

IAEA employee at rest H.H. Rogner served as the author of the passages on atomic energy in the 2014 IPCC report. He participated in the IPCC as a co-opted contributing author[28], and his presence and appearance at the April 2014 IPCC plenary meeting in Berlin was highly unusual[29]. The 2018 and 2022 IPCC reports show the same flaws as the 2014 texts on atomic energy. This real IPCC-gate related to Working Group 3 receives no media coverage, while a few emails between climate scientists of Working Group 1 hijacked in November 2009 turned into a high-profile *climate-gate*, causing a lot of turmoil. This is the result of propaganda. It also proves that IPCC's three Working Groups are of very different quality, with WG3 being infiltrated by fossil fuel and atomic power interests. Those in power in the neoliberalist era know how to mastermind their interests on international platforms and mislead billions of people.

IAEA achieves its second objective by perpetuating the mantra triptych *Renewable Energy, Nuclear Energy, Carbon Capture and Storage* as viable mitigation options to reduce GHG emissions. This triptych permeates the entire climate policy narrative, while distorting the actual reality by putting three options on an equal footing, while only the *Renewable Energy* option is sustainable. Important is that *Renewable Energy* cannot be reconciled with *Atomic Energy* in an integrated electric power system.

IAEA's efforts to preserve the triptych are veiled because otherwise the first and major objective of concealing the facts is jeopardised. The persistence of the triptych discourse is driven by the interests of atomic and fossil fuel industries. Furthermore, outdated computer models employed by economists include atomic power without regard for the inevitable conflicts with renewable electricity from wind and sunlight currents in active power systems. This superficiality puts irreconcilable options side by side on paper, constituting scientific blunders that continue to fester and contribute to sustaining atomic propaganda. IPCC WG3 has some problems to address!

3.4 Announced rebirth of atomic power

While the IAEA lobby operates at international level, the atomic industry actively seeks to preserve its privileges as usual in the highdays of the atomic illusion. The atomic industry in a broad sense includes research centres, university departments specialised in atomic physics, companies providing services for atomic power plants, administrative bodies like EURATOM, etc. To put the shabby, withering atomic industry back in business, climate change is a welcome opportunity. Nothing less than a *nuclear renaissance—rebirth*—was launched, and still looms in the air.

The call for a *rebirth* indicates the languishing state of the atomic industry, which crafts a narrative around a seemingly *viable baby* to perpetuate the practice of dazzling governments, ensuring the continued flow of funds and subsidies—an established practice since the 1950s and 1960s. After the turn of the century, there was an attempt to replicate the *success*[30] of the French atomic programme from the 1980s – a *nuclear renaissance*. The plan was to build mastodon power plants with capacities ranging from 1600 to 1700 MWe in series, and four to six reactors in one park . However, this ambitious approach has already gritted its teeth on three European troublemakers: Olkiluoto in Finland, Flamanville in France, and Hinkley Point C in the UK.

As a flight from these failures, the atomic industry fantasised an alternative: Small Modular Reactors (SMR). This would allow hundreds or thousands to be built, as if there exists a waiting list of cities and towns to welcome one or more atomic energy plants to their territory. SMR is much bleating, but little wool. The technologies associated with SMRs are reminiscent of past failures: fast neutron or breeder reactors, thorium high-temperature reactors, and surely the well-known boiling water technology[32]. Why should a technology, extensively researched for 75 years with massive budgets and plenty of manifest failures, suddenly succeed?

A notable argument against its success is evident in the costs of the few Small Modular Reactor (SMR) plants built—they surpass the cost per MWe of traditional mastodon atomic plants.

Expressed in million US$ per MWe, the Chinese CEFR costs *19.4 million US$* or 15 times the originally estimated price. Similarly, the Russian Akademik Lomonosov costs *10.5–14 million US$* per MWe or 4 times the estimated price. The cost of Argentina's CAREM, which has been under construction for years, has been re-estimated at *14 million US$* per MWe in 2020. The US Nuscale is estimated at *6.6 million US$* per MWe in 2020. The possible start-up would come after 2030[33], like the many other SMR power-plant concepts.

The Belgian MYRRHA project stands as a pioneering design for a lead-cooled breeder reactor, with various objectives. The reactor is intended for research, for the production of isotopes for medicinal use, and also for transmutation of isotopes to shorten the lifetime of an atomic waste particle. The cost of the project is still uncertain, and may rise above €1.6 billion. Several years ago, Belgium extended an invitation to its neighbours to participate, but all countries declined the offer. The success of the partnership campaign seems limited to some interest from Romania.

Proponents of SMR concepts are mainly concerned about subsidies, and lots of public money with firm commitments for guaranteed long-term support. Money and more money from the community, from you and me. Compared to the 1950s and 1960s, nothing new under the sun in the land of atomic power. There is no energy technology on Earth that has received as much long-term support and subsidies as atomic power. The industry seems to regard this as an obvious achievement. However, a fundamental question arises: Should a society still spend money on a 75-year-old technology that has brought more negative than positive outcomes, and will continue to cause serious problems, now and in the future?

Indulging in a risky, expensive, long-term, irreversible liability?

Academic atomic physicists, including Einstein, were the first to see the dangers of atomic technologies and practices. They were critical and independent. In addition, individuals in responsible positions in the industry have opposed the delusive truths, advising society and politicians to stop atomic power. One example is the late David Freeman, once director of the largest US electricity producer, the Tennessee Valley Authority. Also, Peter Bradford, former member of the US Nuclear Regulatory Commission, points out the financial unviability of atomic power.

3.5 Atomic discourse is influential

Sociologists and political scientists highlighted the importance and influence of the discourse[34], a facet often overlooked by techno-economists. When it comes to comprehending policy, particularly in the realm of atomic energy, a purely techno-economic perspective proves inadequate. Words, narratives, interests and institutions have more influence in shaping policy decisions. Atomic energy interests have known this for a long time, and they pay a lot of attention to it.

In July 2007, the Nuclear Forum met with Saatchi & Saatchi and other marketers in Brussels. The subject of discussion was the development of a new strategy to make the renaissance of nuclear power credible among the general public, the young, politicians, teachers, and other key stakeholders. The bumbling engineers who defended atomic power from the 1970s to 1990s are no match for the violence of the new media. If their fees are gorgeous, marketers will sell the Devil to the Pope if necessary, or vice versa, depending on who pays most.

The Nuclear Forum wants a professional approach, as the tobacco industry and Exxon Mobile do. Merchants of doubt are successful in having malicious practices and intentions swallowed by the crowd. A similar approach has been drawn out and applied to atomic power.

Seven steps are recognisable in Saatchi & Saatchi & Co.'s recommendations, as described below, with some comments afterwards. The seven points describe the construction of the atomic energy delusion.

1. *Confuse people's minds*. Avoid clear statements about the experiences with and properties of atomic energy, and prevent others from bringing clarity. Create haze and doubt, giving the impression that *nobody seems to know quite what all these technical features and effects of atomic energy are; it's all very complex*[35]. We, the experts at the Nuclear Forum, are not so sure ourselves. As a layperson in that technical matter, you don't need to know it all. Besides, is there anyone anywhere who would know it all? Apparently, there is no real need to go into depth. This is a waste of time anyway. So why would we need *so-called independent experts*? Surely, this is a waste of money. After all, if we don't really know what nuclear power is and means anyway, it's a bit silly to be *against* nuclear power, isn't it? You are right: *for or against* is a matter of personal preference, something like choosing Pepsi or Coke, or like being a supporter of a football team. Save yourself the trouble and time of looking up and learning about nuclear energy.

2. *Use a modest slogan*. Throw away the arrogant atomic hubris of the 1950s–1980s period. Use as a slogan: *Nuclear power is not the solution, but there is no solution without nuclear power*. This is more realistic and comes across sympathetically.

3. **Assemble a virtual majority.** Do a reverse count of people's positions. In the 1950s–1980s period, the powerful atomic industry immediately labelled any individual with a critical comment or an annoying question about atomic energy as an *opponent*. Saatchi & Saatchi advises the opposite. Any uninformed person now counts as a *supporter* of atomic interests. In this way, you shape a silent majority of supporters. These supporters are not real, but propaganda can go on with *a halo of majority*, even when it is falsified.

4. **Silence informed critics and exclude them from the public forum.** This was explicitly stated at the July 2007 Nuclear Forum meeting in Brussels: avoid any substantive debate with well-informed people on atomic issues. Provide ample advertising budgets to media channels to regularly repeat the Nuclear Forum theses. Traditional media and its personnel are easily persuaded to propagate the Saatchi & Saatchi strategy. Besides, this is just continuation of a practice that has worked successfully for decades[36] for the nuclear industry.

5. **Get well-known 'neutral' experts to confirm the 'necessity' of nuclear power for the climate case.** These are experts without expertise in atomic power, electricity generation, and energy in general. Examples include climatologist James Hansen, psychologist Steven Pinker, and filmmaker Oliver Stone.

6. **Cover up the facts of atomic history, the failures, the dangers, the costs.** Draw attention to GEN4 and GEN5 technology, small modular reactors, thorium, fusion, ..., even if they are just silhouetted birds in the sky. Neglect the need for professional feasibility studies evaluating the financial profitability[37], as is usually done in industry for large, long-term projects when they have to pay with their own money. Disregard cost-benefit analysis and true sustainability assessments.

7. *Present atomic power as an ideal partner for renewable electricity generation.* This is an important capstone as renewable electricity is inexorably growing in importance. But avoid an in-depth study of the proposed partnership. Ominous language about *the lights going out when there is little sunlight and wind* should suffice to proclaim the need for atomic power.

Most of the points above are commonplace in the deception of the busy citizen who has neither the time nor the inclination to delve into energy and atomic power issues.

On point 6, it is worth noting that private electricity companies, having to keep their accounts balanced, made the financial profitability evaluation. Consequently, none of these companies want to invest their own money in atomic power plants. They have dismounted the atomic dead horse.

If some of the electricity generation companies are still involved, it is because the public treasury or the small and medium electricity consumers will bear all the costs. An additional reason is shifting the liability of the atomic waste of the past on to the public. The atomic industry wants to get rid of their atomic liabilities, inter alia the perpetual care for high-level atomic waste.

Point 7 deserves extensive attention because atomic power is a hindrance rather than a partner to renewable electricity. A proper representation in computer models of the real operation[38] of electric generation systems shows how renewable power and atomic power are competing for the same first place in the power supply queue. Prioritisation of one means the loss or potential bankruptcy of the other[39]. This effect has also been practically observed in recent years, when renewable power supply was still at the beginning of its deployment. Proper economic reasoning places the use of power from sunlight and wind before the use of atomic power. However, atomic power plants are so cumbersome and inert, that in practice, the blades of wind turbines have to turn out of the wind, and PV power is not allowed to enter the grid. Atomic power blocks the rapid transition to renewable electricity, and atomic power is completely useless if there are many plants to convert sunlight and wind flows into electric current.

New prophets of the atomic salvation doctrine

The emergence of neo-modernists, armed with narratives reminiscent of the Saatchi & Saatchi approach, has become common in Western societies. Despite their modernism on atomic power being 75 years behind the times, they confidently propagate the atomic delusive truth. Facts, physical laws, and practical objections do not deter them, as they see ignorance as a virtue, guided by the stance that *what they do not know does not hurt*. Engaging in debate with individuals who express their beliefs without considering the history and facts about atomic energy is a challenging and laborious endeavour.

The faithful obedience of traditional media to the propaganda of the Nuclear Forum is puzzling. Even the Belgian Green Parties speak in baffling language about atomic power. A green energy minister equates lack of belief in wind turbines with lack of belief in fourth-generation atomic power plants, particularly small modular reactors. The minister states that SMRs are *flexible, modular, waste-free, no risk of proliferation and so on*. So, she continues subsidising the atomic experiments. Finally, the industry got their unprincipled, no-nonsense green minister who implements what the atomic industry wants. It is easy to know who is going to pay for the green minister's nonsense.

3.6 Dump delusive truth and its disastrous consequences

When the smoke from the technical superlatives about GEN4, GEN5 and SMR clears in your mind, you see the naked truth about atomic power reactors. They are expensive, dangerous water boiling kettles[40] that condemn people today and in the indefinite future to an irresponsible atomic legacy. All power plants generating electricity from steam or gas flows are problematic because of their elaborated fuel cycles, cooling needs, emissions and waste issues.

To avoid writing a long story or additional book, take a careful look at figure 6. It is a depiction that fragments all filibuster, propaganda, and delusions about atomic power. Here is the explanation of figure 6 and its meaning.

Electric power involves the conversion of another energy flow such as sunlight, wind, water, pressurised steam or gas. In the 1880s, such conversions were initiated to provide electric light in advanced cities such as New York, London, Berlin, Paris and Brussels. At that time, drive power for performing work came mainly from pressurised steam, running water, or muscle power. Hence, steam and running water were the obvious source streams for producing the new invention known as *electric current*. With the growing popularity of electricity in the 20th century, and the steep rise in the use of electricity after World War 2, mastodon steam power plants multiplied. Atomic reactors which, like fossil fuel furnaces, also boil water, were part of that explosive growth.

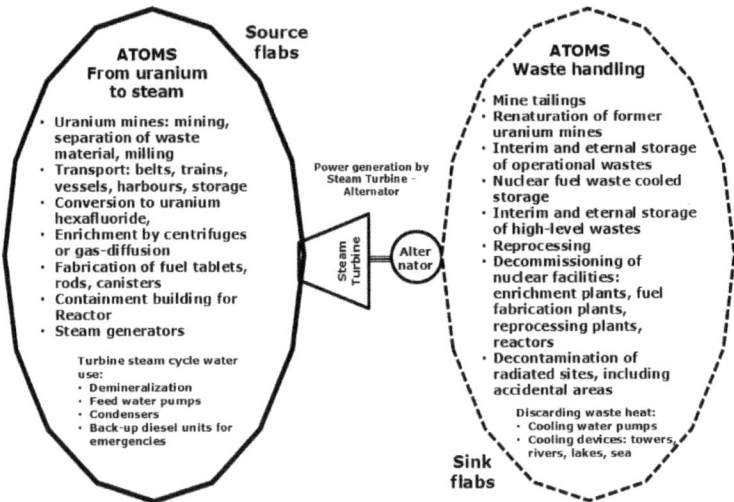

Source flabs

ATOMS
From uranium
to steam

- Uranium mines: mining, separation of waste material, milling
- Transport: belts, trains, vessels, harbours, storage
- Conversion to uranium hexafluoride,
- Enrichment by centrifuges or gas-diffusion
- Fabrication of fuel tablets, rods, canisters
- Containment building for Reactor
- Steam generators

Turbine steam cycle water use:
- Demineralization
- Feed water pumps
- Condensers
- Back-up diesel units for emergencies

Power generation by
Steam Turbine -
Alternator

Steam Turbine

Alternator

ATOMS
Waste handling

- Mine tailings
- Renaturation of former uranium mines
- Interim and eternal storage of operational wastes
- Nuclear fuel waste cooled storage
- Interim and eternal storage of high-level wastes
- Reprocessing
- Decommissioning of nuclear facilities: enrichment plants, fuel fabrication plants, reprocessing plants, reactors
- Decontamination of radiated sites, including accidental areas

Discarding waste heat:
- Cooling water pumps
- Cooling devices: towers, rivers, lakes, sea

Sink flabs

Figure 6: Generating electricity with steam obtained by fission of enriched uranium requires huge and expensive source and sink flabs.

Boiling water requires a fuel. Or would you use electricity? Just kidding[41], you're obviously not going to use electricity to boil water to make electricity. So boiling water requires a fuel: coal, petroleum, natural gas, biomass, or uranium [figure 4]. In existing atomic reactors, enriched uranium is split to obtain the conversion of some mass into energy in the form of heat. The generated heat is then used to boil water, producing steam. Due to technical and safety constraints, atomic reactors deliver steam at moderate pressure and temperature, and it is hence of moderate quality. This steam power is converted into about 1/3 electricity, and 2/3 *waste heat*, which is dumped into the ambient environment. This poor result requires very extensive machinery, investment, people, energy, etc., as illustrated by figure 6.

In the middle of figure 6 is shown the core part of the electricity generation process with steam: a steam turbine, where pressurised steam flies in at high speed, spins the shaft of the turbine, and is then sucked out of the turbine to the condenser where the steam is condensed to water. The rotation of the turbine drives a generator-alternator from which electric current flows[42]. This central segment of the steam power plant is not the problem. Problems come from the required elements before and after this central stage, named here the *source flabs* and the *sink flabs*. These flabs do not refer to the central segment of electricity generation, being the turbine and alternator. They refer to the extensive facilities, operations, provisions, emissions, etc. related to the fossil fuel or uranium fuel cycles to obtain boiling water and deliver it to the inlet of the turbine (source flabs), and to the extensive facilities, operations, provisions, emissions, etc. to capture and process the waste streams of the fuel cycle, residual streams from the turbine, cooling water needs, and so on (sink flabs). In engineering libraries, you find shelves of books detailing the numerous components of such flabs, both in atomic power plants and in any kind of fossil-fuel fired power plant.

The process begins with the uranium mines, most of which are located in distant areas or countries. Mining involves a lot of machinery, investment, people, and energy. Ore coming out of the mine requests initial processing on site, so there is no extra transport of mountains of waste to importing countries. A complicated transport chain is needed to take the raw product to successive processing plants. This requires sea vessels, ports, quays, transshipment, storage, tanks or buildings, trains, inland navigation, and various checks for safety, leaks, and damage.

Extracted fuels also require processing before they are ready for use in power plants. For example, enrichment of uranium is an energy-intensive process via the technique of gas diffusion[43] or by centrifuge. Given the delicate nature of atomic fission, the enriched fuel must be of the appropriate type, packed into tubes, and these tubes organised into bundles. These bundles are replaced at regular intervals, depending on the type of reactor, when the anticipated part of the fuel is spent. Then the bundles go into a water bath that requires constant cooling for many years. The latter is a part of the sink flab, again with many plants, and many unsolved problems.

Fuel bundles of enriched uranium are inserted into a reactor vessel to boil water. The steam produced by the fission of atoms in the reactor vessel is radioactive. Additional heat exchangers are required to obtain non-radioactive steam to power the steam turbines. The spent steam becomes water back in the condenser, which is also a heat exchanger, cooled on one side with huge amounts of cooling water. In hot summers, there is not enough cooling water in the rivers, so atomic power plants may need to run at part load or even remain idle. And so on, and so on, and so on...

Electricity generation without flabs

After the oil price crisis of the 1970s, kaleidoscopic local actions, research centres, and several enlightened politicians in Germany, Denmark, Spain, and other countries, continued to stimulate energy conservation and efficiency, and harvesting renewable energy [section 2.5]. Towards the end of the 20th century, the perseverance of grassroots initiatives and political support pushed an appropriate policy of technological development to harvest electricity from renewable sources, in particular wind and sunlight [section 2.6]. The expensive kilowatt-hours generated before the dedicated policy was deployed went down quickly after the year 2000. The technologies do not need flabs[44] to convert the source energy flows into electricity. Since 2018, wind turbines and PV panels are generating kilowatt-hours at the lowest cost price in human history[45]. Moreover, least cost is not only valid for the financial expenditures made by renewable electricity producers. In environmental and nature terms too, wind and PV technology are 100 times better than the old, outdated steam and gas power plants. Steam and gas plants are fast becoming part of the industrial heritage museum, where youngsters can visit examples of obsolete technology.

3.7 Conclusion on atomic energy

If you are receptive to facts and experiences, the abovementioned discussion highlights why there is no ethical, social, financial, economic, political, or technical argument to spend more time and more money on atomic power. Sadly, this will not be feasible, because an utterly problematic atomic heritage awaits you, especially the young reader, that will require long-term attention and economic resources. Despite promises in the 1950s and 60s that a solution to atomic waste would soon be found, by 2025 no atomic state has a workable solution. So, tucking away deep in Mother Earth's skin is all that remains for them. This is not a solution, because there are more problems that emerge repeatedly than the atomic advocates assume.

Immediate decisions and actions to extinct atomic power plants are advantageous, possible and necessary. These political interventions are advisable before another atomic disaster, *declared as impossible*, takes a huge toll on the population in the affected disaster areas. Delusive discourse and secretive scheming to keep clinically dead atomic power alive are hampering progress towards *Our Common Future*.

A reminder

- Atomic technology was developed to make atomic weapons. Atomic weapons remain the main goal of atomic technology.
- The neo-modernists' *Nuclear Now* dates back to the 1970s. The great financial efforts of those days have been bogged down in financial nightmares and catastrophic accidents. Private power companies refuse to spend on atomic power.
- IAEA is the spider in the web of atomic energy propaganda. The triptych *renewable energy, nuclear power, carbon capture & storage* as equivalent mitigation options is biased. IAEA infiltrated Working Group 3 of the IPCC, and managed to suppress a scientific assessment of the literature on atomic power. This derogates from the essential mission of the IPCC. The traditional media are blind to this *atom climate-gate*.
- In 2007, Saatchi & Saatchi conceived new atomic power propaganda for the Nuclear Forum, traditional media, neo-modernists, and Belgium's green energy minister (2022).
- Atomic power requires heavy source and sink flabs related to its fuel cycle and to the cooling water needs. Atomic power is several times more expensive than electricity from sunlight and wind in commercial terms, and even more so when social costs are considered.

Chapter 4
The delusive truth of the hydrogen energy economy[1]

Like atomic power, the hydrogen energy economy is a delusive truth. Now the truth aspect is the combustion of hydrogen (H_2) with oxygen (O_2) delivering heat while the flue gases are mainly water vapour (H_2O) *without* carbon dioxide (CO_2). As such, hydrogen would be the ideal fuel to bring the CO_2 emissions down. The delusion is the technical-economic set-up of a sizeable hydrogen *energy economy*[2]. In 2022, worldwide industry utilised 95Mt of hydrogen as a *chemical substance* in ammonia fertiliser production, petroleum refining, and steel manufacturing. Hydrogen use in transport and other energy applications were less than 0.1% of global hydrogen use. Almost all this hydrogen came from natural gas or coal reforming processes, causing *more than 1 billion tons of CO_2 emissions*, along with emissions of the more intense greenhouse gases, methane and nitrous oxide.

Vocal proponents claim that hydrogen will play a crucial role in the low-carbon energy future: a claim critics dismiss. The literature now splits into two strands: one strand follows the narrative of hydrogen being a crucial part of the energy future[3], the other points to the danger of spoiling the opportunities of deploying the renewable electricity economy[4]. In 2004, a technically founded publication[5] concluded that the concept of a pure hydrogen energy economy was unrealistic. It is remarkable that Working Group 3 of IPCC did not include hydrogen in its solutions triptych of *Renewable Energy, Nuclear Power, Carbon Capture & Storage*. Nonetheless, hydrogen advocates intertwine their proposals with the three options. Free renewable electricity is the prerequisite for green hydrogen. When lacking sufficient free renewable electricity, delusive atomic power for pink hydrogen is suggested. Carbon capture, use and storage are the lifelines of blue hydrogen based on the use of fossil fuels. The attentive reader will observe that hydrogen does not come ahead of or along with the triptych solutions, but afterwards.

The push towards a hydrogen economy is contradictory: green hydrogen production is expected to be powered by renewable electricity, while the hydrogen hype disrupts the positive momentum of the renewable energy transition. This transition is delayed by diverting massive RE resources, human and financial capital towards hydrogen production. In particular, small-scale distributed renewable electricity deployment will be hampered.

The heralding of hydrogen as the foundation of a new fuel economy confounds energy experts. For years, they had to argue and prove that renewable energy could meet the energy needs of the global population[6], countering claims like *Too little RE* and *Too expensive RE*. Essentially, the hydrogen hype competes for the human and material capital required for renewable electricity serving direct energy needs.

This chapter consists of eight sections.

Section 4.1 recalls how in 2003 the hydrogen hype was launched by the then US president G.W. Bush, known as a friend of the oil industry, together with the then vice-president D. Cheney[7]. Would this launch be a climate friendly inroad against the interests of the oil and gas industry? Parallel with the launch, the US National Research Council made an extensive study, insisting on a *system analysis* of the entire US energy reality and future, and warning about the relative role of hydrogen. Bush's prediction that US children born in 2003 would drive their first car propelled by hydrogen was misguided.

Section 4.2 reports our reading of the European Commission hydrogen strategy for a climate-neutral Europe, published in 2020. The publication is missing the basic attributes of what a strategic document should possess. It is a Eurocentric advertising of the hydrogen hype, without consideration of the real benefits and costs of the announced intentions. As the promises are high, so too are the subsidies flowing from the EU and national states' treasuries. Eurocentrism shows its neo-colonial shadow when *placing hydrogen high on its external energy policy agenda.*

Section 4.3 provides clarity about the peculiar properties of hydrogen fuel. It starts by clearly defining what hydrogen is, and how much energy it holds per kg and per m³. Most hydrogen fuel has to be manufactured, which explains partly its poor economic performance. The other part is due to difficult issues with its storage, hydrogen embrittlement, high flammability, and last but not least the global warming potential of hydrogen leaks in the atmosphere.

Section 4.4 is a numerical analysis of hydrogen as an energy commodity, and the consecutive stadia of production, logistics (with handling, transport & distribution, transfer & storage), and use. A table shows the six colour labels applied to hydrogen molecules according to their manufacturing. Figure 7 shows a typical case of green hydrogen obtained via electrolysis of water for end-use in road transport. From electricity as input energy, battery-powered electric vehicles deliver 69 percent to the wheels and hydrogen fuel cell vehicles around 23 percent. The capital and operational costs of the hydrogen option are also significantly higher.

Section 4.5. Because of hydrogen's inherent and intractable hurdles, the pure hydrogen energy economy is unrealistic. Most of the hydrogen business focuses on hydrogen as a substance for industrial processes. Major derivatives using hydrogen are ammonia and synthetic hydrocarbon fuels. Both sink the green hydrogen ambitions advertised to the public. The ammonia industry causes nitrogen and nitrous oxide emissions. The synthetic hydrocarbons are hydrocarbons, and will emit high volumes of CO_2 when used in aviation, shipping, the military, etc. It is a costly masquerade.

Section 4.6 is a brief wrap up demanding transparency and clarity about the hydrogen affairs. Public policymakers should evaluate key physical, technical, financial and environmental issues from a public interest perspective. The hydrogen rationale is based on a hype, not on facts. The hydrogen related industries may prove their care for a mild climate by urgent manufacturing of carbon free hydrogen for a yearly demand of about 95Mt.

Section 4.7 describes the *announced* 11 million tons hydrogen-ammonia HYRASIA One project in Kazakhstan, contrasted with the 550 times smaller 20,000 ton *realized* project by Yara in Norway. While the Kazakh project promises grand results, its practical and financial feasibility is questionable. The Norwegian project shows the reality of green ammonia production, taking a maximum of design provisions to avoid logistic handlings, such as H2 storage or transport. Up to 40% of the project investments are subsidised via R&D funds.

Section 4.8 recalls highlights from the study and analysis, and formulates clear conclusions, such as: Embarking on megalomaniacal hydrogen generation projects is a waste of energy, money and time. Then, top-quality energy, electricity, is converted into a really problematic fuel, hydrogen. The argument that such conversion is needed to address climate change is false. The contrary is true: a hydrogen energy economy prolongs the use of fossil fuels and distracts societies from deploying the beneficial distributed renewable electricity economy.

4.1 Hydrogen hype launched by G.W. Bush in 2003

Hydrogen is not a recently discovered *energy commodity*. The allure of *clean hydrogen* in power generation and transportation has captivated governments and the public in the 1950s and 1960s[8], and again in the 1970s[9], although it has never built up enough steam to fully take off[10]. In 2024, hydrogen as an energy commodity attracts lots of attention and government subsidies. It is worth finding out who created the new hype. When did it start? What progress has been made since it began?

In 2003, new attention for hydrogen came from the White House in the US, as *President Bush's US$1.2 billion hydrogen fuel initiative aimed to reverse America's growing dependence on foreign oil by accelerating the commercialisation of hydrogen-powered fuel cells to power cars, trucks, homes and businesses with no pollution or greenhouse gases*[11].

Parallel to, but also very different from the Bush initiative, the US

National Research Council[12] appointed a Committee on Alternatives and Strategies for Future Hydrogen Production and Use to address the complex subject of the *hydrogen economy*. In particular, the committee assessed the current state of technology for producing hydrogen from a variety of energy sources. It made estimates on a consistent basis of current and future projected costs, CO_2 emissions, and energy efficiencies for hydrogen technologies; considered scenarios for the potential penetration of hydrogen into the economy and associated impacts on oil imports and CO_2 gas emissions; addressed the problem of how hydrogen might be distributed, stored, and dispensed to end uses—together with associated infrastructure issues—with particular emphasis on light-duty vehicles in the transportation sector.

The US vision of the hydrogen economy is based on two expectations: (1) that hydrogen can be produced from domestic energy sources in a manner that is affordable and environmentally benign, and (2) that applications using hydrogen—fuel cell vehicles, for example—can gain market share in competition with the alternatives.

However, before this vision can become a reality, many technical, social, and policy challenges must be overcome. This report focuses on the steps that should be taken to move toward the hydrogen vision and to achieve the sought-after benefits.

One such benefit was stated by Bush[13] in 2003 as follows: *A simple chemical reaction between hydrogen and oxygen generates energy, which can be used to power a car producing only water, not exhaust fumes*[14]. *With a new national commitment, our scientists and engineers will overcome obstacles to taking these cars from laboratory to showroom so that the first car driven by a child born today could be powered by hydrogen, and pollution-free.*

The Academy report exclusively deals with hydrogen, while noting that alternative or complementary strategies might also serve the set goals. If battery technology improved dramatically, for example, all-electric vehicles might become the preferred alternative. Furthermore, hybrid electric vehicle technology is commercially available today. Biomass-based synthetic fuels could also be used in place of gasoline.

The committee believes that for hydrogen-fuelled transportation, the four most fundamental technological and economic challenges are these:

1. To develop and introduce cost-effective, durable, safe, and environmentally desirable fuel cell systems and hydrogen storage systems.

2. Developing the infrastructure to provide hydrogen for the light-duty vehicle user, which would initially best be accomplished through distributed production of hydrogen, because distributed generation avoids many of the substantial infrastructure barriers faced by centralised generation.

3. To reduce sharply the costs of hydrogen production from renewable energy sources, over a time frame of decades. Tremendous progress has been made in reducing the cost of making electricity from renewable energy sources. But making hydrogen from renewable energy through the intermediate step of making electricity, a premium energy source, requires further breakthroughs in order to be competitive.

4. To capture and store the carbon dioxide by-product of hydrogen production from coal. Sharply reducing overall CO_2 release will require carbon reductions in other parts of the economy, particularly in electricity production.

The committee also formulates several recommendations. It emphasises the critical role for systems analysis, needed both to coordinate the multiple parallel efforts within the hydrogen programme and to integrate the programme within a balanced, overall national energy system. This system is characterised by dynamic changes, issues of timing and sequencing, substantial diversity in options, more-energy-efficient technologies, and it must address safety, security, and environmental concerns.

New solutions are needed in order to lead to vehicles that have at least a 300-mile driving range; that are compact, lightweight, and inexpensive; and that meet future safety standards. Given the current state of knowledge with respect to fuel cell durability, on-board storage systems, and existing component costs, the committee believes that the near-term Department of Energy milestones for Fuel Cell Vehicles are *unrealistically aggressive.*

A nationwide, high-quality, safe, and efficient hydrogen infrastructure will be required in order for hydrogen to be used widely in the consumer sector. The hydrogen infrastructure programme should address issues such as storage requirements, hydrogen purity, pipeline materials, compressors, leak detection, and permitting, with the objective of clarifying the conditions under which large-scale and small-scale hydrogen production will become competitive, complementary, or independent. The logistics of interconnecting hydrogen production and end use are daunting, and all current methods of hydrogen delivery have poor energy-efficiency characteristics and difficult logistics.

Safety: experts differ markedly in their views of the safety of hydrogen in a consumer-centred transportation system. A particularly salient and underexplored issue is that of leakage in enclosed structures, such as garages in homes and commercial establishments. Hydrogen safety, from both a technological and a societal perspective, will be one of the major hurdles that must be overcome in order to achieve the hydrogen economy.

The Research Council points to logistics—transport, distribution, storage—and dispensing systems with end-use equipment as important in a hydrogen energy economy. Hence the recommendation to start with a distributed development and deployment, to realise Bush's hydrogen car dream, as stated above.

4.2 The EU hydrogen strategy for a climate-neutral Europe

In 2003, the European Union had accepted Bush's invitation to join the partnership on hydrogen. Then EU President Prodi stated that *hydrogen* now looks like the best candidate to address sustainable development.

In 2020, the European Commission published *A hydrogen strategy for a climate-neutral Europe*[15], an instructive document for understanding the EU's approach and intentions. Although the title promises a *strategy*, the document lacks the essential components needed for strategy building. For example, fully absent is a strategy's indispensable characteristic of beginning by providing a clear and objective description of the state-of-affairs of the considered item within its realistic context. Contrarily, the first paragraph is a scholarly example of stating the conclusion before the study has started: *All this makes hydrogen essential to support the EU's commitment to reach carbon neutrality by 2050 and for the global effort to implement the Paris Agreement while working towards zero pollution*, with *All this* being no more than some primary school generality about hydrogen.

The European Commission (EC) immediately had to deflate its rash conclusion, in the following paragraphs: *Yet, today, hydrogen represents a modest fraction of the global and EU energy mix, and is still largely produced from fossil fuels, resulting in the release of 70 to 100 million tonnes CO2 annually in the EU. For hydrogen to contribute to climate neutrality, it needs to achieve a far larger scale and its production must become fully decarbonized.* The underlined words reveal the previously accepted conclusion before any meaningful analysis.

The observation *"In the past, there have been peaks of interest in hydrogen, but it did not take off"* is for the EC no signal for a deeper look at the how and why hydrogen failed in the past. The facts are brushed aside, with as a main argument *the rapid cost decline of renewable energy*. A genuine strategy study would investigate the impact of very cheap renewable electricity and performant batteries on the competitive position of hydrogen. Such important issues get no attention in the published strategy of the EC.

The advertisement continues: *Many indicators signal that we are now close to a tipping point. There are many reasons why hydrogen is a key priority to achieve the European Green Deal and Europe's clean energy transition.* This is audacious talk, when the references are *announced plans, planned investments, increased membership of the International Hydrogen Council, projected growth of hydrogen's market share by 2050.* Even announced numbers for nearby years are doubtful. For example: *This Communication sets out a <u>vision</u> of how the EU can turn clean hydrogen into a viable solution to decarbonize different sectors over time, installing at least <u>6 GW</u> of renewable hydrogen electrolysers in the EU by 2024.* Actually, the 2023 tracking reduced the 6 GW to 2.4 GW as the rest was delayed or cancelled[16], with the Hydrogen Europe report adding: The real number that will have come online by the end of 2024 will likely be significantly lower. The 2024 Hydrogen Insights mention an active *global* electrolysis capacity of 1.75 GW, of which 1.15 GW is in China[17]. While the announcements are many times higher than the realisations, the subsidy flows are increasing. For example, on July 29, 2024, Margrethe Vestager, Executive Vice-President of the EU in charge of competition policy, approved a Dutch state aid scheme of €998 million for electrolyser projects[18].

The strategy's expectation of *repurposing or re-using parts of the existing natural gas infrastructure, helping to avoid stranded assets in pipelines* is unlikely due to safety standards and the high exigencies on the materials used in conveyors and stores of hydrogen [section 4.3].

Other weaknesses of green hydrogen seem to be the high production costs in Europe: an average of €7/kg H2, with lower costs in countries endowed with low electricity prices, like Sweden €3.9/kg and Finland €4.8/kg. The high costs result in dependency on subsidies from public treasuries. This reality requires not just a solid business strategy, but further a fully-fledged cost-benefit analysis incorporating the social costs of the pursued *whole hydrogen eco-system.*

The international dimension is an integral part of the EU approach, for advancing supply diversification and helping design stable and secure supply chains. <u>The EU has a strategic interest</u> in placing hydrogen high on its external energy policy agenda, continuing to invest in international cooperation on climate, trade and research activities but also broadening its agenda to new areas. Renewable hydrogen also offers a unique opportunity for research and innovation, <u>maintaining and expanding</u>

Europe's technological leadership, and creating economic growth and jobs across the full value chain and across the Union. This requires ambitious and well-coordinated policies at national and European levels, as well as diplomatic outreach on energy and climate with international partners.

The EC's strategy document emanates the EU interests as prevalent in all its activities in developing countries. Given its limited place for winning the projected huge quantities of renewable electricity, the EU wants to develop Gigawatt projects in other countries, such as Kazakhstan, Morocco[19], Namibia, and Oman. So far, this is presented as mass production of green hydrogen, likely for export to Europe. However, such export over thousands of kilometres brings excessive energy losses, and requires infrastructure investments and maintenance. The EC is silent about such barriers.

It remains unclear how the diplomatic outreach by the EU will handle the impacts of giant hydrogen projects on the national energy and electricity sector of the home country, on its land and water use, and on the populations living in the areas occupied by the mega projects[20].

4.3 The peculiar properties of hydrogen

Hydrogen (H) constitutes about 75 percent of all visible matter in the Universe. On Earth, pure hydrogen gas (H_2) is rare and scattered[21]. Due to its high chemical reactivity, hydrogen readily forms compounds with other elements, creating larger molecules like water (H_2O), hydrocarbons (CxHy), etc. Uncontained hydrogen quickly escapes from Earth into space.

Hydrogen is a fuel that needs manufacturing

All energy used by humans comes from natural flows or stocks, manufactured by nature on the spot or in the past. Such energies are available without manufacturing efforts or expenses for humans. Often, they are a source of big economic profits. Hydrogen is the opposite, it has to be manufactured: a grave economic handicap compared to renewable currents and to fossil fuels.

Energy content

Among fuels, hydrogen has the highest energy value per weight at 141.86MJ/kg, which is advantageous for aerospace applications. However, its energy content per volume is low at 11.88MJ/m³, three times lower than natural gas. Little energy per m³ is a handicap in usual applications, because fuel tanks have a limited volume, and it is better for pipeline diameters to be small than large.

Storage issues

As the lightest gaseous element, hydrogen's condensing temperature is 20°K or -252.9°C. This poses significant challenges for storage. Storing hydrogen in a compressed state requires pressures beyond 800 bar and thick-walled high-pressure vessels. Currently, compressed storage of 1kg hydrogen requires cylinders weighing 33kg, which may be lowered to 20kg through advances in materials science[22]. Liquefaction of hydrogen is highly energy-intensive, requiring approximately 40 MJ/kg H_2, which is 33% of hydrogen's lower heating value. Liquefied hydrogen has a low density: one litre contains only 71 grams of hydrogen. Consequently, storing hydrogen in cryogenic form requires large volumes, leading to extra heat loss[23].

Hydrogen embrittlement

Hydrogen's low viscosity, small size, and light weight enable it to penetrate almost any space, leading to leakages during all stages, from production to utilisation. By being soluble in metals, hydrogen causes gas porosity and reduced strength, a phenomenon known as hydrogen embrittlement. This decreases the ductility of metals due to absorbed hydrogen. To mitigate this, special measures are required, such as selecting stainless steel and nickel-based alloys, protective coatings with nickel, cadmium, or zinc, and using hydrogen removal techniques such as baking and stress-relief annealing. It is also important to limit exposure to hydrogen-rich or corrosive environments.

Hydrogen flammability

Hydrogen-air mixtures are highly flammable, due to hydrogen's broad flammability range: 4–74 percent concentration in air and 4–94 percent in oxygen. A hydrogen–air mixture ignites with only 0.02 millijoules of energy, less than 7 percent of the energy needed to ignite natural gas.

Preventing hydrogen from mixing with air or oxygen in confined spaces is crucial. Even an invisible spark or static electricity discharge from a human body may trigger ignition. Moreover, hydrogen's low electro-conductivity can create electrostatic charges during flow or agitation of hydrogen gas, potentially causing sparks. Therefore, all hydrogen conveying equipment must be thoroughly grounded.

NASA, being a pioneer in using hydrogen as fuel, derived clear lessons from past accidents[24]. A report of the UK gas distributor SGN highlighting the substantial explosion risks of hydrogen gas and devastating consequences, and the need for stringent safety measures, has been long suppressed[25]. A society-wide use of hydrogen would require an encompassing safety apparatus with a multitude of equipment, prescribed practices, rules and enforcement measures. Even very costly apparatus cannot reduce the likelihood of significant accidents to zero.

Hydrogen's peculiar properties imply technical, environmental, and safety challenges in its logistics and utilisation, with significant impact on its socio-economic viability.

Hydrogen as unexpected climate culprit

Leaked hydrogen not only poses fire hazards, it also extends the lifetime of GHGs in the atmosphere. While a hydrogen molecule itself does not trap heat, it indirectly contributes to global warming by prolonging the life of GHGs like methane CH_4, tropospheric ozone O_3, and water vapour. These GHGs are gradually neutralised in the atmosphere by reacting with OH (hydroxyl) radicals. When leaked H_2 reacts with OH radicals, it depletes atmospheric OH, delaying the neutralisation of GHGs and effectively increasing their lifetime.

Four main climate impacts are associated with increased hydrogen levels: longer methane lifetime, leading to increased methane concentrations; enhanced production of ozone in the troposphere, causing photochemical smog; increase in stratospheric water vapour; and changes in the occurrence of particular aerosols.

IEA[26] and IRENA[27] reference Warwick et al.'s[28] finding that hydrogen's Global Warming Potential is 11 ± 5. This number significantly exceeds previous calculations, highlighting the critical need to consider the broader atmospheric impacts of hydrogen in the announced growth scenarios.

4.4 Energy performance of *hydrogen as energy commodity*

Testing the energy performance of an acclaimed *new* energy commodity requires evaluating the stadia *production, logistics* (handling, transport & distribution, transfer & storage), and *use*[29]. The stadia may encompass various technical processes, as exemplified by the multicoloured labelling of hydrogen [table 1].

Production stadium

Electrolysis transforms water into hydrogen and oxygen gases. At 71% efficiency, producing 1kg H_2 with 39.4 kWh energy content requires 55.5 kWh electricity: an energy loss of 16.1 kWh. The average electricity input is 59.7 kWh, accounting for a 5% decrease in electrolysis efficiency during 10 to 15 years of operation[30]. The hydrogen gas is delivered at atmospheric pressure by alkaline electrolysis or at 35 bar by PEM electrolysis. Electrolysis consumes 9 litres of ultrapure water[31] per kgH2. When saline water is used, water input needs several cleaning stages, resulting in significant brine pollution contaminated with chemicals and metals used as catalysts in desalination[32]. Hydrogen from electrolysis powered by renewable electricity is labelled green, and pink when powered by atomic electricity.

Hydrogen production via natural gas reforming has a maximum efficiency of 70%, further reduced by fugitive gas losses. The process emits 10kg CO2 per produced kgH2, and 22kg CO2-eq when adding fugitive methane emissions[33]. Gas-based hydrogen is labelled grey, and blue when the CO2 emissions are to be captured.

Colour	Description
Gold	Few natural H2 sources available on Earth, not requiring manufacturing
Green	H2 produced via electrolysis with renewable electricity
Grey	H2 extracted from hydrocarbons not capturing emitted CO2
Blue	Grey version with methane as hydrocarbon and capturing part of the emitted CO2
Brown	Grey version with coal as hydrocarbon, and capturing part of the emitted CO2
Pink	H2 obtained via electrolysis or via thermochemical processes with atomic energy

Table 1: Multicoloured labelling of hydrogen

Logistics stadium

The simplest *handling* of H2 occurs when it is used immediately—without pressurising and without storage—near the place of production. This may happen when H2 serves as a chemical substance.

Compression: As an energy commodity, manufactured H2 gas usually requires compression. For pipeline transport, an intermediate pressure of 140 to 350 bar is suitable. When hydrogen is used in vehicles, compression beyond 800 bar is typically necessary. The overall compressor work from electrolysis to filled car tank would take approximately 7.87 kWh/kgH2[34].

Transport: Energy use in *pipeline transport* varies widely, depending on diameter and length, pressure levels, and compressor technologies. Gas flowing over longer distances (e.g., 4000MJ/s hydrogen rate over 2000km), requires consecutive compressions. Transport over a distance of 500km consumes about 3.97kWh/kg of conveyed H2, while 13.37kWh/kg is consumed over 3000km.

Liquefaction: As an alternative to compression, hydrogen can be liquefied at -252.9°C for transport and storage. The theoretical minimum energy loss of hydrogen liquefaction is 18%; in practice it ranges from 25% to 45%, depending on plant size[35], or 7 to 13.4kWh/kg H_2[36]. Over long distances, shipping may consume one-third of the liquefied hydrogen.

Since ammonia (NH_3) liquefies at -33°C while at atmospheric pressure, or at ambient temperature at 10 bar pressure, it is proposed as the best hydrogen energy carrier. However, the energy penalty of converting hydrogen to ammonia and back is roughly equivalent to chilling hydrogen[37].

Distribution over hinterland: This stadium is needed when hydrogen would become a widely applied fuel from international imports. A 200 bar distribution network for hydrogen would require about 3.93 kWh/kgH2 for delivery at 150km distance, and 9.83 kWh/kgH2 over 400km[38]. A 100 bar distribution would reduce these numbers by 1kWh/kgH2. Transport over 100km (a radius of 50km around an intermediate transfer/storage depot) would take 1.39 kWh/kgH2[39].

End-use of hydrogen in transport: Currently, hydrogen as an energy commodity is only used in fuel cell powered vehicles or internal combustion engines running on hydrogen. From the electricity generated, electric battery vehicles deliver 69% to the wheels and hydrogen fuel cell vehicles around 23%[40]. Internal combustion engines on hydrogen show efficiencies of 20-30%, whereas hydrogen fuel cells driving electric motors would attain efficiencies of 40-50%.

The option of using excess renewable electricity for hydrogen production through electrolysis, subsequently stored at home for later conversion back to electricity with a fuel cell has an efficiency of 33.5% assuming optimal operation without any hitches.

The energy losses associated with a hydrogen-based economy are excessive and directly related to hydrogen's molecular structure and inherent properties. Consequently, these losses cannot be significantly reduced by any amount of research and development efforts, rendering the concept of a pure hydrogen energy economy unrealistic[41].

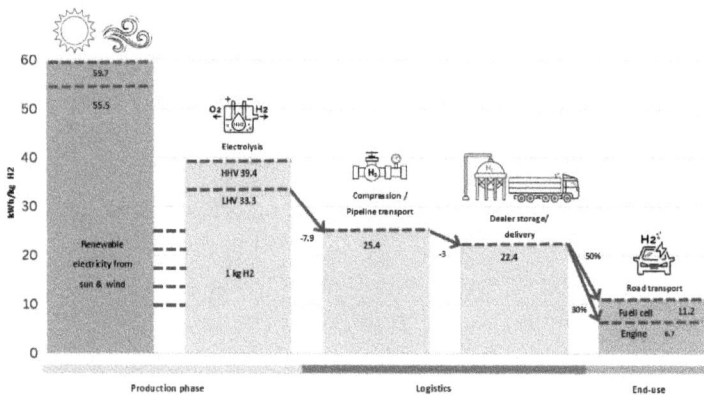

*Figure 7: Hydrogen for road transport, assuming 'minimum-loss conversions'.
1kg H2 is the figure's fixed point. The 39.4kWh HHV is delivered by renewable
electricity via electrolysis at η 71% in a new unit, viz. η 66% over 15 years'
functioning[42]. The 33.3kWh LHV is for use. When electrolysis occurs in areas
with ample sun, wind and water resources, 140 bar pressurised pipeline transport
over 2000km is a minimum requirement[43]. Dealer storage and delivery within
a 50km radius asks for 5kWh/kgH2[44]. Road transport is by fuel cell (η 50%) or
internal combustion engine (η 30%).*

4.5 Hydrogen-derived products and fuels

By now, hydrogen primarily functions as a substance in industrial
activities: oil refineries, fertiliser production and steel plants. *Ammonia*
is a key raw material for chemical fertilisers, while *hydrogen-derived
synthetic fuels* are presented as climate-valid substitutes for fossil fuels.

Ammonia

Ammonia NH3 consists of 82.35 percent nitrogen and 17.65 percent
hydrogen. The lower heating value of liquidised/pressurised ammonia
is 18.6MJ/kg. Most ammonia is used in the nitrogen fertiliser
industry. Annually, about 265Mt of atmospheric nitrogen are fixated
on land: 55Mt natural and 210Mt anthropogenic. The latter consists
of 52Mt fixated biologically; 32Mt from combustion of fossil fuels; via

the Haber-Bosch synthesis process, 126Mt nitrogen is combined with hydrogen to manufacture ammonia. In 2020, the global ammonia production capacity was around 243Mt, with a demand of 183Mt. Approximately 90% of the produced ammonia is consumed on site. Ammonia was generated from natural gas and naphtha (75 percent), coal and heavy fuel oil (25 percent)[45].

Ammonia (NH_3) is a corrosive and toxic gas that can severely pollute air and water, posing a grave threat to ecosystems and to human health. Despite existing infrastructure and regulations, satellite observations reveal industrial NH_3 plants as major emission hotspots, greatly underestimated in inventories by a median factor of 50[46]. In an ammonia-driven economy, the risk escalates dramatically, with potential emissions from pipelines, distribution, storage systems, fuel stations, and combustion sources. Losses and inefficiencies across the value chain result in reactive nitrogen emissions of NH_3, NO_x, and N_2O, with negative impacts on air quality, nature, human health, and climate.

In industrial and agriculturally intensive areas of the EU, critical nitrogen-loads are surpassed[47], as they are globally[48]. There is now *a full stop on the licensing of additional nitrogen-emitting activities* in many regions of the EU, like Flanders (Belgium), the Netherlands, and North-West Germany. Licensing more ammonia production in satiated markets is unlikely. This situation increases the eagerness of multinational companies to produce ammonia overseas.

A spectacular growth of the ammonia industry is announced, pending ample use as an alternative fuel: … *a decade or two after 2050, ammonia energy will have reached 30EJ/y, or 1,600Mt NH3/y. Hydrogen will become 150EJ/y and 20% of it will be transported as ammonia*[49]. Today, shipped ammonia is around 20Mt/year.

There is no carbon in NH_3 and stochiometric conversions are attractive: *Most of the nitrogen in ammonia is converted back to atmospheric N2 during ammonia combustion (4 NH3 + 3 O2 ⇒ 2 N2 + 6 H2O) or ammonia cracking (2 NH3 ⇒ N2 + 3 H2). Practically, however, leakages across the ammonia value chain and undesired reactions during ammonia use would keep the nitrogen cycle partially open, releasing reactive nitrogen compounds like NH3, NOx, and N2O*[50]. A significant stumbling block to the efficacy of ammonia as a climate-change mitigation solution concerns the potential emissions of nitrous oxide N_2O. N_2O is a potent and long-lived greenhouse gas with a lifespan of ~120 years. Its global warming potential is 265 times that of CO_2.

Leakages occur during ammonia synthesis, as well as during combustion and cracking. Total leakages and combustion emissions are assessed to range from 0.5 to 5 percent[51], referring to experience with natural gas shipments and conversions, and to imperfections in the practical use of devices deviating from theoretically perfect combustion in ideal conditions.

IRENA and AEA[52] reflect the vision and interests of the ammonia industry by including *discussions on the direct use of ammonia as a fuel for electric power generation or maritime transport, as well as its indirect use as a hydrogen carrier and a carbon-free energy commodity.* The report is titled *Renewable Ammonia*. However, how can ammonia be renewable? Is a car using electricity from solar panels a *Renewable Car*?

*Ammonia production accounts for around 45% of global hydrogen consumption, or around 33Mt of hydrogen in 2020. Replacing conventional ammonia with renewable ammonia produced from renewable hydrogen presents an early opportunity to decarbonize the chemical sector (...) In 2021, less than 0.02Mt of renewable ammonia was produced, but 15Mt by 2030 is announced, notably in Australia, Mauritania and Oman (...) an electricity price below US$ct.2/kWh is required for renewable ammonia to be competitive with fossil-based ammonia*[53]. This quote underscores the ammonia industry's reliance on fossil fuels, ignoring the immense societal costs of climate change. Accurate financial appraisals that include these costs would mandate immediate use of hydrogen from renewable sources. Western investors, however, expect electricity prices below US$ct.2/kWh for their announced hydrogen-ammonia projects in the global South, exclusive locations, unrestricted access to all natural resources, and likely subsidies and tax exemptions. The language is *de-risk early investment projects*[54], meaning that the public treasury pays for capital and operational expenses of ammonia projects.

The energy efficiency of the best available technology using low-temperature electrolysis Alkaline or PEM is 50 percent[55]. This means that producing one ton of ammonia, which has an energy content of 18.6GJ, requires 37.2GJ of energy.

Hydrogen-derived synthetic fuels

Some energy activities are not grid-connected and require large quantities of storable fuels, making them challenging to power with batteries. Examples include long-distance aviation, ocean-borne shipping, military aircraft, vessels, and rolling equipment. They rely heavily on *liquid hydrocarbon* fuels and they claim unlimited supplies. *Without a ban* on petroleum extraction, oil products will continue to meet their expanding demand. Pressures by the growing awareness among destitute communities, young activists, concerned citizens and scientists spur fossil fuel interests to propose *solutions* for the continued use of fossil fuels. One such solution is said to be blue hydrogen based on fossil gas[56]. By capturing (part of) the emitted CO_2 it becomes the carbon source for fabricating syngas, a mixture of CO and H_2. Although carbon capture is technically feasible, it is financially expensive and not practical on a small scale.

At the bottom of table 2, it is shown that CO_2 emissions during H_2 fabrication exceed the CO_2 input for synthetic fuel fabrication. It is unclear how this surplus is managed.

With a stringent ban on any use of fossil fuels, green hydrogen is seen as a solution for making hydrocarbons without full dependency on fossil fuels. Table 2 documents energy and material flows, and efficiencies of Fischer-Tropsch syncrude and methanol. The inputs of green electricity and of green hydrogen are significant, when fossil fuels are completely excluded.

The blue hydrogen pathway expands the use of natural gas and requires significant investments in installations and equipment. In this context, the role of hydrogen is more a disguise than a solution. Natural gas is at the beginning of the process and liquid hydrocarbons are the outcome at the end. Without complete CCS, the CO_2 created for producing H_2 will be emitted. When the synthetic hydrocarbons are used in aviation, shipping and the military, CCS is impossible, resulting in the emission of all the created CO_2.

	Fischer-Tropsch Syncrude	Methanol
Composition	15% H2 + 85% C	12.5% H2 + 37.5% C + 50% O2
Heating value	11.94 kWh/kg	6.29 kWh/kg
Heat surplus of synthesis	3.94 kWh/kg	0.82 kWh/kg
Heat input for syngas	2.27 kWh/kg	1.01 kWh/kg
Synthesis efficiency	67%	83%
Input electricity	25.4 – 29.0 kWh	10.9 – 12.5 kWh
Input H2	0.44 – 0.46 kg	0.19 – 0.20 kg
Input H2O	4.0 – 4.1 kg	1.7 – 1.8 kg
Input CO2	3.2 – 3.3 kg	1.4 – 1.5 kg
Output	1kg CxHy hydrocarbon	1kg methanol CH3OH
Overall efficiency	41% – 47%	50% – 58%
CO2 averages:		
CO2 production for input H2	4.83 kg	2.09 kg
Surplus CO2	1.58 kg	0.64 kg

Table 2: Green electricity to liquid synthetic fuels: based on theoretical maximum efficiencies. For lost H2 and CO2 mass, minimum-maximum ranges are shown[57].

4.6 Is the *hydrogen energy* economy financially and environmentally affordable?

An energy economic sector is characterised by infrastructures and equipment for handling the energy stocks and flows, and by energy losses during conversion and transfer processes. Before committing to significant investments in research, development and demonstration, machinery and infrastructures for a hydrogen-based energy economy, gaining clarity is crucial. Public policymakers should evaluate key physical, technical, financial and environmental issues from a public interest perspective.

The inherent properties of hydrogen [section 4.3] are the fundamental hindrances for a successful hydrogen energy economy. Section 4.4 documents the poor energy efficiencies of proposed hydrogen applications [figure 7]. Electric battery cars are three times more efficient than hydrogen fuel cell driven cars. In addition, fuel cell vehicles require about double the capital expenditure and at least triple the operational expenses of electric battery vehicles[58].

For *long-distance transport* of hydrogen, two main methods are proposed: pipelines for hauling pressurised gas and ships for carrying liquefied gas. Both methods are so capital and energy intensive that imports from overseas to Europe are not economical; domestically produced e-hydrogen with renewable electricity is invariably cheaper[59]. Despite this, large-scale hydrogen producing projects in distant countries (Australia, Chile, Kazakhstan, Morocco, Namibia, Oman), requesting cross-continental transport mains, are an essential part of the envisaged hydrogen energy economy.

The feasibility of hydrogen energy projects depends entirely on subsidies from the treasury. The EU Commission and some national states provide lavish subsidies, without a guarantee on returns. The rationale for the subsidies is the development and demonstration of new technologies to mitigate climate change. The hydrogen rationale is based on hype, not facts.

If the desire for a mild climate were honest, the industry would substitute green hydrogen for grey hydrogen in the ongoing manufacturing of about 95Mt hydrogen for industrial purposes. The technologies are known and the benefits of substitution too: the avoidance of more than 1Gt CO_2 emissions. According to standard rules of economics, the industrial sectors using hydrogen should include the costs of green hydrogen in the price of their products, like chemical fertilisers, refined petroleum products, steel, ammunition, etc.

Certainly, the *new* solutions proposed so far do not guarantee reductions in GHG emissions. Hydrogen-derived synthetic fuels are hydrocarbons, the combustion of which will emit CO_2 while consuming massive amounts of renewable electricity [table 2]. The associated environmental impacts of ammonia could be excessive for nitrogen and GHG emissions. N_2O formation is most dangerous because of its Global Warming Potential of 265 and its potential to deplete stratospheric ozone. *The ammonia economy would have the same climate impact as the fossil-fuel energy system if 0.4 percent of nitrogen were to be converted from NH_3 to N_2O*[60], considering the overall loss range is likely to be 0.5 to 5 percent. *CO_2 emissions from ammonia* *production amount to 500Mt annually, or 1.4 percent of the global energy-related 36Gt CO2 emissions*[61].

In addition to the noxious atmospheric emissions by hydrogen production, escaped or released hydrogen extends the lifetime of GHG [section 4.3]. Electrolysis for manufacturing hydrogen absorbs significant clean water resources [section 4.7]. Megalomaniacal parks of wind turbines and PV panels disturb wildlife, biotopes and human settlements. Renewable electricity production belongs where people need electricity for their daily use.

To end the continuation of the vast emissions by hydrogen derivatives, what is required is a public interest policy without plundering the public treasury.

4.7 HYRASIA One, announced megaproject of ammonia export from Kazakhstan's Caspian Sea shore

This European project plans to produce 2 million tons of hydrogen for 11 million tons of ammonia annually, utilising water from the Caspian Sea[62]. The project developers have received permission from the local government to install PV and wind farms over a 20,000km² territory on the shores of the Caspian Sea. Figure 8 illustrates the land area that would be occupied by HYRASIA One.

It is planned to abstract around 95 million tons of seawater annually, or 255,000m³ per day. HYRASIA promoters state that the project will not harm the local environment, as the amount of pumped water is *only* 0.03% of the average annual inflow from the main five rivers of the Sea's basin. As compensation they see the discharge to the region's water cycle of 70 million tons of effluents after processing hydrogen and ammonia. Discharging such effluents harms the marine ecosystem, because they include desalination residues, process water, and electrolysers' cooling water. They contain higher concentrations of minerals, metals and other industrial contaminants compared to the abstracted Caspian Sea water. Moreover, 25 million tons of abstracted water is absorbed in the production of 2 million tons of hydrogen and 11 million tons of ammonia, exported and permanently cut out from the local hydrological cycle. Such losses repeat year by year, essentially exporting water from a closed basin without return. These cumulative impacts pose real risks to the Caspian region, located in an arid zone and already scarce of clean water resources.

The project plans to construct fields of 13GW Photovoltaic panels, and 27GW wind turbine farms, together twice Kazakhstan's electricity production capacity of 20.4GW[63]. In 2023, Kazakhstan consumed 115TWh of electricity, around 87 percent from coal and gas. The country will not benefit from the renewable electricity production capacity of the HYRASIA project to decarbonise the country's energy economy, as the planned 113.7TWh electricity generation is intended solely to power hydrogen production and its derivative ammonia.

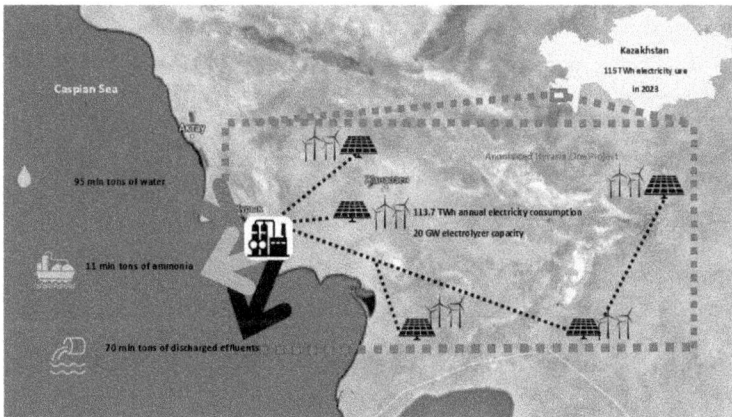

Figure 8: Overview of the announced HYRASIA One project in Kazakhstan

On top of the water and electric power issues, HYRASIA raises environmental and safety concerns. There is irreversible habitat loss for local wildlife and migratory birds due to the vast areas occupied by the megalomaniacal PV and wind turbine constructions[64]. Hydrogen storage and transportation facilities pose fire hazards and risks of atmospheric releases. Ammonia implies contamination risks for water currents and lakes, and for land. Ammonia is known for its toxicity and deleterious impacts on biodiversity, and its nitrogen component is one of the major environmental challenges.

Visiting an existing plant for green ammonia production is highly instructive for assessing the HYRASIA megaproject.

In Norway in June 2024, the second largest ammonia producer in the world, Yara, opened its first 20kt/year ammonia plant, with green hydrogen production capacity up to 3.6kt/year. 24MW PEM electrolysis is driven by hydropower, with annual consumption assessed at 207GWh. The PEM delivers $10tH_2$/day for immediate use, avoiding costly H2 compression and storage. Several treatment steps are needed to obtain ultrapure water for green ammonia production. The layout of the plant[65] shows the combination with grey ammonia production from liquid petroleum gas, increasing the reliability of continuous feedstock for the ammonia synthesis while avoiding H2 storage.

Fresh water is abstracted from lake Norsjø. For the cooling cycles, the lake water seems directly applicable. For the PEM treatment, ultrapure water is needed. Remarkable is the addition of a cold hydrogen venting stack, likely built for safety reasons, however releasing hydrogen into the atmosphere with a negative impact on its GHG concentration [section 4.3]. This real-life project highlights the predominant role of renewable electricity input and the critical importance of water for the electrolysis process. Innovation subsidies for this Yara project cover up to 40 percent or €25 million of the investment.

The announced HYRASIA One project would produce 550 times the output of the Yara plant in Norway. Such 550-factor upscaling is unseen in sound industrial practices.

4.8 Conclusions

Hydrogen has been known for a long time. It is used as a chemical substance in industry. Its use as an energy commodity has been promoted several times but remains negligible. Because natural hydrogen on Earth is scarce, most hydrogen is generated from energy sources, predominantly natural gas and coal. Consequently, manufacturing 95Mt hydrogen for industrial use in 2022 caused more than a billion tons of carbon dioxide, methane and nitrous oxide emissions. Such emissions need elimination to avoid climate collapse. Applying green hydrogen in present industrial processes would be a responsible start. However, only small steps have been noticed, such as Yara beginning in 2024 a 10 ton per day production of green hydrogen for synthesising ammonia.

Announcements of mega projects abound. Hydrogen is advertised as a pivotal component of the future low-carbon energy economy. Granted is the *irrefutable physical truth* that combusting hydrogen with oxygen produces heat and clear water as residual output. Nonetheless, such truth functions as a *delusion*, when non-realistic sequels are built upon it.

Producing one energy unit of green hydrogen needs a minimum 1.4 units of renewable electricity. Giant electrolysis projects exhaust the water resources of countries without an ocean coast. Handling and using hydrogen requires expensive infrastructure, appliances, equipment and control systems for leakages and safety. Transport and storage of hydrogen are energy intensive handlings on top of the wasteful generation process. The hydrogen energy economy is not a sane economic energy option. It unravels in the covered-up continuation of fossil fuel use via blue hydrogen delivering synthetic hydrocarbons for aviation, shipping and the military.

Ammonia production is dislocated from industrialised and intensively cultivated regions because of excess nitrogen emissions. Hydrogen-related activities cause various emissions and impacts, rendering baseless their claim of being a crucial component of effective climate policy. The only climate-friendly hydrogen activity is replacing hydrocarbon-based hydrogen in industrial processes like refineries, fertiliser chemistry, steelmaking, by on-site electrolysis using renewable electricity. It is puzzling why this substitution has yet to occur after the 1994 ratification of the UNFCCC.

The green label of green hydrogen depends on green electricity from sunlight and wind currents, which since 2018 has also been the cheapest electricity ever seen in history. The announced giant projects in developing countries for green hydrogen and ammonia production claim a kWh-price below 2€cents, and hint at Gigawatt wind turbine and solar PV parks. Such parks are a biased concentration of essentially small-scale and even micro generation technologies. Some even suggest producing electricity from hydrogen, likely at a cost price above 20€cents per kWh.

A crucial choice for politicians in every country in the Global South, is how to use their solar and wind resources. The simplest way is to build solar and wind generation units all over the country, and electrify as many energy services as possible, such as electric battery cars. Doing so is following Einstein's advice *Make things as simple as possible, but not simpler*. Distributed community renewable electricity is the proper energy fundament to escape climate collapse, while strengthening democracy, equity, and welfare. The appropriate solutions are negated and obstructed by concentrations of money and power, as showcased by the 2014 coup of the EU's energy conglomerates[66].

Embarking on megalomaniacal hydrogen generation projects is a waste of energy, money and time. Then, top-quality energy, electricity, is converted into a really problematic fuel, hydrogen. The argument that such conversion is needed to address climate change is false. The contrary is true.

While common sense may suffice in denouncing the utopian hydrogen tales, involved interests are often strong and widespread in keeping up deceiving delusions, and getting political and financial support to realise their costly utopia. In the end, it is the citizenry of a region, country or locality that is submitted to the pernicious impacts of ineluctable utopia failures.

Ultimately, hydrogen energy reveals itself as a delusion built on the simple truth that ideal combustion of hydrogen and oxygen is carbon free.

A reminder
- In 2003, then US president G.W. Bush started the hydrogen hype of the 21st century. He emphasised the simple truth of hydrogen combustion, without an eye for the delusive reality, prudently exposed by the US National Research Council.

- The EU hydrogen strategy is a biased belief act, Eurocentric and neocolonial in its approach to the Global South
- The inherent properties of hydrogen itself are decisive for its technical, economic, and environmental failures, such as significant risks, high costs, increasing emissions of GHG and nitrogen when the ammonia path is followed.
- A hydrogen energy economy would prolong the use of fossil fuels and distracts societies from deploying the beneficial distributed renewable electricity economy.

In summary: Hydrogen is the glittering shell concealing the life extension of the fossil fuel economy.

Chapter 5
Fossil fuels: geopolitics for excessive super profits

The salient contribution in this chapter is revelation of the excessive super profits of the energy industry[1]. Many individuals, households, organizations, and companies are affected because they pay for the profits through high fuel bills for heating, electricity, transport, and manufacturing. In 2022, they once again experienced the financial drain caused by huge super profits, prolonged into 2023 and 2024.

In 2021, the pressure by the US on Russia and Europe over Russian gas supplies to Germany began to escalate. The weapon of the artificially created scarcity of oil and gas was again loaded for detonation. Artificial scarcity is the lever to lift excessive super profits[2]. The World Bank assesses annually for every UN country the super profits (also called rents) for all its natural resources commercialised during the year. However, the World Bank results, expressed as a percentage of each country's GDP, are not informative. I converted the World Bank data into US dollars of comparable value. Damian Carrington, an editor at The Guardian, submitted my calculations to professors from leading universities[3] in the UK. The colleagues confirmed the correctness of my calculations and were taken aback by the enormously large sums involved. On July 22, 2022, The Guardian[4] published the results on its front page. This publication had a vast impact, and attention to super profits in US dollars has substantially increased[5].

Rising tensions between the US and Russia-Europe over Nord Stream 2 heightened expectations of escalation. Nonetheless, Russia's invasion of Ukraine on 24 February 2022 could have been avoided in 2021. Apparently, neither Putin nor Zelensky listened to Machiavelli's advice in *The Prince*[6]. For Putin, not to go to war with his weak, outdated army against an ally of the powerful NATO. For Zelensky, not to become totally dependent on foreign powers. The Ukraine war has devolved into a bitter fratricidal struggle, too familiar in European history. What's equally familiar, stretching back more than a century to World War 1, are the propaganda and falsehoods of the warring camps[7]. These methods of obfuscation are applied in extreme ways, and their influence is astonishing, as we see Europe, and in particular Germany, remilitarising.

The traditional media often show little concern for genuine information and critical interpretation. They outdo each other with sensationalism and dubious inventions, such as Russia's *hybrid* war, where it is claimed that Russia sabotages its own pipelines to blame the West. As highlighted by some journalists[8], it is crucial to critically scrutinise media news, ensuring it is based on facts and intelligence by independent and multiple sources. An independent stance, approaching the war with a focus on peace, debunks the propaganda narratives of traditional media. Independent positions are ignored or suspiciously labelled as *friends of the enemy*, a frame openly applied in Russia, but also in the NATO member states.

This chapter reveals the energy-financial aspects of the Russia-Ukraine-NATO war. It serves as a complement, not a replacement, to analyses of geopolitical power from other perspectives[9]. As is often the case in major conflicts, the underlying causes and ultimate motives of the parties remain veiled by unreliable accounts of their own noble goals and the sneaky intrigues of the enemy.

Big Money as a driving factor in wars receives too little attention. Money plays a leading role in the dominant neoliberal regimes, and in all regimes ruled by oligarchs and kleptocrats. It would be peculiar that Big Money would stay on the sidelines of action when war rages, offering an opportunity to gain more money.

Wouldn't money be the main driver of geopolitical conflicts? It seems necessary to investigate the mechanisms of war against oil and gas rich countries, more so because of the links to climate change.

The chapter contains seven sections.

Section 5.1 offers a correct definition of rents (World Bank terminology) or super profits (book's terminology). It is associated with other economic variables such as price, expenditures, revenues, and external costs.

Section 5.2 explains how the super profits in US dollars of the same value are obtained using data from the World Bank and from British Petroleum. Super profits in thousands of billions of US dollars per year are beyond common people's range of imagination; therefore, some references on such excessive numbers are given. Figure 9 illustrates the impact of artificial scarcity by means of embargoes and wars, excluding hostile oil and gas resources from the world market[10].

Section 5.3 is a reminder of the histories explaining the invasions and wars mentioned in figure 9, which coincide with top-score years in oil and gas super profits. It is predominantly oil and gas exporting countries that are the target of the wars launched by the US and NATO countries. Then, the super profits hit record numbers in US$ billions. The hypocrisy in legitimating hegemonic warfare is cynical.

Section 5.4 focuses on impeding Russia's access to the global oil and gas markets under control of the US dollar. The history of Nord Stream 2 reads as a blunt example of how US power imposes its will on its European allies. A US Senate vote of 98 to 2 in June 2017 started a train of sanctions, embargoes and war with the terrorist blasting of both Nord Stream pipelines in September 2022. Europe is pressed to import more polluting shale gas from the US, invest more in weaponry, and prolong the Ukraine war.

Section 5.5 discusses the question: Is there too little or too much oil and gas on Earth? Explaining the real geopolitics of oil and gas over the previous half century is only rational under the condition of too much oil. This novel geopolitical theory allows forecasting where future oil and gas conflicts will develop. *Too much* destroys the hope that oil and gas depletion could stop the climate crisis, and emphasises the benefits of rapid transitions to renewable electricity.

Section 5.6 points to two layers in the super profit stacks. The bottom layer is permanent as a result of the OPEC, OPEC+ policy to obtain revenues for its members. Petrostates depend on super profits to run their economy in a Western style. They prefer stable, almost predictable annual revenues, and are acutely aware of loss of customers. Excessive super profits are irregular and mostly linked to conflict and war, and to the exclusion of OPEC, OPEC+ members from the US-controlled oil and gas dollar trade.

Section 5.7 *Who is cashing in?* and *Who pays?* are two important questions. There are no direct data available to answer the questions in detail. Only hints are possible, for example the huge bills paid by households for heating, transport and electricity.

5.1 What are super profits from oil and gas?

Before turning to the numbers, it is good to know what *super profits* are. When it comes to money, *super* evokes abundant, and indeed the oil and gas super profits are huge sums of money. It is technically accurate that *super profits* are *profits without effort*. They come on top of the *normal profit* earned by entrepreneurs as compensation for capital invested, effort made and risk taken. In the energy industry, extra *profits without effort* are possible due to two factors.

First, the oil and gas reserves in the Earth's soils are a free heritage. The Sun and Earth have been jointly producing fossil fuels for millions of years [chapter 1]. The Sun and Earth do not send invoices to anyone. Bills are invented and applied by the people that seized the resources.

Second, oil and gas are forms of energy with techno-physical properties that are highly desired by industry, agriculture, transport, households, the military, and more actors. Oil, more than gas, is desired due to its high energy density: a limited volume and weight holds a large quantity of energy. It is easily tradable and storable in both small and large quantities, with little or no loss of value. Moreover, oil serves multiple purposes and is now indispensable for various applications. The willingness to pay for oil and gas by users is particularly high when they lack options for transportation, heating their homes, powering production processes, and more.

Another characteristic of oil and gas is of a dubious nature. The unavoidable wasted gas from the use of oil, gas, and coal is released into the air as *gaseous litter*. In 2023, the GHG litter amounted to 37.4 billion tonnes of carbon dioxide[11]. The high costs caused by gaseous litter are not paid by those responsible for its emission. This keeps oil and gas prices low in normal times, even far too low compared to the immense costs caused by fossil fuel use. As a result, the use of fossil fuels[12] has increased dramatically, particularly since World War 2. Despite the growing awareness of irreversible climate change, evidenced by heatwaves, fires, storms, floods, extreme droughts, and other events prominently featured in the media, the consumption of fossil fuels has continued to rise unabated until today.

In industrialised and industrialising countries, billions of people are now addicted to fossil fuels, especially oil for transportation by cars, ships, and planes. Addiction costs money. Most addicts put their last money on the table, allowing dealers to cash in substantial sums of money.

High super profits derived from our natural inheritance, particularly fossil fuel reserves, play a major role in the global economy, especially the *petroleum* states that own and export a lot of oil and gas and obtain richness without effort. A significant share goes to the oil and gas companies assuming most of the techno-economic tasks. Also, traders absorb a big share by means of their control over stocks in circulation and speculation on oil and gas price fluctuations.

Super profits have also caught the attention of global institutions that monitor the economic and financial activities of all countries, such as the International Monetary Fund (IMF) and the World Bank (WB). The WB, in particular, meticulously calculates super profits from various natural resources, including oil and natural gas, for each member state of the United Nations. The WB performs this monk's work every year to keep countries' national accounts consistent. For example, how can Saudi Arabia spend tens of billions of dollars annually to buy luxury goods and weapons if super profits are not cashed? Saudi Arabia lacks the industrial productive activities to generate the many billions of dollars. For a national account to be balanced, revenue must equal expenditure. Balancing that account is impossible without considering super profits. The World Bank presents its results not in billions of dollars but as a percentage of the Gross Domestic Product (GDP) of the various countries, and for the entire world as a percentage of the world product[13]. However, such percentages do not provide insightful information about the actual quantity of super profits. Thus, people do not get a picture of how substantial those profits are.

The bills you pay at the petrol station or to the supplier of your home fuel are more telling than percentages of GDP. There exist direct links between your bills and the magnitude of oil and gas prices and the super profits cashed. However, in many cases, prices are also misleading when they do not clearly state what the price includes.

Price deception in the world of energy, environment, and climate is precarious. Part II sheds light on this issue within the context of the European ETS (Emissions Trading System). Examining that trade, along with the financial scams associated with it, underscores the necessity for publicly available and transparent numbers concerning *money* flows and accumulated reserves in the accounts of various stakeholders.

NGOs and critical authors are advocating greater clarity on money flows. For example, the Dutch NGO *Follow the Money* is mapping the money flows in the EU capital Brussels to expose the extent of lobbyism. Businesses are primarily concerned with money, cash flows, profits, and super profits. All other issues, such as attention to the environment or social problems, receive secondary or no attention. Ultimately, what truly matters for corporates and shareholders is money. How many dollars or other currency individuals pay and where that money ends up. Although not always easy to visualise, this clarity is necessary to promote a fair world. Full transparency must be guaranteed concerning all public funds, taxes, charges, and subsidies that have to do with energy, environment and climate policy. Transparency was a *right* fought for by European citizens of the emerging cities during the Middle Ages, especially on levies applied by the nobility, counts and kings.

5.2 The billions of US dollar super profits, period 1970-2020

During an oil crisis, the spotlight turns to the soaring daily prices of a barrel of oil. The daily price is the conclusion of volatile price quotations on oil trading platforms during the day. The Brent Crude platform is the benchmark in Europe and is also taken as a reference by OPEC. Meanwhile, in the United States, West Texas Intermediate serves as the reference platform for light crude oil with a low sulphur content.

When the supply of a product is low relative to higher demand, the price of the product rises. This economic law applies to almost all products. Prices fluctuate erratically when scarcity is driven by uncertain and rapidly changing factors such as in times of unrest, war, and intense speculation. On trading platforms, the prices are heavily influenced by speculation, resulting in the daily prices becoming volatile phenomena. Reports on oil and gas prices highlight their crucial role in determining the size of energy users' bills. Consequently, during times of crisis, oil and gas traders secure a significant share of super profits[14]. However, the full calculation of actual cash flows and monetary amounts is omitted. An invoice is the product of the unit price and a quantity. Invoices inform about what really counts: *money*. For buyers, invoices imply expenditures, and for sellers they represent revenues. Super profits added to invoices impoverish buyers. Sellers get richer, and this increase in wealth is permanent. Making the big money flows visible and engaging in social debate and climate policy[15] is necessary to find out who earns from the misery of others.

World Bank data, available in summer 2022 for the 51-year period from 1970 to 2020, serve as the basis for the calculated super profits presented in this book. It was the first time these super profits had been calculated in understandable US dollar amounts, as shown in figure 9. The figure consists of 51 vertical bars, each representing a year from the 51 years listed on the horizontal axis. The bars depict the billions of US dollars in super profits at year 2020 purchasing power parity (US$-2020). The dark-coloured bottom sections are super profits from oil; the light sections on top are super profits from natural gas. The vertical axis is divided into increments of US$500bn-2020, marked by horizontal lines crossing the chart at the intervals. The nameplates list the main geopolitical conflicts involving oil and gas extraction from 1970 to 2020. Further clarification and details are provided in section 5.3.

The calculation of super profits consists of two steps:

- The first step involves converting the WB percentages into US-dollar money flows.
- The second step requires adjusting the historical amounts from 1970 to US dollars 2020. This requires an oil price index over the period 1970 to 2020. For the index, I used statistics published by British Petroleum (BP). Super profits in US$-2020 are comparable over the 51-year period, allowing mathematical operations, like additions, averages over selected timespans, etc.

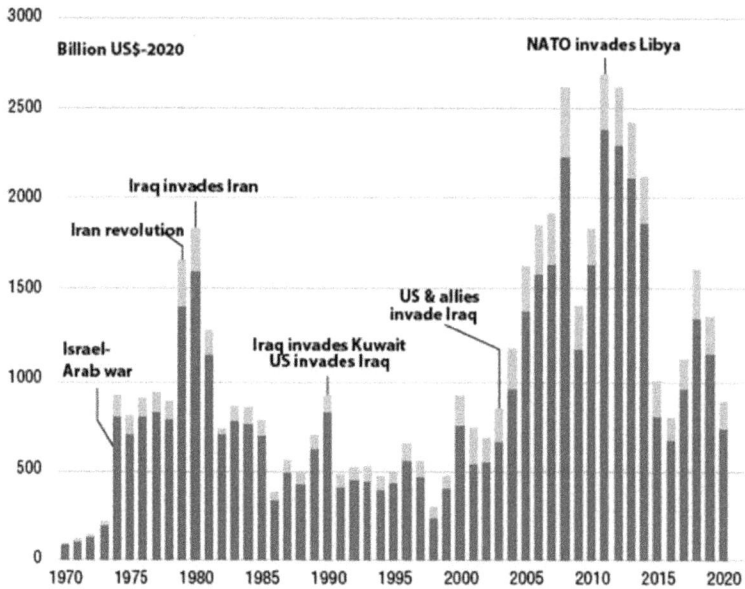

Figure 9: Billions of US$-2020 super profits in the years 1970 to 2020, from oil (lower part of the bars) and from natural gas (light coloured part, on top).

The calculated super profits in the 51 years depict substantial sums of money. They also make big bucks, from US$92 billion in the year 1970 to US$2,696 billion in 2011. In 1970, the charging of super profits was just beginning. In 2011, oil prices peaked as a consequence of the Arab spring and NATO countries' attack on Libya, halting Libya's oil exports, leading to the murder of Gaddafi and leaving behind a civil war.

People like you and me are not experienced in dealing with numbers in billions of dollars. Grasping the magnitude of a thousand billion (a trillion) dollars is challenging. Therefore, a few pointers. In 2021, the entire world spent a total of US$1,531 billion on investments in the energy sector, standing out as the leading industrial investor. The total amount of investment is a fat US$1,000 billion less than the US$2,696 billion super profits from oil and gas in the record year 2011.

In the year 2020, the world's military spending was almost US$2,000 billion, and in 2021 it reached US$2,113 billion. Just imagine the massive amount of money the world's military devices absorb every year. However, the super profits on oil and gas in some years are even greater than the sums consumed by all the world's military apparatus.

Over the entire 51-year period, the accumulated super profits amount to US$52,544 billion US$-2020. The average per year is US$1,030 billion. Notable in figure 9 are the highs and the lows. Super profit declines usually result from low demand for oil caused by an economic crisis. For instance, there was the Asian crisis in 1998, the global financial crisis in 2008, and the COVID crisis in 2020. Highs appear to coincide with military conflicts involving countries with large oil and gas reserves. This is shown in figure 9 with name tags referring to the main conflict hotspots such as Iran, Iraq, Kuwait, and Libya. Due to the absence of the WB figures, super profits for 2021 and 2022 were not calculable at the time of writing. Super profits in 2022 are expected to be extremely high[16], likely higher than the US$2,696 billion super profits of 2011. The accompanying name tag would be *Russia invades Ukraine.*

5.3 A close look at the up and downs in super profits

The political-economic context serves as the backdrop to explain the course, and especially the peaks of super profits. Splitting the 51-year period from 1970 to 2020 into two parts, before and after 2000, clarifies the explanation. All prices and amounts are given in US dollars at the 2020 purchasing power value[17].

The period from 1970 to 2000

Figure 9 starts in the year 1970 with super profits amounting to US$92 bn. In 1970, the price of crude oil in US$-2020 currency was $12/barrel. Oil exporting countries saw Western oil companies making good profits and oil importing countries getting richer and richer. They demanded a bigger piece of the cake, and started making small price moves by mutual understanding. In 1971, the US$-2020 price rose to US$14.3 per barrel and super profits to US$111 bn. In 1972, the price increased to US$15.4 per barrel and super profits US$139 bn.

The OPEC instigated oil crisis of 1973 was totally unexpected. The oil price reached US$19.2/barrel and super profits increased to US$213 bn. The 1973 Yom Kippur war marked the onset of a substantial increase in super profits towards US$1,000 bn, with amounts of US$909 bn in 1974, US$802 bn in 1975, US$899 bn in 1976, US$925 bn in 1977, and US$882 bn in 1978.

The Iranian revolution in 1979 led to a second oil crisis and super profits soared to US$1,659 bn. In 1980, Saddam Hussein (Iraq) invaded Iran but was beaten back. The US was pleased with this invasion, and the aggressor secretly received satellite information from the US. Super profits peaked at US$1,839 bn in 1980. The war dragged on for eight years, burdening Iraq with a lot of weaponry, with a large debt mountain, and with many frustrations.

The West was unprepared for the sharp rise in OPEC oil prices in the 1970s, prompting widespread panic. Efforts went in two opposite directions. Most of the attention and financial resources were devoted to increasing energy supply by opening more oil sources or finding substitutes for oil. Substitutes were natural gas infrastructures, atomic power plants, and bioenergy.

The opposite approach to tackle the energy price crisis involves going full steam ahead for energy conservation and energy efficiency. Many initiatives in this area came from energy users themselves, like sealing gaps, closing windows and doors, switching off lights in unoccupied rooms, etc. The government knew no better than to mandate car-free Sundays. Much of this was improvisation, as knowledge and technology were lacking to manage energy efficiency effectively. Because energy wastage was unimaginably high until 1974, even small interventions could greatly reduce the use of energy.

When the second energy price crisis erupted in 1979, there was more knowledge and technology available to use energy thriftily. Increasing demand unfolded rapidly efficient solutions. While the supply sector was building megalomania, energy conservation and efficiency were reducing the demand for energy. Modern approaches to obtaining renewable energy such as wind turbines and solar panels for heat, along with pioneering projects for photovoltaic (PV) electricity, also emerged.

The setback occurred in the mid-1980s when there was an oversupply of energy and simultaneous decline in energy demand. As a result, crude oil prices fell to the range of US$30-45 per barrel from 1986 to 1997. The Asian economic recession further contributed to a dip, bringing oil prices down to US$28 per barrel in 1998 and 1999. Fossil fuels were again low-priced, and consequently energy was no longer a major concern in a money-driven economy. Energy conservation was fully out of the picture in economies adoring economic growth. Further development of energy efficiency technology came to a halt. The progress of renewable energy technology received minimal attention.

In a belated response to the alarm sounded in 1972 by *Limits to Growth*[18], the UN assembled an international group of experts, led by Gro Harlem Brundtland. They proposed workable solutions to address the two biggest crises afflicting global society at the time: the abuse of nature and the environment, and globally uneven economic development. The culmination of their efforts was the publication of the report *Our Common Future*[19] in 1987.

The neoliberal interests that came to power in the US in 1980, perceived this report as a threat to their agenda of breakthrough in the *Limits to Growth*. The World Summit in Rio de Janeiro in 1992 failed to alter the neoliberal course. It was a missed opportunity to create renewable and efficient energy systems and foster a more equitable world at a measured pace. In contrast, the global use of fossil fuels continued to rise, accompanied by growing carbon dioxide and methane emissions. All the while, in 1992 policymakers worldwide knew, or could have known, that global warming and its consequences were an inevitable effect of the GHG emissions. Those in power ignored the clear warning that the neoliberal growth model was causing irreversible destruction to essential ecosystems, including the clean atmosphere, mild climate, multi-varied biodiversity, and a healthy and pleasant living space for people, animals and plants.

The Ramadan/Yom Kippur war in 1973 and the Iran-Iraq war starting in 1980 were instructive examples of how super profits skyrocket when artificial scarcity is shaped by warmongering. War causes the supply of oil on the global market to stall or fall, thereby creating artificial shortages. Shortage stimulates a panic mood that drives up the price on oil trading platforms. High price signals provide opportunities to collect excessively high super profits, particularly also for traders speculating on oil markets.

The year 1973 is memorable for other reasons too. On 11 September 1973, Chile's democratically elected president, Salvador Allende, was assassinated by the army under General Augusto Pinochet, in a coup orchestrated and supported by the US. Thousands of Allende's supporters were killed, imprisoned, or exiled. It is the beginning of the neoliberal cancer, with Chile serving as a testing ground for plans devised at the University of Chicago. The figurehead of neoliberal ideology was economist Professor Milton Friedman. He equated free market with freedom[20]. The ideology called for the shrinking of government, privatisation of public services, and deregulation, providing unlimited freedom to increasingly powerful corporates. Big Money captured more and more money, power and influence.

In 1971, the US eroded the guaranteed value of the US dollar, by ending its convertibility to gold. While international money circulation continued to be in US dollars, the US no longer took responsibility for its stability. The US could issue unlimited debt to its allies, who thus helped pay for US imperial ambitions.

The period from 2000 to 2020

The dawn of the third millennium casts a shadow over those who knew or sensed it was heading in the wrong direction. After the 1980s, under the influence of Reagan in the US and Thatcher in the UK, the EU and other regions of the world adhered to neoliberal ideology and power relations. This spread the belief in the fetish power of the *free* market[21] to solve political-economic problems. The notion that the market is an institution created and managed by people was lost. Contrary to its name, neoliberalism has little to do with *free* markets as the economic transactions are mainly controlled by giant corporations with monopoly or oligopoly power.

Freedom for the neoliberal powers is synonymous with *anything is possible if you have the money to pay*; their freedom is the arbitrariness of Big Money. Governments treat oligopoly and monopoly power and interests with velvet gloves.

Government was branded as the problem by the first neoliberal US president, Ronald Reagan[22]. Experts and independent public servants who defended the public interest were negated or replaced. The government keeps the political torch lit to keep up the democratic façade, but giant corporations wield the real power. The corporations involved in energy, weapons, chemicals, and pharmaceuticals are extraordinarily active and mediated by money, people, lobbyists, and networks [part II]. Behind the façade, they take the helm to secure their interests, concentrating more and more money power in companies, clans, and individuals. Public debt in the accounts of banks is alarmingly high, and so the sword of public savings always hangs over the heads of common people. But in 2008, when banks and financial institutions overplayed their greedy hands, the governments came to the rescue, covering crimes and scams with a cloak of benevolence and lots of public money [chapter 6]. This is how the neoliberal power system endures.

The collapse in 1989 of the Soviet Union led to independence of many countries annexed after the implosion of the Nazi regime in Germany. This marked a correction of the ill-considered division of the world by the victorious powers at the end of World War 2. From 1989, East and West Germany have peacefully reunited. However, Yugoslavia disintegrated in struggle. Other countries have achieved self-determination.

In 1989, when the Warsaw Pact ended, the dissolution of NATO could have followed, because the *hostile* alliance to be contained no longer existed. The Organisation for Security and Cooperation in Europe (OSCE) was apt to shape and frame a period of peace and prosperity. However, the reality unfolded differently. NATO began expanding eastwards after 1989 as part of the US strategy for world hegemony. This strategy changes suits and bows when the other of the two US parties occupies the White House, but not its content and direction. The corporates and super rich persist and expand their power. They maintain the hegemonic agenda of US geopolitics, as favoured by oil and gas multinationals and the military in first order.

On 11 September 2001, nearly three thousand lives were lost in the terrorist attacks on the Twin Towers in New York, the Pentagon in Washington, and the plane crash in Pennsylvania. The 9/11 terrorism in New York triggered the unprecedented unleashing of power by the same institutions that had orchestrated similar 9/11 events in Santiago de Chile in 1973. It is neither the first nor the last specimen of hypocrisy that has permeated history.

On 18 September 2001, the US Congress (420 votes to 1) and Senate (98 votes to 0) passed the *Authorization for Use of Military Force* to the President, initiating what is commonly called the *War on Terrorism*, started by the G.W. Bush administration. This marked the beginning of an open-ended, secret war of unlimited duration against *those responsible for the recent attacks on the United States*, a war waged against an as yet unidentified enemy[23].

Osama Bin Laden, the mastermind behind the 9/11 of 2001 attacks, was believed to be hiding in a mountainous region of Afghanistan. He was captured alive in Pakistan on May 2, 2011 by US elite troops and killed without recourse. The Afghan Taliban regime was unwilling or unable to extradite him in 2001. In late 2001, the US invaded Afghanistan to eliminate al-Qaeda and oust the Taliban from power. This culminated in a 20-year war, and a hasty withdrawal of Western military forces in August 2021. After many deaths, injuries and widespread devastation, the Taliban regime has regained power in Kabul. As Afghanistan does not exploit oil and gas resources, this 20-year war had no impact on oil prices and super profits.

In 1980, Saddam Hussein became a strategic ally for neo-conservatives in the US, when he served as the *useful idiot* to attack Iran, resulting in an eight-year protracted war. In 1990, Iraq invaded Kuwait, believing that the US would turn a blind eye. However, in the first Gulf War of 1990-91, the US, with a broad coalition and a UN mandate, drove the Iraqi army out of Kuwait. The Iraqi army suffered heavy losses. In this Gulf War, film footage and stories played a remarkable role in shaping public and political opinion. After Vietnam, there was reluctance among both the US public and politicians to engage in another war. Then president George Bush and several senators needed to be convinced of the necessity of this war.

Very influential in turning the seesaw around was the crying testimony of a Kuwaiti nurse refugee, who vividly described how Iraqi soldiers pulled babies out of incubators and left them to die on the cold floor. The story turned out to be a fabrication by the daughter of the Kuwaiti ambassador to the US, who had posed as a fugitive nurse. This incident serves as another warning against fictional stories and theatrical performances that can fool people, including presidents and congressmen, oh so easily. Despite the media-driven narrative, the vote for war in the Senate remained a narrow 52 to 47. Without the media show, the balance would not have tipped so quickly, if at all.

The 1991 defeat made Saddam Hussein a failed strategist and caused many sanctions to be imposed on Iraq, including UN-approved inspections of its military arsenal. A wanton loser, he attempted to complicate the inspections, which increased UN condemnations and caused the sanctions to hit the Iraqi people even harder. But for the grand accusations of Saddam being the bearded devil of the world, credible evidence was lacking. He was not an al-Qaeda henchman, but rather an enemy of it. After the poison gas attack against his own Kurdish population in 1988 and the lost Kuwait war in 1991, weapons of mass destruction were also absent in Iraq.

In 2003, Colin Powell's testimony on alleged weapons of mass destruction from Saddam Hussein rested on fabricated and false allegations. The forgeries were an open secret rather than a surprise. The disastrous war against Iraq in the War on Terror was unleashed by the US with a coalition of willing countries. What is remarkable is the division of Europe between willing countries and countries openly against the war. Willing countries included the UK, the Netherlands, Italy, Denmark, Poland, Hungary, the Czech Republic, Slovakia, Estonia, Latvia, Lithuania, Bulgaria, Romania, and Macedonia. Opponents were Belgium, Luxembourg, Germany, France, the Vatican, Sweden and Switzerland. Spain shifted from being willing in 2003 to openly opposed in 2004. US influence on Eastern European countries is strong by virtue of their membership of NATO. Over the willingness of the UK, the Netherlands and Italy hangs the shadow of major energy corporates like BP, Shell and ENI. The Catholic socialist Tony Blair's active role in starting the war faced opposition within his own party, especially by Jeremy Corbyn. In July 2016, Corbyn apologised on behalf of the Labour party for the war started in 2003 against Iraq. The war calamities in Iraq extend to this day .

Figure 9 illustrates the impact of the Iraq war on super profits from oil and gas. In 2004, they rose to US$1,172 bn, increasing to US$1,629 bn in 2005, US$1,853 bn in 2006, US$1,918 bn in 2007, reaching a peak of US$2,618 bn in 2008. In the same year, the financial crisis began, causing super profits to drop to US$1,406 bn in 2009. In 2010, they rebounded to US$1,837 bn, reaching the record high of US$2,696 bn in 2011, mainly due to the civil war in Libya, with an ancillary civil war in Syria. In Libya, NATO sided with the rebels against Gaddafi, a nationalist dictator with whom France and Italy had previously attempted to reach settlements. When Gaddafi was on the winning side and advanced towards Benghazi, NATO, led by France, initiated airstrikes against Gaddafi's forces. The tide of war turned, and the rebels captured the capital Tripoli in August 2011, leading to Gaddafi's flight and subsequent execution on 20 October 2011. On 31 October, NATO considered its mission accomplished. However, the fragmentation of the rebel front remained unresolved, resulting in a civil war that continues to this day.

After the record in 2011, super profits remained extraordinarily high for three more years: US$2,620 bn in 2012, US$2,430 bn in 2013, and US$2,128 bn in 2014. In 2014, attention shifts to the new focal point, Ukraine, with the coup in Kiev, but immediately followed by the Russian annexation of the Crimean peninsula. After 2014, sufficient supply of oil and gas kept super profits in check. There was a flare-up in 2018 to US$1,610 bn and in 2019 to US$1,350 bn, but the COVID pandemic in 2020 caused a sharp decline in demand for oil and gas, also resulting in super profits dropping to US$878 bn. Nevertheless, they always remain huge sums in being *profits without effort.*

Over the period 1970-2020, a trend of increasing super profits can be observed. The 51-year average of super profits is US$1,030 bn. The 21-year average from 2000 to 2020 is US$1,533 bn and the 11-year average from 2010 to 2020 is US$1,844 bn. The appetite for huge super profits is not diminishing but rising. The sum of super profits is expected to be high again in 2021 and excessive in 2022, due to the Russia-Ukraine war.

5.4 Increasing exclusion of Russia from US-dollar oil and gas trade.

Since 2014, conflicts between the West and Russia have escalated, reaching a critical point in 2021 and early 2022. The eruption of full war was marked by Russia's invasion of Ukraine on 24 February 2022.

The power struggle between the US and the Russia-Germany axis over the construction of the Nord Stream 2 gas pipeline is an instructive example of conflict development, progression, and resolution. Nord Stream 1, operational since 2011, delivers natural gas directly from Russia to Germany through a pipeline on the Baltic seabed. Alongside this, Nord Stream 2 would provide even more cheap and secure natural gas directly from Russia to Germany's northern coast, avoiding fees for transit through other countries, such as Poland and Ukraine. Ukraine was deriving significant economic benefits from the transit of Russian natural gas and held a strategic lever against Russia.

The German gas company BASF-Wintershall, with a 15.5 percent stake, strongly supported the Nord Stream 2 project, and enjoyed backing from the Merkel government. Other participants were German EON-UNIPER with 15.5 percent, Dutch Gasunie-Shell with 9 percent, and French ENGIE (absorbed Gaz de France) with 9 percent. Russia's Gazprom led the consortium with a majority share of 51 percent. The company Nord Stream AG was established and based in Zug, Switzerland.

US oil and gas interests were strongly opposed to Nord Stream 2. In its pursuit of global energy dominance, the US aims to maintain open access to European markets, allowing it to sell surplus shale gas at high price. In 2015, the US ambassador to the EU openly expressed this goal. He took every opportunity to oppose the Nord Stream gas pipelines, linking them to potential harm experienced by Ukraine. With the Kiev Maidan riots in February 2014, the elected president was deposed, and a Western-friendly regime of kleptocrats took power.

On June 15, 2017, the US Senate voted by 98 votes out of 100[25] against the construction of Nord Stream 2. Following the vote, the Senate immediately imposed additional sanctions[26] on Russia, and threats to European companies involved in the construction of Nord Stream 2. During his visit to Europe in July 2018, US President Trump assumed the role of a salesman, promoting US shale gas. He nicknamed the polluting shale gas *freedom gas*, and brokered deals with Poland to export US shale gas to Europe. Germany was bullied for not wanting to stop building Nord Stream 2. Chancellor Merkel's response through the press defended Nord Stream 2 as an important economic project for Germany.

The further story is enigmatic. The Nord Stream 2 pipeline, completed in 2021, was not commissioned due to legal manoeuvres by its opponents. In February 2022, the project was entirely put on hold. On 26 September 2022, Nord Stream 1 and 2 were rendered unusable by virtue of large-scale explosions punching large holes in the pipelines. This resulted in substantial emissions of the GHG methane. The explosions with an estimated force of 100,000 TNT occurred near the Danish island of Bornholm, an area totally controlled by NATO. The Polish president quickly stated that it was a terrorist attack, and therefore must have come from Russia. However, Radosław Sikorski, Poland's former Minister of Defence and Foreign Affairs, thanked the US for the blasts on 27 September: *Thank you, USA*[27]. On 28 September, Sikorski deleted this Twitter message without explanation. Besides a message from Sweden on 3 October 2022, confirming the sabotage afterwards, the Western media's silence on the facts is curious. Or not? Perhaps one can learn more from the concealment of facts than from unverifiable stories that conceal acts and interests.

European newspapers crafted a conspiracy narrative of Russia engaging in hybrid war, sabotaging its own pipelines to exert pressure on its enemies. This seems like a kind of geopolitical masochism. The newspapers did not recall public statements by Victoria Nuland on 27 January 2022, and by Joe Biden on 7 February 2022: both key figures in the US government that declared Nord Stream 2 would *somehow be crossed* in the coming war with Russia.

The sizeable explosions could only be the work of a state apparatus, with approval of NATO, and particularly the US[28]. The explosions are the culmination of the years-long campaign to undermine the Nord Stream projects, and impede Russia's free access to the European gas market. Trump is back in 2025 after a Biden intermezzo. At the end of February 2025, his new policy towards the Russia-Ukraine war is puzzling all observers.

Heavyweight neoliberalism in the US balance does not change when the two sponsor-soaked political parties interchange in the White House. Oil and gas companies and weapons manufacturers were the most powerful lobbyists and funders in Washington politics and throughout the US electoral system. In 2024 the tech-billionaires entered the scheme with seemingly inexhaustible budgets, and less bonded to vested industrial-military institutes and interests. Excessive money in private hands destroys the representative democracies.

5.5 Earth's oil and gas resources: too little or too much?

The 1972 *Limits to Growth* report significantly raised awareness about environmental problems related to depletion and pollution. The 1973 oil price crisis forged a strong link between depletion and the *perceived scarcity* of oil. Authors of doomsday stories assigned a prominent place to depletion of oil resources. Depletion of oil resources has been repeated so much since the 1970s that it lingers until today[29]. The depletion and scarcity of oil were often seen as drivers of geopolitical conflicts, a portrayal upheld by several authors[30].

A handful of colleagues argued that physical scarcity of oil and fossil fuels in general was more than a hundred years away. *Peak-oil* supply[31] in the coming decades is the fully opposite view. The disagreement is not an insignificant nuance on similar insights, because *too much* does mean the opposite of *too little*.

The juxtaposition of the climate issue and the idea of fossil fuel depletion as two threats to humanity is a problematic framing. It is a *very unfortunate reality* that the physical depletion of fossil fuels is more than a hundred years away from now. Contrarily, it would be better if that depletion occurred tomorrow, as addressing the climate issue would become much simpler.

Being misled in the depletion story comes from a misinterpretation of the petroleum R/P indicator, published annually by BP[32]. R/P is the ratio of *Reserves of available oil/Production of oil* in the past year. The indicator states the number of years the current *Reserves*[33] are sufficient to produce the same annual quantities of oil in the future as in the past year.

In the 1970s, BP published R/P values between 40 and 50 years. With *Limits to Growth* freshly released, it is a small slip to accept those R/P values as evidence of the announced, inevitable depletion. However, 50 years after 1973, annual oil production has practically doubled, yet BP's R/P indicator remains between 40 and 50 years. Just swallow: doubled oil use, 50 years later, yet the same R/P range. The solution to this conundrum is simple: R/P is not an indicator of oil scarcity at all. It simply communicates that the global oil sector is prepared to pump enough oil for the next 40-50 years. This R/P story may persist like this, at least well into the next century.

The reality threatening the world is not *too little* oil and gas, but *too much*. With spiralling climate change, even the International Energy Agency has stated that about 80% of the currently estimated fossil fuel resources should remain in the ground, given the atmosphere's overload of greenhouse gases[34]. Those who earn billions of dollars of super profits annually from oil and gas sales are keen on pumping more oil. If any oil is to remain in the ground, it is not their oil but the oil of others, of their nominated *enemies*. Enemies are quickly found if that's what it takes to amass thousands of billions of dollars.

The history of oil over the last few decades can only be understood through the guiding principle of *too much* – too many reserves, suppliers, and supply. The creation of OPEC in 1960, as a cartel of five oil-exporting countries, was aimed at getting a higher price for oil. With *too much* supply relative to demand, prices are low, and there are few super profits to cash in. To obtain super profits, the supply must shrink. This can be done by agreements among exporting producers to limit their own production. Alternatively, it can be achieved by excluding *hostile* exporting countries from international oil trade platforms in US dollars. Such exclusion is implemented through sanctions, embargoes, invasions, or the provocation of civil wars, effectively blocking the export opportunities of countries nominated as enemies.

Describing the exercise of power so bluntly and truthfully is counterproductive to the smooth rollout of the profit-making masterplan. Interventions are therefore given fancy packaging, such as defending democracy, human rights, protecting the population from its dictators. Some dictators are targeted for ousting or elimination. Those with a nationalist agenda for their own country, such as Hugo Chávez, Saddam Hussein, and Muammar Gaddafi, are first in line for elimination. Dictators who serve Western interests are granted a longer life.

With sanctions and even embargoes, achieving regime change is not feasible. This is shown by countries like Iran and Venezuela, as well as Iraq and Libya before the military attacks happened. Sanctions tend to entrench non-Western regimes and exacerbate the population's problems. This can lead to internal conflicts, even civil wars. Civil wars and proxy wars serve the ends of the aggressor best. They may be triggered by foreign elite commandos conducting covert operations on the territory of hostile countries, destabilising regimes selected as enemies.

Based on these observations, sanctions, embargoes and conflicts primarily serve the economic and financial interests of powerful entities such as the multinational oil and gas corporates and the military complex. From this then follows the further question: are the exceptionally high super profits the reason, the motive, the cause of the military conflicts over oil and gas, or are the excessive profits only an accompaniment? Answers to this question lead to entirely different geopolitical theories for explaining past, present, and future conflict hotspots. As long as oil and gas remain important energy sources for world economies, the wars will rage to paralyse hostile oil and gas deliveries. This future Armageddon can only be stopped by fast transitions to renewable electricity from solar and wind currents.

5.6 How do super profits persist and when do they skyrocket?

The fluctuating course of super profits in figure 9 shows that they emerge through two distinct political-economic pathways. One maintains a base of super profits, and another dramatically elevates them in periods of conflict. Both pathways are based on the same economic *law of demand*. If the demand for something significantly exceeds the available supply, prices rise. Conversely, prices fall if supply is significantly larger than demand. Economic textbooks post that higher prices create more suppliers, while lower prices deter them. However, the extraction and sale of oil and gas demonstrate less elasticity than the textbooks suggest. Dealing with naturally manufactured free products [chapter 1] and managing high fixed investments for the extraction and delivery of oil and gas to customers creates inertia, deviating from neoclassical economic theory. Because super profits carry great weight, decisions regarding supply adjustments become highly politicised.

The involved parties include countries, large companies, financial investors, and affluent clans and individuals. They took possession of property rights over the inheritances created by the Sun and Earth. Possession of such rights is a matter of distribution, justice, and fairness, particularly in the context of various groups, such as the Global North versus the Global South. While several economists[35] address this issue, a standard education in economics includes limited exposure to it. Despite the minimal attention given to super profits by academic economists, most corporates actively pursue oligopoly and monopoly super profits. Such extra profits achieve the main goal of companies to make *above-average profits*.[36]

In the oil and gas sector, capturing super profits is a major pursuit for petrostates and multinational corporations. Many oil exporting countries join the OPEC and OPEC⁺ cartel to collectively maintain super profits. When selling prices of oil and gas are exceptionally high, oil and gas corporates can cash in spectacular profits. Weapon-producing corporates benefit from the occasion when spectacularly high super profits coincide with military operations.

OPEC cartels maintain super profits

OPEC (The Organisation of the Petroleum Exporting Countries) was founded in September 1960 by Iran, Iraq, Kuwait, Saudi Arabia, and Venezuela. These five founding countries were joined by Qatar, Indonesia, Libya, United Arab Emirates, and Algeria in the 1960s, and by Nigeria, Ecuador and Gabon in the 1970s. Since 2000, Angola, Congo and Equatorial Guinea have joined, with Angola subsequently leaving, along with Qatar, Indonesia and Ecuador, and membership currently stands at 12 countries. OPEC's headquarters are located in Vienna, Austria, a neutral country since World War 2. OPEC+ includes 11 oil exporting countries that are not members of OPEC: Azerbaijan, Bahrain, Brazil, Brunei, Kazakhstan, Malaysia, Mexico, Oman, Russia, South Sudan and Sudan. OPEC and OPEC+ coordinate their actions to safeguard common interests and prevent disruptions. Besides these countries, exporting countries such as Norway, Guyana and the US apply idiosyncratic policies to maximise revenues from super profits.

OPEC and OPEC+ form cartels to regulate oil and gas supply to keep super profit revenues high, but also stable, as cartel members take a long-term view over several decades. These countries prefer a stable, *guaranteed* income to sustain their economies. They aim at preventing a scenario where excessively high oil and gas prices lead to a significant exodus of customers opting for energy efficiency or alternative energy sources. With oil and gas importing countries, they want to build a customer relationship characterised by *give and take* from both sides. To this end, they prefer long-term contracts. Such contracts serve to mitigate the quantities of oil and gas exchanged on trading platforms, where speculative transactions capture high profits.

When the demand for oil and gas is high, the cartel is stable because every member can get a slice of the cake. However, during periods of stagnant or declining demand, it is much harder to keep the members together. In such situations, agreements are needed on quotas that limit each member's output. Despite agreed quotas, there is always the temptation to produce more than the own quota to take a bigger piece of the cake. After years of experience OPEC and OPEC+ countries seem to have learned that mutual understanding and adherence to agreed quotas bring the greatest benefits for all members and each member individually.

They now dare to antagonise the US. By 2022, Saudi Arabia had already rebuffed the US several times. For example, rejecting US

President Biden's request to increase oil production, maintaining diplomatic ties with Russia, and hosting Xi Jinping on a state visit. Why is the-until-recently-very-loyal-to-Western-interests ally Saudi Arabia acting this way? From a political-economic view, the main explanation seems to be the changed role of the US, now acting as an *exporting producer*. This implies a breach of a long-term customer relationship when the customer itself becomes exporter. Saudi Arabia's leading position in the global oil market is undermined by a US conquering energy dominance. Also, the US pursuit of world hegemony, with accompanying warfare, creates a lot of turbulence and price surges that thwart the OPEC and OPEC⁺ strategy aimed at stability.

Given the politico-military conflicts among OPEC and OPEC⁺ countries, one might expect from a meeting of OPEC members in Vienna more noise than results. Iraq and Iran were at war for eight years. Iraq invaded Kuwait. There is deep distrust and political friction between Iran and Saudi Arabia. Four of OPEC's five founding members are far from being political friends. Yet, OPEC and OPEC⁺ still exist and function. This illustrates that, on the one hand, the oil and gas business operates outside, indeed above, much political squabbling. On the other hand, the deployment of politico-military resources is directed at chosen enemy countries to exclude them from the oil and gas global market. This dispersion suggests that there is a third power factor at play, in which oil and gas interests play a guiding role.

This factor can only be the entente of US multinational oil and gas companies with weapon producers as there is no other such strong concentration of power in the world. Together, they exert huge influence on US governance, wielding immense economic and military power. With a portion of the many billions in super profits cashed by the oil and gas sector, unlimited political power is bought by financing the election campaigns of candidates friendly to the oil and gas sector. This is common and open practice in the US. In 2024, this business-as-usual seems to have been disturbed by the arrival of the techno-billionaires on the US political scene.

<u>Wars lift super profits to excessive heights</u>

OPEC and OPEC⁺ countries are struggling with production cap quotas to collectively limit the total supply of oil and gas exports. The other option to drastically curtail supply is preventing countries with large export volumes from exporting oil and gas. Such an intervention can in practice only be carried out by the world's most powerful country, the US. It is the US that imposes sanctions, forcing its allies to apply them too. Sanctions are a precursor, a warm-up for embargoes on *exports to* and *exports from* the targeted country. *Exports to* usually involve advanced technology or specific products or components. *Exports from* usually concern oil and gas, with in addition its derivatives such as refined oil products. Conditions of hostility, conflict and war are used to argue the imposition of embargoes. War may also result in the destruction of infrastructure for the production and export of oil and gas in the targeted declared enemy country.

5.7 Who earns, who pays?

The staggering amounts of money mentioned in sections 5.2 and 5.3 raise the questions: Who earns? Who pays?

<u>Who is earning?</u>

Those earning are the countries with oil and gas reserves, where extraction completely covers their own demand, leaving a surplus for export. By 2022, the US is the world's largest oil producer, pumping around 16.5 million barrels per day. As a major consumer, the US is not yet a major exporter. Saudi Arabia follows as the second producer with 11 million barrels per day, holding the title of the world's largest exporter. Russia comes in third, producing about 10.7 million barrels a day. While Russia consumes a significant amount domestically, it also has significant surpluses for export. These top three are followed by several countries, for which oil and/or gas exports are a significant part of national income. A country that relies heavily on that income is also called a petroleum state or petrostate.

With World Bank data, one can assess the oil and gas super profits for each recognised UN country. However, this does not mean that all these dollars find their way into the country's treasury. A portion is absorbed by the country's own consumption of oil and gas, while other portions are allocated to private owners of oil and gas wells, to commercial oil and gas multinationals that control the extraction and processing, to traders and speculators, and finally to the public treasury. The latter provides financial resources for the exporting country to implement policies. The distribution among these destinations and the share spent on private companies' profits vary greatly from country to country. This variance affects the struggle to keep super profits high, and the distribution of the spoils among countries.

The countries with large stakes in oil and gas are a mare's nest of diverging interests. First, the US stands out, with its high share of world income: 36 percent in 1970, still 25 percent in 2020. Since the 1970s, the US has pursued energy independence, and this has been achieved with the additional winning of expensive shale oil and gas. This manner of oil and gas extraction is important for the US oil and gas sector to maintain domestic political influence and legitimacy. Additional jobs are created in US states with many conservative voters. Since Trump first came into power, the US has actively pursued global energy dominance, leveraging its highly developed oil and gas sectors. Major US multinational corporations, such as Exxon, Chevron and others, operate extensively worldwide, exerting great influence on domestic and international political systems. Moreover, the US dollar commands dominance in global oil and gas trade. In tandem with its economic prowess, the US boasts by far the world's most powerful military, maintaining over 750 military bases around the world. In 2023, its military spending was US$916 bn, or 37.5 percent of the total global military spending of US$2,443 bn. Notably, NATO spending reached US$1,341 billion, constituting 55% of the world total[37]. President George W. Bush formulated that the US acts *not as any hegemony, but as a friendly imperialism, as evidenced by how others welcome our power*[38].

Second, there are the oil and gas ally countries of the US. Until recently, this was mainly the Gulf Cooperation Council (GCC) states, comprising Saudi Arabia, the United Arab Emirates, Qatar, Oman, Kuwait and Bahrain. Most GCC countries are willing buyers of weapons[39], especially US weapon systems. However, there are also internal disagreements. In the GCC, there was an internal conflict directed against Qatar's more open policy, evidenced by Al Jazeera. Although the dispute has been settled, recent developments include certain GCC countries breaking Arab unity by recognising Israel, a major arms manufacturer and close ally of the US. The Gaza genocide starting October 7, 2023 silenced the Arab countries with Israeli Embassies. The US' most loyal allies are NATO member states. In oil and gas, however, the interests of NATO member states are unevenly divided.

Third, there are the countries with oil and gas resources that lack the technology and capital to independently establish and operate an oil and gas business. They delegate exploitation to Western oil & gas companies, such as Exxon, Chevron, BP, Shell, Total, ENI, and others. Examples of such countries include Nigeria, Angola and Mozambique. There are, however, efforts to take control of more of the industrial activities, for example in Venezuela and Nigeria. Some countries are also exploring cooperation with China and Russia for exploitation of their oil and gas resources.

Fourth, there are those countries that welcome participation from Western companies but strategically retain the majority of shares and profits for the country. A notable example was the 51 percent share of Gazprom, Russia, in the Nord Stream projects, with other shares owned by European companies.

Fifth, there are the countries claiming national ownership and control over their oil and gas resources. They constrain Western interests but do not completely exclude them. Iraq and Libya were examples of this approach before they were invaded or attacked by the US and its NATO allies. Iran, with large oil and gas reserves, has pursued a nationalist course since the 1979 Islamic revolution, leading to strained relations with the US and Israel. Venezuela, under Chávez, distanced itself from the US sphere of influence and nationalised the oil industry.

In response to the nationalist course, the US categorises such countries as hostile and restricts their access to the Western economy with sanctions, embargoes, and military interventions. This exclusion limits these countries' share in the global oil and gas super profits.

The boundaries between the third, fourth and fifth groups are rather blurry. Over the years, countries moved to another group, depending on internal and external changes. Algeria and Sudan are less nationalist now than they were a few years ago. Iran's isolation has tightened and embargoes on Russian oil and gas exports to the West have reached full enforcement. Even then, there are leaks in the embargoes. Sometimes it seems that beyond the political power plays, oil and gas interests follow their own rules.

A full and clear mapping of all financial flows linked to super profits would provide valuable insights. It would reveal which countries and parties are benefiting from the billions of US dollars in super profits. However, such comprehensive overviews do not currently exist. Estimating these financial flows with reasonable reliability is a titanic task. Partial information on the profits of oil and gas multinationals can be found in the specialised sections of financial publications. The published numbers depend on accounting practices which, in turn, require careful study. Petroleum states usually provide only sparse information on their oil and gas activity, especially concerning financial aspects.

Who is paying?

Who pays seems easier to determine than *who earns*. The payers are the buyers who use oil and gas for heating, hot water, industrial uses, transport, etc. In the bills of goods and services, the sellers' expenses on energy are included. This is evident in the price of a loaf of bread, a visit to a restaurant, vegetables from heated greenhouses, and others.

It is necessary to distinguish between countries that consume self-produced fuels, such as the US, petroleum states, Russia and others, and those that import most or all of their consumed fuels.

In self-sustaining countries, internal wealth shifts occur from ordinary users of oil and gas to the owners of wells and shares in oil and gas companies. As national entities, self-sustaining countries do not impoverish. In addition to meeting their domestic needs, they gain extra when exporting oil and gas to high-paying import countries.

Countries without oil and gas pay the bills. The worst-hit are the countries too poor to pay the increased oil and gas bills, especially those that were already short before the price increases. The new oil and gas price crisis is shattering the hopes of billions of people for an improvement in their living conditions. Impoverished nations simply cannot muster the required billions of US dollars.

The question remains: who *does* have the money to pay for the now higher-priced oil and gas flows? Primarily, these are the European countries, with Germany as the wealthiest. These are also the rich countries in East Asia and Australasia, such as Japan, Australia, New Zealand, South Korea, Taiwan, and the semi-rich countries like China, India, Thailand, Vietnam, and the Philippines. Together, these countries make up half the world's population. Both in Europe and the Far East, some countries escape the financial burdens, by belonging to the group of earners, such as Norway in Europe and Brunei in Asia.

Europe is suffering economically due to the military conflict with Russia and the high super profits on oil and gas. A significant proportion of households cannot pay their energy bills or do so with difficulty. Part of the chemical industry uses a lot of natural gas, such as fertiliser producers. High gas prices put European producers at a disadvantage compared to US competitors. European NATO members are now forced to allocate a larger share of their wealth to purchase weapons, including American weapons such as fighter jets.

While European households and companies grapple with the financial burden of rising energy bills, energy multinationals are gaining huge profits. Not only oil and gas companies, but also electricity producers manage to collect extra profits behind a screen of crooked reasoning [part II].

A reminder

- Oil and gas resources are abundant. Due to looming climate change, most of the resources must remain in the ground. Geopolitical conflicts impose embargoes on oil and gas exports from those petroleum states labelled US enemies, so as to cash in excessive *profits without effort*.
- Over the years 1970 to 2020, global super profits at price levels of the year 2020 totalled an astronomical US$52,544 bn, on average US$1,030 bn per year, and US$1,844 bn from 2010-2020, and this yearly figure is likely to be beyond US$3,000 bn in 2022 due to the Russia-Ukraine war.
- The course of super profits is volatile. OPEC, OPEC⁺ policy lays a stable foundation. The exceptionally high annual volumes of super profits occur in years of wars with *hostile* countries where oil and gas exports are truncated.
- Petroleum states, private owners of wells, oil and gas corporates, traders and speculators cash the oil and gas super profits.
- Payers of super profits are mainly rich and semi-rich industrialised countries that have no or insufficient oil and gas resources of their own: European and Far Eastern countries Japan, China, and South Korea. Poor countries of the Global South suffer the most.

Part II
On Politics & Money

Given that the atmospheric GHG concentration is rising rapidly [introduction, figure 1], evaluating existing climate policies is a prerequisite task to comprehend the policy work programme ahead. Figure 10 shows a cascade of questions and answers. It clarifies why this book also covers the impediments to effective climate solutions.

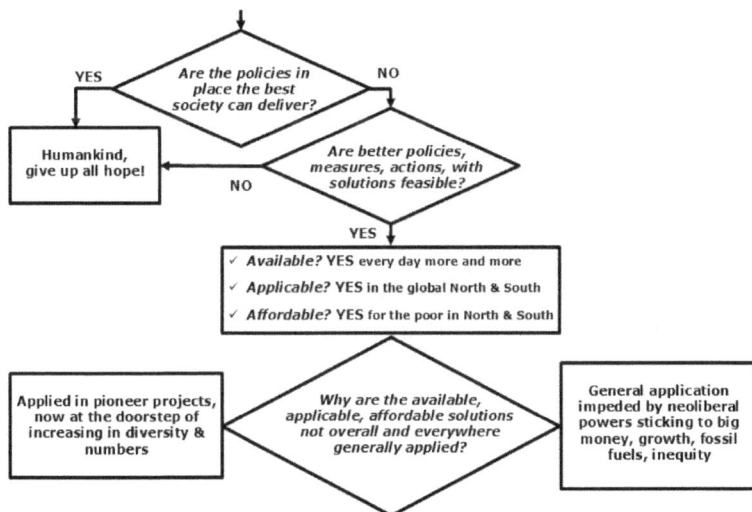

Figure 10: Questions and answers related to climate policies and solutions

The first question is: *Are the policies in place the best society can deliver?* Answering YES, as most politicians and administrations – implicitly or explicitly – assert, implies a dire future: *Humankind, give up all hope!* because the GHG concentration will soar further. However, many concerned citizens, scientists, and activists argue the answer is NO, leading to the second question: *Are effective policies, measures, actions, solutions feasible?* When answering NO, as does the discourse of *there is no alternative for neoliberalism*, and the practice of business-as-usual brings: *Humankind, give up all hope!*

Believing in the feasibility of a salvation path, means three YES answers to the questions: are the solutions *Available* every day more and more? Applicable in the Global North & South? *Affordable* for the poor in the Global North & South?

Then, the political question arises: *Why are the feasible, available, applicable, affordable solutions not implemented overall and everywhere?* Answers to essential political questions are necessarily circumstantial from a variety of angles. At the bottom of figure 10, only two hints are given. The left box recalls that since the 1970s [chapter 2, section 2.5], pioneer communities have developed sustainable energy and convivium demo cases. Over the last few years they have increased in diversity and numbers. Alternatives are real, exist, and progress[1]. The right box identifies the overall impediment to fast deployment of the solutions as being the neoliberal powers that stick to big money, business-as-usual economic growth, fossil fuels, and inequity. The EU ETS is constructed by EU officials and consultants, and orchestrated by a coalition of corporates and lobbyists. It is a remarkable achievement of lobbyism and masterminding[2] by major corporates.

In this part II, important impediments are explored in depth. The results provide foundations for the development of alternative and improved policies in part III.

Part II has three chapters, briefly presented here.

Chapter 6: Neoliberalism and Money

In the Global North, the post-war balance between Capital and Labour started to tilt in the 1970s by virtue of corporates and Big Money conquering increasing shares of global wealth. Liberalism turned into neoliberalism, with three *attributes:* Big Money and corporates mastermind strategic socio-economic decisions via subservient politicians; economic growth is the motor to extend richness and power of the superrich; inequality is seen as normal, charity may cure, not the responsibility of public policies. Neoliberalism leans on three *pillars*: boundless use of fossil fuels; endless access to big financial sources; dominating discursive power via complicit media and neoclassical economists. The mantra *there is no alternative to neoliberalism* dazes people's minds. It is true that neoliberalism has no alternatives to address the major problems of mankind, like climate change. Hence, neoliberalism should be urgently and completely destroyed in order for humanity to have a chance of survival.

Money has various functions: exchange, credit, accumulation, debt, inequality and exploitation. The 2008 financial crisis revealed that *Big Money leans on small money.* Citizens, communities and public politics are the foundation of trustworthy money. Citizens and communities can take the reins of the monetary systems to end neoliberal deception and villain power.

Chapter 7: Money transfers and pricing of goods & services

Money created by national banks rolls in societies via credits by private banks. Prices on goods & services shift money across people, consolidated in savings accounts and capital accumulation. Some goods & services are private, others public. Societal value is private plus public value. However, putting prices on public values is problematic, while societal values are indispensable for good public decision-making. The economists' tool is Cost-Benefit Analysis (CBA), which ranges from practical, over precarious to counterproductive along the stretch of time, depth of doubt, and degree of reversibility [figure 12]. CBA may assist, not replace deliberative strategic decision-making.

Assumptive mathematical economics laud optimal *marginal cost prices* for exchanges in free markets. In practice, marginal cost prices are rare. Corporates apply *fringe prices* to obtain excessive profits. This is illustrated by the billions of euros of swindle profits in EU's emission trading coulisses; speculated GHG emission permit prices at the exchange platforms in Leipzig and London; super profits of European electricity corporates in 2022 disguised by falsely referencing marginal cost pricing.

Public authorities are obligated to claim the handle of pricing fossil fuels in deploying effective climate policies [figure 13].

Chapter 8: EU climate policy debunked

The Kyoto Protocol made trade in carbon emission permits the salient climate policy, at regional and global levels. Mitigation projects in developing countries created offsets[3] for emissions in developed countries. Fraud[4] and perverse impacts on nature and native people dissolved offsets' credibility[5].

Emissions Trading is the vaunted *flagship* of EU climate policy. Detailed analysis reveals the ETS to be a deceit, built by officials and lobbyists, masterminded by corporates like BP and Shell. In 2000, the EU's Green Paper painted a theoretical CAP & TRADE Act of Belief, followed by *opposing facts*. The ETS assigns *free permits in surplus* of the needs, mocking the CAP [figure 14]. Corporates obtained the property rights on the surpluses: stock for speculative transactions at the Leipzig and London exchanges. The posted *fringe prices* feed the discourse that *the market works*, meekly broadcasted by the neoliberal media. Effective TRADE among the corporates didn't happen. In 2012, a separate ETS for the electricity generation corporates created a money pump charging the electricity bills with a climate tax. In 2014, Fit-for-55 allocated to oil and gas dealers the right to install a similar pump charging for fuel use in buildings and cars. A nutshell summary of the actual EU ETS concludes.

Chapter 6
Neoliberalism and Money

In 2025, *neoliberalism* is still the prevailing ideology for legitimising exercised power, acquired wealth, created institutions and institutes, built infrastructures, etc. During the 1970s, neoliberal ideology was developed by extreme economists[6] and right-wing think tanks in the US. Liberalism mutated into neoliberalism by means of the unlimited concentration of money and power in the hands of superrich clans and corporates. After 1980, the ideology gained political implementation with the presidency of Ronald Reagan in the US and prime minister Margaret Thatcher in the UK.

Neoliberalism is an extreme version of liberalism, such that it perverts liberal essentials[7]. For example, the *free market* ideal of liberalism is withered to an empty hull because the *monopoly*, *oligopoly power* of the corporates now prevails in every major economic activity. Free markets only survive at the edges of the megalomaniacal systems of production and trade. Nonetheless, linking neoliberalism to the free market is standard media talk, even in progressive media. They see the market instrument as the culprit of capitalist greed and inequity. They overlook the fact that markets are human-made and regulated institutions for efficient exchange and social networking. The abuse of markets should not lead to rejection of the instrument[8]. Maintaining the confused discourse helps in legitimating the arbitrariness of big money in economic-financial activities. Evidently, arbitrariness is very different from freedom, and annihilating free markets is the opposite of summoning this social institution for the common good.

Politics, economics, and money are inevitably coupled at differing intensities in different contexts. Money has risen in rank with the privatisation of public goods and services, and the intense commercialisation of human interactions, such as the bills of established therapists substituting for the reciprocity of nearby friends. The mantra there is *no alternative*[9] for neoliberalism is widespread. It supports the *business-as-usual* of expanding the commodification of whatever may allow more financial profit. Neoliberalism and Big Money are intertwined, and both merit deeper investigation.

The chapter consists of four sections

Section 6.1 offers a broad overview of the changing world since the mid 20th century, as a context for the items further investigated. After recalling some general evolutions, the attention is directed to energy and its impacts, and to the growth of neoliberalism. Obviously, neoliberalism is irrational. Real rationality is accepting the emergency of preserving human habitability on Earth and avoiding climate collapse.

Section 6.2 describes the three main *attributes* and three crucial *pillars* of neoliberalism. This creates more clarity about the phenomenon of neoliberalism, where the Breakthrough 2 agenda in the 2020s is destroying decent life conditions on Earth. Neoliberalism is this book's Babylon[10]. It should be urgently and fully annihilated for humanity to have a chance of survival.

Section 6.3 visits the world of money to characterise its functions. Aristotle already recognised the exchange and credit functions of money. For currency expert Lietaer, *Money is an Agreement within a Community to use something as a Medium of Exchange*. Under neoliberalism the credit function is captured by excessively rich corporates and clans, shielded behind the façade that *there is no alternative*. However, the 2008 financial crisis revealed the role of money as a means for exploitation, while the power of *Big Money depends on small money.* Given that they are the source and substrate of trust in money, citizens, communities and genuine political power can take the reins of the monetary systems and end the neoliberal deception and exploitation.

Section 6.4 reminds us that money has served benign and criminal ends. Money is used for exchange, credit, accumulation, exploitation and inequal modes of living. The current money systems primarily serve the interests of Big Money and the continuation of neoliberalism. Their democratic legitimation is dubious. It is argued for the transformation of money circulation to the service of democratic projects.

6.1 A changing world since the mid 20ᵗʰ century

Every political period is highly influenced by preceding political periods, and its events and decisions are difficult to grasp without considering longitudinal effects. This concise section is a spotlight on some major political economic, energy and environmental evolutions, mainly viewed from a Eurocentric perspective.

As an opener, see how the world population has grown dramatically: from 2.5 billion people in 1950, to 6 billion in 2000 and 8 billion in 2022. The exponential growth of population was a matter of concern, research and debate in the 1960s. The warnings and suggestions had little influence on birth control by governments, except the one-child regulation in China. This holds the lesson that scientific studies and propositions about societal developments are necessary, but not sufficient to trigger effective social change.

Since 1950, the tenfold growth of material prosperity in the Global North has been enormous, yet very unevenly distributed. The Global South was able to shake off colonialism, but not the dependency and inequity of neo-colonialism, also called coloniality[11]. The globalisation of the world economies in the 1990s occurred in service of neoliberal capitalist growth concentrated in the Global North. The global institutions, such as the International Monetary Fund and World Bank, imposed neoliberal agendas on developing countries. The growth causes depletion, pollution, disruption, and destruction of the Earth's ecological resources, and desperation for the poor majority. Illegal migration is a gauge of hopeless living conditions in several countries of the Global South.

Over the last 50 years of the 20th century, energy systems have undergone significant changes, closely linked to global population growth, and to multiplied production and consumption of material goods and services. The socio-political framing helps in elucidating and summarising current events, shedding light on the contemporary issues at stake.

In the 1950s, more than 90 percent of home heating depended on burning coal or town gas derived from coal. This dependence extended beyond households, as industry and electric power plants also mainly used coal for their operations. Amidst this coal-dominated time, in the villages, children played football in the streets, with their game occasionally interrupted by a passing car.

The use of petroleum surged in the 1960s. Examples include oil-fuelled central heating, large electric power plants running on heavy fuel oil, and growing motorised traffic, shipping and aviation. The availability of petroleum everywhere caused a significant spatial reallocation of human activities. In the 1960s, the delivery of natural gas started in Europe, first replacing town gas from coal, followed by the rollout of natural gas distribution networks in housing estates. Low-priced oil products and natural gas stimulated urban flight of households as well as the spread of industrial and commercial activities. Anno 2024, announced environmental and land-use policies have not stopped the squandering of land and nature.

From the 1950s to 1970s, *practically all public money* for energy research in OECD countries was allocated to atomic power. The announced cheap and clean atomic electricity was supposed to provide all energy services. However, it constituted less than ⅓ of generated electricity, with electricity itself accounting for less than ⅓ of overall energy use. In some nations like France, Belgium, and Sweden, the share of atomic power in electricity generation exceeded 50 percent.

Other nations like Austria, Denmark, and New Zealand, rejected atomic power. Several countries of the Global South were also deceived into investing in atomic power, with a major result being higher financial debts[12].

In the late 1960s, in several countries, youth and workers rebelled against traditions, norms, and power relations that were perceived as outdated and restrictive[13]. Global inequality, risks posed by atomic technology and atomic weapons, and emerging environmental problems gained increasing public attention. Initiatives by pioneers pushed these issues to the international agenda[14], but it was the 1973 oil price hike that awakened the complacent majority in the Global North.

In the 1970s, the course of the world changed. This was not the more humane direction aspired to by the millions of rebels and creative minds both in thought and on paper[15]. It went in the opposite direction – the one desired by the sinister powers of inequality, accumulating wealth in the hands of a tenth of the world population, with on top the 1 percent owning Big Money. Still at war in Vietnam, the US instigated the 1973 September 11 (9/11) coup in Santiago de Chile, assassinating the democratically elected President Allende and thousands of his supporters. The economy of Chile became the experimental field of *neoliberal recipes*. In the 1970s, the post-war welfare state, with a reasonable division between Labour, Capital and Politics in the Global North, arrived on the slippery slope towards breakdown.

Neoliberalism gained influence and political power, starting with Reagan in the US and Thatcher in the UK, and more gradually in continental Europe. Globally, neoliberalism penetrated through economic globalisation. Some industrialising countries like China capitalised on it. With their financial leverage, the International Monetary Fund and the World Bank imposed neoliberal recipes on poor countries in the Global South. The resulting misery for people in poverty received little effective attention, and was reduced to a matter of charity.

In the 1980s, neoliberal power rejected the warnings about limits to economic growth, abuse of nature and the environment, and unequal development. Expanding economic growth to solve the problems forthcoming from previous economic growth is a debased belief. *Breakthrough* the limits was the neoliberal marching order. It ruined the *penultimate* chance of preserving and protecting a hospitable planet Earth[16]. Energy conservation, efficiency, and renewable electricity generation were put on hold. Priority was given to employing overcapacities in infrastructure for natural gas imports, petroleum processing, coal mining, and thermal power plants. In this way outdated equipment remained a source of financial profit, and of rising GHG emissions [introduction, figure 1]. In the 2020s, the neoliberal *Breakthrough 2* agenda is spoiling the *ultimate chance* for mankind to keep the Earth hospitable for human beings.

The 1987 book *Our Common Future*[17] outlines a global approach to environmental and development challenges with *Sustainable Development*, diametrically opposed to neoliberalism. The neoliberal power in the US, with its neoconservative think tanks, insidiously tackled this challenge. Their tactic consisted of sidestepping public discussion about the substantial content, feigned affiliation and support for sustainability. This manoeuvre deflated and distorted the core principles and obligations of sustainability from within. An example: the clear *economic growth to reduce poverty*[18] is cut down to *economic growth* as usual.

The 1992 World Summit on Environment and Development in Rio de Janeiro resulted in a biased version of sustainable development. At the summit, a number of agreements were adopted, such as for the building of international policy frameworks on climate and on biodiversity. The appalling history of following annual COPs shows the poor realisation of the Rio Summit's intentions to *prevent dangerous anthropogenic interference with the climate system*. These shameful events are incomprehensible without understanding the global context and political-economic power relations of the 1990s, in which neoliberalism became the dominant ideology of economists, politicians, media, and a part of the citizenry. Other parts of the citizenry were dazed or silenced by media subservient to Big Money[19].

With a share above 85 percent, fossil fuels—coal, petroleum and natural gas—were dominant in commercial energy use. Their combustion was the main cause of rising greenhouse gas emissions, year after year. These emissions increase the concentration of long-lived greenhouse gases in the atmosphere [introduction, figure 1. As a result, the greenhouse effect intensifies. Anno 2024, weak international, European, and national climate policies have not halted this trend. The war in Ukraine has further diverted the world in the completely wrong direction: climate policy is swallowed in the maelstrom of war, the NATO pushes further militarisation of industrial economies, money and power grabs by energy corporates to perpetuate the use of fossil fuels. The genocide in Palestine proves Wolin's characterisation of US hegemonism as totalitarianism, supporting Israeli crimes. Worldwide, human suffering by war, oppression and poverty is stunning. It places you and me before a dilemma: giving up or uprooting neoliberal vanity and destruction?

In summary: during the period from 1950 to 1975, post-World War 2 policy-making processes evolved from technocratic dictate to technocratic compromise. A middle ground of controversial debate emerged in the years 1968 to 1983. Since 1980, neoliberal power has begun to extend its dominance, which has continued until today. In important cases, the gap between neoliberal discourse and reality is incredibly large. Decoding and elucidating the gaps is not sufficient to stop neoliberalism. Yet, it is necessary in order to pull down the façades behind which neoliberalism conceals itself, proclaiming *there is no alternative to neoliberalism*. The reality is the reverse: *for the future, only alternatives to neoliberalism can rescue humanity*[20]. Neoliberalism is irrational. Real rationality is accepting the emergency of preserving human habitability[21] on Earth and avoiding climate collapse.

6.2 What is neoliberalism?

Since 1980, neoliberalism became the dominant ideology and political economic ruler. The term is everywhere, covering a wide range of meanings from venerated idol to disgusted felon. It cannot be defined in a one-liner. Clarity about its attributes and pillars is needed to identify what should end if humanity wishes to survive on Earth. Publications by S. Wolin and by M. Fisher[22] offered guidance and inspiration in describing neoliberalism here. First its three major attributes are presented, then three main pillars.

Three main attributes characterise neoliberalism:

Attribute 1

Financial power, concentrated in giant corporates and superrich clans, dominates over *subservient politicians in making strategic* socio-economic choices.

The capture of political governance is focused on the strategic interests of Big Money. Distressing societal and environmental problems caused by neoliberal money and power hunger are left over for social institutions, public authorities and politicians.

Most politicians have succumbed to the power of Big Money and its vast apparatus of lobbyists and media. This is visible in extreme capitalist economies, such as the US[23]. The composition of Senate and House of Representatives largely depends on the spent advertising budgets of candidates. Politicians elected by sponsorship, subordinate the public interest to the plans and interests of corporates and the superrich. Politicians are submitted to extensive *lobbyism* to influence the nuts and bolts in law-making processes. Reducing taxes on big fortunes and earnings is one way to make the investments by Big Money in political processes directly profitable. Wolin typified this as *managed, incorporated democracy*. In the EU, blunt sponsoring of elections and elected politicians is not allowed. Lobbyism is more refined in creating and maintaining the *mastermind power of corporates* and clans. The heterogeneity of European countries is reflected in heterogeneous cases of political economic regimes. While the UK is the neoliberal twin of the US, most European countries pursue a mixed economy made up of public and private institutions. However, state-owned companies follow the neoliberal script, such that a country like France with important state control does not behave very differently from the UK. Also in Russia, oligarchs wield the power in a plutocracy. Big Money and oligarchs also play an important role in China's economic growth, but have faced the glass ceiling of the Communist Party. In many developing countries pursuing more wealth via the growth recipes of neoliberalism, Big Money is corrupting leaders and officials. The moral question is who to blame most: the corrupting agents or the corruptible recipients? Or are they equally immoral?

Attribute 2

Profit-driven economic growth fosters the superrich fortunes, while destroying precarious ecological systems and planetary boundaries.

A UN report[24] states that between 1980 and 2016, the richest 1 percent of people took 27 percent of the proceeds of global economic growth. The poorest 50 percent of people collectively obtained only 12 percent. In other words, if an average adult belonging to the 50 percent lowest income group earns 1 dollar from economic growth, the superrich from the 1 percent highest income earn 112 dollars[25]. The poorest people spend their dollar on necessities of life. The 112 dollars captured by the superrich swells their accumulated surpluses. Existing gross inequality increases due to the unequal distribution of the wealth of neoliberal economic growth. The talk of neoliberal economic growth being needed for the poor and for developing countries is an outright lie.

The impacts of destroying numerous ecological systems are real. However they are not detailed in this book for reasons of place, time and focus. They are extensively documented in UN reports, and more and more visible on TV.

Attribute 3

Neoliberalism accepts deep inequalities as *normal* phenomena; hence, social justice is not accepted as a case of societal duty.

In neoliberal terms, inequality is the unavoidable difference between the superrich, who supposedly drive the economy, and the supposedly unenterprising poor. Or: poverty is the guilt of the poor. This framing frees the superrich of their own culpability and ensuing responsibility to reduce poverty and inequality in the world.

Under neoliberalism, charity should suffice to mitigate deep poverty, and to quell street protests or uprisings. Unequal property and income ratios across the various social strata, and vague promises about possible improvements in living conditions on the horizon, lock common people within the logics and fences of the neoliberal corral. Neoliberalism is an amoral ideology, system and practice.

Ethics is never a process of neutral deliberation. Moral scrutiny is always value-based. It takes sides: always for care, equity, justice, dignity, and the good life, and always against harm, inequity, injustice, and the degradation of others and communities. To ignore moral reasons and to refuse to act upon them is to wilfully choose to either harm others, or to treat others unfairly, unjustly or without respect[26].

Neoliberalism is dependent on three main *pillars*, as important as the attributes in comprehending its functioning. The three descriptions end with a *warning*.

Pillar 1

Intensive and unlimited use of fossil fuels in industrialised and industrialising countries, by companies, governments, the military, and wealthy citizens.

Without the uninterrupted supply of the concentrated energy of fossil fuels, globalised industrial economies will unravel, as will their military arsenals. Oil and gas companies gain excessive super profits and leverage these to wield significant political influence, with weapon manufacturers as their close allies.

Warning: fossil fuel use is the major cause of GHG emissions, whose increasing concentration in the atmosphere leads to irreversible climate change with catastrophic impacts.

Pillar 2

Direct control over large money flows and accumulated fortunes, with influence in money creation.

Using big money levers, superrich clans and corporates dominate strategic decisions in the socio-economic sphere. Officially democratic governing institutions are populated by politicians whose election depends on sponsorship by Big Money interests. Many governments in the world are coerced to accept the agenda and actions of Big Money holdings and multinational corporates, because they pursue investments for their constituencies. Global companies know how to maximise their profits from the competition among countries and among states. Concomitant to subservient and deficient politicians is degrading trust of populations in governmental institutions.

Under neoliberalism, large concentrations of money in corporates, clans and individuals eroded the democratic functioning of many nation-states. Big money has become an elusive and arrogant power factor with faint accountability. Until in 2008, the neoliberal financial structures succumbed to their own greed. The reigning neoliberal discourse casts governments as *inefficient actors, overloaded with debt, surviving on loans from private banks.* But in 2008, governments suddenly had to rescue the financial sector. The compliant politicians let central banks give hundreds and thousands of billions of US dollars and euros of state aid to banks and insurers on the brink of bankruptcy. One more black box of lots of money with failing transparency. Cynical bankers and CEOs of corporates are bailed out, while bitching about any government spending for socio-economic purposes.

Warning: private financial dominance disintegrates democracy. Totalitarianism extends inhumane inequality, with illegal and ungovernable migration from poor countries as a corollary.

Pillar 3

Rampant *discursive power* in the Global North and beyond.

The media controlled by Big Money repeat mantras of *free markets*, supremacy of Western ideology, carbon emission permit trading and offsets as best policy instruments, New Deal *business-as-usual*, etc., culminating in the mantra there is no *alternative to neoliberalism*. This mantra is addressed by philosopher Mark Fisher[27]. He divulges the ultimate success of the neoliberal discourse as being the vast indoctrination, killing the search for alternatives. *The lack of alternatives is no longer even an issue*. Taken-for-granted capitalism has colonised the dreaming life of the population, no longer worthy of comment. The old struggle between subversion and incorporation seems to have played out, replaced by *pre-corporation*: the pre-emptive formatting and shaping of desires, aspirations and hopes by capitalist culture. *Alternative and independent* don't designate something outside mainstream culture; rather, they are styles, in fact *the* dominant styles, within the mainstream. All resistance against neoliberal realism is neutralised by creating a pervasive sense of exhaustion, of cultural and political sterility.

The incredible impact of the neoliberal discourse, is the result of a neoconservative strategy and tactics by think tanks and media[28], also employed by Merchants of Doubt. The opponent is not confronted in a fair public debate. Contrarily, opponents are silenced in the tumult of continuous bombardments of images, slogans and advertisements of omnipresent neoliberal media. The tactics are to *infiltrate and take over* initiatives that could develop as a danger to the neoconservative ideology. The neoliberal interests *take over* the strongholds of resistance, defuse their critical content, without deforming the hull, words, and symbols. In this way they confuse and deceive the many. This happened with the sustainable development concept of the World Commission on Environment and Development, and with all delusive truths promoted by financial interests. Who is behind all that cunning? Fisher hammers that *capital* is the ultimate beginning and end of the capture of peoples' minds, spirits and souls.

Fisher's philosophical perspective, fully acquainted with the arts, music, movies, and media, is complementary to the political economic analysis in this book. Fisher also accords with Wolin's analysis, for example[29]: *Put starkly, the crucial political issue of our times concerns the incompatibility between the culture of everyday reality to which political democracy should be attuned and the culture of virtual reality on which corporate capitalism thrives.* While the vocabularies of Fisher and Wolin are slightly different, their findings are chiefly congruent.

Warning: in order to maintain human life conditions on Earth, neoliberalism has to be destroyed in a short time. Neoliberalism is not capable of imagining and creating the necessary alternatives imposed by climate change. Ending neoliberalism is the rational choice.

6.3 The many-headed phenomenon of money

One of the three pillars of neoliberal power is the easy access to unlimited money sources by corporates and Big Money clans. A closer look at the important roles of money is warranted. Stopping neoliberalism involves ending boundless financial capital accumulation, Big Money and superwealth in *private* hands. Typical for Big Money and superwealth is *acquiring* huge amounts of money *without commensurate effort.* Such acquirement happens via legal, dubious, and illegal routes. In addition to the striking size of accumulated private money, its ownership is abused to maintain and expand non-democratic political power and influence. Amoral use of money is also pervasive, most visibly in excessive consumption by superrich crooks in a world of widespread poverty.

The neoliberal entanglement is a pyramid game. The organisers of the game win massively, their supporters receive a portion, while the public incurs the losses. It reflects the unequal division via wealth of the 1 percent superrich, 10 percent rich, and the remaining 90 percent – among whom 50 percent, half of the world's population, are desperately poor in property and income. Individually getting out of the pyramid scheme seems perilous; tiny or modest interests of common people cause them to endure the cunning of the superrich and their cronies.

People's money is different from Big Money. Most of people's money consists of revenues obtained by rendering services to society. The income is not spectacular; subsistence income allows life to be lived in an honourable way. Vulnerable people, making ends meet for the month on a small auxiliary income, lack sufficient money for an easy going life. Insufficient income for a decent life[30] is the injurious situation of billions of poor people in the Global South.

Chapter 1 treats the question *What is energy?* A legitimate question is also: *What is money?* Whereas the study of energy is firmly rooted in physical sciences, in the money world prevail societally constructed rules and beliefs. Answers on questions like how money was created and comes into being, what it is, and what it is for, are circumstantial. The presently dominant neoliberal rules and beliefs underpin a world of inequity and conflict. The future era3 necessitates other rules and beliefs. Articulating a persuasive vision of money as *a public good and a democratic constitutional project of self-government* is essential[31].

Money is conceived by people

Money was not in the pockets of Adam and Eve. Money is a human invention. Aristotle observed two main functions: money as a practical medium in the exchange of goods and services, and money as an arrangement, an agreement between the citizens of a community.

Money as a medium is an intermediate good or token[32] in the exchange of goods and services among human beings. Using such tokens substitutes for barter trading. Exchanging goods and services is simplified, boosting trade operations and increasing the prosperity of the involved parties[33]. However, it is unknown whether money emerged first for easier exchanges. Anthropologists see earlier traces of money as a tool for the instalment of credit, used for building public utilities such as water supply, temples, market places, etc. Accumulated wealth and the reputation of industrious citizens in a community enable the address of sizeable community challenges by realising vaster projects. *Money is, above all, a subtle device for linking the present to the future*, stated John M. Keynes.

Money for exchange and money for credit can help organise the political community in a mutual and equitable way, agreed Aristotle. He disagreed with the accumulation of wealth and money by private individuals for only or mainly private ends. When industrious citizens do acquire greater property, they should spend it *moderately* on themselves and generously on others[34].

Aristotle's philosophical wisdom had little impact on human behaviour. The rich mainly display *greed and selfishness* in extreme degrees under neoliberalism. Political and administrative potentates use credit extensively for megalomaniacal erections and for military conglomerations and wars. In this, money is a handy tool to make citizens pay for the follies and crimes. This was so for imperial wars in the Roman empire, by Charles V in the 16th century, and for decades for the US hegemonic wars, largely financed via US dollar dominance. Money in unequal exchange, credit and debt, and brute power[35] played an important role in bringing about immoral, unequal economic development in the world[36]. Colonialism followed in the footsteps of overseas explorations by a handful of European nations. Standard colonialism implied also looting of gold and silver from occupied territories. Plundered gold and silver that arrived in Europe from Latin America between 1503 and 1660, a volume of 185 thousand kg of gold and 16 million kg of silver, are recorded in the Archives of Seville[37].

During the 18th century, capitalism unfolded in Europe. Capital is accumulated money. Karl Marx[38] analysed the reversal of the original exchange process of *Goods*[(a)] - *Money* - *Goods*[(b)] into the accumulation process *Money – Goods – Money*+. The capitalist starts from a bunch of *Money* to buy factors of production such as machinery, coal, raw materials, and labour force by hiring workers, in order to acquire a larger bunch of *Money*+. Money as a means turns into money as an end[39]. In the leap from *Money* to *Money*+, labour is treated as a commodity and a major source of surplus value. The public character and social relation of money in the ideal vision of Aristotle was narrowed to unlimited accumulation of private money by capital owners on the one hand, and to degrading exploitation of workers on the other hand. The combined exploitation of the many and accumulation of money among the few have caused huge social, economic, political, and military crises in the Global North and in the Global South.

Money is an ongoing human invention

The functioning of money in a society relies on each person trusting that fellow human beings foster the same trust[40]. Under the previous condition, money remains widely accepted as a means of payment and of credit. When money circulation was fully performed with coins, these contained a precious metal such as silver or gold. During some periods the percentage of precious metals was above 90 percent and in other periods below 50 percent[41]. When paper money was substituted for coins of precious metals, interchangeability of paper money against gold was guaranteed. Too much paper money in circulation causes inflation, meaning a devaluation of the currency. Hyperinflation leads to crumbling of a currency. The inflation rate is a signal to ease or to limit money printing, making more paper money. However, rabidly fighting light inflation comes at the expense of employment and a more equitable distribution of wealth.

In the Global North, cashless or digital money, numbers in accounts at banks or at stock exchanges, is now the main *currency*. It is a flexible form of money, and especially pliable in adding money, as long as the state guarantees the additional money volumes. Since the state legally represents all citizens of a country, the guarantee commits every citizen without her or his explicit approval.

Money continues to exist because of the general trust by a vast majority of common people in expectations and promises attached to the numbers in personal accounts at banks. When large parts or the majority of people become suspicious about the established currency, the money system fades and will likely crash.

Trust and money's imaginary nature are not very different from trust and the imaginary nature of many social institutions, including modern forms of governance[42]. Delusive truth and deceit exert substantial influence on the functioning or paralysis of societies. Money is also a malleable, adaptable institution, not fallen from heaven, but human-made.

<u>Money since World War 2</u>

At the end of World War 2, the US was the overwhelming victor and economically and materially unharmed[43]. In 1944, before the end of the war, all 44 Allied nations accepted a new international monetary and financial order at Bretton Woods (US). New global structures were created, such as the International Monetary Fund (IMF) and a forerunner of the World Bank. The aim was to build a stable, open world economy, with virtually fixed exchange rates among national currencies and vis-à-vis the US dollar. The US dollar became the world reference currency, with the guarantee that dollars were redeemable in gold. US planners consolidated American power by basing international monetary policy on the asset that the US Treasury held – gold: the US held three-quarters of the world's monetary gold reserves by 1950[44].

Through their opposition to Nazism and Fascism in Europe, left-wing challengers to traditional power emerged strengthened from World War 2. An understanding between Capital, Labour and Politics was needed in most Western European countries[45]. This balance of interests paved the way for Western welfare growth, in which the larger part of the population shared. This growth was admittedly at the expense of the Global South, while thoughtlessly damaging nature and the environment. This mix of positive and negative evolutions fomented two major post-war world problems: global inequitable development and fast-growing environmental disruptions. The socio-economic peace treaty between Capital and Labour in the wealthy nations of the Global North crumbled in the 1970s, and was disbanded by neoliberalism. From 1980 onwards, the power of Capital soared with concentrated accumulation of money at the top of the inequality pyramid[46].

In 1971, US President Richard Nixon ended the exchangeability of the US dollar to gold. Practically all countries of the Western world, using the US dollar as an international reserve currency, had no alternative choice of reserve currency. The US increased the amount of dollars to boost its own economy, swell its military apparatus, and finance the Vietnam War and subsequent US wars. By buying and holding large amounts of US government bonds, subservient allies paid a significant share of the bills. The politico-military power of the US, and the pervasive use of sanctions and embargoes, still manage to establish the US dollar as the world currency. The events of 2022 [chapter 5] reconfirm the might of US-dollar hegemony in the Western world.

After Iran and other countries came under US embargoes, the US/NATO force has, since 2022, pushed Russia and China out from Western trade flows. How China and Russia will use their dollar reserves is unclear. US$300billion of Russian reserves have already been confiscated, with Germany suggesting giving this sum to Ukraine to pay its foreign creditors and pay for more US arms. To support the West's arms supply to Ukraine, the IMF has lent Ukraine seven times its quota – despite this large a loan being against the IMF rules, despite Ukraine being at war, and despite the fact that this loan obviously cannot be repaid[47].

China and Russia are the most developed economies in the BRICS+ group, also striving for an alternative to the US dollar hegemony[48]. This is done by settling their mutual trade flows in the countries' currencies, and in attempts to extend trade among Global South countries. Most non-Western countries did not go along with the US embargo on Russian exports of oil and other products. US diplomatic efforts in the Global South since 2022 aim to counter this evolution, pinning down countries in the US-dollar sphere of influence.

The Nixon move in 1971 was a cancellation of the 1944 Bretton Woods accords. Normally, this would also signal the end of the IMF and the World Bank. However, dismantling the IMF and the World Bank would reduce the power of Western capitalism in the world. Moreover, internationally spread, well-paid bureaucracies are self-sustaining, often with dire consequences[49]. The IMF and World Bank have embraced the neoliberal ideology, and imposed neoliberal beliefs and rules on the Global South. The *structural adjustment* programmes paid little attention to the even greater poverty imposed on billions of people. Opponents[50] of the neoliberal agenda proposed an *International Monetary System and a New International Order.* They intended to defend the interests of the Global South, but were no match for the neoliberal juggernaut. They learned about *the inescapable politics of money. Those who wield power control money. Those who manage and control money wield power. An international monetary system is both a function and an instrument of prevailing power structures*[51].

The circulation of money is a product of power centres, and the arrows should be pointed at these power centres[52]. Under neoliberalism, not government but private capital controls money power. Big Money manages to enrich itself, even or even more during the greatest disasters that afflict societies. Corporates, clans, and individuals conquer more strategic power in societal affairs of particular value for their interests. Politicians shrivel into subservient valets. They accept and protect the property and excessive money flows to the rich. The governmental system is in charge of absorbing most of the socio-economic debris of inequality and of derogated public goods. Professional politicians hold up the smokescreen of representative democracy in their mutual struggle *over the unenviable prize of ruling the void*[53].

In the years 1980 to 2008, the influence of neoliberalism was extending and technocrats were given full freedom in pursuing anti-inflation policies. Stocks and flows of money were regulated by adjusting interest rates as an expression of the cost price of money. Banks and shareholders enriched themselves through higher share prices and through swelling financial speculation balloons. As neoliberal doctrine dictates, governments played a subordinate role[54]. In this ideology, retreating governments ceded the creation of the *public good* money to national banks that assist *supposedly neutral private* banks.

Official financial *neutrality* is hiding the gradual impoverishment of the many and the continual enrichment of the wealthy top layer. The greed of too-much-money owners is insatiable, and their financial pyramid scheme caused the 2008 banking crisis. A huge mass of *securities* turned out to be speculative hot air. Banks and other financial institutions in distress had to find hundreds of billions of dollars at short notice to avoid bankruptcy.

Where did those billions of dollars come from? Then big money needs *society* to bail out the banks. Instantaneously, national banks conjure billions of dollars out of thin air. For example, in March 2009, Ben Bernanke, chairman of the US Federal Reserve, assigned US$85 bn to the ailing insurer AIG. When asked how this was possible, he answered: *We just use the computer.* The special US programme[55] to combat the 2008 financial crisis would provide support to many agencies, including homeowners with high home mortgage payments. Afterwards, it turned out that only private banks and corporations received the billions of US dollars. The US has again added billions of US dollars in March 2023 to bail out a bank in Silicon Valley. Similar money creation escalated when fighting the COVID crisis in 2020-21.

There is no way that today's international debt overhang can be repaid. That is as true for the United States as it is for Global South debtors. The US Treasury owes much more to foreign governments in the form of their holdings of US securities than it can foreseeably repay. It has post-industrialised its economy, and has committed to spending enormous sums abroad, while its dependency on foreign imports is rising and its prospects for collecting its existing debt claims on deficit countries are looking shaky[56].

The statement *money is power, power is money* raises the question: which of the two is ultimately dominant? In ongoing business, it is money as chapter 5 reveals. In crisis moments of the financial system, it is societal power. It follows that ultimately societal, political power of the citizenry is the founding agent. The 2008 crisis divulged: *Big money leans on small money.* The citizenry delivers the fundament of monetary systems: *trust in the currency.* But the citizenry let financial institutes and Big Money use and abuse the trust.

When rejecting and ending neoliberalism, democratic societies can create another financial system supporting Sustainable Development. It will be necessary to *use the computer* to delete the few happy fortunes at banks, exchanges, tax havens, islands with exotic names. The enormous debts loaded on to most of the Global South are not the result of honest economic and political relations. Throughout history, debt has been one of the tools that has served to build and reaffirm all kinds of hierarchies and inequalities. Debt has been a powerful means of exploitation, subjugation and enslavement, which over time has taken on different disguises[57]. The debt of the poor countries has to disappear together with the private big money balloons in the Global North.

The neoliberal economy will crash: So, what? For the survival of humanity on Earth, neoliberalism must crash.

6.4 Politics and money

Money is an instrument to do good or bad. Because of its good uses, money persists and is wanted by all. But when it accumulates to Big Money, it is a source of unchecked power in a society driven by a neoliberal ideology. The question is whether the current distribution and circulation of money are legitimate. A fresh look at money circulation is inspiring, especially for local communities pursuing monetary sovereignty.

Money serves benign and criminal ends

Money makes the world go round are the words of a cabaret song. Money speaks a language without words, well understood by people. A savings account bolsters peace of mind. Losing money provokes concern. Money matters to people. Money is a suitable tool to push or pull indecisive people in selecting socially desirable pathways. Intelligent public authorities may apply well-adjusted levies or subsidies. Effective financial stimuli are fine-tuned, taking into account the diversity of contexts and existing inequalities[58].

Money plays a significant role in climate policy. This starts with the correct definition of GHG emissions as *gaseous litter*. This assigns liability for temperature rise and the ensuing damages and losses to the emitters. Proper liability for emissions would greatly promote international justice, as the Global North and its wealthy top layer are responsible for most of the GHG litter. For the Global

South, the financial debt created by the neoliberal regime is a heavy burden. Cancelling these debts, actually transferring promised funds, compensating losses and damages, ... are useful uses of money[59].

Concentration of hundreds of billions of dollars in private hands creates a financial shadow world, where huge sums of dollars fly around the Earth at electronic speed. Super-rich, mafiosi, crooks, ... accumulate fortunes that harm society and the planet. Besides exchange, credit, and accumulation, big money plays the main role in exploitation of people and nature, and distorts the socially useful use of money.

A documented example of abuse is *gentrification*: in historical cities, superrich people buy historical buildings, houses and flats that they hardly use. Households with an earned labour income cannot compete with Big Money. Thus, the social fabric in historic cities disintegrates. This example is telling for how concentrated Big Money in private hands stands in the way of a just and sustainable society.

More attention and money should go to public projects providing necessary social goods and services, such as security, independent justice, sound governance, reliable information, accessible education, healthcare, appropriate mobility, etc. However, the neoliberal powers and their media propagandists constantly criticise investments in creating a liveable and prosperous society. Again and again, there are austerity proposals so that more money can flow from the less fortunate to the far too rich people.

Are the current money creation and circulation legitimate?

Professional politicians have divested their responsibility over the essential socio-economic public instrument money. Most authority has been delegated to the central bank[60], described as a special part of the state administration. Yet the central bank acts at its will, *politically neutral* and *officially impartial*. In practice, the central bank assigns priority to private banks' money needs when allocating credits. In this way, the size of the money supply is determined. Private banks should obey a framework of rules drawn up by the central bank. Greedy banks have proven to be unreliable, as shown by the crisis of 2008 and the Silicon Valley Bank collapse in 2023. Billions of dollars were supplemented to bail out unreliable private banks. The global money supply is highly affected by the unsatiable profit hunger of greedy people, linked to private banks and other financial institutions.

In neoliberal states, central banks strictly constrain the monetary space for public socio-political objectives. The parsimony is ostensibly argued to control the assumed profligacy of public authorities and governments. Actually, central banks largely determine the size of the public budget and the associated budget deficit. Only in crisis situations is political governance visibly indispensable to underwrite massive money creation to bail out failing banks. Caps on government spending and debt are loose and porous when the interests of the superrich are at risk. The ambiguous construction in which central banks and private lenders determine money circulation and allocation is not a model of democratic legitimacy. Governments are used as unbounded guarantors, loading the burdens on to the citizenry via austerity programmes.

Money circulation in the service of democratic projects

A democratic use of money requires a halt to neoliberalism. Legitimisation of excessive wealth and accompanying super profits should cease on moral, political, and legal grounds, followed by corrective action. Investigative journalists reveal money flows to tax havens and criminal money laundering. Their disclosures deserve political and regulatory follow-up with the elimination of such money and practices. Also helpful is mandatory *energy conservation* by extremely heavy taxation or complete bans on excessive and harmful consumption by the superrich.

An enforceable, democratic, and legal obligation is *full transparency and clarity* about all money flows and money pots related to public affairs. The need for such an obligation is obvious in pricing oil, gas and electricity, the EU's emissions trading systems, atomic power and hydrogen subsidies. Full transparency in a *follow the money* practice is a prerequisite to obtain public data for democratic far-reaching policies. A lack of transparency encourages the growth of cheating and scams. The EU commission should be the first to provide clear accounting of the money flows and pots in its climate policy.

Stephanie Kelton[61] offers a fresh perspective on monetary thinking. She highlights the difference between money creators (the banking system) and money users such as firms and households. Fiscal rules differ between the two. Money creators do not have to adhere to the strict equality between spending and income because they can, even should, create a reasonable amount of money to keep the economy thriving. The government's fiscal deficit does not matter. What matters are the deficits in good jobs, education, health, other public goods and in democracy. Kelton refutes the trumpeted contention that government borrowing makes private sector borrowing more expensive, curbing economic wealth. The reverse is true, as government borrowing creates money off which lenders earn.

Her proposals are *conclusive when a country is monetarily sovereign*. Then, the security and welfare of its citizens can be prioritised without too much concern about how to pay for it. But monetary sovereignty has two important features. One, the country currency is not exchangeable against anything that is or may be in short supply, like gold. Two, the money creator does not borrow in foreign currencies out of control. Because of the dominance of the US dollar, there are few monetarily sovereign countries in the Global North. Practical application of Kelton's propositions requests conformity with other contextual conditions, which have to be shaped politically.

With the development and growth of millions of small-scale living communities with bottom-up power that also adopt and wield the financial levers, more and more steps can be taken towards greater equity and financial equality in society. In well-run local communities, local means of payment are also emerging, in parallel with national and international forms of money[62]. In autonomous communities that conquer and guard monetary sovereignty, the virtuous principles of Kelton are manageable. The use of money is then consistent with sound economic management of the real economic wealth and resources available to communities[63]. Aristotle would be satisfied with this benign role of money in community life.

Some lessons from the exploratory trip in the world of money

Money is not a phenomenon obeying physical laws. Money is a multifaceted, human-made tool. When communities from local, through national, to partly international level, set clear and transparent socio-economic goals of wealth production and distribution, money is a helpful instrument. Each community has more or less bounded resources and capacities to create wealth, goods and services of various types[64]. The full deployment of political-economic instruments may safeguard creative activity and processes from suffocation in bureaucratic labyrinths. Possible tools are *truly free markets*, Ostrom institutions[65] for self-governance over communal goods and services, money as a public medium of exchange and credit to promote transactions and investment. The public central bank can work through private banks to judiciously screen the numerous investment plans. But the cut is kept on excessive profits and super profits earned without effort.

The emergence and growth of super profits are symptoms of the lack of free markets. Production and exchange of economic goods and services is then dominated by oligopoly and monopoly corporates, mocking the idol of free markets. In this neoliberal context money is a means of exploiting people, not least in the Global South. The money is accumulated and preserved as private fortunes, with subservient politicians executing the neoliberal agenda, up to warmongering.

The incredible challenge of reconquering and rebuilding democratic political institutions is in front of you. One of the tasks is fine-tuning money creation and circulation to realise the transformations ahead.

A reminder

- Since the 1980s, neoliberal ideology and power has heedlessly caused irreversible damage to nature and the climate.
- The ongoing Breakthrough 2 of neoliberalism is irrational in annihilating the ultimate chance of humanity's survival.

- Money is used for exchange, credit, accumulation, exploitation, and inequal modes of living. Money working depends on the trust of the citizenry in its value, i.e. political power prevails over money power.
- Present money systems are not democratically legitimated. Destroying Big Money by using the computer is an important lever for making neoliberalism irrelevant.

Chapter 7
Money transfers and pricing of goods & services

Looking at money from various angles is warranted due to its salient role in societal functioning. In a monetary zone, money is shaped by government with the national bank or federal reserve, which cares for printing paper money and stamping coins. More simply, it is *using the computer*[1] to add billions of digital dollars to the accounts of private banks or other financial institutions. This chapter looks at how the available money mass moves around in society in its multiple functions of exchange, credit and debt, savings and capital accumulation, source and vehicle of exploitation, inequity, and imperial modes of living. However, a full view on the myriad transfers, exchanges, flows and stocks of money is beyond reach, and is thus not pursued in this chapter. The chapter is half presenting basic economic concepts and methods, and half factual cases of pricing in European energy and climate policies and practices.

Chapter 7 consists of 5 sections:

Section 7.1 starts with the generic term *goods & services* for items wanted by people and organisations. Hence, they may spend money to obtain them. The spending differs according to whether goods & services are private or public. Inherent attributes and property rights explain why a particular good or service is private, or public. Neoliberal interests pursue the privatisation of goods &

services, also when their public character is essential, for example in health care, education, security, etc. The various types of public goods for life on Earth for all people reveal their importance, followed by the importance of politics to ensure their availability.

Section 7.2 is a brief review of Cost-Benefit Analysis (CBA), the default methodology for the assessment of large projects with significant impact for a long time. CBA processes societal values, being the sum of private and public values. However, applying CBA ranges from practical, over precarious to counterproductive along the stretch of time, depth of doubt, and degree of reversibility. CBA can assist but not replace strategic decision-making.

Section 7.3 collects some notes about pricing being linked to money transfers in exchanges. The economic theory about marginal cost pricing depends on non-realistic assumptions. Prices set in practice are a kaleidoscope for maximising the profits of sellers. The novel concept of fringe price debunks the imaginary of marginal cost pricing.

Section 7.4 discusses factual cases of manipulated prices to make common people pay oligopolistic corporates. Speculative fringe prices at emission permit exchanges are the symbol that emissions trading is working. Billions of euros of swindle profits are covered up as windfalls. The deceit with artificial permit markets was already illustrated in 2005, but neglected by the European Commission. Electricity corporates exploited the oil and gas turmoil in 2022 to gain billions in profits.

Section 7.5 highlights the two opposite ways for pricing fossil fuels like oil and gas. Very high prices for both are an economic necessity because of the enormous damage they impose on nature, the environment, and the climate. For effective climate action, public authorities are obligated to claim the leading role in pricing fossil fuels.

7.1 Public and private goods & services

Which goods and services are public or private is recognised by the inherent characteristics of both types, and additionally by specific property rights assigned to various public items. Different societies apply different property assignment rules, for example about who owns fossil fuels under the ground.

Inherent characteristics

One inherent characteristic is the *degree of rivalry* among candidate users of a considered good or service. High rivalry is related to something like eating an apple, or receiving a haircut from a barber. Only one person can benefit from the single apple or from the barber's time, hence excluding all *rivals* of this specific consumption. Rivalry is low when the consumption by one does not hinder the consumption by others, like using solar light for electricity generation, or gazing at the stars at night. Some goods start at practically zero rivalry, such as a freeway at a very low traffic rate; however, an increasing number of users may cause *congestion* that may intensify and destroy the service, in the case of a traffic standstill.

Another inherent characteristic is the *feasibility of access control and partitioning for use* of a given good or service. For example, partitioning the atmosphere is not feasible, which precludes its privatisation. Access to the atmosphere for GHG dumping is difficult to control, especially when the emissions are diffuse. Four categories of goods & services are identified by combining low or high rivalry, with low or high partitioning access control effort:

	Low effort for control	High effort for control
High rivalry	Private goods	Common pool resources
Low rivalry	Club goods	Public goods

Club goods are public goods whose use is reserved for club members, excluding all others. *Common pool resources* is a term created by Ostrom for what is called *commons* by Hardin and others. Examples are the goods & services supplied by nature for free. When the use is intense, rivalry occurs and the probability of exhaustion or destruction increases when access is not rationed. Both categories are mostly public by character. The *public goods* category of low rivalry are items that can be multiplied by human investment, such as public transport facilities, hospitals, public schools, etc. Control effort is high in situations of easy *freeriding*, i.e. use of the good without contributing to its realisation or maintenance. The usual example of freeriding is using public transport without a ticket[2].

Property rights

Given the extensive and competitive demand for most goods & services, their distribution requires rules for organising *who gets what* via one or another system of rationing. An institutional method of rationing is private ownership of property rights by persons or legal organisations, registered companies, etc. The owners are privileged in obtaining the fruits of their private property, given that property rights are exclusive, transferable, and enforceable. *Exclusivity* means that all benefits and all costs related to the ownership and to the use of the property belong fully to the owner. No roll-off of negative externalities or free supply of positive externalities should occur. *Transferability* of property rights among sovereign agents makes private property efficient, by acquisition, ownership, and passing on of property according to the willingness-to-pay of the new owner. *Enforcement* of property rights safeguards the property from incursion or theft by third parties. These three main attributes of property rights require monitoring and protection by entitled authorities for public governance.

In general, economists favour private property with the empirical observation of people caring about their own property, but tending to neglect the property of others and public property. Philosophers Aristotle and Locke emphasised that the right to property is limited. A view on private property is formulated by McClaughry[3]. Property should be acquired through *personal effort* as a reward for diligent industry and fair dealing. Property implies *personal control* and individual responsibility. Property is relative to *human need*; accumulation beyond the necessary is surplus wealth. Property should be productive, yielding goods or services for exchange with others in the community. Concentrated wealth means concentrated power, to dominate others and protect privilege.

A major goal of the neoliberal Breakthrough 1 since the 1980s has been *privatising public assets*. Some public companies were qualified as lame ducks, such as the UK's Central Electricity Generation Board in the 1980s. However, very successful local, public electricity and district heating companies, such as the German Stadtwerke, were main targets and good loots for neoliberal raiders. Neoliberal interests also absorbed parts of the public social services where profit-making was expected, such as elderly care, postal services and security services. Under neoliberalism, private capital accumulation[4] prevails over common people's living conditions.

Vital public goods & services

For the vast majority of people, *public property* makes societal living feasible and pleasant when the public goods & services are of sufficient quantity and quality. A few examples are: provision of security and safety by good laws, legal institutions, police forces, courts; medical services for all citizens from children to the elderly; guaranteed housing with negligible monthly bills for energy and maintenance; educational and scientific institutions; infrastructure for mobility and transport, for water management, waste collection and processing; natural parks, nature and environmental protection facilities; democratic political institutions serving the whole society and a care for the future. The latter is essential because public authorities are responsible for the provision of all the other public goods & services.

Communal property is in the hands of an association of mostly private owners, for example: irrigation systems of small landowning farmers, or a wind turbine in the neighbourhood owned by a cooperation.

Open access goods and services have no owner and therefore are called *res nullius* or no one's property. Open access land was abundant in the times of small human populations. They are now endangered by depletion, pollution and destruction caused by the excessive growth of material production and consumption. Neoliberal growth does not respect the *limits* imposed by nature. Such a reckless attitude and behaviour cause *irreversible losses* to the mild climate, biodiversity and numerous amenities.

All kinds of public goods are essential for community life, for the active community citizens, for the more passive citizens, and even for the superrich who shun common people. Despite living in a parallel world inaccessible to common people, the rich also benefit from public goods. They mostly escape from contributing, given that they evade paying taxes. They are *freeriding*, similar to people using public transport without a ticket.

Democracy is primarily good governance of the enormous treasure of public goods & services. The life and wellbeing of all people on Earth depend on nature and environmental goods & services. The political institutes of the world, regions, nations, and local authorities are responsible for the provision of sufficient high-quality public goods & services.

7.2 Cost-Benefit Analysis based on societal values

Large-scale investment projects with an impact on their surroundings and the wider environment are generally argued with a Cost-Benefit Analysis (CBA) at hand. A CBA is mostly a voluminous bundle of documents, prepared by officials, academics or private offices. A prerequisite for CBA studies to add value to societal decision-making is their foundation on societal values. This section starts by explaining what societal value is. Then, feasibility spaces of CBA are shown. The section ends by pointing to alternative decision-making methods, based on transparent deliberation activities. The attention then goes beyond the 1-dimensional monetary yardstick.

Societal value

Societal value is the addition of private and public values, as explained with the help of figure 11. To optimise the production and use of private, public and societal values, methods for decision-making were developed. An extensive description here would be overkill.

A minimum familiarity[5] is worthwhile for understanding how flawed political decisions about the common good mainly concern the Earth's climate.

	Private money €, $, £, …	Public goods & services are crucial for societal life. Assigning monetary values, ranges from precarious to impossible	Societal value = Private + Public
DEBIT	**(1)** **Expenses**	+ Monetized *negative* externalities measure reductions in quantity & quality of public goods & services, by polution, depletion, disturbance, destruction, morbidity, mortality …	**(1)** **Costs**
CREDIT	**(2)** **Revenues**	+ Monetized *positive* effects of more or better public goods & services	**(2)** **Benefits**
	(2) – (1) + = Profit – = Loss		(2) – (1) + = Higher welfare – = Lower welfare

Figure 11: Private money + Public goods & services = Societal value

An important facet of democratic societies consists of *well-balanced shares of private and public property*. The pursued shares are country-specific as they depend on cultural, historical, legal, and socio-political factors. Societies strongly infested by neoliberalism can only redress their skewed balances by *using the computer* to cut the private big money fortunes [Part III].

Nonetheless, money matters for everybody. Denying this fact is either fooling yourself or trying to fool others. Do you know someone looking forward to earning a lower salary next year than this year? Managing the personal, family, cooperation, company budget in a clever way according to their own needs and ends will minimise one's financial problems. Personal, private autonomy in money management is generally the best practice, contingent on the availability for all of a sufficient budget for access to a dignified mode of living. To terminate the omnipresent improper inequalities, uprooting global neoliberalism is a necessity.

Figure 11 is a schematic representation of how private and public money interact. In money transactions, the two main positions are DEBIT - duty to pay, and CREDIT – right to receive. In the case of private property, the transactions are predominantly pecuniary Expenses and Revenues. The world would be simple if it stopped here, as hardcore neoclassical economics assumes. However, next to private goods & services, there are more public ones. The monetary value of some public goods & services is roughly known. For most public goods, assigning monetary values is precarious, and for some impossible. What is the monetary value of a stable, mild climate on Earth? Or redefined: what is the monetary value of human survival? While you are still stupefied in looking for an answer, many economists infected by the hubris of assessing the value of all – also immeasurable – public services, fabricate *shadow prices* in their Cost-Benefit Analyses.

In order to be helpful in making societal decisions[6], a CBA must cover all costs and benefits to society wherever and whenever, and upon whomever they fall.

All Costs = Expenses + monetised negative externalities; all Benefits = Revenues + monetised positive effects of more or better public goods and services. A *clean atmosphere*, not overloaded by GHG emissions leading to irreversible higher concentrations, is such an essential public good supplying several public services. It is societally relevant to have a view on when, where and how a CBA may be a helpful instrument to decide about the future.

Feasibility space of CBA

Between full rejection of the CBA instrument and dogmatic belief in baseless numbers, one may search for delimited spaces wherein CBA could *assist, not replace*, strategic decision-making. Figure 12 shows a 3-dimensional space with domes pointing to increasing complexity levels. A comprehensive assessment of public values first faces long spans in future time[7]; second, doubts expressed as risk, uncertainty, to ignorance; third, the looming danger of reversibility declining towards tipping points into irreversibility by permanent loss without valid substitutes.

The dimensions of stretching future time, degrees in doubt, and declining reversibility, define a 3-dimensional space. In the sub-spaces where the accuracy of the monetised values is reasonable, CBA may be helpful. In figure 12, the virtual domes visualise complexity from minor to excessive. Near the origin of the three-dimensional space, the context is standard and manageable. Doubt in terms of risk, a future time span counted in years, and flexible reversibility, together make CBA feasible and helpful when performed with the utmost care.

Beyond the feasibility dome, the situation is grading towards complexity: under uncertainty, probabilities are subjective; the time span runs in decades and rigidity reduces degrees of freedom in reverting failing systems, weakening their resilience. Such conditions make CBA problematic and the results contingent on many assumptions. When performed carefully with explicit attention to the contentious issues, CBA can still play a subservient, partial role in decision making.

Beyond the second dome, complexity dominates because doubt turns into ignorance, very long spans in time eye eternity, and precluded reversibility is the doorstep to irreversibility. Under such circumstances, CBA is *counterproductive* because it presents opinions and guesses as knowledge. This is economics in Utopia.

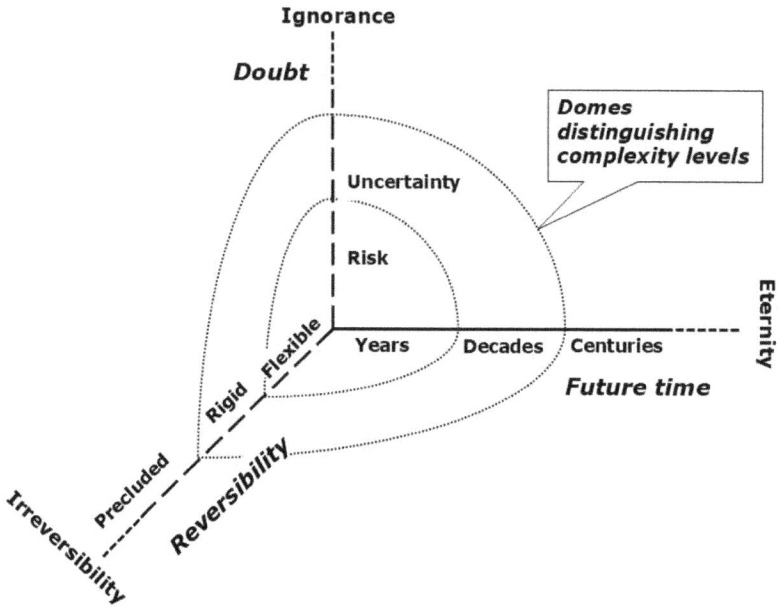

Figure 12: Decision making context framed by future time, doubt, and reversibility

A broader view on societal decision making

Weighing values across time spans beyond decades, prospecting doubt beyond risk, and low reversibility that precludes important options in the future, requires *analytical tools beyond CBA*. Complex reality demands better science, characterised by more humility and less hubris[8], with a focus on *what we don't know* as well as on *what we do know*. More plural and conditional methods such as multi-criteria mapping are proposed[9]. *Socio-ecological resilience* provides a conceptual framework to embrace surprise when it offers opportunities for structural change to avoid greater catastrophes or to change conditions that are neither desirable nor tenable[10]. The necessary architectures for decision making and agreement are of a different nature to standard CBA.

7.3 Prices of goods and services: uniform in theory, kaleidoscopic in practice

Money is vastly transferred in many ways among many agents and many agencies. In the financial sector, billions of dollars are permanently on the move in search of profit making. In industrial societies, money is moving permanently from consumers to producers and from producers to the suppliers of production factors[11], mostly with banks as intermediaries.

Money flows also between the public and private parts of society: taxes of all kinds, paid by the constituency to public authorities, mostly at national, federal, state or municipal level. In the reverse direction, subsidies, grants, allowances, etc. flow from public treasuries to private entities. The public money flows are submitted to *strict rules of transparency and openness*. Every public money flow should be earmarked: Which tax is levied or subsidy assigned? What is the amount of money? Who are levied and who are beneficiaries? It was over 800 years ago, in 1215, that the Magna Carta installed a transparency requirement, heralded as the seed of Western parliamentary democracy.

Money and price

Money as an exchange intermediary is the result of a price times exchanged quantities. The money transfer may occur in a bilateral contact between seller and buyer. When for a particular good or its ready substitutes, many prone sellers face many prone buyers, a market structure emerges. Since Adam Smith, economists had been interested in economic exchanges and in markets. In the final quarter of the 19th century, neoclassical economics started crowding out classical economics. This is paired with more mathematical formality and less attention to reality and social aspects, like distribution of the economic fruits.

Exemplary is the formal theory of the competitive market: quantities of *some* goods are offered by numerous sellers and demanded by numerous buyers. In theory, all members of both groups are free to join or leave the market. This kind of relative free choice is the pretence for neoliberal talk about free markets, freedom by trade, liberal freedom, capitalist freedom, in practice ending in arbitrariness for money owners.

With ample assumptions about human preferences and optimising behaviour, simple mathematics reveals an equilibrium between aggregate demand and aggregate supply at an installed price and corresponding quantities. In theory, the equilibrium guarantees a maximum sum of wealth for the market participants, split as consumption enjoyment for the buyers and profit for the sellers. The promises of maximum wealth are fascinating. However, imperative are the strict conditions the related market equilibrium should obey. The equilibrium price should be *uniform* for *all buyers*, and should be *equal to the short-run marginal cost* of the *aggregate supply*.

Neoclassical theory assigns a bliss role to uniform pricing. University of Chicago economist G. Becker stated: *Because prices are so important, lectures on microeconomic theory can be said to be lectures on price theory*[12]. The practice of pricing is rather the opposite of the theory: not elegant and simple, yet messy and complicated. University of Louvain economist L. Phlips observed: *The reason for the difficulty into which uniform pricing is likely to fall is that real life firms do have at least some monopoly power and can use marketing techniques to keep their markets separate, so that price discrimination is generally possible. Discrimination might be as common in the marketplace as it is rare in economics textbooks*[13].

In practice, firms pursue the attainment of above average profits[14]. Free market working is annihilated by monopolistic power, and by the capture of excessive rents, profits without effort [chapter 5]. Nonetheless, the idols of free markets and of uniform prices remain worshipped by neoclassical economists and lip served by neoliberal Big Money interests. The economics religion infected the official climate policies of the capitalist countries in the Global North, with the EU pretending to carry the flag of global climate policies. Salient examples are the *advocacy*[15] for two major climate policy instruments. One is the Global Uniform Carbon Price, or a *harmonised flat tax* on every CO2-eq ton of GHG emitted. The real diversity in the world disqualifies global uniform carbon pricing for effective climate policy[16]. The other instrument is the set-up of perfect artificial markets for a global trade in GHG emission permits, with the EU's Emissions Trading System as the exemplary case [chapter 8].

This section sheds more light on marginal cost pricing theory and fringe pricing practice.

Marginal cost pricing

To attain the bliss equilibrium in a competitive market, sellers should charge the uniform price equal to the short-run marginal cost (SRMC) of the aggregate supply of all sellers in that market. The SRMC is that part of the total costs needed to produce the last (marginal) unit to meet the demand. Mostly the SRMC corresponds to the variable cost. While the theory is year-by-year taught to millions of economics students, its actual implementation is scant. Recommending SRMC pricing outpaces by far the actual trials to apply it.

While the theory hinges on the *ideal competitive market*, implementation experiments were most advanced in pricing electricity by the French state *monopoly company* EDF[17]. Electricity is a transient non-storable power flow, requiring a permanent[18] equation of demand and supply. A quarter or full hour timespan is used in systems of *real-time* pricing. Smart meters for all end-users can lift such pricing from concept to application. The SRMC of producing a kWh by an integrated power system is practically equal to the fuel expense of the last capacity running to meet the total demand. The SRMC differs with the shifting total demand for electricity, and is well-known as the system Lambda λ. The mathematical and graphical representation of deriving hourly λ values is straightforward[19].

The idea of an ideal selling price equal to the mere fuel expense of the marginal supplying unit puzzles non-economists: How can a producer cover all the expenses with sale prices at the height of only variable cost? Theoretically this enigma is solved by the implicit assumption of either *perfect competition*, or in case of an electricity monopoly producer, by the assumption that perfect planning results in an *optimally composed* electricity generation park. In the real world, assumptions about perfect and optimal remain wishful thinking. However, when the deviation between assumption and fact is reasonably small, marginal cost pricing may still function as a beacon for practical pricing, for example of hourly electricity consumption. However, when the deviations are too large, the theory of SRMC is no longer valid, and the quagmire of *fringe pricing* opens.

Fringe pricing

Fringe pricing is a new concept, necessary for the identification and clarification of the big gaps between applied prices and the economic reference of marginal cost prices. Both terms, *fringe* and *marginal*, refer to the *edge* of an activity. This presence at the same place is a source of confusion and a veil for deceit. However, marginal cost pricing and fringe pricing are fundamentally different.

The term *fringe price* is indispensable for describing the nature of prices established at trading platforms. The economic theory of market forces is built on the interaction of the *aggregate* demand of all buyers with the *aggregate* supply of all sellers in a given market. If all the demand and all the supply is actually involved, then the resulting price is a real *market price*. When only ¼ or ¹⁄₁₀ or ¹⁄₁₀₀ of the turnover in a market participates in the price-setting process, the marginal cost of the fringe will likely deviate more and more from the marginal cost based on all supply and demand.

A marginal cost price is the pinnacle, the end-result of a full aggregate of marginal cost curves of sub-marginal activities. When the aggregate changes, so does the marginal cost price. No genuine marginal cost price emerges from a market activity without submarginal reality.

Distinctly, fringe prices refer to a limited activity at the edge, *detached* from the aggregate of the majority of activities[20]. Speculation at so-called *market* exchanges is a major creator of fringe prices. When a significant share of the demand and the supply in a specific market is not implied in the construction of the market equilibria, the generated prices are fringe prices, not genuine marginal cost prices. Fringe pricing is happening for different ends.

My experience has been that it took time to explain the concept of *fringe price* to economist colleagues, before the *eureka* moment happened. While metaphors always fall short in comparability, the distinction between marginal cost price and fringe price may be better understood when looking at governments wielding power in a country. In a democracy, the citizens of a constituency elect representatives forming a government, as the pinnacle of an ordered, inclusive society (like an inclusive free market will reveal proper marginal cost prices).

However, the government of a country may have obtained power via non-democratic ways. Such ways may range from illegal practices within a democratic hull, blatant interventions to suppress opponents, up to bloody coups like the 11 September 1973 one in Chile. Such governments represent only a fringe of the population; they do not represent the people (like fringe prices do not represent free market outcomes).

The democratic and the non-democratic governments exist at the same place in society, use the same buildings, use the same taxes paid by the citizenry, represent the country at the United Nations, etc. However, the two government types differ and are irreconcilable.

7.4 Fringe pricing in the EU's energy and climate policies

The existence of dubious prices is experienced in practical life, and also evidenced by literature based on facts. Prices are often *symbols* to mislead people by upsetting the link between price and money. The most important and reliable indicator in financial matters is *money* as numbered quantities with dated guarantees about ownership. Firms' financial accounts and investment appraisals are based on cash flows and available money.

Prices are adaptable, multipurpose, volatile, and flawed when neglecting the value of external goods & services [section 7.2].

Especially in public financial matters, full transparency and clarity are necessary for a trustworthy community life. The super profits on oil and gas were opaque when expressed as percentages of GDPs. Expressed in US dollars-2020 value they became understandable by all [chapter 5]. In a democratic society, public budgets, tax returns, subsidy assignments, investments and spending, etc. are transparently exposed to the citizenry. In autocratic states and managed democracies, opacity and confusion hinder transparency.

Lack of transparency and dishonest cunning with billions of euros is observed in the EU's climate policies based on market-based economic talk, with the EU ETS as a major case. Examples are described in this section.

Fringe prices at trading platforms

In the 8-year period 2005-2012, practically all ETS permits were donated for *free to all* companies participating in the EU ETS. The electricity corporates received around 60 percent of the total volume of ETS free permits. A surplus on top of the permit numbers needed for submission to the ETS boards was allotted, as is standard practice in environmental permit assignment. When all agents get ample free permits, the propensity to trade permits is absent[21].

Notwithstanding the surplus of free permits, exchange platforms for permit trade opened, because trade is an essential component in the efficiency proof of market-based instruments. The financial departments of electricity corporates have experience in speculative trade of fossil fuels or materials they process. In addition, financial speculators were invited to help in shaping speculative activity at the permit exchange platforms. Because the involved quantities at the edge were minor, it was possible to inflate speculative prices to incredible heights of €25-€30 per permit for posting on the exchange boards. The price symbol of the EU ETS was created. In 2007, the spot price crashed to zero, but the symbol was revived in phase 2 of the ETS.

The major role of the daily fringe price creation at the exchanges was to keep up the symbol of market functioning, essential in the façade of the EU ETS [chapter 8]. Electricity corporates with millions of captive customers use the posted permit prices to legitimate the tariffs they applied in the invoices paid by non-ETS customers.

Windfall or swindle profits

In the muddled state of the EU ETS in the years 2005 to 2012, electricity generation corporates saw an outstanding opportunity to cash super profits. They pointed to price quotes on the speculative trading platforms for ETS permits and then levied a *climate surcharge* on the bills of non-ETS electricity users[22]. A small climate surcharge per captive customer means billions of euros of super profits for the oligopoly corporates. ETS supporters call these billions of super profits euphemistically *windfall* profits. In this context windfall is an incorrect, deceiving name, according to Keynes who used the term *windfall* for something very exceptional. Monopoly profit cashing and rent skimming are improper practices, once upon a time – before neoliberalism became victorious – criticised by economists concerned about the public good. The true name is *swindle* profits[23].

For phase 1 [2005-2007], super profits are estimated at €10 to €60 per year for an average household consumption of 3350kWh/year. German electricity oligopolies thus collected €6 to €8 billion. For Belgium, the skimming was estimated at €1.2 to €1.5 billion per year. Due to a lack of clear financial data on the ETS, stated monetary amounts are always estimates.

The immoral rent skimming ended due to public protests and the fear of the corporates that the EU ETS could crash on the swindle. As revealed in chapter 2, section 2.7, the corporate sector in 2014 wanted the *EU ETS as a flagship climate and energy system*. After 2012, the electricity sector obtained a separate position and treatment in the EU ETS, with an organised system of charging climate levies on their captive customers [chapter 8, section 8.6].

Tradable Green Certificates as an early warning of deceit with artificial permit markets

Chapter 2 [section 2.5] mentioned the failure of tradable green certificate systems in the development of renewable electricity technologies. In Flanders, the failing TGC has siphoned hundreds of millions of euros from less well-off households to richer households, investors and electricity corporates[24]. Power corporates raked in hundreds of millions in super profits with outdated technology and with biomass known for its dubious sustainability record, such as palm oil.

The uniform price for every certificate or MWh of renewable electricity generated was a fringe price at the edge of the imposed yearly quota of generated renewable electricity. Because the quota had to go up, the uniform price approached the penalty level, and was known in advance. The uniform price was applied to all generated renewable electricity, either coming from obsolete domestic refuse incinerators or from novel technologies in their infancy. The first kind captured fat profits, while the latter could not fully deploy with the uniform remuneration per MWh. The spillage of money was high.

Electricity corporates exploit oil and gas turmoil in 2022

This item ties in with the discussion of super profits on oil and gas [chapter 5]. In 2022, European gas prices rose to unprecedented levels due to the artificial scarcity created by the war in Ukraine and embargoes on Russian oil and gas exports. The same year, the electricity corporates in Europe charged high crisis prices for electricity, legitimising the price hike by referring to the high prices of natural gas driving up the price of electricity traded on the Leipzig trading platform for electricity, EPEX[25]. It is a case of super profit capturing by a combination of war-driven gas scarcity and fringe pricing.

In the EU ETS, the permit fringe price serves to disguise the fact that ETS companies *do not pay* for carbon emissions. In 2022, the electricity fringe price fetish pursues high revenues for oligopoly electricity producers by *making customers pay* for non-existing costs. It is another case of billions in super profits, paid for by captive electricity customers.

The discourse covering up the invoices with super profits, is as follows: *the sudden high customer tariffs for electricity are the logical economic effect of higher marginal cost prices noted on the EPEX.* The loud or tacit support for this discourse by neoclassical economists is a consecration of the EPEX notations as valid marginal cost prices under all circumstances. It is propagated as an indisputable truth, without investigating whether the theory of *marginal cost pricing* holds validity in the gas price crisis created by sudden embargoes on natural gas supplies.

Marginal cost pricing of electricity is fine when the electricity generation park is *optimally composed.* Then the application of marginal cost prices implies that the obtained revenues *recover exactly all expenditures* of the electricity producer. The revenues obtained must also cover the fixed costs of investment in all plants including a normal return on capital. Such cost recovery is balanced if and only if the fleet of power plants for electricity generation is *optimally composed*[26].

Optimal composition requires each type of plant to have the right capacity to meet the demand of all end customers at the least cost. In practice, there is a lot of noise on that optimal composition and on a number of assumptions. However, the sudden and sharp natural gas price hikes completely disequilibrate the existing electric power generation systems, and annihilate the relative optimality of the generation systems.

Then the EPEX platform price hangs on the edge, far too high and detached from the reality of power plants not burning natural gas. Hence, it is a *fringe price.* In 2022, the EU electricity corporates showed once again that they are not too shy about robbing billions of euros from the electricity customers who depend on them.

Post scriptum

All above examples of cunning to obtain super profits happened or still happen in the domain of energy and climate policy-making. It is deplorable to observe how corporates only chase money without moral brakes, in matters of survival importance for the climate, nature and thus humankind. How is this possible? What explains the easy escape by the electricity corporates from regulators, politicians, academics, and the media when they cash billions in super profits with flawed arguments?

7.5 What is the right price of fossil fuels?

About fossil fuels, this book informed like: The Sun and Earth manufactured fossil fuel resources for free [chapter 1]. Fossil fuels cover about three quarters of the global use of commercial energy. Who seized the property rights over the petroleum and natural gas resources, reaped enormous super profits, as do corporates active in the winning, processing, trade and sales of oil and gas [chapter 5]. Combusting fossil fuels is the major cause of GHG emissions and of global warming [introduction].

Warranted high prices for fossil fuels

In the energy world and in society, the dominating discourse is about cheap, low-cost fossil fuels.

In reality, these low costs do not exist and never existed, because of the numerous and dauntingly large harmful side effects of their use [section 7.2]. The public damage costs of fossil fuel extraction and use are not included in the bills paid, yet passed on to the environment, nature and future generations.

In summary: fossil fuels are *very high-cost* energy, while *low-priced* and *low-spending* for the past and present generations. The latter begin to experience the huge damages as a corollary of the destabilised climate.

Very high fossil fuel prices are warranted for charging the full damage costs on top of the expenses for extraction and processing fossil fuels. If all the harmful externalities of oil and gas were really paid for, oil and gas would today be a small industry, not the powerful mastodon masterminding the largest economies in the world. Clever budget management stimulates households and companies to control their bills, by reducing consumption and exploring alternative energy sources when oil and gas bills soar. High fossil fuel prices will help to prevent the profound societal issue of climate change from further escalating to climate collapse that threatens all human life on Earth.

However, what are problematic are the high prices charged by petroleum exporters and oil and gas, coal, and electricity companies, amassing super profits. Setting the true required social prices is the duty of public authorities serving the common good.

Oil & gas prices set by industry or by public governance

Fundamental differences between oil and gas interests versus public authorities setting the sale prices of oil and gas are shown in figure 13. The first difference is how the price levels of oil and gas are formed. The oil and gas industry installs price levels via organising artificial scarcity in the markets. On top of prices that guarantee a stable base of sizeable super profits, there are sanctions, embargoes and wars, which generate extremely high usury prices [chapter 5]. The prices pursued by public authorities would be the outcome of a wide variety of applied instruments aimed at progressively increasing financial burdens on fossil fuel extraction and use. This would certainly start with the elimination of the enormous subsidies for fossil fuels[27].

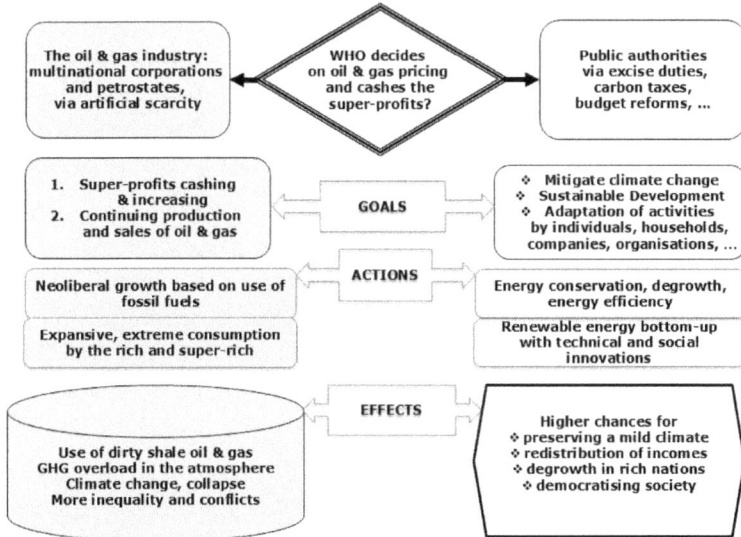

Figure 13: Opposite paths for determination of oil and gas prices and for collection of associated super profits, with opposite Goals, Actions, and Effects

The second difference is the kind of *goals* that are pursued. For the petrostates and the oil and gas industry, it is not just cashing in and increasing super profits year after year, but also continuing to produce and sell large volumes of oil and gas. In other words, extending the life of the fossil fuel industry despite increasing greenhouse gas emissions, and additional overburdening of the atmosphere. For the public interest, maintaining a mild climate is the main goal. This goes hand in hand with the pursuit of Sustainable Development for all Earth's inhabitants [part III]. This will require profound changes with adjustments in the activities of individuals, households, companies, and institutions. Initiatives by billions of individuals grow robustly when based on economic rationality. The rectification of oil and gas prices and incorporating charges on climate and socially harmful activities are crucial instruments.

The third difference is the *actions* attempted. The oil and gas industry plays the central role in the neoliberal power structures of the US with impacts on many nations in the world. Fossil fuels are an essential pillar in ensuring neoliberal wealth and wielding of neoliberal power. The ongoing pursuit of material growth strengthens the position of the superrich, enabling their expansive and extreme forms of consumption. Their lavish lifestyles serve as an inspiration for those less affluent, including the poor, to aspire to similar standards. In contrast, for the public good, energy conservation and natural degrowth of industrial economies are crucial steps in achieving a more sustainable society. Public actions should foster a complete transition to renewable energy supplies. Financial support, technological research and development, public services such as public transport, and other services are available from the revenues generated by proper taxation of fossil fuels.

The fourth difference is the expected *effects*, listed clearly at the bottom of figure 13.

For effective climate action, public authorities are obligated to assume the responsibility of pricing fossil fuels by abolishing subsidies for fossil fuels, and gradually increasing levies on fossil fuel use. At EU and member state level, there is little enthusiasm for assuming this task.

Hence, local authorities, communities, and grassroots initiatives will have to take over the responsibility. In this way, tax money can be channelled toward more meaningful and effective purposes.

Can energy monopoly profits bring beneficial impacts?

Are high monopoly profits in the fossil fuel and electricity sectors also incentives for enhanced energy efficiency and more renewable energy? The answer is both yes and no.

Yes, for the affluent part of the population, who, in addition to paying high energy bills, can still invest enough money to improve the energy efficiency of their homes and equip them extensively with solar panels for hot water and electricity, home batteries, computer control systems, electric cars, etc.

No, for cash-strapped households. High energy bills burn their last savings, leaving them unable to invest. Energy conservation in these households is not the result of cutting futile consumption, but stems from uncomfortable, even painful, cuts in living standards. No mention is made of the billions of poor people in the Global South who have been hit hard by the war in Ukraine. Property and income inequality are intertwined with the challenges and opportunities of accelerating energy transformation. Policies without detailed and bold solutions to reduce, and where necessary, eliminate inequality cannot provide credible solutions to the challenges of climate change.

Some also suggested that the profiteering energy corporates would spend their super profits on the energy transition. This vague hope from politicians is an example of *wishful thinking*.

Distinguishing between fossil fuels and electricity is obvious. On the one hand, fossil fuels should be phased out as an energy commodity, and serve merely as providers of raw materials. On the other hand, electricity shifts to the most central, almost the only, provider of commercial energy for human activities [figure 4]. The future of electricity lies in local harvesting from sources such as sunlight, wind, water and geothermal currents.

With super profits, energy corporates can invest in large-scale renewable power generation, mainly offshore wind turbines. Those projects serve to secure their profits in the future, which includes inhibiting and discouraging small-scale renewable installations [chapter 2]. This counteracts rather than promotes the transformations needed to ensure the future of humanity.

For the future, politicians express the hope that the companies and individuals most responsible for the disastrous state of the atmosphere, climate, nature, animals, plants, habitats, etc., will find solutions on their own. This *business-as-usual*, just getting on with it, is deeply ingrained, exacerbating the existing problems. The snail's pace of promised change from above falls short and arrives too late to implement the transformations necessary for human survival on Earth.

A reminder

- An important facet of democratic societies is *well balanced shares of private and public goods, services, and property*.
- Cost-Benefit Analysis is an instrument to *assist not replace* public strategic decision-making.
- Both linked to the *edge of a particular activity*, a marginal cost price covers all of the activity below the edge, very different from a *fringe price* referring to the edge only.
- Lack of transparency and dishonest cunning with billions of euros is observed in the EU's energy and climate policies based on market-based economic talk.
- For effective climate action, public authorities are obligated to assume the responsibility of pricing fossil fuels.

Chapter 8
EU climate policy debunked

International climate policy is heavily influenced by neoclassical economics about markets and pricing. For example, Nicolas Stern[1] frames climate change as a huge market failure problem. In the Working Group III IPCC reports, price-induced mitigation of GHG emissions prevails. Policy instruments, such as taxes, levies, subsidies, and tradable emission permits belong to the economics toolkit. Internationally, the EU assumed pole position in GHG emissions trading.

The EU's climate policy flagship is the Emissions Trading System (ETS). After the 1997 COP3 in Kyoto, it took 7 years to conceive, and a 3-year trial period from 2005-2007. Ten years of precious time were lost in a matter of high urgency. Moreover, the hailed flagship is actually a floating boat, requiring many re-riggings after havoc. Its designers and crew disguise its poor performance by engaging in relentless excessive praise of a mythical artificial market mechanism. The praise drums drown out critical thinking and democratic debate about the system.

I point out that the EU ETS is a salient case of delusive truth. The truth is the formal mathematical theory of the imaginary perfect market. Bringing life to the formality requests vivid exchanges of emission permits obtained at active auctions. Opposite to this ideal market functioning is the busy alchemistic activity by thousands of officials, academics, and lobbyists in the ETS policy labyrinth. The questionable activities and products are shielded by neoclassical economics propaganda about superior performance.

The open access book *Pricing Carbon Emissions. Economic Reality and Utopia*[2] offers an extensive analysis of the EU ETS, as being masterminded by a handful of corporates with BP and Shell in the vanguard. The essence of EU climate policy is turning freely given emission permits[3] into *bankable and tradable private assets*, available for financial speculation[4]. Shaping the EU ETS is done by big GHG emitters, warranting a brief comment and a few questions about lobbyism.

Lobbyism

In autumn 2022, the European Parliament was shocked by a bribery case. Qatar paid European parliamentarians to mute criticism of its human rights record. The scandal is a rather irrelevant quack in the wide pool of Brussels lobbyism. In this pool, matters of significant importance are masterminded by corporates and Big Money clans. Legions of lobbyists[5] create balloons of deceit and complacency, shielding politicians, officials and Big Money strategists from criticism.

Regularly, NGOs[6] or journalists sharply comment on the prevalence of lobbyists in Brussels, in Washington and in other cities where policies are crafted. While such criticism provides consoling reading by affirming *you are not the only one annoyed by lobbyism*, it has no impact. Critics would do better to address how lobbying mechanisms function, and most importantly, which outcomes are fabricated by lobbyism. Outcomes are policy documents and instruments favouring Big Money, with the burdens rolled off on to society and nature.

Policy mechanisms and their resulting outcomes largely escape independent scrutiny and evaluation. The EU policy and lobbyist bubble in Brussels evaluates itself. Praising the ETS is part and capstone of the lobbying process, and draws established environmental NGOs into the intricacies of European politics. It is worthwhile considering four questions:

Q1: Given the tumult about the Qatar scandal, why is there no louder outrage about extensive and continuous lobbyism by corporates and Big Money?

Q2: Is indignation at lobbyism reconcilable with praise and support for the outcomes of lobbyism activities, such as the EU ETS?

Q3: Why is the impact of corporate lobbyism on energy and climate policy not abated, yet propagated by *comitology*[7] platforms?

Q4: What explains mass media's constancy in supporting the products of lobbyism and deceit?

Corporates and Big Money do not spend € millions on numerous lobbyists to shoot their own feet. Their aims are to escape financial burdens and obligations, protect business-as-usual, and strengthen neoliberalism while skipping Sustainable Development. Under neoliberalism *masterminding*[8] politics substitutes for *capturing* regulation. Big Money designs policies for administrations to execute. Chapter 8 unravels the EU ETS as the hindrance to *effective* climate policy for industry.

The chapter consists of eight sections.

Section 8.1 on money drivers in climate policy questions the effectiveness of financial incentives for emission mitigation when low-carbon alternatives are lacking. The fantasy of artificial markets is an imaginary bend around industry's rejection to pay for their GHG emissions. Industry is unwilling to make expenses without the perspective of making profit. This is the red thread of chapter 8. The section rounds up by recalling global emissions trading, accepted in 1997 at COP3 in Kyoto.

Section 8.2 identifies the EU ETS as the result of corporate masterminding. It lets the European Commission float its emission trading flagship as long as industry gets free permits. The acceptance of the opaque system was pushed by two biased examples One was the BP in-house reduction of emissions by plucking low-hanging fruits in its energy efficiency garden, hulled as a tradable emissions experiment. The other was the US scheme for reducing the sulphur dioxide emissions of its coal-fired power plants, in no way comparable with due GHG mitigation by an amalgamation of industries in the EU ETS.

Section 8.3 refers to the European Commission's Green paper of the year 2000. It is an act of faith in CAP & TRADE. However, the opposite of the act happened. There is no effective CAP in the EU ETS, and there is no TRADE among industrial companies. The reduction in the GHG emissions of the European industry is the result of de-industrialisation in Europe, economic crisis, and renewable electricity generation. The development of photovoltaic and wind turbine technologies was stimulated by policies being the opposite of trading concepts [chapter 2].

Section 8.4 tests the performance of the ETS on major attributes that were promised in the 2000 act of the EU Commission. Promised broad coverage became limited participation of industries benefiting from free permits, which turned into bankable and tradable assets. Promised efficiency gains through equalising the marginal abatement costs of all sources only materialised at price zero (free permits); trade had no impact. The promise of little bureaucracy created an enormous flood of documents, structures, adaptations, exceptions, consultancy contracts and an opaque labyrinth. Announced price induced innovations by the ETS are debunked by several electricity corporates ordering coal-fired power stations in the year 2008. Discursive power keeps up the ETS façade.

Section 8.5 clarifies why the electricity generation corporates wanted separate treatment in the ETS after the year 2012. Fast growing grassroots renewable electricity generators became a major challenge for their business. Their transition to renewable electricity was indispensable. They wanted reliable sources to finance stranded assets and investments in large-scale generation such as offshore wind parks. Their electricity customers had to pay a carbon surcharge on the bought electricity. A money circulation mechanism was created, starting with purchases of permits at exchanges where permit prices are shaped by speculators.

Section 8.6 focuses on the permit prices posted by the exchange platforms. It is argued that the posted prices are fringe prices as explained in chapter 7 [section 7.3]. When there is continuous excess supply beyond the demand of a thing, the thing is characterised as refuse or waste, and prices become negative, meaning: the supplier of the thing has to pay to get rid of the excess. For the electricity corporates, symbolic fringe prices are the wished-for references, easy to manipulate via speculation and marks for legitimating the inclusion of carbon surcharges on their invoices.

Section 8.7 informs about the EU ETS2 proposed in the Fit-for-55 package of the EU's Green Deal. ETS2 is created for the oil and gas industry. For consumed fuels in buildings and transport vehicles, the users must pay extra to fuel suppliers for emissions permits. In reality this is imposing indirect taxes on the constituency. The Green Deal is Eurocentric neoliberalism pure and simple, and does not respect the basic principles of taxation in democratic governance.

Section 8.8 gives a nutshell summary of what the EU ETS really is. This leads to the question: *What to do with the ETS?* My answer is that the elimination of the ETS will be a liberation. Wipe it off the table, and there is room for effective policies. The alternative is not a heavy uniform tax on the industry's GHG emissions. The EU officials have neglected lots of evidence about the failings of emissions trading systems; such an attitude is to characterise the officials as *guilty of negligence.*

8.1 Money drivers in climate policy

Money is a driver of human and corporate action. People spend most of their money efficiently on compelling needs and personal desires, while avoiding expenditures that do not provide tangible benefits or returns. Corporates act similarly. They use professional procedures when spending large amounts of money. For significant long-term investments, they carefully estimate their expected cash-flow returns in advance[9]. They skip expenditures that do not yield a financial profit, such as spending on a better environment. Even knowing the necessity of emission reductions, companies resolutely reject any payment for their GHG emissions, paying taxes, levies or fees, or buying emission permits.

Effectiveness of GHG emission taxes/levies

It is observed that people and companies are profligate with free and cheap things. When those things become expensive, they tend to use them less. They rearrange their activities, or look for better technological solutions. In this way a tax on GHG emissions may function as an appropriate lever to lift people to less carbon-intensive activities. Such lifting happens successfully when good alternatives are available at affordable prices for the public. When at present the conditions are such that decarbonised solutions are particularly arduous and technologically out of reach, imposing (high) taxes may result in (substantial) financial burdens for those required to adapt.

See the problem of automobility. Applying higher taxes on car fuels encounters a lot of resistance. An alternative to excessive car usage is reliable, comfortable, and regular public transport. The latter requires better land use planning and infrastructure, including safe and suitable spaces for pedestrians and cyclists. Such alternatives require considerable time and financial investment. But without such alternatives, levies are rather ineffective in reducing GHG emissions, bring hardship for those who are not well-off, and foment resistance, such as the yellow vests in France.

Electric vehicles are another low-carbon option. In the Global North they were introduced at the luxury end of the market; in China mainly according to cities' needs. The spread of electric vehicles over the full span of the automobile markets is likely. When accessible to all car-driving citizens, gasoline and diesel can be taxed forcefully in order to ban fossil fuels.

Fossil fuel intensive businesses face situations of underdeveloped alternatives at present. High levies on their carbon emissions are cash drains and meet strong resistance. Companies react something like this: *you, government, are taking away our money that we need to invest. So, nothing will come out of your climate policy!* Negotiations with companies are crucial for binding commitments to the development of GHG emission-free products, processes and technologies.

Neoclassical economists fantasise about an artificial market in emissions permits as a successful bend to circumvent corporate aversion to spending money on GHG emissions reductions. On paper, with graphs and mathematical formulas, such an imagined market seems deceptively simple. The imaginary promises an extraordinary score on effectiveness, on efficiency, on equal treatment of participating companies, and on administrative simplicity. These four performance criteria are valid yardsticks, widely accepted in the community of environmental economists.

Academic economists and their trainees in public administrations were enthusiastic about the announced artificial market in emissions permits with the promised performance[10]. Little criticism is to expected from that corner. Mathematical formality is the bedrock of theoretical truth regarding the EU ETS. Criticising mathematical formality per se is pointless.

Feet on the ground about money spending by ETS regulated companies

A preliminary question hangs over the EU climate policy endeavours: Is it justifiable to tax GHG emissions by European industry while similar emissions from industries outside Europe remain untaxed? The question is answered differently. *YES* by those who believe that Europe should play a *leading role* in the world to save the climate. *NO* by those who expect *carbon leaks* from such higher taxes, because most European big industry is integrated within the global industry. Taxing the operations in Europe may result in reduction of the European industrial activity. Europe would then import even more products from outside Europe, creating more emissions globally. More European manufacturing jobs would be lost and global transport gone up. These reasonable arguments are to be considered seriously, when designing climate policies. At the end of this chapter, it will be evident why no leakage by the applied climate policy is observed in Europe.

ETS companies' actual expenditures on acquiring permits and on emissions reductions are minor. Their position is: *No carbon tax at all. Not in vain did big industry in the 1990s block the EU Commission's proposal for a phase-in[11] of a carbon tax! The industry is against taxes, against levies, … against anything that causes expenses without revenues.*

The top goal of industrial companies and corporates is maximizing profits, making above average profits to get the financial means to satisfy their stockholders and realize sub-goals[12]. It is naïve to build climate policies on other premisses. It is best to remind the industry's contention for constant awareness. It is the red thread for exploring the labyrinth of the EU ETS.

In the late 1990s, energy corporates led by BP, Shell and the chemical industry emerge as advocates of a tradable permit system for GHG emissions. The anti-tax coalition of the 1990s puts on a new suit. It is dressing up as a coalition[13] in favour of emissions trading[14]. An indelible imprint on the new suit is: companies participating in the ETS *do not pay* for their GHG emissions. Replacing a trivial but nonetheless transparent and documented tax with an opaque artificial market had its reasons. From the cradle of the EU ETS in the late 1990s until anno 2024, many cardboard screens, pennants, adornments and newspeak[15] have been created. Their removal is due in order to expose the delusion of the EU's emissions trading.

Kyoto COP3 and emissions trading

Public attention to global warming and subsequent climate change did not emerge until the 1980s. In 1988, the UN World Meteorological Organisation and the UN Environment Programme jointly founded the IPCC. The first IPCC report was published in 1990, just in time for the 1992 World Summit in Rio de Janeiro. This helped the summit to deliver a Climate Convention. Its goal was to *prevent dangerous anthropogenic interference with the climate system*. The Convention emphasised that it would be a common task among nations *on the basis of equity and in accordance with their common but differentiated responsibilities and respective capabilities*[16].

To further develop and implement the goals of the framework convention, a series of Conferences of the Parties (COP) were planned. Following COP1 in Berlin in 1995 and COP2 in Geneva in 1996, the anticipation was that COP3 in Kyoto in 1997 would yield workable global policies to combat climate change.

However, instead of fostering solid cooperation, the Kyoto protocol negotiations were marked by a cynical power play, won by the US. During the scheduled closing day of 8 December 1997, Vice President Al Gore[17] arrived with a pivotal neoliberal message: The US would accept the Kyoto Protocol[18] only if it included a *global trade in emissions permits* as the mechanism for regulating the mitigation of greenhouse gas emissions.

Most COP attendees and government officials heard about emissions trading for the first time in their life. Until today, emissions trading is unclear to most politicians, citizens and organisations, as their information is limited to the adulation stories on EU sites, in the traditional media and in the neoclassical economics literature.

At Kyoto 1997, the EU reacted to the US proposal with both bewilderment and sharp criticism. At the time, the EU wanted to accept global emissions trading as a secondary measure, insisting that countries should first implement individual emission reduction measures. Faced with the steadfast position of the US, to secure the US signature on the agreement and to ensure the subsequent COP4 in Buenos Aires in 1998 could take place, COP participants conceded. The EU had to accept emissions trading and swallow its legitimate critical reservations. In fact, the lobbying work of the anti-tax coalition in the 1990s had ensured that the EU Commission was not equipped with climate policy instruments before COP3 in 1997.

8.2 Corporate Masterminding

It is remarkable how the EU Commission completely reversed its position on emissions trading after COP3. It made a U-turn from critically against to ardently in favour of emissions trading. This seems to be a confession of faith: emissions trading heralded as the new saviour of climate policy. Or less pompous: corporate lobbyists could claim the scalp. The EU Commission recognises the dominant power of neoliberalism, accepts raising the façade of the ETS, and prioritises the interests of industry under all circumstances. This is along the red thread guiding the EU's climate policy.

The EU Commission's conversion fits into the plans of BP, Shell and the chemical industry. Their invisible hand is guiding the EU Commission further towards emissions trading. It is a stunning display in political *masterminding* set up by the so-called *politically neutral* corporate industry. It achieves its goals with little effort, stays out of the spotlight and precludes eventual harmful effects. The EU Commission officials, with the cover of professional politicians, set up the ETS construction and are responsible for it. To keep a close eye on official and political affairs, corporate industry offers free feedback and advice through its lobbyists. The participation of stakeholders and their lobbyists in *comitology* meetings is legislated in the 2003 EU Directive on emissions trading. Comitology is rubberstamped lobbyism.

It is attribute #1 of neoliberalism that politicians meekly fulfil the agenda of the corporates. The formerly anti-tax and now pro-emissions trading coalition foresees additional measures to solidify the EU Commission's total policy reversal. One measure is maintaining legitimacy by broadening the coalition and keeping it broad. This is done by controlled openness with freedom of opinion. The involvement of outsiders such as academics or environmental NGOs is encouraged. As long as they *accept the credo of the ETS*, critics are more than welcome in the bureaucratic labyrinth that unfolds. Ceaseless propaganda hides the delusive truth of the system.

Biased examples to make EU ETS acceptable around the year 2000

Examples stretch to imitation. One of the techniques used for persuasion is the *just look at this example* argument. This is justified if things are comparable. It is fallacious when the comparison is inappropriate. For example, the system taken as an example differs in fundamental properties from the proposed ETS scheme. The facts and results of the proposed example are taken out of context, obscuring its mechanisms. Two biased examples were disseminated during the advocacy in favour of GHG emissions trading at the turn of the century. Notwithstanding the falsehood, the advocacy moulded beliefs and opinions.

Biased example No.1. In the years 1998-2001, BP organised in-house GHG emissions reduction across its numerous plants. BP reported 10-20 percent emissions reduction and US$650 million savings. The achievement was applauded: *The oil & gas giant BP recognises climate change as a problem, and shows that emissions trading is a win-win solution. Proof that corporate profit and climate care go together; you know Profit and Planet.*

Sobering up for a moment: how can an internal BP project with no permits, no price and no payments for using the atmosphere as a GHG wastebin be a model for an economy-wide ETS? How can it be called *trading* without a traded product and without real financial transactions?

The corporate internal BP project is actually replicating the normal business of standard companies, known as *picking low-hanging fruit*: reduce energy use if it is profitable for the company. The noteworthy aspect of this initiative is not its innovative character, but rather that such common practice was adopted by BP, a multinational corporate in oil and gas.

In no way could the BP project be considered a suitable example for GHG emissions trading. Yet it was advertised as an example of successful carbon trading, and BP obtained a generous grant from the UK government for experiments with carbon permit trading in the UK.

Biased example No.2. The US system established in the 1990s for regulating sulphur dioxide (SO_2) emissions. While it is reasonable to draw parallels between policy instruments aimed at reducing sulphur dioxide and those targeting GHG emissions, comparisons should be grounded on scientific evidence and factual analysis[19].

The relative success of the US sulphur emissions reduction system depends on some key features. One is its application to a single industrial activity in one established regulatory environment: coal-fired power stations in the US, known in full detail by the EPA (Environmental Protection Agency). In fighting acid rain in the 1980s, the EPA initially imposed strict technological requirements, mandating coal-fired power plants, whether new or old, to install specific sulphur scrubbers. Coal plant owners protested the rigid obligation as being inefficient. The EPA changed course, from technical prescriptions to actual reductions of SO_2 emissions. The flexibility of the new approach allowed coal plants to reduce emissions with simple and inexpensive interventions, mainly substituting low-sulphur coal from the Western US for high-sulphur coal from the Eastern US. This substitution was cheap due to low rail transport tariffs.

Flexibility and low costs to reduce SO_2 emissions are the real success factors of the so-called trading of SO_2 emissions permits. All permits were issued free of charge to the electricity generation companies. Even the few permits that were sold at an experimental temporary auction were reimbursed by the EPA. There was virtually no trading between differently owned companies. The lauded SO_2 emissions reduction system was poor in permit trading.

The physical, economic and political realities of the amalgamated CO_2 emissions from Europe's diverse industrial sectors differ fundamentally from the US SO_2 emissions by coal power plants.

The US experiment shows that the conditions of success are not present in the EU to build the CO_2 emissions trading system proposed on paper. Yet, in the masterminding deceit it was an influential just *look at this US example of SO_2 emissions trading* argument.

8.3 The EU Commission's act of faith in emissions trading ignores reality

The EU Commission's shift towards emissions trading at the turn of the century is regrettable. Designing the ETS took from 1998 to 2005, with 2005-2007 as a test period. Ten years of wasted time, as if GHG concentration in the atmosphere did not go up by 17 ppm [figure 1].

In 2000, the Commission published its *Green Paper on Greenhouse Gas Emissions Trading within the European Union*. It was an act of faith to garner support from national politicians, the public, NGOs and from industry. Yes, also from industry, because the environmental staff of many companies was convinced that emissions trading was not the proper policy instrument.

The act of faith is an ideal CAP & TRADE system: governments decide on the CAP, being the maximum number of available emissions permits for the coming years, and ceiling on the allowed total emissions of all ETS companies together. Every emitting company must surrender one permit per tonne of GHG emissions produced in a year by the 1st of April of the following year. A missing permit is subject to an additional fine of €100. An artificial market in permits should emerge as a trade-off between a fixed limited *supply* of permits (the CAP) and the summed *demand* for permits by all ETS companies. A CAP smaller than total demand creates scarcity in the artificial market, so the permit price exceeds zero. To obtain enough permits to surrender, companies have two options. Either lowering the need for permits by abating their own emissions, or buying permits at auctions or from other companies with a permit surplus. The latter is trading or TRADE, from which the highly vaunted efficiency would follow *automatically*.

The logic of CAP & TRADE in summary: Efficiency is the result of trade. Trade works when the permit price is above zero, due to scarcity of permits[20]. Scarcity exists when the CAP is smaller than the sum total of the actual emissions of all companies combined. The EU ETS has not met any of the fundamental conditions in any year, and is not expected to do so in the future.

Immediate sobering: there is no CAP in the EU ETS

Figure 14 shows how the so-called CAP numbers are significantly above the real emissions. The horizontal axis of figure 14 represents time, marked in years and showing the ETS phases. Phase 1 was a trial period over three years (2005-2007). Phase 2 ran over the 5 years from the beginning of 2008 to the end of 2012. Phase 3 extended from 2013 to 2020, and the ongoing Phase 4 is set to run from 2021 to 2030. Contrary to the Green Paper, the phases are not isolated, but blend into each other and transfer accumulated surplus permits.

The vertical axis shows million tonnes of CO_2-eq emissions. The lower curve shows permits surrendered, representing equally the actual tonnes emitted by all ETS companies. In the years 2005 to 2008, the actual emissions exceeded 2,000 million tonnes of CO_2-eq emissions. They fell to 1,368 million tonnes in the year 2020. The upper curve shows the so-called CAP, every year larger than the actual emissions. As such, the so-called CAP is no incentive to cut GHG emissions.

Nonetheless, the word CAP appeases those claiming *there is no difference to the climate whether you travel Brussels-Lyon by train or by plane, because both trips are covered by the ETS CAP.* Following such blindness, you can emit without concern: the virtual CAP takes over your responsibility.

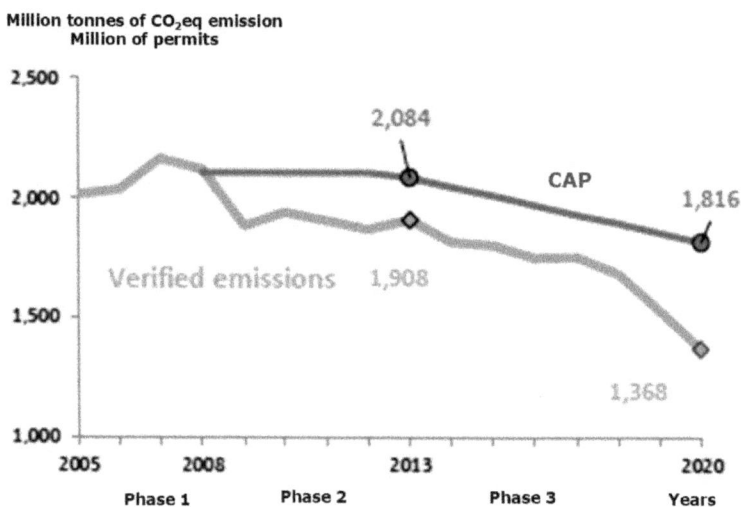

Figure 14: The number of permits in the CAP exceeds verified (=actual) emissions for all years from 2008 to 2020. Source: Marcu et al. (2021), p.21

Figure 14 shows a drop in actual emissions after the year 2008. Not an ETS result, yet due to a sharp economic downturn during the financial crisis. Also, year after year, emission-intensive activities have relocated outside Europe, with China being a favoured destination for low wages and high profits. The ETS did not affect the industrial exodus from Europe. Additionally, autonomous innovations in industrial economies improve equipment and processes, mostly with lower use of fossil fuels.

The decline of verified emissions in 2017-18 is the result of more renewable electricity generation, thanks to technological innovation developed outside the ETS. The innovation happened by means of a financial support mechanism being the opposite of a market-based chimera like green certificate trade. Grassroots communities and people were the active agents, not the corporates [chapter 2].

8.4 Announced first-class performance of the EU ETS is only propaganda

Neoclassical economic publications describe emissions trading as a superior tool but they overlook the practical complexities and conditions of real markets. The EU Commission's anno 2000 *Act of Faith*[21] demonstrates the neoclassical doctrinaire utopia. It seems like a religious conversion, gazing towards heaven, forgetting the realities on Earth. Seven questions about the promised ETS performance are answered.

1. Who can benefit from the EU ETS?

In 2000, the EC stated that the ETS would cover many, including medium-sized, GHG emitting sources. By the ETS launch in 2005, the many were limited to around 11,000 large installations in Europe. Under the cover of the ETS, installations are shielded from non-ETS climate policy measures. The neoclassical doctrine states that additional measures would distort the purity of market dynamics and trade. The doctrinaires did not acknowledge the absence of a real market and trade within the ETS itself. See the case of aviation.

Aviation *within* Europe entered the ETS in 2012, with more involvement since 2022. By virtue of its ETS membership the aviation industry remains shielded from more focused policies, such as taxing kerosene or progressive levies on frequent fliers.

The *enjoyment* to be part of the ETS increases when some corporates, like Shell, *earn profit* from speculation on the Exchanges. *Environmental care is not an item of expense for corporates*, but a source of profit.

2. How do participants obtain permits?

The 2000 Act of Faith argues for auctioning being the proper way to bring permits into the ETS. Member States sell their CAP share of permits. Companies buy the quantity of permits they need through a robust bidding process. Technically, economically, and legally defensible as the most direct, efficient, and fair procedure to feed a CAP & TRADE system.

Purchasing permits implies expenses for ETS companies, which reject spending much money on environmental care. Consequently, the auctioning path was abandoned already before the ETS launch in 2005. Companies received free permits, with electricity companies absorbing about 60 percent of the gifts.

From 2005 until the end of 2012, all permits were practically free of charge[22]. Many more allowances than required for annual compliance led to excessive *surplus of permits*. The financial crisis of 2008 further inflated the stockpile of excess permits, accumulating to a surplus stock of at least 2.2 billion permits by the end of 2012.

According to the Act of Faith, phases should annihilate surplus permits at their closing. Evidently, the big surplus would crash the speculative price on the trading platform to zero, as happened at the end of phase 1. To avoid a second display of a sinking flagship, the EC purged the 2012 excess situation by allowing 1,750 million surplus permits to flow into phase 3 from 2013 to 2020.

The standard practice in environmental regulation is licensing permits to emit substances activity-by-activity, taking into account the unique situation and context of the sector to which the activity belongs. Issuing *surplus licenses* to company activities is common practice for precluding activities that are interrupted by a shortage of permits when approaching the end of the licensing period. Hence, the existence of surplus licences is normal in standard licensing practice.

The yearly assignment of free ETS permits to thousands of activities equals the standard practice, however with important caveats. First, the ETS surplus permits remain the property of the polluters, versus in standard practice the permits dissolving at the end of the licensing period. Second, in a true CAP & TRADE system, surplus permits are a *contradiction in terms*[23].

3. Is Efficiency a trump of emissions trading?

The claim that ETS guarantees optimal efficiency follows from economic theory about the ETS being assumed to be a market. The problem of the ETS advocates is to prove ETS is a market, when it is not.

A market is composed of an aggregated demand curve and an aggregated supply curve, whose crossing sets a positive price. No aggregated demand for permits exists because the permits are free gifts. The aggregated supply is represented by the administrative CAP, being beyond the aggregate of required permits. The true price of permits is zero.

Given this situation there is no propensity of emitters to trade permits. The 'trade' is limited to speculative exchanges at the platforms in Leipzig and London. The speculative price is then labelled as *the price of the ETS permits*, as a fig leaf for missing real trade.

In 2000, the EC Act of Faith annexe announced € millions in efficiency gains. Such numbers hang on unrealistic assumptions about propensity to trade by *heterogeneous* activities. No economic sector will transfer millions of euros to another sector to obtain emission permits. As observed in the US SO2 scheme for coal power plants, there was little trading among *homogeneous* activities.

4. How light is the ETS bureaucracy?

Market-based advocacy paints ETS as a market melting red tape in environmental regulation. Public authorities would only have to fix the CAP, and then take a step back. The *market* would take over without bureaucracy. Visibly another grave deceit by the ETS advocates. To launch the ETS, years of preparatory administration were needed. An EU Directive was enacted in 2003[24]. This act was followed by 20 years of complicated adjustments, additions, omissions, exceptions, exemptions, new versions of the Directive, etc.

The ETS is a vast bureaucratic labyrinth[25] where civil servants, academics, NGO staff, legal advisers, and lobbyists[26] in particular, find considerable opportunities to construct idiosyncratic fantasies and to cash high fees. They expand the labyrinth and take care that the deceit remains accepted.

They are not focused on the emissions reduction results of ETS companies. Their main objective is to keep up the façade that the *market is working*, with the speculative prices on the trading platforms as a fig leaf. Their self assessments provide no clarity over what that platform price represents.

Whoever enters the labyrinth is sucked into the ETS community. The newcomer accepts the credo, the elementary theoretical frames, the numerous assumptions, and is then ready to help in maintaining the façade. Being part of the dominant thinking is the simple way to safeguard the short-term self-interest of academics, NGOs, etc. Critically observing, analysing, testing, and forming a truthful picture of the EU ETS are all uphill battles against vested interests.

The public depends on traditional media for information about the ETS. But the media personnel also lack the authorisation, time, enthusiasm, courage and knowledge to assess the ETS. Mostly, they rely on the European Commission or European Environmental Agency data and reports.

5. Is there ETS price-induced innovation[27]?

Technological innovation is key in mitigating GHG emissions

towards zero levels. Policies of specific innovation of diverse renewable energy technologies (PV, wind turbines, etc.) are most effective and efficient in maturing the production, at never-seen low expenses and environmental impact [chapter 2]. Neoclassical economic academics rejected such successful policies. They stated that the ETS would *induce innovation* automatically by means of the settled permit prices delivering the induction forces.

However, no effective innovations are observed in the ETS. The opposite is clearly visible: from 2008 to 2020, European electric power corporates continued *ordering and building coal-fired power plants*. For example, in the Netherlands: ENGIE 800MWe in Rotterdam; RWE 1,560MWe in Eemshaven; EON-UNIPER 1,070MWe in Maasvlakte. The three plants of 3,430MWe started in 2015-16. Coal plants are carbon bombs, not innovations[28] to reduce GHG emissions to zero.

6. Why didn't ETS deliver price-induced innovation?

A quick answer is: *free permits do not provide induction force for innovation*. By virtue of free permits allocated in excess, the Leipzig and London exchange prices are mere speculative phenomena.

This quick answer is correct. It can be completed with the red thread of companies not paying for permits, or for environmental innovations. Companies expect subsidies[29] because spending on environmental care doesn't bring them any financial revenues.

The permit surplus is a permanent and unavoidable tumour of the EU ETS. The tumour demands care but no cure, as it is integral to the functioning of the system as a carbon emission permits licensing tool. Starting from 2012, years of palaver were spent on a mechanism for managing the surplus of hundreds of millions of permits. In 2019, the *Market Stability Reserve* (MSR) was added to the ETS administrative juggernaut. The MSR is a mechanism to oversee and adjust the amounts of surplus permits, focusing on regulating the surplus, not on eliminating it. This is additional proof that the EU ETS does not intend to create a genuine market mechanism, with real bills for corporates.

7. Why continue with this ETS system?

Big industry obviously wants to keep the ETS to legitimise its *business-as-usual approach*, without costs and shielded from other policy initiatives. Similarly, the technocracy that feeds on the ETS does not intend to give up their fantasy garden. Ambiguity and inconsistency are a paradise for lobbyists who preserve the delusive truth. Those who should be looking after the public interest, EU institutions and officials, continue to adhere to the neoliberal belief that the *market on its own* can fix environmental issues. Short-sightedness and fear of losing face are *throwing good money after bad*. ETS stakeholders do not fade away, while taxpayers and energy users carry the burdens of the ETS bureaucracy and commerce [section 8.5].

Some scientists[30] and NGOs[31] recognise the deceptive design of the ETS. However, many NGOs get wrapped up. They enter and get stuck in the ETS labyrinth and offer superficial criticism. This role aligns with the interests of major businesses, because it supports the continuation of the ETS narrative and practices.

8.5 The post-2012 ETS: electricity generation corporates go solo

From 2013 onwards, the ETS is split into two separate sections. Splitting is a schism of the ECs Act of Faith, whose principal selling point was high efficiency thanks to uniform treatment of all emission sources in one market. Since 2013, electricity generators form a separate segment, with separate legal regulations. The other sectors and companies remain under the old regime of free permits.

At the end of the 1990s, the fossil fuel multinationals BP and Shell were leading the setup of the ETS. Later, the electricity companies' influence increased due to their robust lobbying networks within EU Member States and in Brussels. At its inception, the ETS served to shield the *business-as-usual* of all industries from effective climate policy by receiving free permits. Up until 2012, this strategy seemed to align with the interests of all industrial sectors, including those of electricity generation corporates. They were the largest CO_2 emitters with new coal power plants under construction.

The ETS flagship would have floated on if unforeseen pirates hadn't appeared on the horizon, threatening the positions of electricity generation corporates. The pirates are millions of small electricity generators from natural currents, wind and sunlight. Since 2008, the cost of renewable electricity has been falling rapidly. An increasing number of local cooperatives, small businesses, energy communities, local governments, households, and farmers began installing their own solar panels and wind turbines.

In the years 2009-2012, the alarm bells rang at the headquarters of the electricity corporates. Continuing with the *business-as-usual* approach would lead to the demise of the electricity corporates. Facing this pressure, the experienced strategists designed a new strategy: betting fully on renewable electricity, but generated in large-scale installations, like offshore wind farms, PV fields of tens to hundreds of MWe, and the expansion of large-scale energy storage systems. Another strength is their acquired data and tools for managing and controlling electrical systems. A positive outcome of the U-turn in strategy is the reduction in GHG emissions by more renewable sources, evidenced by the downward trend in the emissions curve shown in figure 14.

The main concern of the oligopolies is: who pays for the new strategy? Piles of money are needed for *stranded* investments such as in the coal-fired power plants, still under construction in 2012. Large-scale mega-projects, like offshore wind parks, are also expensive; far more expensive than localised production of renewable electricity. For instance, in 2023, 1 kWh of electricity from offshore wind costs US$-cent 7.5, and from onshore wind US$-cent 3.3[32]. Political cover for the new strategy of the oligopolies is desirable.

In 2012, the ETS electricity generation corporates shifted their focus from business-as-usual to securing funding for transformation while safeguarding their profit-making business model. Procuring money from the constituency works best under the banner of climate policy. Much of the 90 percent common users of electricity wish to contribute to effective climate policy. So how could the corporates smartly organise the fundraising?

Charging free permits on end-users' bills is no sustainable option. This happened during the first years of the ETS, but was revealed[33], causing a great deal of disgust. It is smarter to devise a robust system of cash flows to raise the corporates' accounts. Through the purchase of emissions permits at auctions, the corporates gain legitimacy to levy a carbon surcharge on sold electricity.

During ETS phase 3 from 2013 to 2020, power companies received progressively fewer free permits. Their package of permits to be submitted annually is therefore gradually more composed of saved permits and of permits bought at auctions or from industrial companies with surplus. In the electricity companies' accounts, the item *Expenses for buying ETS permits* is growing. Also growing is the item *Revenues from climate surcharge on electricity sold* charged on the bills of all electricity customers.

Figure 15 shows the mechanism of money circulation put in place within the new separate section of the ETS. At the top right, *ETS electricity generation companies* are mentioned. They are linked to financial speculators through shadow companies active on the platforms[34]. These speculators can manipulate platform prices.

The purchases of permits at auctions by electricity producers mean *Payments* to the auction authorities. These payments are overcompensated by *Surcharges on electricity bills* (upward arrow at the right in figure 15). Surcharges are paid by *ETS industrial companies* and *Non ETS electricity customers* including a group of *Vulnerable customers* (the horizontal arrows at the bottom of figure 15 feeding the upward vertical arrow).

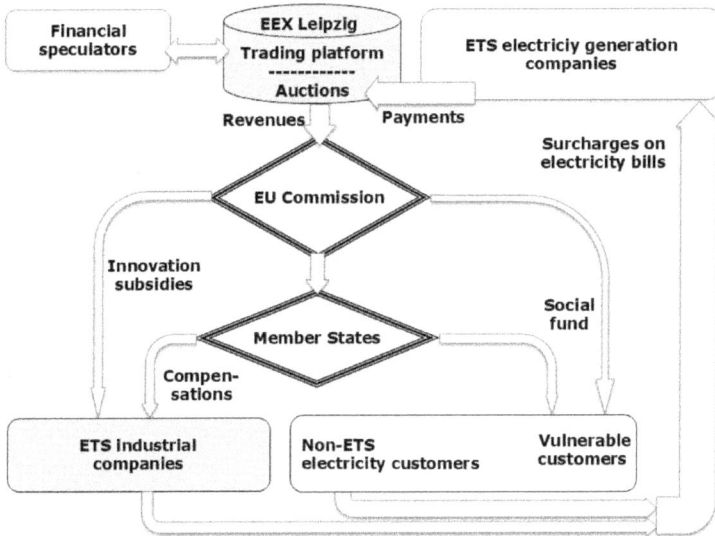

Figure 15: Money circulation pump in the EU ETS electricity generation segment (numbers of euros are not mentioned because they are only partially available and not verifiable)

The middle part of figure 15 describes the role of the *EU Commission and Member States.* They receive *Revenues* from the auctions. The EU Commission transfers a large portion of the Revenues to the Member States, retaining a part for its own operation and Innovation grants to ETS companies. Companies from the other ETS section receiving free permits protest the payment for *indirect emissions* via the surcharges on their electricity bills. They usually receive compensation for the part of their electricity used in the installations covered by the EU ETS.

Indigent, vulnerable customers who already have problems paying their regular electricity bill obtain support from a *social fund*, partly financed by auction revenues. The EC wants to avoid yellow vest protests.

Who finally pays the bills? Ordinary non-ETS electricity customers such as small businesses, public services, educational institutions, hospitals, sports clubs, households, etc.

No data is published about climate surcharge money billed on non-ETS electricity customers' invoices. Some researchers[35] denounce the lack of clear and complete data in the EU ETS. Their criticism does not trigger an investigation into *why* the data remain concealed. The secrecy about the money flows in public policy-making destroys an essential component of democracy.

Non-electricity ETS companies stick to *business-as-usual* as before: free permits, no hassle. At the start of Phase 3, the system is drowning in the transferred surplus from Phase 2. As a result, auctions are pushed forward to the end of Phase 3, and a mechanism to *stabilise the 'market'* is installed in 2019[36]. The EU ETS flagship was again rigged to float through Phase 3 to 2020 and then into Phase 4 from 2021 to 2030. The EU Fit-for-55 package provides for a new ETS2, essentially a money pump as shown in figure 15, created specifically for and by fossil fuel traders [section 8.7].

8.6 Permit prices posted on ETS trading platforms

Daily ETS permit prices are posted on two recognised trading platforms: the EEX in Leipzig and the ICE-ECX in London[37]. Speculative sales and purchases are typical on these platforms. The platforms welcome *financial players* from outside the ETS to keep speculation alive. Average day prices are published, without underlying data on supply, demand, who the parties are, and what financial flows are involved. Respect for the *public good* is fully absent.

Companies may sell or buy ETS permits among themselves without passing a trading platform. Long-term bilateral contracts are common in trading natural gas and oil.

Quoted prices on trading platforms

Every trading day of the year, a positive permit price is posted[38]. Around 280 players speculate on the ETS trading platform in Leipzig.

At permit auctions, less than 20 buyers show up. Speculators hide in ghost companies. As for the operations, it is unclear who did what and why. Insight requires a lot of information about how much is traded by whom, however this is not provided by the trading platforms.

For ETS adepts, posted prices are *proof* that *the ETS market is working*. This is shorthand talk. What happens on the ETS platforms is not healthy market functioning. The existence of large, permanent volumes of surplus permits [figure 14] refers to a particular economic situation. When the supply of *something* permanently and seriously exceeds the demand, that something's price will fall to zero and below. *Something* is then called *waste*. In the artificial ETS system, posted ETS permit prices fluctuated between €80 and €100 during 2023, and between €60 and €80 during 2024. What does the posted price actually represent?

ETS prices are fringe prices

Transactions on the platforms deal mostly with small volumes of permits. Speculators seek short-term profits from the cumulative effect of their trades. They also serve the electricity generators to maintain a targeted price range for the proper functioning of their money circulation pump [figure 15]. One result of their speculative activities is the *posted permit price* on the platform.

Apart from its role for speculation, what other significance does the platform price hold? In Phase 1 and in Phase 2, all permits were given for free[39], resulting in surplus for almost every participant and for the system as a whole. What is the link between permits received for free and a price on a speculative trading platform? Apart from the fact that companies with too many received free permits may speculate more easily, there is no other economically significant link between the two.

In the ETS with all permits given for free, the daily price on the platforms is only applicable to the permits involved in that day's speculative transactions. It has relevance for speculators at the edge (fringe) of the broader emissions and reduction activities. The fringe price is the *symbol* that *the market works*. For big industry, it is the licence to obtain free permits for their assessed emissions, possibly even earning from surpluses.

The fringe effect is observed on any trading platform that does not represent the full quantities of supply and demand. The fringe effect is stronger as the distance increases between the financial escapades at the fringe and the actual economic activities that should have an effect on price formation. When the link between the two breaks, as it did in the financial sector in 2008, the consequences are disastrous. On this subject, legal and financial experts have provided revelatory information[40].

8.7 European Green Deal and emissions trading

EU climate policy continues to rely on delusive emissions trading theory. On 14 July 2021, the EC published a 4,053 page document for the Fit-for-55 package as implementation of the *European Green Deal*. The mish-mash of documents is a thick crop for consultants, lobbyists, civil servants, NGOs, academics, et al. One of the documents is a 14-page readable communication[41], with an overall picture of the planned regulations. Such communication is inherently incomplete and deprived of legal value. Yet, it clarifies the main lines of the policy, some critically reviewed here.

Eurocentrism

Fit-for-55 is entirely focused on Europe, on Fortress Europe. This may be expected from European institutions, but exaggerated eurocentrism lacks the universal vision necessary for proper alignment with a global approach. The package overlooks climate change being a world-wide common responsibility.

The EU Commission approaches the non-European part of the world with an instrument[42] of mandating non-European companies to buy ETS permits on their exports to the EU. Export products in question are aluminium, cement, fertilisers, steel, electricity, and others whose production takes place in the EU covered by the ETS. Once such obligations are implemented, it is said the number of free permits given to companies in the EU ETS could be reduced. There are many gaps to plug before the proposed mechanism would work. It will mostly make consultants happy, as it will provide work for years to come. Lawyers will also be on the hook, due to the inevitable litigations before the World Trade Organisation[43]. And the ETS companies benefit when it will take a long time, as in the meantime their free licences are guaranteed by the 2018 version of the ETS Directive.

This insular approach not only displays a mode of arrogance towards the non-European world but also neglects the broader, equitable distribution of responsibilities in addressing climate issues.

Economic growth

Continued economic growth in the EU is paramount, with naive faith in neoliberal economic recipes. The narrow approach is hidden under a bold verbiage of *international solidarity, transformational change, socially just transition,* etc. Fit-for-55 prints text like *sustainable Europe in a sustainable world, sustainable growth, sustainable competition, sustainable fuels,* etc. Despite the many pennants with sustainable lettering, genuine *Sustainable Development for Our Common Future* is neither a real objective nor a guiding principle in current EU policy. It is only window-dressing.

Fit-for-55 prepares a *low-carbon neoliberalism*. It proposes reducing the use of fossil fuels to achieve carbon neutrality by 2050. This date is so distant that it doesn't matter too much for today's politicians, most of whom in 2050 will have retired, if not passed away.

Life extension of neoliberalism

The EU Commission's Energy and Climate policy directorates bow to the wishes of multinational corporates. Fit-for-55 literally puts this on paper, as evidenced by the following quotes from the EU Commission text (my underlining):

1. *It (the package) ensures that* <u>*industry can lead the transition,*</u> *and gives it the certainty it needs for boosting investment and innovation. It focuses on taxing energy resources in line with our climate goals and environmental objectives. The package translates the polluter pays principle into practice.*

   For the EU Commission, the polluters are only households, schools, hospitals, and other small users of electricity and fuels. This is so in the existing EU ETS, which mainly rates non-ETS electricity users to provide ETS revenues[44] [figure 15].

2. *The European Green Deal is a* <u>*growth strategy,*</u> *and as outlined in the EU's updated Industrial Strategy, the Fit-for-55 proposals offer significant opportunities to develop, deploy and export low-carbon technologies and green jobs. In reviewing the environmental and energy State aid guidelines, the Commission will pay particular attention to ensure that they mirror the scope and ambition of the European Green Deal*[45].

   The European Commission does not question the growth of aviation, nor how its benefits and burdens are spread over frequent fliers and communities affected by airports, noise pollution, and climate change. In 2022, the EU growth strategy has been taken at speed by the US, with realignment of geopolitical relations in which the war in Ukraine plays a key role [chapter 5]. The war has prompted the relocation of industrial activities from the EU to the USA. The show of force and martial activities also mean a setback in the phasing out of fossil fuels. While climate change continues to dominate disaster news, the focus of both media and politics is intensely fixated on war and ongoing threats of more war.

3. The Fit-for-55 package introduces an additional <u>*emissions trading ETS2*</u> for the use of fuels in road transport and buildings. This ETS2 provides *revenues* paid by users of buildings and vehicles, as *tax warehouses and fuel suppliers have only limited possibilities themselves to reduce emissions*[46]. ETS2 states: *25% of expected revenues will* <u>*in principle go to*</u> *a new Social Climate Fund to tackle*

energy poverty and mobility problems for the vulnerable low and middle-income households, transport users, and micro-enterprises.

Fearful of street protests by vulnerable people, the European institutions are unwilling to hold the superrich accountable. *In principle*, 75 percent of the generated revenue goes to fuel sellers and the European Commission. This is effective taxation of citizens without democratic approval. As in the existing ETS system, it is opaque how much which groups in society pay, and who receives what amount for which reasons. The oil and gas industry wants a money pump for itself, just as the electricity companies already have [figure 15].

The stalemate over the Magna Carta began in England in the year 1215, focusing on rights and methods of imposing taxes on the residents of a town or region. This conflict concerns a crucial aspect of the democratic functioning of communities and states. According to the Magna Carta principles, taxes should be levied only by those who have been democratically elected to represent the community. The amounts must be reported and accounted for in publicly accessible, usually parliamentary documents. Negating this basic democratic acquis strengthens anti-democratic forces.

To verify the accuracy of the annual national accounts of nation states, the International Monetary Fund (IMF) monitors which official and name-tagged taxes and subsidies the nation states apply. Evidently, nation states should execute their tax and subsidy authority in a proper and transparent way. The Fit-for-55 package violates the essential democratic principles. Entrusting power over taxes on energy use to energy suppliers is not conducive to the democratic functioning of countries or the EU as a whole. It is inconceivable what Fit-for-55 wishes to enact, and that professional politicians, academics and media meekly go along with it.

The transformation pursued by Fit-for-55 supports neoliberalism as the dominant societal paradigm, excluding genuine Sustainable Development. Fit-for-55 is pursuing a low-carbon neoliberalism by announcing *climate neutrality* by 2050. The EU Commission relies on big industry – which requests massive subsidies – to come up with large-scale renewable energy projects and the announced hydrogen energy economy [chapter 4]. Even atomic power has already been given the *green label* by the European institutions. It is a disastrous path, which the traditional media is happy to carp at. It is high time to find and choose the only path with a realistic probability of salvation.

8.8 What is the EU ETS in reality? What should be done with it?

The preceding analysis reveals the insidious deception behind the advertised CAP & TRADE narrative of the year 2000. Already the 2003 EU Directive on ETS had revealed the deceit. The CAP & TRADE slogan served as a façade to disguise the arrangements serving big industry.

In a nutshell...

- The ETS is not a true CAP & TRADE system. There is no CAP and there is no TRADE. There is only daily speculation on the ETS permit trading platforms.
- The ETS has not delivered an iota of innovation for carbon emissions reduction.
- The ETS is controlled by big business, and ensures that companies do NOT pay for the emissions they cause, nor for measures for emissions reduction.
- The ETS is only about money, mocking climate policy. The EU Commission and ETS companies keep the money flows opaque and secret. The outside world has to be satisfied with a few numbers about auction *revenues* and their public spending.
- The permit price quoted daily on the EEX trading platform is a speculative fringe price. Proponents of the ETS use that price as proof that the *market works*. In reality, it is a symbol and fetish that misleads and silences discussion.
- The ETS was created to ensure *business-as-usual* for large companies. Anno 2024, this is still the case for all participating companies, except electricity generation companies. After 2012,

these companies use a *money circulation pump* [figure 15] to get their stranded assets and new strategy paid for by non-ETS electricity users.

• The ETS *business-as-usual* system grants free permits to GHG emitting companies. This is common environmental policy practice, heavily criticised by the first emissions trading advocates[47]. In systems of permit licensing, assigning surplus permits is standard practice. Normally, surplus permits expire at the end of the regulatory time spans, mostly one year. Not so in the ETS: the permits become the companies' private property. ETS is *environmentalism* that cost companies nothing, but may even be a source of profit.

• The ETS is a bureaucratic machinery. This is standard for administrations granting permits, as a lot of knowledge and information per company is required. With the ETS, the machinery is squared by the accompanying chimera to hide free permits behind a CAP & TRADE façade, and still allow money to flow to participating companies. It is an opaque labyrinth for citizens.

The EU Commission and business sectors are too late in understanding the very danger of climate collapse, and consequently that GHG-free technology is inevitable. A switch from business-as-usual to *money circulation pump* for the fossil fuel industry is in the pipeline of the Fit-for-55 package. It is an anti-democratic approach because it puts the decisions regarding surcharges and cash flow management into the hands of private companies. The pseudonyms used of scheme, system, and mechanism cannot disguise the true nature of the ETS as being a financial tax on non-ETS energy users. A heavy bureaucratic ETS bestowing swindle profits on polluting companies is incredibly harmful.

Also very important: there is no trace of any vision and plan within the EU Commission to quickly discontinue the ETS instrument. This is what the evident aspiration should be, because scrapping means achievement of the real goal of climate policy: deep and full emissions reductions. On the contrary, maintaining the ETS as a tool has become the goal of the bureaucracy in Brussels and in member states, with tens of thousands of consultants, lobbyists, advisers and civil servants in its wake.

What to do with the ETS?

The people, and the youth in particular, have been deceived for twenty-seven years. Some with an active interest in climate policy did engage with the ETS behemoth. They faced a wall of ETS supporters. Critical NGOs and individuals revealed the fraud of emissions trading.

However, BP, Shell, other corporates and the EU Commission deliberately constructed and deployed a flawed system. The masterminding of such an extended policy machinery, keeping up its façade, is a blunt success of the corporate industry's pecuniary interests.

Twenty-seven precious years of time have been lost for reducing GHG emissions in industrial processes. The moral responsibility for this loss is heavy for any individual who is to blame. *That is not us. It is them*, the CEOs in their private jets moving swiftly around the globe to hasten the destruction of the planet. *It is they* who helped build and maintain the ETS behemoth of deception. The EU's climate policy is an emperor without clothes, but for twenty-seven years the court of lobbyists and officials have concealed the nakedness.

What is done is done. You cannot change the past. A person can only learn from it. Take the hint *Every disadvantage has its advantage*[48]. When your sour feeling about the cheating is digested, can you see some *advantage*? Urgently needed is a full understanding of why the so-called superior EU climate policy did not achieve significant results in reducing GHG emissions. This gives strength and encouragement to apply other, really effective climate policies [figure 10].

The elimination of the ETS will be a liberation. If the ETS were really the best policy to tackle the climate issue, then humanity would be stuck with an unsolvable problem. Take the ETS and ETS2 Fit-for-55 package off the table, and there is room for effective policies.

How will it proceed if the citizen remains belittled?

As long as politicians and people adhere to neoliberalism, big business will remain the *master-minder*. Then the ETS will continue to exist as long as the corporates benefit from it. They fold the complicated, opaque system according to their interests. As irreversible climate change increasingly threatens the survival of human life on Earth, complacency and further wasting of time are intolerable.

The alternative is NOT to apply a heavy tax on industry's GHG emissions. A tax on emissions is only effective if carbon-free solutions are available. Then a well-targeted tax or other financial instrument can boost indecisive companies, or penalise polluters who refuse the available alternatives. The solution is the development and deployment of carbon-free technologies and a ban on carbon-emitting technologies.

Lessons learned?

In the period 1998-2002, the EU Commission, then fabricating the ETS, conflicted with Member States leading in renewable energy technology. The Commission's favourite was a *tradable green certificate* market. Germany and other Member States worked with diversified support for the various technologies.

The Renewable Energy Directive included an obligation to evaluate the two applied systems by the year 2005 at the latest. The evaluation studies were carried out at the initiative and expense of the EU administration. Scientific reports confirmed the success of the *German approach* to achieve swift and cost-effective results. Moreover, the evidence of the failure of an artificial certificate trading system was presented with clear facts and numbers. It was a suitable testing case for the *artificial market* as a new policy instrument.

One could have learned from the disastrous experiences in green certificates, *before the launch of the EU ETS*. The market-worshipping EU Commission turned out to be blind and deaf. They knew but did not want to know. In legal terms, this attitude is called *guilty of negligence*.

A reminder

- The EU ETS was set up by corporates with BP and Shell in the vanguard, for *business-as-usual* with no payment for GHG emissions. Since its launch in 2005, EU ETS is a provider of free permits.
- The ETS is no CAP & TRADE: there is no CAP, and there is no TRADE. The ETS did not bring innovations for cutting GHG emissions. It is a waste of precious time, blocking good policy-making directed by innovation.
- Daily trades on the EEX trading platform provide posted prices based on speculation with small amounts of emissions permits. This is not proof that *the market is working*.
- Since 2013, a money circulation pump surcharging non-ETS electricity customers is the core component of the separate ETS construct for electricity generators.
- The ETS imposes *climate taxes* on non-ETS electricity customers, without political mandate and transparent information about the money flows. This violates foundational principles of democracy wherein citizens' constituencies approve tax raising.

Part III
Making the
Common Future

Part II provides analysis of the current state of climate and energy policy, revealing that the policies in place are veiled by verbose documents. Both global and European energy and climate policies maintained and reinforced vested interests and practices rather than constructing the necessary disruptive transformations. Evidently, shortage in mitigation efforts results in poor outcomes for globally reducing greenhouse gas emissions. However, drastic and urgent actions are needed to preserve a mild climate and functioning ecosystems.

Today, a majority of people around the globe are convinced of the severity and urgency of the environmental and social challenges. People from every corner of the planet, spanning all beliefs and age groups, are deeply concerned and committed to shaping a sustainable future. The world is buzzing with many ideas and proposals on problems such as inequality, growth, moderating consumption, changing energy use, and so on. While many authors explicitly address the "What?" and "Why?" of these challenges, the "How?" and "Who?" mostly remain blurred in *"we should"* phrasing and discourse. Skipping "we" phrasing is needed to bring How and Who to the foreground.

How will the world change? What is your place, your duty? Eternal questions, today confronting even those dazed by an imperial mode of living. Since the first human communities on Earth, stories and myths[1] have been proclaimed to give meaning and structure to communal existence, keeping the conflicts between people manageable. The future is a twilight zone filled with a mixture of probable, detestable and desirable images. An artist's quote to consider[2]: *"To live is living with narratives. Without narratives, we do not exist. Neither as individuals nor as a group. Once upon a time, narratives provided coherence and meaning. They connected the past to the future, assigning meaning and direction to the present. They held a community together. They told of its origins and its development. Each individual got a place and each event a meaning. In the confusion of a transition time, we can only tell narratives of conflict and collapse. The new world is only detectable in the debris of the old."*

Science searches for probable paths. It cannot offer certainty because the future is by definition uncertain. Dealing with uncertainty is rational processing of natural laws, human characteristics, sociological laws, facts, and possible events.

Part III has two chapters, briefly presented here.

Chapter 9: Transformation of energy systems and human societies

Era3 Sustainable Development (SD) built on small-scale renewable electricity generation is the substitute for Era2 neoliberalism based on fossil fuels. The full SD substance shows that the 3Ps mantra *Planet, People, Profit paralyses action by omitting the key P-dimension of Politics-Public Policy.* Energy transformation means: fossil fuels rest in the ground; end all atomic power; electricity as provider of commercial energy; all electricity is renewable. 100% renewable energy systems are *possible, desirable,* and *necessary. Bottom-up small-scale* electricity generation will stop carbon emissions at the global scale, and improve the life conditions for the majority of the population. Large-scale renewable electricity is more expensive, disturbing the grassroots projects.

Related to the transformations emerge topics such as energy conservation, sufficiency, and *natural degrowth* by ending fossil fuels and thermal power generation with its enormous fuel cycle source and sink flabs. Good provision of electricity needs clear definitions of *security*, *reliability*, and *priority*. The chapter concludes with three prospects: era3 energy must not meet the bad habits of neoliberalism devouring fossil fuels; capacity redundancy is a keystone of renewable electricity; the future new electricity reality requires a new electricity economics theory.

Chapter 10: The human and societal character of transformation

Human and social sciences are essential in understanding and promoting transformations. A few highlights from philosophy, psychology, and political sciences are presented. Philosophers, from Aristotle to Latour, address the human condition. Mimesis and myths have been inherent to human societies since their nascency. Savoir is suggested to complement the human passions Avoir, Pouvoir, Valoir. Psychologist Maslow's *human needs* pyramid ranges from physiological needs to personal self-actualisation as a goal. Social psychologist Fromm combines personal and societal characters. Personal disposition balances *having* versus *being*. The social structure, its values and norms, influence the balances of individuals. The realisation of Fromm's New Society features depends on illusory actions by benevolent people in power.

Political philosopher Wolin reveals US hegemonic politics, perverting democracy and evolving to totalitarianism. His advice about turning the tide is prudent and wise, yet pessimistic.

Power for controlling people for good or for evil follows four stages: inform/convince; entice/bribe; oblige/coerce; remove/eliminate. Contravening power requires particular implementation of the stages.

In public economics, self-interest is a positive attitude, different from perverse selfishness and greed. Self- and common balanced interests promulgate societies. Ostrom's approach of self-governance is applicable at local and global scale. Moral philosophers on the ethics of climate change add ethical content and context to climate policies.

Part III has no chapter with conclusions and recommendations. The draft versions of chapter 11 about strategic management of the climate crisis and related problems did not comprise the out-of-the-box visions, viewpoints, vanguards, ... essential elements of transformation. Leaving the drafts aside, an essay about transformative conditions and actions is written to conclude the book.

Chapter 9
Transformation of energy systems and human societies

Transformation implies disruptive changes in essential parts of systems. Not minor adjustments or slight modifications, but 180-degree changes in direction and substance. Most publications on climate, transition and societal transformation mention *energy* as one factor among many. The attention to energy ranges from superficial to extensive.

Factually, almost all GHG emissions are related to the use of fossil fuels. Hence, drastic and urgent cutting of their use is evident. However, the cutting does not happen, as shown in the introduction [figure 1]. Politicians, officials, academics, media and many activists fall short in properly placing the energy issues at the centre of climate policy-making. The extensive and relentless lobbyism by fossil fuel corporates and petrostates is certainly an important factor of the political immobilism.

This chapter clarifies energy's role as a feeding substrate for the type of human societies built upon it. On the one hand, energy enables human activities. On the other hand, the political economy in human societies decides who controls the energy systems.

Control over energy and associated technology exerts penetrating influence on how particular societies function. Substituting equitable and ethical politics for destructive neoliberalism cannot succeed without deploying the proper energy systems. Energy and technology merit the spearhead role in climate policy, for their strong impetus for societal transformation. A total and immediate ban on fossil fuels is the emergency brake to avoid climate calamities. This ban will unravel the neoliberal regimes. A spearhead does not exclude, nor minimise, the significance of other factors like Actors, Ideas, Interests, Institutions, and Infrastructures [figure 2].

Chapter 9 has six sections:

Section 9.1 presents the relation energy-society as intense interactions. As a replacement for Era2 neoliberalism based on fossil fuels, Era3 Sustainable Development (SD) relies on small-scale renewable electricity generation, flanked by energy conservation and efficiency. Specifying the substance of SD unveils the flawed and misleading 3Ps mantra *Planet, People, Profit*. The mantra paralyses thorough action because it omits the key P-dimension of *Politics-Public Policy*, hinting at other P-factors like *Peace* and *Participation*.

Section 9.2 is a summary of the energy transformation agenda, advanced by several energy experts. The four main components are: letting fossil fuels rest in the ground; ending atomic power immediately; electricity provides practically all commercial energy in society; all electricity comes from renewable energy sources, especially sunlight and wind.

Section 9.3 discusses two themes under the title *Sufficiency*. One is conservation of commercial energy, in particular of fossil fuels and of electricity from centralised fossil or atomic power plants. The other is about growth versus degrowth.

Section 9.4 reveals that 100% renewable energy systems are *possible, desirable*, and *necessary*, also argued with the information of chapter 2. Opting for *bottom-up small-scale* electricity generation rather than forced *top-down large-scale* can stop carbon emissions at the global scale, and improve the life conditions for the majority of the population. The section ends with the conditions of clear choices and of urgent action.

Section 9.5 provides answers to some practical questions related to overall bottom-up small-scale renewable electricity generation. There are differences between *security, reliability*, and *priority* in the provision of electricity. The layered character of required reliability, and the possibility to adapt the service to the diversified layers, explain how reliability can be guaranteed in various ways.

Section 9.6 offers three prospects on renewable electricity in the coming years. First, era3 energy must not intend to continue the bad habits of neoliberalism dependent on fossil fuels. Second, a major problem ahead is the high redundancy of PV capacity installed causing grid congestion. Addressing congestion issues requires new regulations. Third, a new electricity economics theory is due because free power supplies in the future are fully dependent on nature's generosity.

9.1 Renewable energy as a precursory condition of societal transformation

Building on the information of chapter 2, figure 16 shows the coherence of transformations in energy systems and in societies from Neoliberalism in Era2 to Sustainable Development in Era3 [figure 5].

Energy systems under the horizontal line are substrates for human activities above the line. Energy facilitates civil activities, economic, social, cultural, ...; it also enables war, colonisation, oppression. All activities, beneficial or evil, require energy. Energy technology evolves continuously through intensive interactions with society. Developments driven consciously are paired with unforeseen changes and circumstances. New energy availability anticipates changes in society.

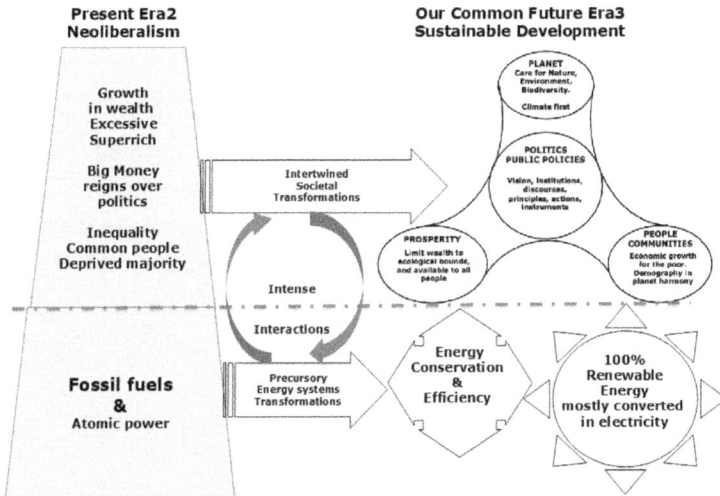

Figure 16: Transformations in energy systems and societal structures for deploying Sustainable Development on 100% Renewable Energy

Neoliberalism against Sustainable Development

Neoliberalism is the final phase of Era2, because it sees no alternative for itself[3] [chapter 6]. Its mania for growth requires ever-increasing use of fossil fuels, which still account for about 80% of commercially traded energy. In 2023 atomic electricity covered 9.4% of global power generation, or about 2% of global energy supply[4]. Petroleum in particular enables reckless growth, immoderate consumption and megalomaniacal projects because it can deliver *massive quantities of concentrated energy on command.* It fits seamlessly with the desires of the superrich and of hegemonic countries, maintaining giant military forces and military bases beyond their own borders.

Without ending neoliberal power in society, the use of fossil fuels will not stop. Without ending the use of fossil fuels, irreversible climate change will not stop. Without mild climate conditions, humanity will wither and neoliberalism will anyhow stop too.

The rational choice is to quit era2 and urgently transit to the necessary, possible and desirable future of era3. The societal model of era3 is Sustainable Development. Its energy and technology substrate consists of energy conservation and efficiency, and renewables, mainly renewable electricity.

Sustainable Development for Our Common Future

Sustainable Development (SD) is a programme of radical socio-economic change, proposed in 1987 by the World Commission on Environment and Development[5]. The report addressed environmental degradation and unequal development. These unresolved challenges of post-World War 2 liberalism are today much heftier after four decades of neoliberalism, which deliberately subverted the essence of SD [chapter 6, section 6.1].

While some details of the 1987 WCED-report are dated, its essence remains relevant and imperative. The SD mission statement is: *Humanity has the ability to make development sustainable – to ensure that it meets the needs of the present generations without compromising the ability of future generations to meet their own needs*[6]. This statement begins by expressing humanity's responsibility in making SD, a part seldomly cited. Only the second part is widely cited as an SD *definition* without attention to substance. The mission refers to a goal setting, not elaborating on substance. It is the substance that informs about the task of making development sustainable.

Therefore, three substance themes are recalled with quotes from the WCED-report:

1. Growth control[7]: *Demographic developments in harmony with the changing productive potential of the ecosystem. Consumption standards that are within the bounds of the ecological possible and to which all can reasonably aspire.*

2. Redistribution[8]: *Overriding priority to the essential needs of the world's poor. Many problems arise from inequalities in access to resources. Economic and social justice within and amongst nations. Economic growth for the alleviation of poverty.*

3. Processes of change in Political, Economic, Social, Ecological systems[9]: *Exploitation of resources. Direction of investments. Orientation of technological development. Institutional change: the real world of interlocked economic and ecological systems will not change, the policies and institutions concerned must.*

These foundational ideas have not been surpassed by better alternatives[10]. Neoliberal societies lack consensus on content and application of SD in practice. This is due to opposing worldviews and conflicting interests. While neoliberal documents are stuffed with sustainable and sustainability labels[11], neoliberalism *is by its very nature opposed to any notion of sustainability*[12].

The *Planet-People-Profit* or *3Ps mantra* is a pernicious distortion of SD. The 3Ps mantra cancels[13] the all-important *P of Politics, Public Interest and Policy*, while this is the most substantial aspect of SD. Like blades of a windmill without a rotor, 3Ps speak lacks the active core for societal dynamics[14]. It showcases the impact of neoliberal discourse.

The 3Ps mantra is utilised by corporates, lobbyists, ill-informed students, NGOs, and others. It is a handy bottom line in corporate reporting for obtaining a *socially responsible corporation* label, without jeopardising excessive profit-making.

EU energy and climate policy skips SD as a guiding principle and frame to curb neoliberal growth, to respect natural boundaries, to address the diverse needs of its many people and reduce inequality. Political action and institutions must undergo urgent changes to deploy SD. The minds and hands of today's politicians seem unprepared for this task.

Sustainability assessment of investments, events, activities, technologies, etc. is an indispensable tool for supporting decision-making. The criteria adopted for structuring the assessment should reflect at least the 4Ps and the full substance of SD.

The only appropriate energy substrate for sustainable development consists of renewable energy, energy conservation and efficiency. Conservation and efficiency were crucial in overcoming the energy crisis of the 1970s until the mid 1980s. Then the attention of energy users, companies and public authorities faded due to the neoliberal breakthrough 1. A few buds survived in initiatives by NGOs, local governments, public enterprises, and knowledge centres. Since 2018, renewable electricity has been fully ready for global deployment [chapter 2].

9.2 Components in the transformation of energy supply

Energy supply reduced to its techno-economic essence is about technology and money. Then rationality in analysis and findings is appropriate in fulfilling four tasks. Two tasks are nasty, hard nuts to crack in eliminating outdated technologies. Two tasks are rosy with the deployment of promising alternatives.

Nasty task 1: Letting fossil fuels rest in the ground[15]

Fossil fuels are the elephant in the room. Almost everyone is concerned about the escalating threat of climate change, and knows that the use of fossil fuels must stop, immediately. Various action groups, NGOs, and concerned scientists are launching campaigns to push professional politicians to take decisive action, and to discourage financial investors from funding fossil fuel extraction. However, the success of the actions has been disappointingly slow and negligible at the global scale.

On the one hand, small cracks are appearing in the fossil fuel fortresses through combinations of sustained bottom-up actions with some prominent politicians and judges. Notably, the Hambacher Wald actions in 2018 and their subsequent efforts have hindered brown coal mining in North Rhine-Westphalia. Denmark's climate law represents a positive shift, taking deliberate, albeit small steps to curb Danish natural gas extraction. Similarly, Norway would cancel three oil and gas exploration blocks in the Barents Sea[16]. These actions are still baby steps in the right direction.

On the other hand, there is the terrifying power of oil and gas multinationals fuelled by super profits, now linked to the war in Ukraine [chapter 5]. In 2022, the US conquered its pursued energy dominance. The reaction of the EU and practically all countries in Europe is deeply worrying. For example, Germany, once a leader in the Energy Transformation[17], is now obsessed with importing liquid natural gas and shale gas, and has extended the operation of brown-coal power plants. The climb out of the fossil fuel abyss has been interrupted by a severe downturn.

Keeping fossil fuels in the ground by persuasion, incentives, coercion[18], ... has only moderate success. It is also far too slow and results are uncertain. They are water pistols aimed at a giant fire. More effective actions are needed to make fossil fuels irrelevant.

Nasty task 2: Ending atomic power immediately

See chapter 3 on atomic energy, and its conclusion [section 3.7]. Contrary to super profits in fossil fuel sectors, atomic power generation is a money crunching activity. Neither private investors, nor informed re-insurance companies are willing to take on the risks of atomic projects. Without big subsidies by big states, atomic energy would soon wither. Without atomic weapons, the interest in atomic technology would be reduced to scientific, medical and industrial applications.

Rosy tasks

Promising solutions in energy are like roses, beautiful, and endowed with pleasant fragrances. However, the thorns of roses advise caution. Electricity is the rose in the future energy supply. Electricity itself does not cause emissions. Electricity is a wonderful phenomenon with many benefits if generation and use are done in a safe and clean way.

Energy transformation follows two main axes. One, electricity as the practically only commercial[19] energy carrier for human activities. Two, extracting practically all electricity from natural flows, mainly sunlight, wind, water and geothermal.

Electricity serves practically all commercial energy needs in society

Everything on electricity for everyone was the slogan painted in large script on the service vehicles of the Belgian electricity company EBES in the 1970s[20]. At that time the company believed in the promises of atomic power to provide massive amounts of safe and cheap electricity. Times and reality have changed. Half a century later the adapted call is *everything on renewable electricity for everyone, and predominantly harvested locally in communities.*

Electric current is generated by people from source energy flows. The current is short-lived: Once generated, it instantly flows to places to provide final, usable energy such as light, drive power, heat. The phenomenon[21] electricity is created and dissipated in fractions of seconds. If not immediately consumed at the place of production, it must pass through the electric grid to other useful applications, before it ends up in the ground.

Access to interconnected grids is subject to a myriad rules. Technical rules ensure synchronous functioning of all producers by respecting frequency standards and place-dependent voltage levels.

Administrative rules regulate information exchange, important for clarity about the financial terms for compensating the power delivered by producers. The set rules can either complicate or facilitate access to the grid and proper interaction, depending on who sets the rules and enforces them[22]. Therefore, creating fair rules that are focused on public interest goals is a critical political and regulatory task, conceptually and practically.

After World War 2, electricity production has seen rapid expansion. Large electricity companies operating as legal or de facto monopolies managed generation, transmission, and distribution. Public control over their operations and selling prices was mostly inadequate in many countries[23].

In the 1990s, the EU decided to establish a single market for electricity. This changed the playing field, with more opportunities for independent producers, including producers of renewable power. However, the EU plans only partially succeeded, also due to opposition by power corporates and by some member states. In 2024, the dominance of monopoly-oligopoly companies is still omnipresent. In France and in its electric vassal state Belgium, French state-owned EDF and semi-state-owned ENGIE wield decisive influence. In Europe, the power corporates are fellow competitors. EURELECTRIC is their European federation, influential in the Brussels lobbying bubble, with the Magritte group as an additional lobbying vehicle for the 2014 a coup [chapter 2; section 2.7].

Thermal power generation, whether using fossil fuels or uranium, is technically, environmentally and financially outdated. Thermal power has long been unsound, due to the huge unpaid costs [chapter 6, figure 11]. Moreover, since 2018, thermal power can no longer compete with electricity generated from sunlight, wind, and water, in terms of naked expenditures. The enormous source and sink flabs of the intricate fossil and atom fuel cycles with additional cool water cycles require huge economic resources. Moreover, they entail the awkward risks of irreversible climate change, long-living atomic waste, and destructive accidents.

Ending inefficient thermal power generation guarantees significant cost savings and reductions in environmental damage and risks. Their scrapping is a real *natural degrowth* measure. Ending fossil-fired thermal power generation cuts at least 18 billion tons of CO_2 emissions[24]. Ending atom power generation brings very high savings in economic resources, while atomic risks will be phased out and the burdens on future generations of eternal atomic waste will no longer grow.

All electricity from renewable energy sources, especially sunlight and wind

In 2014, energy corporates organised a coup against the flourishing small-scale renewable energy projects in several European countries [section 2.7]. To continue their business model, including selling electricity to captive customers at high profit margins, they claim priority for their large-scale generation assets, overriding small-scale activity by Independent Generators of Own Power. In 2015, the negative impact by the coup was visible in the broken growth of the small-scale grassroots renewable electricity projects in Germany.

Forward-looking policies in Germany and Denmark had developed photovoltaics, wind turbines and other technologies for harvesting renewable energy [chapter 2]. The success of this bottom-up approach was due to several factors: creativity, perseverance, and advocacy of grassroots NGOs; support by some resilient politicians at various policy levels; convinced scientists and practicians; the confluence with society-wide innovations like electronics, new materials, ICT, nanotechnology, and biotechnology. Besides, the failures of atomic power and the growing threats of climate change reveal the need for renewable energy. The fortunate situation is that since 2018 small-scale electricity production is the best choice for people on crucial criteria like finance, climate and environment, security, and safety. It leads to more peace with nature, social interaction and personal satisfaction. It is by far the most rational choice, personally and societally.

9.3 Sufficiency

Sufficiency indicates a mode of living pursued in order to realise Sustainable Development. It is a lifestyle in between deprivation and excess. When this lifestyle is generalised, the rich accept or are mandated to accept frugality, banning the imperial mode of living[25]. The bridge between sufficiency and addressing inequality is short.

Conservation of commercial energy, mainly fossil fuels, is the road to sufficiency in energy use. Conservation means limitations on energy-intensive activities, via replacement by high-efficiency alternatives or by a complete halt to those activities. Commercial energy use is a measurable and manageable item, and a first candidate to introduce sufficiency in society. A specific case of sufficiency concerns the levels of required reliability in electricity provision. Excessive reliability exigencies, uniform for all end-uses, are customary in power systems of wealthy countries. Accepting dissimilar reliability guarantees depending on end-uses and power deliveries by variable renewable sources is a smart case of attaining sufficiency at least cost.

First questions, then answers

Since the 1970s, Amory Lovins[26] has been a pioneer in renewable energy and efficiency. He experienced that energy corporates never ask *What do people need energy for?* yet always have the ready answer: *More oil, gas, coal, nuclear power plants.* The response to the oil price increases of the 1970s was a rush to build new energy supply infrastructures. Hence, the 1980s witnessed a surplus supply of fossil fuels and electricity, stifling ongoing energy conservation initiatives and further progress in energy efficiency technology[27].

Energy conservation and efficiency

When the range of renewable energy sources provides the necessary utility energy, its two natural allies are energy efficiency and energy conservation. The difference between the two is important.

Energy efficiency does not intervene in people's activities, but reduces the amount of energy required to perform an activity. To this end, technical measures and/or best practices are usually sufficient. Improved technical efficiency sometimes leads to increased activity, as a result of lower expenditures. This is the *rebound effect*. An example is substituting LED lamps for incandescent light. The far lower electricity consumption of LEDs may lead to more LEDs being installed and more hours of use[28].

Energy conservation means intervention in the activities of people, and their associated goods & services. Such intervention is a major societal challenge[29]. The key questions are: Which activities are necessary, desirable, and possible for what purposes? What type and amount of energy is justified for a given activity?

Setting limits to human behaviour and related activities is standard practice in communities. The selection of limits, and the monitoring and enforcement of compliance all depend on the available institutions.

Capitalism, particularly in its extreme neoliberal form, has broken many boundaries, leading to disastrous outcomes. For the parasitic superrich, anything is possible, up to the extremes such as having a private island as a home, the exclusive private hotel yacht, the private jet, and space tourism. In contrast to neoliberalism, Sustainable Development does involve limits: *levels of consumption that respect ecological limits and are applicable to all world citizens with reasonable expectations*[30]. Indeed, establishing limits to prevent destruction of planetary ecosystems and to address human inequality is essential for the survival of humanity.

There is work to be done to curb the idiocy of Branson, Bezos, Musk and the like, and ban space tourism as a crime against humanity and future generations. Such intervention to limit extreme consumption will undoubtedly stir controversy. Yet the scope of energy conservation efforts must be expanded further, particularly targeting air travel[31]. About 11% of the world's population uses air travel. More than half of aviation's GHG emissions are attributable to 1% of the population[32], partly overlapping with the 1% superrich who travel by private jets. There are plenty of arguments in favour of radical reductions in aviation.

Applications of energy conservation cut across neoliberalism on its main features, and include steps towards a more equitable distribution.

Growth versus degrowth

Energy conservation is linked to proposals advocating for *lifestyle change*[33], economy of sufficiency, and *degrowth*[34]. Degrowth is not a new idea. In 1881, John Stuart Mill discussed the concept of a stationary state of the economy. In 1972, *Limits to Growth* boosted environmental consciousness in the post-war world. Since 1972, Herman Daly[35] advocated the steady-state economy with a broad range of arguments, such as population growth control and resource scarcity as requisite themes in the 1960s-70s, distributional justice, and moral growth.

Nowadays, degrowth ideas receive particular attention in Europe. Spokespersons from the Global South treat degrowth with caution because SD includes *economic growth for the elimination of poverty*[36].

In the Global North, scientists and activists concerned about climate change differ in their support of degrowth. Opponents use different social and tactical arguments. Social concerns are that the least affluent will bear the heaviest burden, with low-wage earners particularly vulnerable. Trade unions fear job losses in the industry. Tactical points are that growth is needed to fund the transition, as heavy investment would be needed. How heavy is not explained. The scale of investments depends on the choices made by present and future generations. Degrowth proposals often stiffen politicians' resolve, leading them to shut out any suggestions about change. Industry fears loss of profits.

Degrowth advocates point to the catastrophic environmental and natural impacts of economic growth so far, and question the sincerity of *green growth* proposals. However, practical plans for society-wide degrowth are elusive. General narratives about degrowth, as an end in itself and with high promises about the effects, are not very persuasive.

Most cogent is to treat degrowth *not* as an end in itself. Decrease in material throughput is a natural, positive element of disruptive transformations in energy systems and in societies to stop destroying Earth's ecosystems. This result of the transformation towards sustainable energy systems and societies is called *natural degrowth*[37].

Thoughtfully implementing energy conservation unravels existing regimes. It is a task riddled with pitfalls and much public debate. A major contention is where to start cleaning the societal stairway of uneven consumption. Beginning at the top is the logical way to clean a stairway. Referring to COP27 in Egypt, a comment was: *A conference, 70 participants of which landed in private jets, recommends me to cycle more.* This critique reflects outrage at the hypocrisy of top-down policy-makers.

Beyond mere outrage, other compelling reasons reject neoliberalism and its relentless pursuit of economic growth, including ethical objections, strategic considerations, and practical necessities.

It is possible to consider social and tactical aspects without impeding beneficial degrowth of Western consumption. Addressing the overabundance of stuff and waste disenchanting life of people[38] may start by asking over and over again: *What does one need the energy and matter for?* Is it for basic living needs, or for excessive consumption destroying biodiversity, resources and amenities of nature?

9.4 100% renewable energy systems are possible, desirable, and necessary

100% renewable energy systems will derive all electricity from renewable sources such as sunlight, wind, water, geothermal, and other renewables. The majority of energy needs will be met through local, small-scale production, complemented by limited, large-scale production from more costly sources like nearshore or offshore wind turbines. Integral to a 100% renewable future are robust measures for energy conservation and efficiency, which will serve as solid partners in ensuring a sustainable and reliable energy supply.

Pursuing net-zero emissions by 2050 is ineffective, too little, too late. It includes the biased goal of substituting renewable energy for the present quantities and types of energy in a neoliberal setting and forecasting. It chases delusive truths like atomic power and the hydrogen energy economy. It mainly hinders and blocks the deployment of the sustainable renewable energy systems, crucial for human survival on Earth.

A liveable future requires liquidation of fossil fuels in the hands of big-money promoters of the growth economy. In its place comes sustainable renewable energy from millions of communities. Direct harvesting of electricity from sunlight is the most promising option: possible, desirable, and necessary.

Possible

The technology for harvesting light and wind from the environment for conversion into electricity has developed from the bottom up and on a small scale. This small-scale nature aligns with the diffuse characteristics of light and wind, which do not naturally aggregate into dense flows. Otherwise, water flows naturally concentrate in rivers and lakes, and can be artificially accumulated in reservoirs behind dams. This explains the dual nature of water as a flow and as a stock energy source. Biomass fuel provides stock energy. However, large dams and biofuels generally receive moderate to poor ratings in sustainability assessments. Additionally, their potential annual generation of electricity is limited and more costly than solar and wind electricity. Hence, large hydro dams and biomass cannot meet the global demand for electricity.

Photovoltaic panels and wind turbines are essentially small-scale technologies. Aggregation to large capacities equals collocation of many small-scale units. This is clear in the aggregation of individual PV cells to panels, and panels to a roof, or to a field.

Meanwhile, Dutch innovator Cell Technologies is demonstrating the Blade, a small-scale vertical axis wind turbine for private households, with yearly generation of around 2500kWh in most locations without favourable wind conditions. The scale of the large wind turbines has grown to 10–12MWe turbines. There are also plans to build a giant 15MWe turbine. Wind turbines above 10Mwe are categorised as medium rather than small, and their locations are restricted to offshore or in distant places. There, the shaft height and blades' length of these mastodons seem less disruptive. They are preferred by the giant companies and their supporters. Still peculiar, since large-scale wind turbines at sea generate more expensive electricity than the smaller turbines on land. Below is the data on onshore versus offshore wind, for the year 2024[39].

Source: IRENA[40] (2025): numbers for the year 2024	Onshore wind	Offshore wind
Investment cost in US$2024 per kW	1,041	2,852
Capacity factor[41] in percent	34	42
Cost of power generated in US$-cent/kWh	3.4	7.9

Conclusion: technologically and economically, small-scale from the bottom up wins out against large-scale from the top down.

Desirable

Globally, sustainable development represents the cooperative efforts of all well-intentioned people towards *Our Common Future.* The connection with renewable energy is intrinsic. Small-scale renewable electricity from the bottom up is an important element of community development, which is preferable to superrich corporations that control the energy supply, and pursue even more profits and super profits, even at the cost of sanctions, embargoes, conflicts, and war.

Necessary

Climate change and impending climate calamities are global issues. Energy transformations to prevent and mitigate them are global tasks. Therefore, solutions must be globally applicable in the coming years. The technologies that enable bottom-up, small-scale generation of electricity from natural flows like sunlight, wind, and water, are user-friendly. They do not require a university degree, making them accessible in all places, in all countries. Particularly noteworthy is the role of women, who traditionally collect wood in rural regions of

Africa, Asia and Latin America, and are now effectively managing PV installations in their villages. This grassroots development has begun and can spread at lightning speed. Local cooperatives and local power companies can build and operate wind turbines and water turbines in nearby brooks or rivers. Reliance on donors from the Global North will decrease. China and India, as major producers of PV panels and wind turbines, will take a burgeoning position in the Global South.

When the industrialised countries roll out the small-scale approach from the bottom up, this visionary solution will be techno-economically optimised. This will make renewable electricity cheaper in developing countries and boost it as an important energy substrate on which further development can thrive.

In the Global North too, small-scale renewable energy from the bottom up is the most sensible approach. This includes the implementation of smart local grids for buildings, neighbourhoods, cities, industrial parks and farms, alongside passive and active use of ambient energy in buildings. Encourage the deployment of somatic energy by providing the facilities that allow people to walk, cycle, and use their hands for more gentle gestures than only pressing buttons. Concentration projects such as offshore wind farms can play a complementary role, but should not displace small-scale bottom-up development. However, with the lobbyism of the big energy companies and their coup in 2014, the displacement scenario is in full swing. It is reinforced by the EU support measures for environmental and energy projects adopted by EU commissioner Joaquín Almunia in 2014. The 'Fit-for-55' package is a deleterious policy of a similar kind [chapter 8, section 8.7].

Clear choices needed

Thermal power generation is quickly becoming obsolete, as it is no longer competitive and carries significant risks, burdens and ballast. Maintaining atomic power or adding gas power plants is a sheer waste of money and disrupts a robust renewable electricity policy from the bottom up. But what is best for the community and the future is not what the political agenda and politics of big administrations such as the World Bank and the European Commission advocate, propagate, and impose in regulation.

Urgency is crucial. Therefore, what is due is superfast electrification of virtually all economic activities, as well as superfast expansion of small-scale power generation. They are financially, economically, socially, environmentally, and politically better than using fossil fuels and uranium for longer. Avoid half-hearted approaches, as they are expensive, risky, and unpredictable in terms of impact. Moreover, they hinder the sustainability solutions.

9.5 A bird's eye view on practical issues

The total revolution in energy land, namely: electricity for all commercial energy applications, all electricity from renewable flows of sunlight, wind, hydro and geothermal, and small-scale bottom-up generation in millions to billions of plants, will turn the current energy world upside down, flipping the hourglass[42].

Evidently, the big-money energy interests of the fading regimes will spread doubt by any means they control. Listen to the neo-modernists with their neo-ideas that failed over the previous 75 years. Read and see the media educated on neoliberal thinking and broadcasting, ringing the alarm bell. *This cannot and must not happen, lights will go out on days with too little wind and light. People want energy security. We will still need fossil fuels beyond 2050, and more nuclear power.* Such deceiving stories by Merchants of Doubt confuse susceptible people, facing a novel inexperienced future. Some practical issues deserve consideration.

It is frustrating when the electric current is interrupted during a not-to-be-missed programme on TV. The probability of such outages should be very small. However, zero probability is hard to guarantee even with high redundancy in expensive reserve capacity. For example, a storm triggered by climate change could knock out electrical distribution lines. Such vulnerability is greater in a pyramidal system organised from the top than in small-scale electricity systems, built from the bottom up. The example does not intend to sidestep the issue of days with *low wind and sunlight*, but to broaden the discussion about vulnerabilities in electricity supply. It is necessary to mark the distinction between *security, reliability,* and *priority* in this context.

Security means having enough electricity daily to meet all reasonable needs. If electricity users can demonstrate adaptability, flexibility and sometimes patience, security is fairly easy to ensure. For the rich North, security is taken for granted by almost everyone. For billions of poor in the Global South, security is an important stepping stone to a manageable supply of electricity.

Reliability means that at every moment there is sufficient supply of electricity to meet the immediate demand for all purposes of customers, regardless of their location. Achieving this level of reliability is more demanding and significantly more costly than ensuring basic security of the electricity supply. Electricity travels at the speed of light and cannot be stored as an electric current. *Storing the energy in electricity* requires two operations: first converting electric current into a storable form of energy, for later conversion of the stored energy back into electricity.

For households, a home battery can store a reasonable amount of kWh, making it a viable option for daily use. For larger communities; bigger battery systems are deployable. However, during extended periods of 'low wind and light', current battery technologies[43] fall short of providing an affordable solution for sustained reliability. Then a reliance on supply from other, sometimes distant, regions may be needed to maintain the desired reliability (see below).

Priority in electricity supply may exist for privileged applications of certain users. Priority may depend on the application and/or on the user, as well as on priority management regulations. Many applications in hospitals deserve the highest priority. The operation of traffic lights and safety equipment also stay high in the priority list for obtaining power. When it comes to private use, rich users can buy priority in systems driven solely by money[44]. But other orderings are conceivable, so that the financially vulnerable are not always at the tail of the priority list.

Required reliability is layered: high, medium, low

An eye-opening example in advance. The surgery service in a hospital requires the highest reliability level. That is why hospitals have on-site emergency generators. Right now, these are mostly diesel engines; in the future, these will be hefty batteries. Pumping water to refill a reservoir can be done with electricity at low reliability, as it is not harmful to delay pumping for quite some time when enough water has been previously buffered.

In people's homes with sufficient energy security, there are many applications with electrical appliances, whose power consumption ranges from a few watts to several kW (1000 watt). The desired reliability of delivered electricity is tiered from high, through middle to low depending on the application. In general, high reliability is for light, communication, electronic applications such as TV and audio, food, personal hygiene, and ventilation. Medium reliability suffices for motor drives in fridges, freezers, vacuum cleaners, and air conditioners. Low reliability is acceptable for non-urgent thermal applications such as filling hot water boilers, washing, tumble drying and ironing clothes, washing dishes, non-time dependent cooking or baking. Car batteries can provide can provide flexibility because charging at home can be spread over time.

The high-reliability needs require such things as light, communication, telephone, and need little power, ranging from a few Watts to a few tens of Watts. The medium-important needs require an average power of tens to several hundred Watts. Thermal applications absorb hundreds of Watts to one or more kW. Increasing the efficiency of appliances reduces the required power. For example, one-digit Watt LED lights are now replacing two-digit and three-digit Watt incandescent lights.

Instantaneous control of devices allows the shifting of power demand over time - spanning seconds, minutes, or hours, depending on the application. Dynamic pricing can signal the optimal times for such shifts, benefiting the overall power supply in a specific community and making processes like battery recharging most cost-effective. End-user choices will be automated, and easily programmable to optimise services. When the stratification in desirable reliabilities is properly integrated into the demand management programmes for every electricity customer in the future, the likelihood of disruptive shortages is significantly reduced. Then, home and district batteries will suffice to achieve the desired levels of reliability. A higher reliability level can be obtained by back-up from central storage and grid interconnection. These measures are sufficient to ensure a range of *diverse optimal reliability levels* for all end-uses and end-users.

It is recommended to adapt houses and other buildings to require minimal commercial energy. This can be achieved through *passive gains* of sunlight and heat in winter and coolness in summer. Well-placed insulation and thermal inertia are key, so that the demand for heat on cold days and for cooling on hot days is low[45]. Then heat pumps are sensibly applicable. *Active* electricity generation with solar panels, or better full solar roofs and even walls is now an obvious choice, given the low and falling price of PV cells. Furthermore, solar energy can provide heat for sanitary purposes during summer, spring and autumn.

In electric systems fully powered by renewable flows, sufficient continuity of electricity supply can be ensured. This is achieved through combinations of demand management, exchange of electricity over local to continental grids, and storage of energy recoverable as electricity without greenhouse gas emissions. Storage techniques include chemical energy in batteries, potential energy in water reservoirs, flywheels, pressurised air, and upcoming novel storage technologies. With so many solutions available, it is important to know that renewable energy remains at the forefront of progressive, ongoing innovations[46].

9.6 Prospects on renewable electricity in the coming years

Three prospects are signalled. First, renewable electricity in the future is not intended to continue the bad practices of neoliberalism. Energy demand and supply for Sustainable Development will be structurally different than at present. Second, redundancy in generation capacity and in electricity supply at peak moments will grow, and requires the proper regulatory approach. Third, there is a need for a new electricity economics theory and handbooks.

Renewable electricity is not continuing the bad habits of fossil fuels

The era2 of narrow-minded selfishness of the superrich, and the less rich who mimic them, with *I want it all, here, now*, has passed. It no longer needs to be tolerated. If humanity is to survive to 2050, humans must quickly realise that they are subordinate to nature, whose ecosystems and their functions set limits on what is available, where, and when. Human aspirations and activities must align with the variable generosity of nature. This kind of sufficiency happens when the entire energy supply utilises the variable flows of sunlight, wind, water and geothermal provided by the Earth and Sun for free [chapter 1].

Small-scale bottom-up electricity generation does not serve to perpetuate the unsustainably bloated production-consumption systems and associated warfare, typical of the Global North as of 2025. On the contrary, renewable electricity from the ambient environment is the most crucial factor for the elimination of neoliberal excesses. The bottom-up electricity-centred system aligns with the goals and attributes of Sustainable Development, contrasting sharply with the problematic elements and pillars of neoliberalism. Ending thermal power generation is a significant step in natural degrowth. Energy conservation and energy efficiency will reduce the spillage of commercial energy. Institutes delegated by the numerous neighbourhood communities develop the rules of full-sized decentralised electricity supply systems in era3 civilisation.

Capacity redundancy is a keystone of the renewable electricity supply

Imagine the year 1925: a lecture on the future of the automobile. The speaker concludes his analysis with: *the main problem of the automobile in the future is the excessive number of automobiles on the road, far too many*. Bulldog laughter and boos of disbelief in the hall.

Back to 2025: the excess of cars is a big problem. Human communities are affected by it, and they want to limit the number of cars in their living environment. The source of the problem is redundancy, i.e., an abundance and surplus of available capacity. The observable standstill of most passenger cars during most of the day reveals that capacity factors are low. Measured on the basis of average time on the road, 5-10% is likely an accurate range. Measured based on the use of horsepower that car engines can deliver, it is likely less than 5%. In the Global North, many people consider it *normal* to own cars that they use so little, while spending a considerable portion of their income on car ownership.

PV panels are still falling in price, and the cheapest roofing material in 2025 is a solar roof made of PV panels. This is so in smart new buildings or renovations. If a large proportion of buildings are constructed as solar buildings, tens to hundreds of Gigawatts of electricity generation capacity will become available in large cities and counties. During sunny hours this capacity could provide far more power than all operational applications could absorb. Wind turbines will exhibit similar, less extreme, redundancy.

Consider windy, sunny days, when all hands-on deck are searching for a use for the surplus electricity. Excessive electric power on the grid means overvoltage, a condition much more problematic than undervoltage. Overvoltage causes electricity-using appliances to catch fire. However, no panic needed, because there is a simple solution. Although people cannot control when natural flows are available, they can easily bypass excessive flows. For example, wind turbines can turn their blades out of the wind currents, and PV panels cease delivery to grids where voltage levels approach the upper limit because the inverters between PV panels and the grid will halt PV generation.

Isn't there a problem with redundancy then? Yes, significant problems arise from the question: *who* should partially or fully switch off her/his installation? This is a matter of choice and policy. And, as you guessed: this is where the big conflict arises between *large-scale top-down* supply and *small-scale bottom-up people-owned* installations.

Is politics ready to propose the right vision and regulation on this political priority for the benefit of common people?

The future new electricity reality requires a new electricity economics theory

Teaching *Electricity Economics* in era2 was adapted to its energy realities. In contrast to utopian neoclassical economics, applied electricity economics was firmly linked to the physical-technical facts and laws of electricity generating plants and systems. Thermal power plants, for instance, had different fuel costs, and could operate at full load, part load or spin idle *on command*. Mathematical models proved very useful in seeking the best investment decisions and for the least-cost operation of such optimally composed electricity generation systems.

In era3, electricity generation is fundamentally different because it will be almost entirely based on natural currents. Human beings cannot command natural currents to flow at their will. Bypassing available natural currents is easily done. Light and wind have no fuel costs. On water and geothermal, it is possible to discuss how to set a usage price if alternative uses of the sources are possible. However, for most natural currents this is not a reason to charge a usage cost. The theories and models valid in era2 have become obsolete and collapse like a house of cards. This is evidenced by negative kWh prices when supply exceeds demand, and thus electric current is considered as waste.

A new theory of electricity economics is necessary to underpin the three key decisions. Which production capacities are allowed to supply to the grid in times of redundancy? What is the remuneration in return for delivered electricity to the grid? What price should customers pay for grid electricity? Suggestions[47] for answering the questions have been proposed, yet developing the full new theory is a significant task[48]. The new theory is urgently needed for an effective and fast deployment of future electricity supply systems.

A reminder:

- A total and immediate ban on fossil fuels is the emergency brake to avoid climate calamities. This ban will unravel the neoliberal regimes.
- As a replacement for neoliberalism, Sustainable Development for Our Common Future relies on small-scale electricity generation from sunlight, wind, water and geothermal energy flows, which also promotes energy conservation and enhances energy efficiency.
- The 3Ps mantra 'Planet, People, Profit' is flawed and misleading. It paralyses thorough action because it omits the key P-dimension of Politics, Public Policy.
- Degrowth is not an end in itself, but a natural outcome and result of transformations to new energy systems and related societal revolution.
- Redundancy in electricity generation from free renewable sunlight and wind flows, which humans cannot control but can easily bypass, requires a new theory of electricity economics and novel regulations.

Chapter 10
The human and societal character of transformation

Chapter 10 broadens the scope of the book with social sciences' insights about human and societal characters. The transformation from neoliberalism to Sustainable Development, is a *human-societal work by insurgent women and men*. Actors, agents, decision-makers, inventors, teachers, coordinators, and leaders live in communities. They stand up for a variety of reasons intertwined with and beyond techno-economic interests. The human and social sciences are most essential for understanding and promoting the upcoming life-saving transformations.

As a techno-economic researcher, I visited some territories in the social sciences: philosophy, psychology, political philosophy, political sciences and sociology[1]. Such visits are superficial because a visitor is not a professional. Particular fruits emanating from the work of social disciplinary experts are plucked. Please, remember my limitations when reading this chapter.

The chapter consists of eight sections.

The sections 1 to 4 report about the visit to the social sciences literature. Then follow two sections from my workshop in political economy, one about how societal power is exercised, the other about self-interest. Section 7 is about local and self-governance in communities, and section 8 about climate change ethics.

Section 10.1 recalls contributions of philosophers from Aristotle to Latour. Mimesis and myths have been inherent to human societies since their nascency. The three human passions of Avoir, Pouvoir, Valoir are complemented by Savoir as a fourth. Mark Fisher and Bruno Latour oppose the neoliberal discourse supremacy.

Section 10.2 is a brief presentation of psychologist Maslow's ideas about *human needs*. To his five-level pyramid from physiological needs to personal self-actualisation, Maslow later added cognitive, aesthetic, and transcendence needs. He specifies self-actualisation with 15 characteristics and 7 behaviours, not all attainable by one person, given that perfect human beings do not exist.

Section 10.3 presents multidisciplinary social psychologist Fromm's book *To Have or To Be?* People cultivate a balance as a personal disposition between *having* and *being*. Shifting towards the *being mode* offers a more fulfilling existence. The social structure, its values and norms, influence the balances attained by individuals. Fromm studies the interactions between the human and societal characters. As a democratic socialist, he adheres to a radical humanism, and designs the features of the New Society. However, his proposals cannot work due to their dependency on benevolent actions by those in power.

Section 10.4 presents political philosopher Wolin's book *Managed Democracy and the Spectre of Inverted Totalitarianism*. It is a wealth of factual information and life-long study about the political clockworks of the United States of America, domestic and global: *superpower US, blessed hegemon of the globe*. This allure covers the perversion of democracy and the growth of a totalitarian regime, masterminded by Big Money. Wolin shows how neoliberalism has been able to burgeon since the 1980s. His advice about turning the tide is prudent and wise, however overly pessimistic. The section is completed with brief notes about today's political science views on climate change and policy.

Section 10.5 concerns power: what it is, and how it is used for good or for evil. From experience, four stages are recognised in the use of societal power for controlling people: inform/convince; entice/bribe; oblige/coerce; remove/eliminate. Insurgents for preserving human life on Earth need contravening power, requiring a particular implementation of the four stages.

Section 10.6 discusses public economic views on self-interest, which is different from selfishness and greed. A proper balance between self- and common interests promulgates thriving societies.

Section 10.7 contains a part on local governance, and introduces Nobel prize laurate Elinor Ostrom's theory and practice in self-governance.

Section 10.8 presents the work of moral philosophers on the ethics of climate change. The text is based on a Routledge handbook of applied climate change ethics, and on a document of the World Commission on the Ethics of Scientific Knowledge and Technology.

10.1 Philosophers on human motivations

Philosophical ideas about human motivations on three topics are presented: mimesis and myths, human passions, and neoliberal discourse supremacy in the 21st century.

Mimesis and myths

Humans affect each other when interacting and by living in communities. Imitation is a prominent mechanism of mutual learning. Young people or other newcomers to a community learn its customs, norms, rules, etc. Spontaneously and by education, they adopt most of the institutions via positive imitation.

A negative expression of imitation generates the human desire to obtain what the other human has or owns. Philosophers[2] call this negative imitation and desire *mimesis*, being the fundamental origin of rivalry and fighting among people. In his book *Things Hidden Since the Foundation of the World*, Girard emphasises the inherent anthropological character of mimesis.

Primitive communities subdued the rivalries and related violence with myths telling of the dangers of mimesis. At times of supreme mimesis and bitter rivalry in a community, the bundled violence was diverted on to a scapegoat. S/he was loaded with the evil of the community and sacrificed. This common super-violence deflated the tensions and allowed the community a restart. Later on, sacrificed prophets were often adored as symbols of wisdom and courage. Ancient societies created mythological religions, with significant and enduring impacts on their political, social and economic institutions.

Human passions

Aristotle, Kant, Ricœur, and other philosophers recognise three main passions motivating people. *To have (Avoir)* is possessing property, things, and money. *Wielding power (Pouvoir)* is exercising influence or control over others. And *Valoir is securing respect* for esteem, status and prestige.

According to Kant, human passions are not directed towards objects, but reflect desires related to other people. According to Ricœur, *Valoir* depends on *Pouvoir*, and *Pouvoir* depends on *Avoir*. In this view, the ordering of human communities is ultimately built on economic grounds, on the possibility to satisfy the basic physiological and safety needs. This accords with the significant role and impact of economic drives. Aristotle mockingly observed that around noon, philosophers dwelled in numbers at the doorsteps of the mansions of rich people, as candidates to be invited to the meal.

Savoir as knowledge, diligence, skill and knowing[3] is a fourth passion. *Savoir* is important for all people in their search for personal development and spiritual meaning. It may be expressed visibly by artists and art lovers, writers and readers, craftsmen, and scientists. *Savoir* may eventually mitigate the weight and impact of Avoir. Human history contains periods of cultural excellence in which *Savoir* competed with *Avoir* as an inspirational factor in society. This will probably occur in era3 of human civilisation, when the struggle for the basic means of existence no longer dominates many people's lives. *Savoir* relates to the cognitive, aesthetic and transcendence needs added by Maslow to his five-level pyramid [section 10.2], and is a main strand in Fromm's analysis [section 10.3].

Fisher and Latour: Neoliberal discourse supremacy in the 21st century

In his 2009-book, *Capitalist Realism*, Mark Fisher[4] addresses the widespread sense that not only is capitalism the only viable political and economic system, but also that it is now impossible to imagine a coherent alternative to it. While ideologically excoriating the state, neoliberalism surreptitiously relies on the state, plainly evident during the banking crisis of 2008.

A brutal state of affairs, profoundly inegalitarian, where all existence is evaluated in terms of money, is presented as the ideal. It is like a pervasive atmosphere, acting as a kind of invisible barrier constraining thought and action. Capitalist realism can only be threatened if it is shown to be in some way inconsistent and untenable.

Neoliberalism has sought to eliminate the very category of value in the ethical sense. Everything in society should be run as a business. Emancipatory politics must destroy such appearance of *natural order*, which is inherently dysfunctional. Environmental catastrophe is Real. The cause of eco-catastrophe is an impersonal state structure which, even though it is capable of producing all manner of effects, is precisely not a subject capable of exercising responsibility. The required collective subject does not exist, yet the global crises demand that it be constructed.

In an era popularly described as post-political, class war has continued to be fought, but only by one side: the wealthy. The resurgence of bureaucracy in neoliberalism is more than an atavism or an anomaly. The vices are engendered by the structure: replacing the whole managerial and banking class with a whole new set of (*better*) people would not improve things. The ultimate cause-that-is-not-a-subject: *Capital.*

The goal should not be to take over the state but to subordinate the state to the general will. The proliferation of certain kinds of mental illness and the increasing urgency of dealing with environmental disaster make the case for a new collectively managed austerity. From a situation in which nothing can happen, suddenly anything is possible again.

In 2022 interviews about how to inhabit the Earth, Bruno Latour[5] raises the question: *How is it that an entire civilization, confronted by a threat they were perfectly aware of, did not react?* The problem is that ever since the 1980s, we have been disoriented. Now, Gaia puts us on notice.

The new ecological class needs to say: '*We are more rational than you, the liberal bourgeoisie, because for the whole of the 20th century, you could* *not be bothered understanding that the fundamental situation into which production was inserted was the planet's conditions of habitability, and because you really stuffed those up. You are irrational.'*

Dependence on a territory and on others is the fundamental issue: that what you depend on defines who you are. This relates to the place of living, the community, and the fundamental question of *habitability*. A landscape, a land, a new land, is now opening up at our feet, before our very eyes. Questions are opening up again. Obviously, it's difficult and distressing ... but what a relief!

Latour wants to engage all disciplines in a back to basics, step by step approach without prejudices. His advice is: *'Let's go and see'* as the usual method for dealing with problems.

10.2 Psychologist Maslow's needs analysis[6]

In order to better understand what motivates human beings, Maslow first developed a five-tier hierarchy of human needs, which he later extended. The five-tier hierarchy is depicted as a pyramid: at the bottom *physiological* needs, then *safety and security*, next *belonging and love*, followed by *esteem*, with *self-actualisation* at the top. This arrangement suggests physiological needs as conditions for survival up to the more creative and mental oriented self-actualisation. Different authors mention slightly different needs under the five level-headings, for example:

Physiological: air for breathing, water, food, shelter, clothing, sleep and rest, ... The human body cannot function optimally if physiological needs are not satisfied. Maslow considered physiological needs the most important as all the other needs become secondary until these needs are met. Anno 2025: in the wealthy part of the world, meeting the physiological needs is considered as a right. However, half of the world population is lacking an *ethical existence minimum income*[7], necessary for a decent standard of life.

Safety and security: family, financial security by income and property, public services like medical care and education, protection, law and order, ... Human safety needs are already apparent in childhood.

Adults living in developed nations want safety in emergency situations due to war and disasters. Need for safety is why people hold a savings account, purchase insurance, or tend to prefer accustomed life conditions above change.

Belonging and love: social ability, friendship, trust, intimacy, sense of connection, feeling loved, receiving and giving affection and love, … This need includes both romantic relationships as well as ties to family members, friends and social groups.

Esteem, encompassing self-esteem by means of confidence, dignity, mastery, independence, being a unique individual, and esteem from others by way of reputation, status, prestige, and accomplishment, … For esteem and obtaining acceptance, people want to be engaged in social and community activity via a profession, a hobby, volunteering work, and more.

Self-actualisation: achieving a person's full potential, seeking personal growth, including creative activities. Maslow describes this level as the desire to accomplish everything that one can, and *to become everything one is capable of becoming.* Individuals may select personal capabilities, like becoming an ideal parent, a top athlete, artist, or inventor, … It is believed that few people reach this level, but all people may enjoy moments of peak experiences.

Once the joining of the five needs motivating the actions by people was interpreted as sequential from bottom to top. In later work Maslow stated that the order of the levels is not completely fixed. For some, esteem outweighs love; others may self-actualise despite living in material poverty. Generally, human behaviours are motivated by multiple needs simultaneously, and priorities for needs may also shift due to external factors.

In 1970, Maslow extended the five-stage model by adding cognitive and aesthetic needs, and later transcendence needs.

Cognitive needs: knowledge and understanding, curiosity, exploration, need for meaning and predictability, facilitating personal growth, comprehension, and a deeper understanding of life and its complexities.

Aesthetic needs: appreciation and search for beauty, balance, form, etc. in art, music, nature. Physical beauty may be complemented by emotional and psychological satisfaction derived from experiencing order and elegance. It leads to a deeper sense of satisfaction and harmony in life.

Transcendence needs: pursuing altruism, spiritual connection, helping others achieve their potential, desiring to connect with a higher reality, purpose, or the universe. It may include mystical, natural, aesthetic experiences, the pursuit of science, religious faith, and so on.

Maslow identified *15 characteristics* of self-actualisers, merely achieving their own potential:

Perceive reality efficiently and tolerate uncertainty; Accept themselves and others for what they are; Spontaneous in thought and action; Problem-centred and not self-centred; Unusual sense of humour; Able to look at life objectively; Highly creative; Resistant to enculturation, but not purposely unconventional; Concerned for the welfare of humanity; Capable of deep appreciation of basic life-experience; Establish deep satisfying interpersonal relationships with a few people; Peak experiences; Need for privacy; Democratic attitudes; Strong moral/ethical standards.

There are *7 behaviours* leading to self-actualisation: Experiencing life like a child, with full absorption and concentration; Trying new things instead of sticking to safe paths; Listening to your own feelings in evaluating experiences instead of the voice of tradition, authority or the majority; Avoiding pretence and being honest; Being prepared to be unpopular if your views do not coincide with those of the majority; Taking responsibility and working hard; Trying to identify your defences and having the courage to give them up.

It is not necessary to display all 15 characteristics to become self-actualised, and it is not only self-actualised people that will display particular characteristics. Self-actualisation is not to be equated with perfection. Anyhow, the set of perfect human beings is empty – there are none, concluded Maslow.

10.3 Social psychologist Fromm: *To Have or To Be?*

Erich Fromm was next to social psychologist, also a psychoanalyst, sociologist, philosopher and democratic socialist. Inter alia, Fromm explored the interdependence among the character structure of individuals and socioeconomic structures. He highlights two fundamental modes of human existence: *To Have*, dominating Western industrial societies with its emphasis on possession and material wealth; *To Be*, prioritising genuine experiences, independence, and the active engagement of one's faculties.

Fromm argues that the prevailing *having* orientation, characterised by an insatiable desire for wealth, power, and status, not only shapes individual identities but also perpetuates societal structures that prioritise material gain over genuine human fulfilment. The having mode of existence necessarily produces the *need for power*, to control other living human beings, to break their resistance, to maintain control over private property. Private property desire produces the desire to *use violence* in order to rob others in overt or covert ways. *Language*[8] is an important factor in fortifying the having orientation.

That the having mode and the resulting greed necessarily lead to interpersonal antagonism and strife holds true for nations as it does for individuals. For as long as nations are composed of people whose main motivation is having and greed, they cannot help waging war.

The *being* mode offers a path towards a more fulfilling existence, emphasising the importance of relationships, creativity, and personal growth, with independence, freedom, and the presence of critical reason as prerequisites. The main ethical goals – overcoming greed and hate – cannot be realised without an insight into reality.

The experience of *sharing* makes and keeps the relation between two individuals alive; it is the basis of all great religious, political, and philosophical movements. When the movements ossify, when bureaucracy manages the people by means of suggestions and threats, the sharing stops.

Both to have and to be tendencies are present in individual characters. As such they form a duality, a dipole. *To have* owes its strength to the biological factor of survival. *To be*, share, give, sacrifice, owes its strength to the specific conditions of human existence and the inherent need to overcome personal isolation by oneness with others. From these two contradictory strivings in every human being, it follows that the *social structure*, its values and norms, decides which of the two strivings dominates the other.

The two extreme groups, respectively manifesting deeply ingrained and almost unalterable types of having or of being, form small minorities; in the vast majority *both possibilities are real*, and which of the two becomes dominant and which is repressed depends on *societal factors*[9]. The distribution of the described attribute is quite common in human behaviour. For example, opinions of pro/anti atomic power are similarly distributed, and are affected by advocacy and advertising [chapter 3].

The will to give, to share, to sacrifice

In the dominant discourse, the having mode of existing is said to be rooted in human nature, unchangeably. A similar dogma states that people are basically lazy, passive by nature, and that they do not want to work unless being driven by the incentive of material gain, or hunger, or the fear of punishment. This widely accepted dogma determines the methods of education and of work. Actually, the dogma defends the prevailing social arrangements as *following the needs of human nature*.

In contrast, the truth is that both the having and the being modes of existence are potentialities of human nature, that the biological urge to survival tends to further the having mode, but that selfishness and laziness are not the only propensities inherent in human beings. Human beings have an inherent and deeply rooted desire to be: to express their faculties, to be active, to be related to others, to escape the prison cell of selfishness.

Fromm gives the example of workers' strikes as situations manifesting human strivings for giving and solidarity. Many workers accept severe hardships in order to fight for their own dignity and the satisfaction of experiencing human solidarity. It is as much a *religious* as an economic phenomenon[10]. The same needs have been affirmed and expressed in many communes throughout the centuries, whether religious, socialist, or humanist.

Social character is the blending of the individual psychical sphere and the socioeconomic structure, with the thesis that a new society can be brought about only if a profound change occurs in the human heart – if a new object of devotion takes the place of the present one.

Determining the role of social structure

The socioeconomic structure of a society moulds the social character of its members so that they *wish* to do what they *have* to do. Simultaneously, the social character influences the socioeconomic structure of society, acting either as cement to give further stability to the social structure or, under special circumstances, as dynamite that tends to break the social structure.

The relation between social *character* and social *structure* is never static, since both elements in this relationship are never-ending processes. A change in either factor means a change in both. Changing first the socioeconomic structure to generate a *new human* is an invalid claim. Also invalid is first changing the nature of human beings – their consciousness, their values, their character – to then build a truly human society.

A religious attitude is an aspect of the human character structure: human devotion motivates the conduct. Through his analysis, Fromm advocates for a societal shift towards the *being* mode as essential for addressing contemporary challenges and fostering a sustainable, equitable future. His work remains crucial for understanding the potential for human and societal transformation, urging every individual to evaluate their own values and priorities in pursuit of a more harmonious and meaningful existence.

Fromm's Radical humanism

Fromm adheres to radical humanism, whose shared ideas and attitudes are[11]:

- Production must serve the real needs of the people, not the demands of the economic system.
- A new relation must be established between people and nature, one of cooperation not of exploitation.
- Mutual antagonism must be replaced by solidarity.
- The aim of all social arrangements must be human well-being and the prevention of ill-being.
- Not maximum consumption but sane consumption that furthers well-being must be striven for.
- The individual must be an active, not a passive, participant in social life.

While this list is impressive and still valid after half a century, the weakness is that in every bullet the word *must* appears. The question is: *how and who* is going to realise the must?

Features of the New Society

The first requirement in the possible creation of the new society is to be aware of the almost insurmountable difficulties that such an attempt must face. But those who have not given up hope can succeed only if they are stubborn realists, shed all illusions, and fully appreciate the difficulties[12]. Fromm's vision involves a transformation from a society where individuals are primarily consumers and spectators to one where they are active participants in shaping their communities[13] and broader societal structures. The idea of forming hundreds of thousands of small, face-to-face groups as deliberative and decision-making bodies represents a radical decentralisation of power. This approach aims to foster a more engaged and informed citizenry, where the local and communal become central to political life.

The emphasis on decentralisation extends to both industry and government. Fromm highlights the dangers of centralised power structures—referred to as the megamachine. He warns that the erosion of critical thinking and individual agency paves the way for authoritarian leadership, and may lead to fascism. Fromm's proposal for decentralisation within industries and government to smaller, more manageable units is grounded in the belief that such structures encourage participation, accountability, and a sense of community. By empowering smaller entities within enterprises and advocating for government functions to be delegated to small districts, Fromm envisions a society where individuals can meaningfully engage with and influence the political and economic spheres of their lives.

Overall, Fromm's thoughts present a compelling case for reimagining democratic participation and economic organisation. He reconsiders the scale and structure of societal institutions and explores more human-centric approaches to governance and community life. The realisation of his vision of a more engaged, equitable, and humane society requires significant societal and cultural changes.

Gentle critique on Fromm's propositions

Fromm's plea for a new social and psychological revolution skips crucial political factors and actors. There is no identification of reactive versus proactive agents, nor of various interest groups in society, their known and hidden networks, bureaucracies, etc.

For example[14], *The task is to construct a healthy economy for healthy people*, is followed by: *The first crucial step toward this goal is that production shall be directed for the sake of "sane consumption"*, and further, *At this point a most difficult practical question arises: Who is to determine which needs are healthy and which are pathogenic?* and *This cannot happen overnight or by decree, but will require a slow educational process, and in this the government must play an important role*, while *the tremendous power of giant corporations' big hold on the government, which becomes stronger daily, and on the population via thought control through brainwashing*.

For the reader, it remains unclear *what kind of government* must play an important role. It seems necessary to first break the injurious controls by Big Money over governments and over peoples' minds [chapter 6].

To achieve a society based on being, all people must actively participate in their economic function and as citizens. Hence, our liberation from the having mode of existence is possible only through the full realisation of industrial and political participatory democracy. This demand is shared by most radical humanists[15]. Government functions must be delegated to relatively small districts where people can still know and judge each other and, hence, can actively participate in the administration of their own community affairs. *Active and responsible participation further requires that humanistic management replace bureaucratic management[16].*

Clearly, Fromm's small districts organised by democratic participation depend on *delegated* government functions[17]: *Women must be liberated from patriarchal domination; A Supreme Cultural Council, charged with the task of advising the government, the politicians, and the citizens in all matters in which knowledge is necessary, should be established; A system of effective dissemination of effective information must also be established.*

Fromm's propositions with a political impact are typified by a *must*, with expected realisation by entities wielding power. There is a lack of clarity over whether he points to incumbent neoliberal entities, or to *new* entities, and if so, *which* new entities? The undefined political perspective fails in finding realistic paths of change. An established *megamachine* of power never delegates real power to democratic entities. In history, people did take, and conquer societal power, because waiting to receive it from incumbents is a dead end. In 2025 corporate and neoliberal discursive power is far more influential than in 1976. Radical humanists cannot build on established governments to change society's course. Revolt is a crucial factor in every revolution, like women did without vainly waiting to *be liberated from patriarchal domination by a Supreme Cultural Council.*

No workable political programme is available at the end of his highly recommended book, because Fromm did not identify the socioeconomic enablers of transformation.

10.4 Political sciences on climate change

The major part of this section introduces the book of Sheldon Wolin. It is followed by contributions in the recent literature.

Political philosopher Wolin: Managed Democracy and the Spectre of Inverted Totalitarianism

The mainstream media in the Global North broadcasts images and comments that overwhelmingly conform to the neoliberal ideology. The media postulate the superiority of neoliberalism without alternatives. Big Money power, economic growth for the richest part, inequality, imperialism, colonialism, military superpower, sanctions, embargoes, border walls, etc. are presented as *normal*.

Western citizens lack sober observation and assessment of the political systems governing their lives and the future of their children and grandchildren. The seminal research of Sheldon Wolin offers an unrelenting, comprehensive and consistent analysis of the US political system and its exploits. The book dates from 2008, with a new preface in 2010. In 2025, Inverted Totalitarianism is no longer a spectre, but a reality. This section provides a trailer to entice wider readership.

Superpower US, blessed hegemon of the globe

The imaginary of the US as a superpower, the hegemon standing above international law, dates from the Cold War period, when the US dumped World War 2 ally, the Soviet Union, *without whose contributions and horrific sacrifices the Allied victory would have been highly problematic*[18]. In April 1950, the US National Security Council stated: the US must *accept the responsibility of world leadership. This means mustering clearly superior overall power in its most inclusive sense, such as: Intensification of affirmative and timely measures and operations by covert means in the fields of economic warfare and political and psychological warfare with a view to fomenting and supporting unrest and revolt in selected strategic satellite countries*[19] of the USSR.

Totalitarianism's Inversion, Democracy's Perversion[20] describes how the US democracy metamorphosed into a totalitarian regime, organised as the *inverse* of the 20th century totalitarian regimes, which were founded on mass mobilisation around—atrocious, immoral, vain—myths, imaginaries represented by its leader-architect and its entourage, broadcasted via full control of the public media, infesting the minds of the majority of the population. The regime controlled all sectors of society, including the economy.

In the inverted version now deployed in the US, the myths and imaginaries are similar, also pursuing world hegemony. *Myth presents a narrative of exploits, not an argument or a demonstration. It does not make the world intelligible, only dramatic. In the course of its account the actions of the myth's heroes, no matter how bloody or destructive, acquire justification. They become privileged, entitled to take actions that are morally denied to others. No need to tally the Iraqi civilian casualties*[21].

The political system is not by personal rule but driven by abstract totalising powers. The system succeeds by encouraging political disengagement rather than mass mobilisation. It relies not on public agencies, but on *private media* to disseminate propaganda reinforcing the official version of events. The US president-leader is not the system's architect but its product, a construct of public relations wizards and of party propagandists. Those who counsel the titular head of Superpower supply the hubris that confuses opportunity with capability and grossly underestimates the resources needed to accomplish the grandiose goal of world hegemony.

During the presidency of G.W. Bush (2000-2007), the US invaded Afghanistan and Iraq, framed by the Bush Doctrine: *We are not just any hegemon. We run a uniquely benign imperialism ... it is a fact manifest in the way that others welcome our power. Pre-emptive war entails the projection of power abroad, usually against a far weaker country. It declares that the US is justified in striking at another country because of a perceived threat that US power will be weakened, severely damaged, unless it reacts to eliminate the danger before it materialises*[22].

In the case of Iraq, the script for applying the pre-emptive doctrine produced a disaster. The Superpower's toll – thousands of innocent lives, widespread economic devastation and social dislocation, and years of military occupation – was unintended rather than deliberate. The conqueror wants to avoid actually governing conquered land. A globalising power wants military bases abroad, trading partners, markets, and consumers: suzerainty, not an old-fashioned empire[23].

The sole form of protest against the pre-emptive war and the repression policies of the administration took place not in the Congress, the courts, or an opposition party, but outside 'official channels', in the streets where hundreds of thousands of ordinary citizens organised themselves to protest the actions of the administration. Equally striking, the administration consistently ignored the protesters. The major media, attentive to official cues, followed suit with belated, condescending, and minimal coverage[24].

In the highly structured marketplace of ideas managed by media conglomerates, sellers rule and buyers adapt to what the same media has pronounced to be 'mainstream'. Free circulation of ideas has been replaced by their managed circularity. The result is an essentially monochromatic media. In-house commentators identify the problem and its parameters, creating a box that dissenters struggle vainly to elude. The critic who insists on changing the context is dismissed as irrelevant, extremist, 'the Left' – or ignored altogether. A more sophisticated structure embraces the op-ed page and letters to the editor. In theory everyone is free to submit articles or letters, but the newspaper chooses what suits its purpose with meagre explanation of standards for acceptance – although it is obvious that the selected opinions represent limits set by the editors[25].

Hypocrisy is widespread and deep-rooted. This is quite problematic because hypocrisy undermines trust among people, among nations. Trust among people is an essential factor in democratic societies.

The hypocrisy of the enemy is exposed and criticised. Their own hypocrisy covers and accepts the criminal acts of Western hegemonic power executed by the US, NATO allies, and Israel. Murdering unarmed citizens, often children, in occupied land is daily practice by the Israeli military, part of an Apartheid regime (Human Rights Watch 2021; Amnesty International 2022). The genocide on the Palestinian people seems to be a piece of the US hegemonic plan.

Adding a hopeful comment:

Wolin's remarkable book ends[26] by asking how the people, people like you and me, can turn the tide of neoliberalism. He argues: *Without democratisation of people themselves, the democratisation of politics will* *be purely formal. Self-democratisation increases by virtue of one's own activities. It requires the individual to participate in public life, to shape public, open policy, which in principle is accessible to all who wish to be part of it. Popular political interventions are, <u>at the national level</u>[27], inevitably episodic and fleeting. The People will <u>never</u> dominate politics. A united populace is no longer possible, and may not even be desirable. Instead of One People, it would be preferable to have democratic citizenship. Most likely <u>to be cultivated in local, small-scale forms</u>. The quality of public debate must change significantly. This depends on the recapture of the media from commercial hands.*

Wolin's assertion that *The People* will never dominate politics is correct for the top-down centralised mastodon regimes of neoliberalism, yet requires nuancing. The techno-economic and social realities of era3 remove '*never*' in Wolin's position. Full transformation is realised bottom-up by the people themselves. The result is not a large pyramid with centralised power at the top. Even benevolent central power is episodic and ephemeral, as it is quickly alienated from the living world of 90% of the People.

Era3 needs a network of numerous, diverse power centres spread across the world, continuously created and renewed[28]. The sum of millions of power centres scattered across the communities of people is stronger than the neoliberal central bastions. The future geopolitics may root out colonialism[29], militarism and widespread destruction of ecosystems.

Recent political literature on climate change

In the recent political and sociological literature, I was unable to find publications as factually and analytically rich as Wolin's book. Paterson[30] sees power as the central organising concept, directing attention less at specific institutions but instead to a much broader set of social processes, all human activities and relations. Climate change is every day, mundane, implicated in the normal dynamics of our societies. Much climate politics is thus *implicit*, logically contained in an activity, decision, initiative, or conflict, even if climate change is not mentioned explicitly.

Some people think that climate change is not political but instead an economic or technological question. The economy and technology are indeed important but it is a mistake to think that they are themselves not political. Technical and social change are always closely intertwined. Making a contrast between technology and behaviour is a false dichotomy.

Paterson criticises definitions of climate change as a simple *emissions problem*, a *market failure*[31] problem, or a *global commons* problem, and underscores the importance of how integral fossil energy is to the modern world. His discourse of decarbonisation between weak and strong phasing out of fossil fuels sheds light on an explicit anti-capitalist framing of climate change. Capitalist obsession with economic growth and capital accumulation; dominance of the profit motive; constant externalising of social and ecological costs; persistent inequalities and injustices; structural power of business within politics. Conflict is at the heart of climate politics, an *inherent* dynamic, with concrete interventions involved in the pursuit of decarbonisation occurring at myriad scales, by diverse actors with their own logics. Identification of an enemy or a single effective site of struggle is rather difficult.

Paterson calls the shaping of climate change action *cultural political economy*. He refers to forces opposing low carbon transitions and powerful emotional forces[32] around practices such as driving, flying, meat-eating, or air-conditioning, that produce cultural resistance to low carbon transitions.

Interestingly, the important tension he first identified between drastic, urgent elimination of fossil fuels and addressing all other socio-political processes, Paterson[33] dissolves by stating that both are needed. Or: in addition, *spearhead actions* are needed as constantly biting demolishers of the neoliberal system.

A good deal of recent work on climate change politics has focused on the urban scale[34]. In cities key carbon-generating systems are located physically, organised techno-economically, and governed politically.

At the forefront of climate political action, several authors criticise present policies. For example, Ajl[35] questions the language, keywords and agendas of Green New Deals. They are instruments for governing capitalism, rather than for destroying it. Others[36] address the geopolitics of green colonialism, requesting global justice and eco-social transitions. Themes of extractive economies, degrowth, colonialism, debt, inequality, and feminism are brought up in the societal transformations needed for averting climate collapse.

10.5 Practical experience about how power is applied

The headquarters of neoliberalism, the energy corporates and the weapons industry, are concentrations of money, power, prestige and influence[37]. They paralyse or corrupt a large part of the people, graduates and mandarins of the system. The supremacy of neoliberalism leaves only room for small changes to neutralise criticism. Now that even the superrich can no longer deny the calamities of climate change, they accept a slow shift towards *net zero emissions*. The EU *Fit-for-55* is the implementation of this neoliberal programme [section 8.7]. This is muddling through as in the 33 years from 1992 to 2025. Dominating neoliberal power paralyses disruptive change.

Power is a concept used in everyday life, politics, social relations and in energy theory. Power is the amount of force exerted per unit of time. If the force is strong and delivered over a long period, the power is big and enduring, as opposed to an episodic surge or explosion of energy. An explosion is intense but short-lived. This occurs in rebellious actions by way of emotion, anger, or resistance to self-experienced gross injustice.

How to empower

Power is employable for different purposes, and in many directions. It can impede or occasion motion, stimulate or disrupt change.

There is use of power for Good and for Evil. Characteristics of power for Good are the possibilities of self-determination[38]. This includes having access to people, institutions, infrastructures, solutions, and prosperity and also being invited to participate in activities, and the right to speak and be heard[39].

Power for Evil dominates the world and the media today. The images that flood children, young people, and adults every day via TV, internet, movies, series, ... have predominantly evil, violence, crime, ... as the main theme, without context and clarification. Neoconservative ideology and arrogance in the US pushed neoliberalism to the political forefront in the 1980s. Linked to this was the new cult of the successful top manager, trained and certified in the complex dynamics of organising, managing and applying power[40].

They are no choirboys, the powerful of neoliberalism and their servants of various ilk, from sturdy security guards to cunning lawyers. They specialise in deception and controlling and directing dossiers that concern them while hiding in the shadows (masterminding[41]). Lobbyism plays a major role in this, including sometimes bribes and blackmail. Based on experience[42], it is possible to infer a pattern of *how power is exercised*. Exercise of power for Good is widely publicised and glorified in the media, for example when a company donates to a nature restoration project. The exercise of power for Evil, with lobbyism, bribes and blackmail, happens covertly, as invisibly as possible. To avoid reputation damage, *third parties* are hired to carry out unsavoury activities in the interest of the power holder. Using power efficiently is the general rule: to achieve an intended result, the least amount of power and resources is pursued.

Four stages in applying power

Power in operation exerts force on persons. The force either makes persons move or paralyses them, this according to pursued objectives. For a power centre, two groups of persons are important. On the one hand, persons belonging to or connected with the power centre. On the other, persons outside the power centre, in actual or potential contact or interaction with it. The exercise of power vis-à-vis the two groups differs formally, in its packaging and manner. Nevertheless, on both groups, four successive stages of activities to move or paralyse persons are applied: 1) inform/convince; 2) entice/bribe; 3) oblige/coerce; 4) remove/eliminate. The stages shift from soft to hard means, from efficient and effective interventions to costly and risky ones.

By *informing and convincing*, a roughly estimated ⅔ majority of the population listens to the dominant societal power centre's narrative. Upon conviction, that majority accepts the stated framework of thought and values, and associated paradigms. This acceptance legitimises the power centre and its influence. It explains the excessive role and impact of big media on social functioning[43]. Add *enticing and bribing*, which appeal to people's interests, and the agreeing majority increases.

The less applied stage 3 and the exceptional stage 4 affect small to tiny parts of the population. They are nevertheless of great importance to neoliberal power centres for nipping in the bud or smashing germinating *contravening power* created by activist agents for change. Both sides, power centre and activists, experience more damage beyond stages 1 and 2. The damage in terms of exposure and experienced impacts is much worse for the activists, and extreme if elimination means death. In many countries, this is the fate of social, environmental, political, legal, and media[44] activists, wherever oligarchs, plutocrats, dictators, fascists or deceiving democrats set the tone.

Contravening power

Fright, paralysis, laziness, and complacency are bad counsellors when the water is at your lips. What matters for transformation is contravening power. There are few manuals about dealing with and overcoming neoliberal powers by means of self-awareness, perseverance and agility. Agility reduces the likelihood of hostile attacks and exposure to evil power. Agility also helps to bypass cynicism, a dangerous mood fostered by delivering overly difficult efforts for too long and in vain.

A strong source of will is knowing that thorough transformation is the only path to a humane world, the era3 of human civilisation. After World War 2, heavily armed Western aggressors were defeated by peoples in the global South yearning for independence. Some peoples used non-violent methods of resistance. Others were forced into armed guerrilla strategy and tactics with severe consequences, as in Vietnam, Afghanistan, and in Palestine since 1948, facing extreme genocide in 2023-25. Their struggles are instructive for developing resistance to coercion and elimination. It is also instructive to explore how neoliberal centres of power organise and function. Knowing and understanding the opponent is part of a successful strategy in any showdown.

How to acquire and execute contravening power?

The four execution stages of evil power are evaluated on their applicability by contravening power. The stages, considered next one by one, overlap and interact in practice.

Stage 1 *inform/convince*. To some extent, the media determine everyone's perception. For many to a large extent because they lack the resources, time, money, networks and education to delve into the background and context of the messages. Mass media owned by the superrich play a particularly pernicious role in the battle for highlighting crucially important ideas for the future. They propagate delusive truths and fake news, and stifle attention to contradictory substantive debates based on facts, observed actions and explicating mechanisms. Neoliberalism is rooted in right-wing ideology and far out from democracy and free markets. It is shifting from conservative, over neoconservative, to far-right. Alliances with fascist ideas and forces lurk more and more.

Resistance by independent, critical media is indispensable. They run on limited financial resources and their information mostly does not reach a majority of the population. They explain falsehoods and lies in the traditional media[45], and extend their influence. To inform and convince people about the road to era3, brainwashing is neither a desirable, nor a necessary method. Expanding centres of active citizens and honest politicians are committed to civic initiatives, experimental projects[46], exploratory discussion groups, cooperatives, etc. Fact-based examples and consistent narratives about future perspectives exert great appeal.

The economic-financial superiority of electricity generation from harvested natural flows of sunlight, wind, water, and heat is rising by the day. False allegations about shortages of materials, about major waste problems, about too much space occupation, etc. cannot stop solar power overwhelming fossil fuels. Factual truth confluent with the true interest of the majority of people is irresistible. Just see it and tell it everywhere.

Stage 2 *seduce/bribe*. The money power of the superrich today is enormous. In the neoliberal context, it is an illusion to be able to build a greater countervailing power in money. The Achilles heel of super-wealth, its weakness, is the extremely high, and still growing, inequality in property and income. In the Global South, the *ethical existence minimum income* is still denied to 4 billion people, half the world's population. They long for the better life touted by Aristotle.

Unstoppable migrations have taken off, and will not quieten down until era3 is spread globally. In the Global North, the invisible catacombs of the 21st century are spreading, due to continuing streams of *illegal* refugees and desperate vulnerable people. They are people who possess practically nothing, have little to lose, and can only gain through societal transformation. Their alliance with the oppressed sections of the middle class, and with the few defectors of the higher class, forms the basis of effective social power.

Actors for and of change and revolution are increasing in number and determination in rich countries. Movements like Youth for Climate and Extinction Rebellion, individuals and families adopting a climate-conscious mode of living, prefer community values above money accumulation. These radical movements and changes are difficult to capture and control by power from above.

Power from below can be achieved faster and stronger with a broad multicultural and interdisciplinary vision of the future and society. It is buzzing on all sides, in every stratum and disciplinary direction. The challenge comes down to putting them together into an irresistible, unbreakable and positive force. A laminar junction of perspectives and insights from all disciplines would provide solid support. It is not money that counts, but vision, willpower, persistence, and agility. Dare to question entrenched beliefs, look through and behind delusions. Don't be fooled.

Stage 3 *oblige/coerce*. As long as traditional politicians meekly carry out the will of Big Money, the legal and judicial power obliges and coerces in the wrong direction. There are contravening initiatives on several fronts, like proposals to demolish unjust privileges of the rich in private law[47]. Participatory democracy attempts[48] to broaden formal representation. Legal court cases require governments to respect their promises, or suing for climate-damaging behaviour by companies and individuals.

Building contravening power at stages 1 to 3 is absolutely needed. There will be successes and failures. But can these stages eliminate the organised bastions of neoliberalism? How can stage 4 contribute?

Stage 4 *remove/eliminate*. Brutal, direct elimination of the superrich and their bastions is rather a script for Hollywood movies. The better and feasible path is to make the powers of neoliberalism *irrelevant, meaningless and therefore useless*. This will happen in era3, starting in the energy substrate via the global spread of *grassroots small-scale electricity generation from the bottom up*. Interacting with it will follow the rollout of Sustainable Development for Our Common Future through globally dispersed, local initiatives. Let the big mess of neoliberalism rust, go around it on all sides.

Eliminating neoliberalism with its vast powers for Evil is the most challenging part for community governance. Elimination is necessary, possible and desirable. Certainly it will happen: it will be either by Sustainable Development substituting neoliberalism in due course, or by full devastation of all decent human life on Earth when the fossil fuel industry, the military complex and Big Money continue on their business-as-usual path, the neoliberal Breakthrough 2.

10.6 Public economic view on self-interest

Financial interest, selfishness, and greed are components of the neoliberal ideology and practice. Yet, self-interest is different from selfishness. Take care not to replace economic utopias and dystopias with social ones assuming a new kind of human beings with lasting goodwill and giving to others[49]. Personal Benefit/Cost ratio tests are inherent in human life, attitudes and decisions.

Self-interest is not selfishness[50]

Self-interest is an ineradicable force occasioning positive and negative effects. Some traits of self-interest in social functioning are similar to the working of gravity in the physical world. Gravity is a continuously operating and omnipresent force. Still, science is puzzled about the fundamentals of this force. Gravity brings order by keeping things in place or in balanced motion, avoiding chaos. Overcoming gravity forces is a daily activity of acting and moving people. Such an escape from inertia avoids order degrading to stagnation. When people are enterprising, or architects design physical constructions, they all take gravity into account.

Self-interests of people, individually and collectively in groups, clubs or communities, are to some extent affecting their modes of living, motivations and passions. Self-interest is omnipresent like gravity. When designing social institutions, considering the force of self-interest is always needed to obtain workable and robust solutions. Institutions based only on goodwill are not robust[51].

The positive effect of human self-interest is to provide appropriate solutions to most problems in a society. Taking care of oneself is generally the most effective and efficient way of practical living for people endowed with adequate healthiness, diligence, and opportunities. A person does not always know very well what to want, to have or to be. However, a person usually knows better than others think they know for her or him. This also concerns selecting the most appropriate solutions to satisfy the desired mode of living, and obtain suitable goods and services in an appropriate manner. In exploring and choosing, the person benefits from considering the broad context and specific constraints, including its limited assets and budget. Leaving choice to people as sovereign, self-determining individuals is a valid constituent of democratic governance.

In practice, exercising personal sovereignty is severely constrained when lacking the *ethical existence minimum income*, and through a lack of reliable information. Correct information is a public good, to be freely available. Today, private interests bombard people with low quality information, infested by advertising, deception and crime. In modern times, it is a challenge to compose a personal consistent and comprehensive worldview.

Too little self-interest may deteriorate to forms of self-loathing and neglect. Then the community must take care of persons who do not sufficiently care for themselves[52].

Immoderate self-interest degrades to selfishness, greed, and narcissism. Selfishness causes negative effects for other people and community life, but also for the selfish individual. It makes vigorous cooperation and solidarity precarious to impossible. Selfishness is not conducive to one's own happiness, given that humans are social beings.

True evaluation of all Costs and Benefits

When true evaluation of all costs and benefits of technologies, projects, policies, etc. is performed, the yardstick *Benefits exceeding Costs* is useful for monitoring the effects of societal transformations. Only considering money as a motivating factor is flawed and misleading. In a widely outreaching endeavour of transforming society, looking over the walls of economics is necessary and instructive.

Benefits and costs are partly material, partly mental; some are private and some public [figure 11]. Positive personal, private material and mental results are necessary to obtain and maintain people's contributions and support for the common good. In transformative episodes, mental, ethical and spiritual enriching is a prevailing factor for a significant share of the population.

Between self- and common interests

When physiological, safety and security needs are covered, people enjoy a decent life standard. Owned property for *personal* and *functional* ends can be *restricted* property by the obligation to help one's fellow beings, providing room for *common* property, which a group shares in the spirit of a common bond[53]. It implies a shift in the individual character from *to have* towards *to be*, opting for personal growth needs, such as cognitive, aesthetic, self-fulfilling, and transcendent needs. *Mutual cooperation* is overcoming greed and hate in striving for and attaining *to be* ethical goals.

Cooperation ranges from two individuals forming a couple, over a variety of communal relationships among many people, to citizenship of political entities. In effective cooperation, participants rank their self-interests in *having* subordinate to the shared common interests. Successful cooperation is enriching for all participants. Nevertheless, cooperation is threatened if it is possible to stealthily escape its duties while retaining the benefits[54].

How individuals behave depends on several factors, including their moral beliefs, the context, the matter under consideration, past experiences, and the prevailing type of social control. Social control is a community responsibility to keep its members functioning within the boundaries of common interest. Controlling people's behaviour opens up a wide spectrum of options on socio-political regimes, from participatory democracy to autocracy[55], with a great many varieties in between. In the highly diverse world several action levels exist. The United Nations at the highest level, followed by a colourful kaleidoscope of national and federal states, cities, neighbourhoods, institutions and agencies[56].

10.7 Local governance and self-governance

Notes from the literature on local governance are followed by an introduction to Ostrom's seminal work on self-governance.

Local governance

Governance[57] refers to the conditions for ordered collective action, while government refers to the formal institutions of the state and their power to decide and enforce decisions. Governance includes actors and institutions from government and beyond. Responsibilities and roles are blurred, while the respective powers are interdependent. New governing techniques relate to *steering and guiding* rather than *command and control.*

Self-organising networks are possible. In general, many models of governance want systems to be effective and efficient, following the rule of law, participatory, consensual in decision-making, accountable, transparent, responsive, equitable and inclusive. A long list of conditions to attend to!

Bouckaert[58] formulates a comprehensive view on *effective local governance.* In local governance, bottom-up ownership is important to develop a legitimate, coherent, and trustworthy governance system that is owned by all actors in the system, especially local actors.

In the broad span of local governance, Bouckaert identifies five types, listed along their increasing scope. *Corporate* covers single and autonomous public sector organisations and entities. *Holding* covers a range of organisations that belong together and need a consolidated governance. *Public service* implies the responsibility and accountability for the performance of a local system of organisations. The service will only be effective in collaboration with the private sector, the not-for-profit sector, and even organised citizen clusters. *Supra-structure* reaches beyond institutional infrastructure in referring to ideas, ideologies, values, and cultures. It implies a two-way interaction between organisational hardware and software. *Systemic local governance* is about macro governance and includes the major features of a local system, mostly defined by legal and political frames such as checks and balances, key allocation mechanisms of resources, key rules for decision-making (elections and other participation mechanisms), and distribution of the local power balance.

Governance at a local or a subnational level is different from governance at other levels of government. Local governance is separated: mostly *legally*, in most cases even *constitutionally*, and also *politically*. Even when levels are separate, they are intertwined, related, and networked in a *marbled* multi-level governance context. Interdependency becomes tangible when competences between levels are reshuffled during moves of centralisation or decentralisation. Compared to central governance, a culture of local governance implies more engagement, participation, and voice, which results in different decision-making processes. In combination with more tangible service delivery, this may result in different levels of perception and satisfaction with outcomes. As a consequence, local governance becomes increasingly different and distinctive from central governance. These observations are applicable by means of *excellence* in the supply and use of renewable electricity locally generated from ambient natural energy flows like solar light and wind. Owning the extraction and provision of energy is a solid foundation for local governance[59].

Local governance, closely related to *engagement* and *participation*, is impacted by its interactions with citizens[60]. This allows for more direct democracy. Democratic governance and trust are mutually conditional. A crucial variable for trust is user satisfaction and citizen perception of service delivery. Both the absence of corruption in the process and the quality of public services as its outcome are positively related to citizens' trust in public administration. Building and maintaining trustworthiness need special attention. The three trustworthiness bases are ability, integrity, and benevolence.

Ability refers to structuring the processes and obtaining outcomes. It needs local capacity and competence to deliver services, to control crises by means of sound policy-making in designing, deciding, implementing, and evaluating in collaboration with citizens and their local communities.

Integrity relates to a strong sense of justice, individual and organisational. It implies honest, open, and visible arrangements and mechanisms for responsible and accountable local governance. Commonly used strategies focus on integrity, transparency, and independent oversight.

Benevolence accords with a general culture of doing good for the community, by being inclusive and guaranteeing access for all to local services and policies. It is realised by leaving no one behind, non-discrimination, participation, subsidiarity, and inter-generational equity.

With such bases, Sustainable Development can materialise as a socio-political reality.

Ostrom: self-governance in practice and theory

Nobel laureate Elinor Ostrom[61] is a pioneer in the study of how *self-governance* works in local communities. Bottom-up cooperation between sovereign individuals is a matter of commitment and methodology[62]. Only goodwill does not lead to the necessary robust structures[63]. The sustenance of cooperation is persevering contributions by *sovereign* persons. Nonetheless, sovereign persons repeatedly weigh their contributions against their obtained benefits of the two options: participating in the communal approach or staying outside for individual realisation of pursued ends. The balance between acquired benefits and own contributions must remain equilibrated. To maintain the equilibrium, Ostrom presents three puzzles to solve[64]:

1. Establishing clear, appropriate *new rules*, when rules are missing or existing rules are inadequate to achieve robust, stable forms of organisation for self-governance among sovereign actors.

2. Credible *commitments* in terms of contributions by sovereign individuals, framed by mutual trust, reciprocity and equity.

3. Mutual *monitoring*, coupled with enforceability of compliance with the rules and with pledged contributions.

Without *monitoring*, the participant's *commitments* are not reliable, not credible. Without credible commitments to contributing, there is no sufficient basis and reason to propose *new rules*. Trials of self-governance will then fail.

Mutual supervision may lead to rather nasty situations[65]. A separate *policing* institution is then preferable, belonging to the juridical corps in democratic states. Evidently, the governance of cooperation pursues transparency, effectiveness, efficiency and fairness. This requires rules of governance suitable for the community assets under governance such as *smart grids* to support small-scale renewable electricity generation in the community. Rules work best when tailored to the specific context, being local communities, as well as to other levels such as the national and super-national electricity systems. Understanding well, the coordinating and auxiliary components of the multi-level system are there to fully support local small-scale renewable electricity generation. Today their growth and autonomy are hindered and smothered by the central commandos in the neoliberal regime [chapter 2].

Ostrom's methodology is tried and tested and is useful for organising climate policy at local to global levels. High degrees of self-initiative and self-governance are conditions for realising energy and societal transformations.

10.8 Climate change ethics

Climate change is a multi-faceted crisis of existence by threatening life on Earth, of governance by people in power, of ethics: climate change harms, and the responses to it are unequal and unjust[66]. People causing the least GHG emissions are the most adversely affected by climate change[67].

Recognising a problem as a moral concern is a moral value or a moral reason, articulating the distinctions between right and wrong, good and bad, and what deserves respect and what does not. These distinctions are made to ensure that others are not harmed, and not treated unfairly or unjustly, or without the dignity and respect they deserve[68]. Ethics is never a process of neutral deliberation. Moral scrutiny is always value-based, and it takes sides: always for care, equity, justice, dignity, and the good life, and always against harm, inequity, injustice, and the degradation of others and communities[69].

In setting climate targets, ethical foundations of climate policy and centrality of concern for justice should be taken seriously. How timid or aggressive GHG emission reduction should be is mainly an ethical question. Physically a total ban on fossil fuels at short notice is possible[70]. About the ethical assumptions underlying specific targets, more transparency is obtained by applying principles in three categories. First, *procedural issues* (consultation, ethical accountability). Second, *technical feasibility and predictability*. Third, *content of climate policies* (protection, respect for ethical and ecological norms)[71].

The World Commission on the Ethics of Scientific Knowledge and Technology (UNESCO) prepared a report on Ethical *Principles for Climate Change Adaptation and Mitigation*[72].

Vigorous policy of mitigation holds major challenges for the political and societal implementation of solutions. There is a debate about the approaches and mechanisms to tackle climate change, with conflicts of interest between different groups. Clarification of the ethical principles is important[73].

Ten ethical principles for climate change mitigation provide a frame for ethical handling, and some are highlighted here.

Cultural diversity presupposes respect for human rights and fundamental freedoms, and gives voice to a more pluralistic framework of worldviews and diversity in practice. Different nations should engage in genuine ethical dialogue that respects global climate justice and equity.

Interdependence of life on Earth entails that the survival of one species contributes to the survival of others. All other species and life-support systems make human life possible.

Intellectual and moral solidarity of humankind implies cooperation of the peoples of the world, beyond national boundaries, gender, age and ethnicities. Solidarity offers a solid ethical foundation on which to base responsibilities according to affordability and needs, particularly towards affected individuals and populations, and more broadly towards the environment and future generations.

Global justice is conceived as fairness through actions and programs on health, education, and economic opportunity, in helping poor countries on the path of welfare for the poorest people[74]. Global justice should also take the interests of non-human animals and the health of Mother Earth into account. Although the *no harm* principle is in the Preamble of the UNFCCC, many countries do not seem to observe this principle in their policies and actions. All nations have ethical duties and a legal responsibility to avoid harming others unnecessarily by avoiding unnecessary activities that increase GHG emissions.

Resilience is associated with the development of strategies that promote procedures and systems that lead communities to optimise the resolution of climate-related disasters through self-organisation and feedback mechanisms at various levels of society, but most effectively at the local level. It is important to identify gender-sensitive strategies to respond to the environmental and humanitarian crises caused by climate change[75].

Sustainability in terms of climate change considers frugality, renewable energy, and reforestation.

Integrity of Scientific Research refers to essential ethical values, such as integrity, truth and respect for reasoned argument and evidence. Climate science has an important societal impact – only ethical science can have and must have a moral impact on society. Some of the general principles of scientific and research integrity are: honesty in presenting research goals, methods and results; reliability in performing research and in communication of results; objectivity; impartiality; open communication; fairness in giving due credit to the work of others; education and responsibility for future science generations[76].

Conclusion: Such ethical imperatives will ultimately affect and challenge prevailing political and economic systems since the trajectories of contemporary economic and political practices are leading the global community towards unacceptable consequences.

Re-visioning current worldviews and questioning deeply entrenched perspectives that will allow for the emergence of a more considerate and caring human community that responds to the vulnerabilities of nature and their fellow human beings will have to be articulated and inculcated. The principles enumerated above seek to contribute to the development of this noble purpose[77].

A reminder:

- Mimesis, violence, and myths have been inherent to human societies since their nascency. The human passion *Prestige* rests on *Power*, and Power on *Property*. Fischer's critique on neoliberalism is merciless, yet invigorating. Latour suggests a *Let's go and see* approach to save the habitability of the world.
- To his five-level pyramid from physiological needs to personal self-actualisation, Maslow added cognitive, aesthetic, and transcendence needs. Self-actualisation is a human's purpose, requiring particular characteristics and behaviours. Yet the perfect human does not exist.
- Fromm's book *To Have or To Be?* identifies individual and societal characters, and their interaction. Whether *to have* or *to be* dominates depends on the social structure, its values and norms. Shifts from have to be improve peoples' lives. Fromm's radical humanism and a New Society cannot be realised by the incumbent powers in neoliberal societies.
- Politics holds a central place in energy and climate policy-making. Neoliberalism controls the managed democracies of the Western national states, and has evolved to totalitarianism in service of Big Money, with the fossil fuel and arms industries in the cockpit. Given the subservient role of formal political institutions, radical new views and initiatives are needed.
- Self-interest is a positive property, when not perverted by selfishness and greed. Bottom-up self-governance can take institutional shape via three steps: creating new rules, credible commitments by involved citizens, and monitoring for enforcement, as described and tested by Elinor Ostrom.
- Ethical imperatives will ultimately affect and challenge prevailing political and economic systems since the trajectories of contemporary economic and political practices are leading the global community towards unacceptable consequences.

Transformation viewpoints: shape paradise or slip into hell

Throughout the writing of this book, the evidence of necessary transformations amplified, while strengthening the view on the *single narrow path* of action to overcome the climate change crisis. Such a path stretches out to the future, from the coming months to the completion of a sustainably developing global world. Arrival at this end goal is contingent on the narrow paths of pioneers taking the right direction while enlarging over time to broad boulevards full of people.

The collection of viewpoints intends to elucidate the direction and conditions for protecting and multiplying the grassroots pioneer initiatives. It emanates from a strong appeal for facts and testable rationality, avoiding baseless hope in solutions offered by corporate captains and politicians striving for money, power, and vanity. The approach is interdisciplinary by covering energy-technology, political economy, and socio-political topics. Consider this interdisciplinary essay as a pioneering exemplar. The variety of know-hows, specialties and disciplines will contribute in the transformations to era3. Every added discipline to the lamination of the here- covered disciplines is an asset[1].

While most of the contents are plucked from the book's chapters, the essay is not a summary, nor structured like its chapters. Standard strategic planning methods[2], abiding by business-as-usual frames, cannot deliver the proper insight and strategy. They fall short in covering the long-time and universal perspectives, inherent to climate change and its global impacts. Conceiving transformation requires viewpoints from outside and beyond the present business-as-usual, the narrow dry dock of mainstream climate policy literature and practice. Forecasting compelled in mental tunnels rebuffs disruptive visions and solutions. Back-casting from imagined future landing points is a better approach.

Inspired by Paule Amblard's commentary on the exposed Apocalypse tapestries of Angers[3], the format selected for presenting the transformation viewpoints is an exhibition of text panels. They inform about facts, concepts, actions, clockworks, and visions on the present state of the world and how the near future of humankind may unfold.

You are invited as a visitor to stroll around in this exhibition, a map of which is shown in figure 17. Please, select panels as you see fit. Most panels start with an explicative caption. The format is open for more panels with analysis, information and perspectives that are now missing. The exhibition format tells us that books are momentary, one element in a kaleidoscopic literature, and open for criticism and compliments. An exhibition also winks at the Arts, requesting from visitors the effort of understanding, interpretation and projection. The intention of this exhibition is also to invigorate for decisive active agency with your talents and specialties in your living space.

In the entry corridor, two panels inform about the framing of the analysis. One about the author's background and disposition; one about the interesting historic example of St. John's Revelation.

In the transit room, panel 3 introduces climate change and neoliberalism as interacting problems.

In room A: *Only transformation has a chance to avoid climate collapse*, transformation is described in one panel, followed by three panels about the three major areas of application, one being the hazard of neoliberalism and its dangerous breakthrough illusions.

In room B: *Neoliberalism made irrelevant by Emptied substance and Removed pillars*, exhibits six panels with proposals to remove the pillars under neoliberalism to dissolve its substance. By removing the fossil fuel pillar, the irrelevance of neoliberalism will be apparent given it cannot generate any sustainable alternative.

In room C: The triangle Nature – Individuals – Communities, figure 18 is added to remind about known aspects in the Nature-humankind relationship. The panel on Nature focuses on climate change and ethics, or immediately involving the human disposition. The latter is more developed in a panel about individuals and another about communities.

When leaving the exhibition, a panel with salient findings and suggestions is shown, without being either a summary, or a conclusion. The transformation of era2 now dominated by neoliberalism into era3 encompasses more dimensions and disciplines than the book covers. However, the focus on spearheads and urgency, universality and equity, is worth publishing as it is [panel 18].

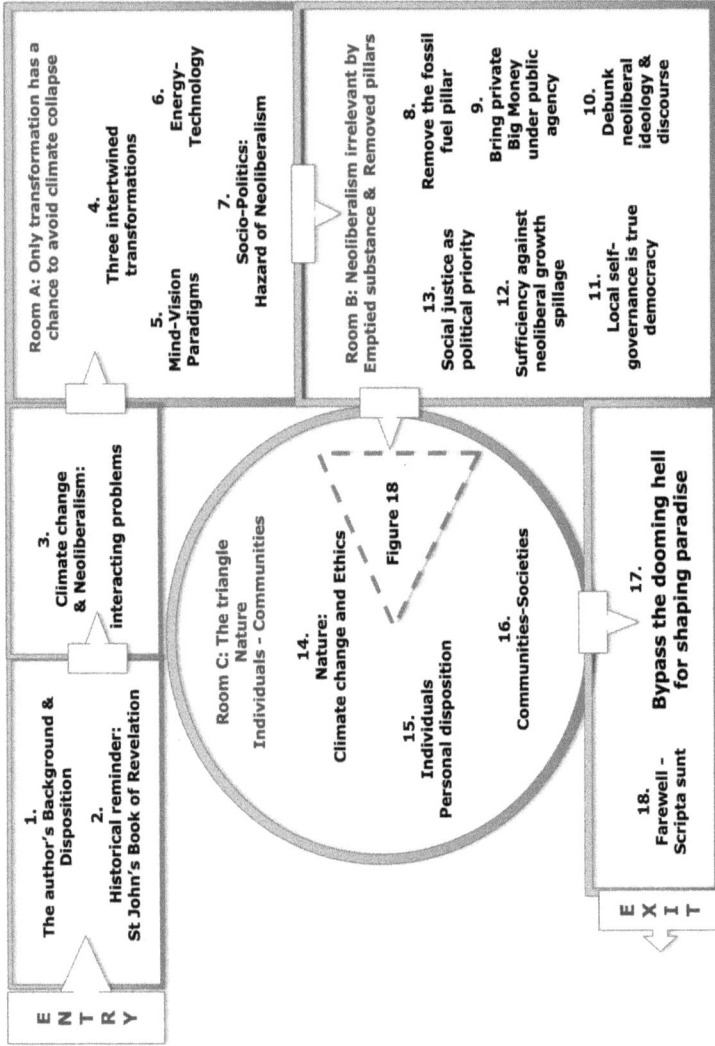

The author's Background & Disposition

1.
The author's Background & Disposition

2.
Historical reminder:
St John's Book of Revelation

3.
Climate change
& Neoliberalism:
interacting problems

Room A: Only transformation has a chance to avoid climate collapse

4.
Three intertwined
transformations

5.
Mind-Vision
Paradigms

6.
Energy-
Technology

7.
Socio-Politics:
Hazard of Neoliberalism

Room B: Neoliberalism irrelevant by Emptied substance & Removed pillars

8.
Remove the fossil
fuel pillar

9.
Bring private
Big Money
under public
agency

10.
Debunk
neoliberal
ideology &
discourse

11.
Local self-
governance is true
democracy

12.
Sufficiency against
neoliberal growth
spillage

13.
Social justice as
political priority

**Room C: The triangle
Nature
Individuals - Communities**

14.
Nature:
Climate change and Ethics

Figure 18

15.
Individuals
Personal disposition

16.
Communities-Societies

17.
**Bypass the dooming hell
for shaping paradise**

18.
Farewell -
Scripta sunt

ENTRY

EXIT

Figure 17: Map of the Exhibition "Transformation viewpoints: shape paradise or slip into hell"

Panel 1
The author's background and disposition

Caption

Involved citizens see the world through different lenses, dependent on mental frames and vantage points. Obtained perspectives hang on patchworks of assembled insights and experiences. They are affected by practical experiences at work and in daily life, by processing information, by discussions with friends and opponents. Mental frames are also intuitive, unclearly delineated, and not carved in stone. They change over time. By the confinement of their own lens, a person's worldview covers only a fraction of reality. The coverage is enlarged by integrating a variety of perspectives. This is the purpose of reading, debating, studying.

Telling you my background as an author and my disposition as an academic citizen helps you in qualifying the analysis and propositions of this book and transformation viewpoints[4].

Background as author

At high school, history and philosophy were favourite themes, yet mathematics prevailed. University bachelor's in engineering, master's in engineering economics. As a student working at the Port of Antwerp, participating in the ardent 1973 dockers' strike: a lab of popular activism, pride and politics. PhD on CHP, combined heat & power generation. Research of energy topics: electricity planning, costing, pricing of atomic plants and independent CHP units; Grid access and tariffs; energy efficiency; energy from waste. Environmental topics: planning, state-of-the-environment reports, climate change.

Contributions to IPCC's Working Group 3 during 1998-2014. Advisory reports for politicians and administrations, also beyond Europe in energy projects by international aid agencies.

A 1999-2001 political function in the Flemish government. Thanks to the www, international academic research became my first interest, with EU energy and climate policies as the main topic. Retired since 2016, more time available for socio-political literature. This enhanced my attention to interdisciplinary work, convinced that all types of knowledge and disciplines are necessary in addressing the huge challenges of today[5].

Disposition as academic citizen

In the middle of the 20thcentury born in Europe, a privileged place and an epoch of economic wealth and growth. An *imperial mode of living*[6] was and is much in evidence. This creates a painful ambiguity in actual climate change denial[7] and mental willingness to escape climate collapse. Frustration from this ambiguity may penetrate into this book. While my work and visions are mainly European, they are not mainstream. From inside the European bubble, I fiercely criticise the EU's energy and climate policymaking. Not for pleasure, yet out of need due to the alarming state of the world[8].

On the payroll of the public treasury, academic staff have specific responsibilities, such as:

- Autonomy as a condition for scientific honesty.
- Integrity and objectivity in all circumstances.
- Non-neutral against abuse, crime, deceit.

Science is a public good. Lucky scientists serve society, the people, the commons, the future.

In joyful life, choose *to be* over *to have*[9]. Money is an adequate servant, but perfidious master.

Academic Motto:

Prefer to speak true words receiving blame, above deceiving advice in soliciting praise.

Panel 2
Historical reminder:
St. John's Book of Revelation

Caption

The reference to the Apocalypse in the book's Preface emphasised the possibilities of salvation by humans themselves. During the writing process, I became more and more acquainted with St. John's revelation, and its unexpected relevance for today's peoples and societies, also engulfed in a very perilous state. This book's reference to the Apocalypse does not imply adherence to Christianism or to one of the later religions forthcoming from Christianism. Only the ca. 300 years of the transformation of the pagan Roman Empire (with the Eagle as a symbol) to the more humanistic Christianity (with the Cross as a symbol) are considered.

If St. John had not been an exile, it is unlikely he would have found the vantage, time and focus to compose his Book of Revelation.

This essay hooks up at the Apocalypse, the Revelation of St. John the Divine[10], exiled at Patmos. He intends to invigorate the nascent Christian communities. The new beliefs face harsh hostility and rejection by the kaleidoscope of pagan religions and usual worldviews. Regularly the hostility flips over in severe persecution of Christians by the vested powers in the Roman Empire with its many occupied territories. Turning Jesus of Nazareth's bequest into an irresistible force of transformation was then like a mission impossible.

Resolute choice and perseverance with the new worldview was requested by the prophet. The announced catastrophes are one side of the bifurcation of the future, leading to perdition and hell. The opposite direction is a magnification of human life, a spiritual way leading to heaven, a paradise for converted people. St. John's profoundly humanistic approach addresses all human beings. The radical Christian insurgency was in need of a strategy, hidden in symbolic language and images to avoid being recognised and immediately being quashed by Roman power. The Book of Revelation stipulates the crucial steps for overcoming the enormous challenges.

First, the forces of change are the *individuals and small communities* enlightened by the new belief in a less violent, more equal society for all people. Disciples of high moral standard are tenacious without doubt or compromise at the crossroads of choosing between good and evil. They revitalise their spiritual essence, and persevere in the profound transformation of being. The dominant ideology of inequality, amorality, and violence of the Roman Empire is disproved and replaced by the evangelical message. Frugality prevails over accumulating wealth. The transformations request radical U-turns in the minds, personal and societal characters and modes of living.

Second, the new society demands *new societal institutions*, totally different from the existing ones, whose destruction is unavoidable. The tapestry of Angers shows repeatedly the *destruction of Babylon*, a concealed reference to the Roman Empire as a source of evil. Today, the majority of the world population and world peace are victims of hegemonic, totalitarian states and their neoliberal ideology, escalating since the 1970s. Neoliberalism exhibits a growing unequal spread of power and economic wealth over the world. Power and wealth are concentrated in the Global North, wielding discursive, monetary and military supremacy. The pursued goals are an escape from Hell, and by ethical living win the paradise of Heaven, a life in enjoyable conditions with fellow citizens.

Third, the above two main tasks are supported and embedded by insight and understanding of the state-of-the-world. St. John keeps the awareness vivid by telling horrible stories of four horsemen representing conquest, war, famine, and death, of seven-headed monsters of a different nature. The rogue Antichrists are preaching deceiving discourses, delusive truths, fake religion. The enlightened followers of the liberating way should identify and reject the flawed messages. Messaging Christianity is nonetheless a dangerous endeavour because of the persecutions by the cruel forces of Rome (Babylon).

Panel 3
Climate change & Neoliberalism:
interacting problems

Caption

The *Carrying Capacity* of the Earth's ecosystems has been heavily exploited since World War 2, and now extremely stressed. The state-of-the-world in 2025 is very worrisome, not by accident. It follows from deliberate neglect and wrongdoing by neoliberal think-tanks, corporates, the superrich[11] and their slipstream[12]. *Climate Change*, a direct effect of Global Warming, is the salient driver of the unchecked deterioration of nature, the environment and human living conditions.

The Earth's climate is a unique system, for millennia[13] active in many ways: from a gentle provider of amenity, abundance, energy ... to furious forces of torrential storms, severe droughts, wildfires, due to climate change. Climate change is an *irreversible* physical process, *caused by human activities.*

The *irreversibility* makes stopping GHG emissions a real *urgent duty.* Due action time is accountable in days and months, not the usual distant target setting.

Climate change is gauged by the rise of the average ambient temperature on Earth. Mild ambient temperatures result from the *beneficial natural* greenhouse effect. GHG emissions from human activities cause *disastrous anthropogenic* greenhouse effects. Warming increases due to the steadily thicker blanket of GHG in the atmosphere. The thickness is accurately measured by the concentration[14] of GHG.

Further warming can only be stopped by ending the rise in concentration. The rise in concentration can only be stopped by ending the yearly Gigaton emissions of GHG.

The yearly Gigaton emissions of GHG can only be stopped by *ending combustion of fossil fuels.* Combustion of growing amounts of fossil fuels is one of the three pillars of *neoliberalism*[15]. Fossil fuels provide US$ billions super-profit to petrostates, oil corporates, speculators[16]. Control over money creation, flows, and stocks is another pillar of neoliberalism. Big Money masterminds strategic socio-economic processes via subservient politicians. As such democracy is managed in regimes metamorphosing to *totalitarianism*[17]. Effective climate politics are impossible under neoliberalism. Ending neoliberalism is a *necessary condition* for escaping climate collapse. Either, pyramidal empires and states disintegrate to splintered and fighting entities.Or, emancipatory grassroots activists build inclusive and cooperating communities.

Only countervailing power by uprising people can *make neoliberalism irrelevant.* Ca.10% of the world's people lives wealthily; Ca.50% lacks an ethical living minimum income. A full *transformation* of all human societies shocks the wealthy part of the world.

Nonetheless, escaping climate collapse is beneficial for all living and future people.

Room A: Only Transformation has a chance to avoid climate collapse

Panel 4
Three intertwined transformations

Caption

In the jungle of new green deals, change talk without walk, transition, COP meetings, unreliable mainstream media, daze, deceit, wars, genocide supported by the hegemonic leader of the Western so-called democracies gliding into fascist practices, atomic power and weapons propaganda, hydrogen fantasia, ... transformations are urgent to avoid hell in era3.

Due are three major mutually reinforcing transformations: mind-vision; energy-technology; socio-politics. Such comprehensive scope implies that all sciences, disciplines, practices, peoples' experiences have to work together to realise the overall transformation to a promising era3, with bounded climate change and pleasant living conditions for the many.

Transformation implies supersession of an old identity and the acquisition of a new one[18]. The new is irreconcilable with the old. Era3 is a tabula rasa of the era2 inequalities and annihilation of Earth's living systems. Era3 is non-continuation of the energy uses, politics, lifestyles and visions of era2.

Transformation is qualitatively different from transition.Transition is anchored at Business-as-Usual, with discussed adaptations too little, too late. Transformation is ignited and expanded by spearhead action breaching neoliberal fortress walls. Three mutually reinforcing transformations are mind-vision; energy-technology; socio-politics.

- Mind-Vision: The *power of the word*[19] drives out neoliberal daze, lies, deceit. Paradigms are systems' fundaments, of shared social agreements about the nature of reality[20], focal points for human strivings and the basis for effective—not only proclaimed—values[21].
- Energy-Technology: Renewable electricity drives out fossil and atomic fuels. The spearhead is people-owned electricity from ambient light, wind, water, geothermal

flows. Grassroots renewable electricity bears socio-political agency in new community systems. Rejecting and burying the obsolete technologies and practices of neoliberalism implies an *enormous degrowth* in capital and material intensive processes, and embracing all new *effective and sustainable* technologies and practices.

- Socio-Politics: Sustainable Development (SD) drives out neoliberalism. SD is the future human-societal edifice, constructed by enterprising women and men. Neoliberalism becomes irrelevant by destroying its *pillars* and dismantling its *attributes*.

Transformations occur by necessity to avoid harm and by will to attain favourable goals. *Necessity* is due to the fast, irreversible increase of global warming. *Will* is related to the majority's advantages of a mild climate and of Sustainable Development.

Panel 5
Mind-Vision Paradigms

Caption

Mind-vision is the first to address leverage point[22] in transformation processes. Intervening in systems at the level of the paradigm hits a leverage point that totally transforms systems. There is nothing necessarily physical or expensive or even slow in the process of paradigm change. In a single individual it can happen in a millisecond. All it takes is a click in the mind, a falling of scales from eyes, a new way of seeing. Whole societies are another matter. They resist challenges to their paradigm more strongly than they resist anything else. Donella Meadows refers to Thomas Kuhn[23] for answers to the question *how do you change paradigms?*

Ideas affect a person's mind, vision, motivation, attitude to speak and to act. Ideas as myth, narrative, ideology, paradigm frame political constellations. Immaterial ideas range from ephemeral to lifelong, yet mindsets are changeable.

Paradigms are the foundation and legitimation of socio-economic systems. Adoption of paradigms by people and societies is voluntary, mimetically spontaneous, enforced. Since 1980, neoliberalism has expanded its reign from the US and UK to most of the world. Money, economic growth, and inequality dominate peoples' lives.

Superrich clans and corporations wield uncontrolled power shrouded in myths. Like the rhetoric of *free markets, there is no alternative, cheap fossil fuels, life in outer space, ...*

Neoclassical economics is a *theoretical utopia* that conceals politics wasting diversity[24]. Present economies are highly biased by virtue of counting private expenses only. The more important public costs and benefits are deliberately obscured by Big Money. Exemplary cheap fossil fuels talk, while irreversible climate change entails immense costs.

Salient neglects of public costs are depletion, pollution, degradation, destruction, extinction. Exemplary is littering the Atmosphere with greenhouse gases, atomic and chemical particles; Oceans and seas with plastics, oil spills, effluents; Outer space with discarded objects.

GHG emission is *Gaseous Litter*, as it is discarded into the environment without care. This genuine definition reframes the assumed privileges, responsibilities and duties. Legality requires litterers stop littering, to clean up litter, to compensate for its impacts.

Imagine the Rio Summit in 1992 had adopted the genuine GHG definition with its legal impact. The Conferences of Parties (COPs) record would differ from day to night caused by neoliberalism

Panel 6
Energy-Technology transformation

Caption

Without energy there is no life, nor living. Energy is an indispensable substrate of human activities and civilisations. Civilisation Era1 was based on renewable energy; Era2 extracts ever more fossil fuels from the Earth; Era3 will again be entirely based on renewable energy with electricity for commercial supplies[25]. Advanced technologies in electronics, new materials, data analysis, communication, etc. are instrumental in converting *free energy* from the Sun and Earth to commercially available energy, in particular electricity, being as it is the highest quality of all possible energy forms.

Energy use is indispensable in every activity of living beings, as well of human beings. All energy on Earth comes from free solar, atmospheric and terrestrial sources. In Era3, *electricity* is the substitute for fossil and atomic fuels[26].

In the 1880s the generation of electricity, the king of energies, began: top quality, clean, useful for all valuable and peaceful applications. Not so for the unsustainable, imperial lifestyles of the wealthy.

Every year now, fossil fuels for generating electricity cause 18 billion tons of CO_2 emissions[27]. Fossil and atomic fuels cook water or heat gases to drive turbines for generating electricity. Such technology requires expensive and risky fuel cycles and discards emissions and waste[28].

Since 2018, solar light and wind flows have generated the cheapest electric kWh ever. Technology makes small-scale renewable electricity plants tremendously cheap[29].

In Era3, renewable electricity meets the commercial energy needs for the global citizenry. Urgent full conversion to renewable electricity merits priority in investment decisions. Since the 1990s, grassroots initiatives in Germany and Denmark have shown the way.

In 2014, villainous European energy corporates lobbied EU commissioner Joaquín Almunia. He allowed state aid for large-scale wind at sea and PV fields, and for atomic power. This coup jeopardised grassroots initiatives, and delayed the urgently needed energy-technology transformation.

Blocking and sabotaging the fast and full roll-out of local renewable electricity is criminal. Hindering deployment of small-scale renewable electricity plants is irrational.

Technology and real economics counting all costs can deliver *abundant low-cost kWh*. They are incredibly strong fundaments for Sustainable Development by communities.Renewable electricity generation can be deployed *fast* and in *all communities* of the world. It can offer energy security for all inhabitants of the world. In this way it is the most crucial factor in ending the use of fossil fuels.

Electricity is *top quality* energy. Electricity is used *efficiently* in various applications for numerous ends. Renewable electricity is the *spearhead substitute* for fossil and atomic fuels. Renewable electricity means *natural degrowth* by closing thermal power plants.

Electricity is not suited to long-distance transport by aviation or ocean-borne shipping. Electricity falls short in driving fighter planes, aircraft carriers, and other war machinery. Exclusive use of electricity matches a peaceful world of exchange and cooperation.

Panel 7
Socio-Politics: Hazards of Neoliberalism

Caption

Neoliberalism is the extremist version of liberalism. It renounces the positive liberal values on liberty[30] and human dignity; it deforms crucial attributes such as free markets, private property, appropriate rewarding of entrepreneurship and dedicated engagement. Oligopoly and monopoly corporates skim huge super-profits. Big Money operates an opaque financial machinery, with tax havens whitewashing criminal money. Federal reserves and national banks make common people pay for the greed of financial clans (2008 financial crisis).

While the word neoliberalism is frequently used, a common understanding of what neoliberalism precisely covers is not fixed. For more clarity in the fight to make neoliberalism irrelevant, the attributes and pillars of neoliberalism are defined. This is followed by a briefing on the neoliberal Breakthroughs 1 and 2.

Attributes

A1. Financial power, concentrated in giant corporates and superrich clans, dominates over *subservient politicians* in making *strategic* socio-economic choices.

A2. *Profit-driven economic growth* fosters the superrich fortunes, while destroying precarious ecological systems and planetary boundaries.

A3. Deep inequalities are accepted as *normal* phenomena; social justice is not a case of societal and political duty.

Pillars

P1. Intensive and unlimited use of fossil fuels in industrialised and industrialising countries, by companies, governments, the military, and wealthy citizens.

P2. Big Money has direct control over large money flows and accumulated fortunes, and influences money creation.

P3. Rampant *discursive power* to spread the neoliberal ideology in the Global North via media concerns, and imposed on the Global South.

Annex: Neoliberal Breakthroughs 1 & 2

Neoliberal Breakthrough 1

In 1971, the US affirmed its hegemony by imposing a lopsided US-dollar regime on the world. The 1973, 9/11 US instigated coup in Chile opened an experimental field for neoliberal recipes. In the 1970s, the post WW2 *Welfare State* in Europe and in the US arrived on the slippery slope towards breakdown. Corporates and Big Money have subdued politics fully since Reagan (US, 1981–88) and Thatcher (UK, 1979–90). The *Limits to Growth* 1972-warning is reviled and negated with debased talk about dauntless economic growth solving the huge problems created already by earlier smaller economic growth. The fall-out of Breakthrough1 is today's state of nature, climate, environment and society.

Neoliberal Breakthrough 2

The 2001, 9/11 attacks on the World Trade Center and the Pentagon, symbols of financial and military power, were met with a response from the US neoliberal cloud. The immediate US response was endless *War on Terror* against an enemy whose nature, number, and location were largely unknown. The policy was packed in predominantly Christian mythology, summoning the US citizenry as participants in a sacrament of unity and in a crusade to *rid the world of evil*[31]. Preemptive war was put into practice against Afghanistan (2001), Iraq (2003), Libya (2011), and Iran (2025). In 2022, the US reconfirmed its hegemonic power via the US-dollar regime, the submission of its allies, the isolation of Russia, and the incessant support for Israel's Apartheid and genocide in Palestine. Atomic power and hydrogen are heavily subsidised, despite having been proven to be clumsy technologies. They augment the problems instead of contributing to solutions[32]. Breakthrough 2 surfs on the talk that *there is no alternative to neoliberalism*, while it is an irrational abolishment of the *ultimate chance* for human survival on Earth.

Managed democracy and Totalitarianism[33] are everyday more visible. Ending and fully rejecting neoliberalism and its Breakthrough 2 push is crucial for humanity.

Room B: Neoliberalism irrelevant by Emptied substance & Removed pillars

Panel 8
Remove the neoliberal fossil fuel pillar

Caption

When some object that another energy future is impossible, think of the smartphone: an absolute impossibility at the beginning of this century turned into a ubiquitous device within a decade. Quantum physics, nanotechnology, micro-electronics, information and communication for bottom-up system control, new materials, photovoltaics, power electronics, batteries, conversions of electricity into radiation such as LED, laser, microwave, ... support the transformations.

Next to fossil fuels, it is worth being attentive to other extractions of Earth's treasures, such as water, metal and nonmetal minerals, forests, etc., in particular when they play a role in the replacement of fossil fuels. This book is focused on spearhead policies to address climate change as priority #1.

Extracting, shipping, and processing fossil fuels and uranium is unduly risky and expensive. Electricity from light, wind, water, and geothermal currents is incredibly safe and cheap. Electricity is *top-quality energy*, efficiently convertible for many end-uses without emissions. Electricity is not apt to serve megalomaniacal follies like space travel, predatory wars, etc. One billion wealthy people are addicted to fossil fuels, especially to petroleum derivatives.

Seven billion other people spend a significant part of their income on fossil and other fuels. More than half of humans on Earth can barely afford a small consumption of fossil fuels. Many inequalities among human beings are interwoven with unequal access to fossil fuels. Dissolving fossil fuel use is part of dissolving inequality.

In the years to come, renewable electricity stands in for practically all commercial energy. Generating technologies are available, applicable, and affordable, when realised bottom up.

People's electricity in communities is indispensable for terminating fossil fuels.

Small-scale distributed generation is affordable for all communities in the world. It is manageable by households, small companies, cooperatives and local authorities.

Energy autonomy is a firm foundation for community governance. *Global applicability* is essential for mastering the climate crises.

In poor settlements, all-time availability of electricity will be suboptimal by Western standards. Yet, every renewable kWh is progress, without liabilities in health and pollution.

Abundance of electricity supply from redundant PV capacities is the likely future. Redundancy will be a tricky, luxury problem for regulators in avoiding grid congestion.

Nature delivers the currents for generating renewable electricity; humans adapt. New electricity economics theory substitutes for the merit order of fuel driven generation[34]. The so-called electricity market disappears, as do negative prices of electricity.

Panel 9
Bring private Big Money under public agency

Caption

Money is used for multiple purposes with either good or bad ends: exchange of goods & services, savings, credit, capital accumulation, power to influence and control political processes, extortion of people, creating deep inequality. The distributions of property, and income and spending, are heavily skewed. A minority of people owns most money, hence the majority owns least. About half of the global population does not obtain the *ethical living minimum income* for buying the goods & services needed for a decent life.

Making neoliberalism irrelevant implies democratic authorities creating new financial systems for Sustainable Development. It will be necessary to *use the computer* to delete the happy few fortunes at banks, exchanges, tax havens, and islands with exotic names. The neoliberal economy will crash: *So, what?* For the survival of humanity on Earth, crashing neoliberalism is a blessing.

Money is an *agreement within a community* to use something as a medium of exchange[35]. Once, communities conceived money as a tool for easier exchange and credit for public projects. A monetary system only functions when the citizenry has *trust in the currency*. Generalised trust is a crucial aspect of functioning societies and economies.

Monarchs and private oligarchs capture the money tool for accumulation and wielding power. Nowadays, the fully institutionalised monetary systems are exploited for power and extortion.

Small money differs from Big Money. Small money is earned by personal diligence or is assigned by communities. Small money is used for buying goods & services, savings, repayments of credit, gifts, ...

Private Big Money thrives on super-profits, subsidies, speculation, intrigues, crime, ...Big Money extracts natural and public treasures, and squeezes workers and consumers. Big Money masterminds politics, and financial institutions, including national banks.

Small and Big money are intertwined. Big Money greed caused the 2008 banking crisis, divulging: *Big Money leans on small money*. Federal reserves, national banks created US$ billions of new money by *using the computer*[36]. Fraudulent private financial banks received the created money, enriching the wealthy top layer.

The deficit crisis of public budgets is called in to load the burdens on to common people. Official financial *neutrality* is hiding the gradual impoverishment of people.

Public democratic control of the monetary systems is necessary, desirable and possible. When *using the computer* works for creating money, it can also work for annihilating money.

Modern Monetary Theory[37]

Money's principal duty is supporting economic activities for the public good of the communities. To this end, public authorities create the appropriate quantities of money, disregarding deficits. Prioritising the common good is only conclusive if the public authority is monetarily sovereign. The trusted currency is not dependent on gold, nor on foreign currencies beyond control.

Local currencies enhance community sovereignty and autonomy, preventing gentrification. Community monetary systems are pushing back the US$-dominated financial world. Such push back will deflate US hegemonic power and military adventures. A more peaceful world is on the horizon when neoliberalism is dissolved.

Panel 10
Debunk neoliberal ideology & discourse

Caption

In the history of mankind there are plenty examples of the influential role of ideas, myths, symbols, images, language, narratives, discourses, ideology, paradigms, ... to *exert influence and obtain legitimacy* for actions, institutions, distributions of property and wealth. In present times, the role of ideas is exceptionally important. Next to legal, executive, and juridical powers, the media are seen as the fourth power with a significant and enduring impact on major sections of society. Neoliberalism uses discursive power in various ways to the detriment of democracy. Sheldon Wolin, Mark Fischer, Chris Hedges, Noam Chomsky, and many other authors have addressed the dangerous evolutions and practices.

Ideas, narratives, and paradigms are factors of high leverage to *maintain* or *transform* systems. Lobbies and media sicken human thought with *there is no alternative to capitalism*[38]. Capitalism is proposed as the only system compatible with *human nature* and *economic law*. This deceiving falsehood is based on a perverted human nature and biased economics.

Big Money imposes a pervasive sense of exhaustion, of cultural and political sterility. Neoliberal ideology precludes all mindsets beyond business interests and having money. Never-ending propaganda conceals the deep gaps between ideology and reality.

Lobbyism booms in Washington, Brussels, State capitals, administrations, universities, ... At the end of 2022, Qatari money corrupted EU parliamentarians, followed by media outrage. Why is there no outrage about the continuous huge lobbyism by corporates and Big Money? Why do the media support and praise the outcomes of lobbyism, like EU's Green Deal? What explains the media's constancy in supporting the products of lobbyism and deceit?

Delusive truth is far more effective than blunt fake news. Delusion is built on a truth, like Archimedes lifting the Earth on the lever mechanism. E=mc2 is a physical truth; atomic power is an expensive, risky, unethical delusion. CO2-free H2 combusting is true; fake hydrogen economy means life extension of fossil fuels.

The triptych *Renewable Energy, Nuclear Power, Carbon Capture & Storage (RE, NP, CCS)*: Juxtaposition of incompatible options pervasive in official climate policy talk. Nuclear power and redundant renewable electricity conflict and are mutually exclusive. Atmospheric CO_2 was reduced by natural CCS creating hydrocarbons over millions of years. Mechanical CCS is cumbersome and expensive, seldom applied, and is much talk without walk.

The triptych Planet, People, Profit is a flawed reduction of Sustainable Development. Neoliberalism cancels the central P of Politics, including Public Policies, Participation, Peace.

Refusing to characterise GHG emissions as *gaseous litter* [panel 5]. Neoclassical economists state: *present generations reducing GHG emissions bring offers*. The truth is: by polluting the atmosphere, present generations capture amoral privileges.

Panel 11
Local self-governance is the condition
for real democracy

Caption

Wiping out corporates and superrich clans dominating society via *obedient politicians* can only be realised by means of local self-governance in cities and communities. The pioneering experiments in the Global South (e.g., Zapatistas in Mexico) merit generalisation, also in the Global North. The episodic and fleeting popular political interventions[39] can be solidified by local ownership of the least-cost energy supplies. Information and communication technology is available, while know-how capabilities are widespread across communities. Peoples' trust is the Achilles heel of a currency, and can annihilate the digital billions of Big Money.

The main passions motivating human activities are *money, power, prestige, and knowledge*[40]. *Whoever wields power controls money. Whoever controls money wields power*[41]. The outcomes of the catch-22 money versus power depend on contextual factors.

In the context of ongoing neoliberalism, money commands power[42]. Big Money and corporate strategic socio-economic interests are served by obedient politicians. Nonetheless, the Achilles heel of money is the *trust of citizens* in the currency. The trust will evaporate on the evidence that money is *impotent* against climate change.

In an exceptional context like the 2008 financial crisis, political power presides over money. In 2008, Big Money and subservient politicians abused the trust of a passive citizenry. While ideologically excoriating the state, neoliberalism surreptitiously relies on the state[43].

In a democracy, public goods and good life for all are ranked above private greed. National banks best use the computer to eliminate digital private Big Money.

Large investments in crucial public goods & services are financed by public credit. Cities and local communities create complementary currencies for local goods & services. Money for local exchanges and community projects mitigates poverty and gentrification.

Renewable electricity is locally generated by households, cooperatives, public companies. Energy disappears as a vehicle for super-profits, war-mongering, extortion of common people. Owning energy is a firm basis for wealthy local economies in the Global North and South. Energy ownership is a prerequisite for the robustness of societal transformations.

Emancipatory ideas emerge because neoliberalism cannot create alternatives. Climate change facts break up neoliberal ideology and parasite bureaucracies. Critical thinking dissolves delusive truths, lobbyism, deceit media, and money as a vice guide. Invigorated women and men are the diligent agents for a democratic community.

Local authorities delegate duties and means to coordinating levels, counties to states. The goal is not to take over the state but to subordinate the state to the grassroots' will.

From a situation in which nothing can happen, suddenly anything is possible again[44]. New living conditions boost participation and socio-psychological well-being.

Feasibility and robustness of democratic local governance are guaranteed by novel solutions: Technological swaps from material-intense mechanics to light electronics at nano scale. Nano sciences provide cheap performant photovoltaics, power electronics, batteries, ... Smartphones, www, AI, ... for Information and Communication at local and global scale.

Liberated from neoliberal irrationality, human capital can flourish for the common good. Intellectual capabilities are enhanced by joining people's wisdom with modern inventions. Understanding and know-how spreading over communities allows people to dominate politics[45].

Panel 12
Sufficiency against neoliberal growth spillage

Caption

Sufficiency and economic degrowth are not new ideas. In 1881, John Stuart Mill discussed the concept of a stationary state of the economy. In 1972, *Limits to Growth* boosted environmental consciousness in the post-war world. Since 1972, Herman Daly[46] advocated the steady-state economy with a broad range of arguments, such as population growth control and resource scarcity as requisite themes in the 1960s-70s, distributional justice, and moral growth [panel 13]. By virtue of their imperial mode of living, the GHG emissions of the richest 1% account for more than twice the emissions of the poorest 50%. The elite will need to reduce their footprint by a factor of at least 30.

Sufficiency indicates a mode of living pursued for realising Sustainable Development. Lifestyles between deprivation and excess imply lower and upper consumption limits. Democratic institutions can set, monitor and enforce specific limits.

Limits to human behaviour and related activities are standard in ethical communities. Frugality is a main component of sustainability[47]. It requires a discernment of the distinctions between needs and wants.

Economic growth enriching Big Money and corporates hides the *wreckage of previous growth*. Growth expands resource extractions and littering of land, water, air, and outer space. Amoral neoliberal growth opposing Sustainable Development is socio-economically irrational[48].

For example, depending on massive quantities of fossil fuels are:

• The military apparatus for aggressive wars.
• Long-distance transport by aviation and ocean-borne shipping.
• Abuse of outer space.
• The imperial mode of living of the wealthy, superrich and their slipstream.

Vigorous mitigation holds major challenges to its political and societal implementation. In the 1970s, ecological, economic and ethical arguments promoted *steady state* economics[49].
Western degrowth advocacy as a response to neoliberal growth

is received with mixed feelings. Developing countries defend their rights to *economic growth for the elimination of poverty*[50]. Promising degrowth narratives in general, as an end in itself, are not very persuasive.

Beneficial scaling down particular socio-economic activities is *natural* degrowth. Stopping fossil fuel extraction and use is a significant reduction of wasteful activities. Rejecting the atomic power and hydrogen energy delusive truths is a further scaling down. Talk about expensive transformations is hardcore deceit; an artificial barrier to sustainability.

Renewable electricity generation by small-scale personal or community owned plants is efficient. Substituting *renewable electricity* for fossil fuels fully transforms economic activities. Next to low expenses, the real costs of renewable electricity are low and manageable. No heavy heritage of depletion, pollution, extinction and radioactive waste is left over.

Panel 13
Social justice as political priority

Caption

Inequality is a primary indicator of a society's insanity. The wealthy corporates and clans will not cure the dysfunctions of inequality. Except for a few odd cases, the first goal of too-rich people is to get richer. Private Big Money has to be liquidated [panel 9]. Governance by people at the grassroots with a firm ethical compass is the way to turn over the neoliberal course. UNESCO and the *World Commission on the Ethics of Scientific Knowledge and Technology*[51] offer thoughtful insight and recommendations, further developed in academia[52].

Neoliberalism based on greed and conflict is the opposite of ethical human cooperation. To address climate change, cooperation is due in adaptation and mitigation. For both fields, scientists have defined principles for advancing ethical approaches.

For adaptation, the main principles are: *avoiding harm, fairness in the distribution of burdens and benefits, equitable access to medical, scientific and technological developments, the moral solidarity of humankind, and environmental sustainability.*

Fairness assigns special consideration to the poorest countries and people. People causing few GHG emissions are most adversely affected by climate change[53]. Being least responsible, they face great vulnerability and direct exposure to climate change.

Mitigation requires vigorous policy with justice as a central concern. Given that GHG emissions are rising, climate activists insist on deep and urgent cuts. The intensity of GHG emissions reduction is mainly an ethical question[54].

Global justice is one of ten ethical principles proposed for climate change mitigation[55]. Fairness in health, education, and economic opportunity for poor countries and people. Dignity and justice, non-discrimination and equality for each and every human being[56]. All nations have ethical duties and a legal responsibility to avoid harming others.

Migrants engendered by climate hazards begin to demand their human rights. Climate migrants will flood the gates of fortunate populations living in temperate regions[57].

Intellectual and moral solidarity of humankind by cooperation of the *peoples of the world*. Human fate and destiny reach beyond national boundaries, gender, age and ethnicities. Solidarity is an ethical foundation for responsibilities according to affordability and needs.

Resilience lead communities and cities[58] towards self-organisation and feedback mechanisms, resolving climate-related problems at various levels, but most effectively at the local level. Renewable energy offers security of energy supply to the whole world. Renewable energy is *a sine qua non* condition for humanity and the environment.

The UNESCO ethical imperatives challenge prevailing political and economic systems. Revise current worldviews and perspectives for a considerate and caring human community. Distinguish subsistence from luxury GHG emissions, and restrict the latter more stringently[59]. Mandated energy conservation officiously includes steps towards more equity.

Poor countries' financial debts preclude *ethical living minimum incomes*[60] for the world's poor. There is no way that today's international debt overhang can be repaid. That is as true for the United States as it is for Global South debtors. Deliberate dismantling of the financial bomb is better than suffering its explosion.

Room C: The triangle
Nature – Individuals – Communities

Nature's sources make living feasible. The free sources are forthcoming from the Sun and Earth's atmosphere, water, and land. Astonishing biodiversity, *the variability among organisms and other ecosystems and the ecological complexes of which they are a part*, has made Earth a uniquely habitable place for humans. They created cultural diversity as *the manifold ways in which the cultures of groups and societies find expression. These expressions are passed on within and among groups and societies*[61]. As long as human beings consider themselves a natural part of nature with respect for all other parts and for ethical principles, harmonious co-habitation of humans with nature and among peoples is possible.

However, some populations did and do pursue supremacy over nature and over other populations. Supremacy and superiority at industrial scale is significantly harming nature and biodiversity. Once nature is no longer able to fully assimilate the harms, they cause deteriorating impacts. *Irreversible* impacts destroy *the ability to maintain and to restore the functional performance of systems*[62], which are crucial for sustainable life conditions. Climate Change is one such irreversible impact. Figure 18 is a schematic view of human society as a metabolism embedded in Nature. Free sources such as high-quality matter and energy are delivered by Nature, converted for peoples' ends, and the low-quality residuals are discarded to Nature's Sinks.

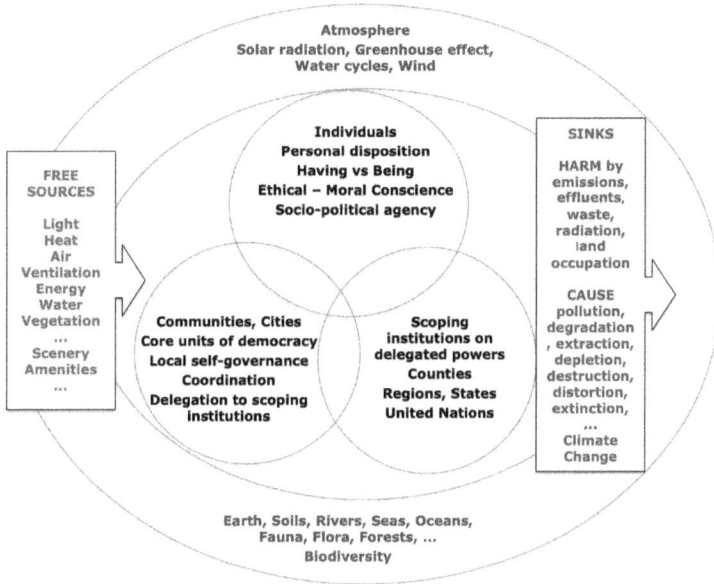

Figure 18: Nature encloses and supports all life on Earth.

Fundamental changes in the *mankind-nature relationship* are a prerequisite, a sine qua non, for addressing climate change, loss in biodiversity, loss of life quality for the majority, and more.

The human disposition of being exploiter and master over nature and over other humans, needs to be reversed to *respecter and associate of nature and fellow humans.* The reversal will be reflected in its use of energy sources, in lifestyle change from imperial to frugal, in decreasing inequality among people. The order: *first Nature – then mankind* is a necessity for a sustainable future. If the now dominating groups and ideologists think the suggested reversal is soft-headed, their self-deceit will end when climate change unchains the incredible power of Nature, devastating their artifacts. The supremacy over Nature belief is an illusion with fatal consequences.

Panel 14
Nature: climate change and ethics

Caption

It is outside the scope of the book to describe here the unmeasurable extent, depth and diversity of Nature's role in the life of all humans. The focus is on climate change and ethics, creating a direct link to mankind's activities and disposition.

The Sun and Earth created the Atmosphere and mild climate, Nature and copious biodiversity. Humans, a creature of biodiversity, assigned holiness to Air, Water, Land, and Fire-Energy[63]. Homo sapiens emerged as a unique species developing practical mental capabilities. Myths helped the formation of peaceful communities[64], albeit warring with other tribes. Religions and ideologies framed states governing several communities and tribes.

Humans' foraging transited to agriculture, exploiting carbon beyond replacement[65]. Stored surplus harvests generated expansive hierarchies, armies, profound social inequality. Learning evolved to craftmanship, industrialism, technological bursts in today's Anthropocene. Industrial success is based on wild exploitation of Nature. The related huge costs are deliberately neglected by the beneficiaries of industrialism.

The exploitation implies *corporate colonialism* towards the global South. *Nature is commodified as natural capital*, and submitted to the financial greed of corporates. The practices, packed as *nature-based solutions*, mostly override indigenous interests[66].

Neoliberalism is a socio-economic, ethical failure by its destruction of crucial life supports. Claiming masterdom over nature is highly destructive and amounts to self-deceit. *Irreversible loss* means *eternal wrecking* of unique natural systems and amenities.

Application of the Precautionary Principle[67] intends to preclude irreversibility. Act anticipatory to avoid morally unacceptable, scientifically plausible but uncertain harm. Unacceptable harm is inequitably imposed and is threatening to human life and health.

Sustainability assessment informs decisions on *go/no go* for proposed technologies or projects. Appropriately responding to the challenges of climate change faces common obstacles[68], like:

- Priority given to short-term social consequences, prejudice and bias, cognitive constraints;

- Inappropriate methods of cost-benefit analysis, financial discounting and impact assessment.

Integer assessment requires reliable, independent experts, public inputs and deliberation. Mandating full indemnity insurance on risky projects is a *better safe than sorry* approach.

The integrity of scientific research on climate change is pervaded by uncertainty[69]. Science provides the consensus of experts' scrutiny of accumulated evidence, yet no certainty.

The important societal impact of climate science asks for *good science*, and *ethical criteria*. Essential ethical values are integrity, truth, and respect for reasoned argument and evidence.

Only ethical science can have and must have a moral impact on human society.

Panel 15
Individuals – Personal Disposition

Caption

The Universal Declaration of Human Rights is recalled, while being aware of the little actual respect for it nowadays. Inequality in property and income is revealed by gaps between the state of inhabitants in the present world: of 100, ten are too rich, twenty own adequate means, sixty are too poor. Inequality is the lead cause of littering by GHG emissions. Inequality hinders measures to address climate change adaptation and mitigation, and affects the personal disposition of individuals, with the rich ones mostly *living in denial* of the dangers.

Recognising the inherent dignity and the equal and inalienable rights of all humans, being a foundation of freedom, justice and peace in the world[70]. Individual rights are entirely valid without distinction of any kind, such as race, colour, sex, language, religion, political or other opinion, national or social origin, property, birth or other status. Today's actual implementation of the Universal Declaration of Human Rights is disappointing.

Most rich people are infected by neoliberal ideology, and addicted to an imperial mode of living. High income people, well informed and concerned about climate change, *live in Denial*[71]. Their GHG emissions remain high, despite awareness triggering personal actions and gifts. The demand for luxury goods and frequent flying is not affected by uniform financial tax policy.

Energy corporates shift the culpability for climate change to consumers of oil and gas. Uniform carbon taxes or emissions trading are falsely described as problem-solving policies. The burdens of applied financial instruments ultimately land at the purses of common people.

Uniform financial instruments discriminate when property and income are unequal. Neoclassical economics are a cloak for the generalised political defection on climate policy.

Citizens, individually and in groups, have to address climate change. A complacent personal attitude is often argued by pointing to others with a similar attitude.

"My impact is as tiny as a drop in the ocean" and *"If I abstain, others will fill the gap"*, to be rebutted by: *"I act because my*

contribution cannot be missed in reaching the crucial goal."

In an individual context, a considered mindset can suddenly emanate. All it takes is a click in the mind, a falling of scales from eyes, a new way of seeing[72]. YOU as a human being can swap fast.

Problematic is generalising this swapping to cover all of society. No longer stumbling forward, but now pointing at the anomalies and failures of neoliberalism. See the essence of the global society's sustainable future, spell out the steps to reach it.

Keep speaking louder and with assurance from the new world. Skip reactionaries. Find active change agents and the vast middle ground of people who are open-minded[73].

The global majority of humans are dissatisfied and want change up to transformation, through fear of climate collapse and war, poverty, socio-economic opportunity, dignity, will, ...

Individual characters balance tendencies towards *to have* and *to be* living modes[74]. The *To have* mode is characterised by an insatiable desire for wealth, power, and status. *To be* fosters relationships, creativity, free personal growth, and critical reasoning.

Which of *both possible modes* becomes dominant or repressed depends on the *societal context*. Societal structures prioritise either material gain or genuine human fulfilment.

The experience of *sharing* makes and keeps the relation between individuals alive. Sharing is the basis of all great religious, political, and philosophical *movements*. Local self-governance for Sustainable Development is the great era3 movement.

Be part of the positive era3 movement!

Panel 16
Communities – Societies

Caption

Grassroots people and community power are known from pioneer projects and episodic successes. In 1975, inhabitants of Wyhl, nearby villages and Freiburg im Breisgau initiated bottom-up renewable energy development in Europe. Social scientists[75] have contributed to community self-governance by spelling out their constitution, conditions and criteria of performance in multi-level contexts. Socio-political transformation for a human era3 will advance along the crumbling of neoliberalism to irrelevance. Today's political institutes and bureaucracies will undergo transformations.

Rebellion against atomic plant building at the Upper-Rhine started in Wyhl-Freiburg in 1975. The community's initiatives started the development of renewable energy in Germany[76]. The Wyhl-Freiburg protesters were scientifically and technologically forward looking. They debunked the myth of neutral expertise and exposed the pro-nuclear coalition interests. They created expertise in technical, socio-economic and local governance matters.

The community was a catalyst for solar technologies and sustainable business practices. In the 1970s, energy corporates trampled renewable energy developments and projects. In 2014, via a coup, the corporates captured the technologies for large scale applications.

Community self-organisation enhances resilience in climate change adaptation and mitigation. Resilience measures the ability of individuals and local communities to bounce back. Resilience is constituted by the cultural and spiritual reservoir of peoples[77]. Agency by necessity can turn into agency by will and purpose.

Elinor Ostrom[78] pioneered in the study of how *self-governance* works in local communities. How sovereign individuals cooperate bottom up is a matter of commitment and methodology[79]. Equilibrated balancing between own contributions and acquired benefits is a crucial factor. Clear appropriate rules, credible commitments, and mutual monitoring are due.

Government refers to formal state institutions and their power to decide and enforce decisions. Governance[80] refers to conditions for ordered collective action, also by self-organising networks. Main criteria are: participatory, consensual, transparent, responsive, equitable, inclusive. A legitimate, coherent, trustworthy governance system is *owned* by all, especially local actors[81]. *Public service* implies responsibility and accountability for performant local organisations.

Separate governance levels are intertwined and networked in a marbled multi-level context. A culture of local governance implies more engagement, participation and voice by citizens. Local governance becomes increasingly different and distinctive from central governance, by means of excellence in the supply and use of renewable electricity locally generated.

Engagement and *participation* in local governance allow for more direct democracy. Democratic governance and trust are mutually conditional. The three trustworthiness bases are ability, integrity, and benevolence[82]. With such bases, Sustainable Development can materialise as a socio-political reality.

In 2025, managed democracy and inverted totalitarianism[83] prevail in the Global North. The US top-down *democracy incorporated* has metamorphosed into a totalitarian regime. The regime's pursuit of world hegemony is slightly veiled by propaganda and myths. Pre-emptive war entails the projection of power abroad, usually against a far weaker country[84].

Hypocrisy accepts criminal acts of Western hegemonic power of the US, NATO allies, and Israel. Murdering unarmed citizens and children in occupied land is daily practice of the Israeli military. As with the Nazi regime, international law and organisations are negated and trampled.

The political challenges are incredibly big and dangerous. Only grassroots power can and will fight human extinction. The driving force is creating millions of local governance systems all over the world. They are effective and robust by fitting personal disposition and technological evolution.

Panel 17
Bypass the dooming hell to shape paradise

Caption

In 1987 the WCED proposed Sustainable Development as the way to address the two major post-war problems: environmental destruction and unequal development. Since 1990, the scientific evidence about global warming has been available, clear and instructive. The then predictions of expected climate change impacts by climatologists are nowadays visible all over the globe. Neoliberal prophets and captains mocked the warnings and overruled the sustainability options. Their lip service to Planet-People-Profit is a façade for increased extraction, litter, destruction, and inequality. Every year since, the guilty negligence caused tens of billion of tons of greenhouse gas emissions and irreversible higher concentration in the atmosphere [figure 1].

The average ambient temperature on Earth is rising abruptly. Biodiversity deteriorates through shrinking and parcelled habitats, and species extinctions. Generous nature, a gentle climate, astonishing landscapes, and pleasant amenities dwindle. Human instigated natural calamities multiply. Conflicts and wars intensify.

Countries once known as democracies today meet all criteria typifying a totalitarian regime. Inequality wrecks the soundness of humankind. Poverty below ethical living minimum income deprives development for billions of poor people. In wealthy countries, greed, loneliness, fear, and obesity intensify the loss of happiness[85].

The physical, social, political, and mental state of the world is at worst caused by many factors. Global warming and climate change are singled out as irreversible, global, kindling threat. The primary life support systems for human living and comfort are increasingly devastated.

Such features urge unrelenting spearhead policies to stop the warming. The spears are directed at the use of fossil fuels, a crucial pillar of neoliberalism. This implies frontal confrontations with Big Money and corporates. Vigorous public agency dilutes private Big Money, and debunks neoliberal ideology and myths.

The spears are operated by growing numbers of common people, your neighbours. They know their lives and the futures of their children and grandchildren are in danger. Extinction of the human species is likely, as numerous other species have been extinguished. Agency by necessity may turn into agency by purpose and will.

Ending fossil fuel use requires replacement by other energy options. The 1950s-60s claim of atomic power as a cheap, safe, and abundant substitute failed. Due to its inherent properties, hydrogen is a vain alternative.

Renewable electricity can be generated from natural flows light, wind, water, geothermal. Nanotechnology raises the performance and decreases the costs of photovoltaics and wind. Already now, small-scale technologies deliver the cheapest electric kWh ever seen.

Electricity is clean top-quality energy. It is efficiently convertible into many energy applications. Being a current, storage requires conversion and equipment like batteries or hydro reservoirs. Electricity is not fit for long-distance aviation and shipping, nor for war or space littering.

Exclusive use of electricity entails a stop to neoliberal waste and immorality. Renewable electricity is *a sine qua non* condition for the environment, because a stable mild climate is *a sine qua non* condition for humanity[86].

Locally generated, free renewable electricity is a solid basis for socio-economic activities. Grassroots techno-economic power supports socio-political transformations. No persons and no disciplines are excluded in realising the three major transformations. When joining the many in a strong lamination, all blows are resisted and hindrances overcome.

Neoliberal drift towards the abyss is left by grassroots pioneers creating surges for survival. The mission is fast multiplication of the surges globally, and their gradual connection.

Panel 18
Farewell – Scripta sunt

This book is offered as a tiny redemption for climate change caused by post-war wealthy people. I belong to that group. Travelling all over the world created a significant historical carbon debt.

Post-2000 research has alienated me from mainstream economics and politics. Due to its independence and integrity, neoliberal media have silenced my work since 2020[87]. Fortunately, I enjoyed the imposed exile position. It offered undisturbed time and vantage points beyond daily turmoil.

May I recommend to you a visit to the *Apocalypse* & *Le Chant du Monde* tapestries in Angers[88].

Bibliography

Ackerman, B.A. and Stewart, R.B. (1988). Reforming environmental law: The democratic case for market incentives, *Columbia Journal of Environmental Law* 13: 171-199.

Ajl, M. (2021). A People's Green New Deal. London: Pluto Press.

Amblard, P. (2017). Saint Jean l'Apocalypse. Traduction de l'École biblique et archéologique française de Jérusalem, illustrée par la tapisserie d'Angers. Paris: Éditions Diane de Selliers.

Avelino, F. (2021). Theories of power and social change. Power contestations and their implications for research on social change and innovation, Journal of Political Power 14(3): 425-448.

Bamberg, S. (2023). From consumers to citizens – grassroots initiatives for system transformation, in Gatersleben, B., Murtagh, N., eds. (2023), Handbook on Pro-Environmental Behaviour Change. Cheltenham: Edward Elgar Publishing. pp. 387-403.

Banks, J.S. and Hanusek, E.A., eds. (1997). Modern Political Economy. Cambridge: Cambridge University Press.

Barlow, N., Regen, L., Cadiou, N., Chertkovskaya, E., Hollweg, M., Plank, C., Schulken, M. and Wolf, V., eds. (2022). *Degrowth & Strategy: how to bring about social-ecological transformation*, Minneapolis, MN: MayFly Books.

Becker, G.S. (1971). Economic Theory. New York, NY: Alfred A. Knopf.

Bertagni, M.B., Socolow, R.H., Martirez, J.M.P., Carter, E.A., Greig, C., Ju, Y., Lieuwen, T., Mueller, M.E., Sundaresan, S., Wang, R., Zondlo, M.A. and Porporato, A (2023). Minimizing the impacts of the ammonia economy on the nitrogen cycle and climate. PNAS Earth, Atmospheric, and Planetary Sciences 120 (2023) 46 e2311728120.

Böhm, S. and Sullivan, S., eds. (2021). Negotiating Climate Change in Crisis. Cambridge: Open Book Publishers.

Boiteux, M. (1956). La vente au cout marginal. Revue Française de l'Énergie, 113-117.

Bossel, U., Eliasson, B. and Taylor, G. (2004). The Future of the Hydrogen Economy: Bright or Bleak? Journal of KONES International Combustion Engines 11 (1-2): 87-111. https://afdc.energy.gov/files/pdfs/hyd_economy_bossel_eliasson.pdf

Boström, M. and Lidskog, R. (2024). *Environmental Sociology and Social Transformation*. Key Issues. Abingdon: Routledge.

Bouckaert, G. (2023) Effective local governance, in Teles, F. ed., <u>Handbook on Local and Regional Governance</u> (2023). Cheltenham: Edward Elgar Publishing. pp. 26-38.

Boulanger P-M., Couder, J., Marenne, Y., Nemoz, S., Vanhaverbeke, J., Verbruggen A. and Wallenborn, G. (2013). Household energy consumption and rebound effect, HECoRE (Final Report). Brussels: Belgian Science Policy Office.

Bourdieu, J. and Heilbron, J. eds. (2024). Pierre Bourdieu. Return to Reflexivity. Cambridge: Polity Press

BP (2021). *BP Statistical Review of World Energy*, British Petroleum, <u>www.bp.com</u>.

Bradford, P. (2012). The Nuclear Landscape, Nature 483: 151-152.

Brand, U. and Wissen, M. (2017). The Imperial Mode of Living, in Spash, C.L. ed., Routledge Handbook of Ecological Economics. Abingdon: Routledge. pp. 152-161.

Brown, D.A., Gwiazdon, K. and Westra, L. eds. (2024) *The Routledge Handbook of Applied Climate Change Ethics*. Abingdon: Routledge.

Brunnengräber, A. and Di Nucci, M.R., (eds.) (2014). Im Hürdenlauf zur Energiewende. Heidelberg: Springer VS.

Bryson, J., Sancino, A., Benington, J. and Sørensen, E. (2017). *Towards a multi-actor theory of public value co-creation*. Public Management Review 19(5): 640-54.

Cebon, D. and Ainalis, D. (2021). Written Evidence submitted by the Centre for Sustainable Road Freight. HNZ0020.

Cline, W.R. (1992). The Economics of Global Warming. Peterson Institute for International Economics.

Cornelis, L. (2019). Openbare Orde. Liber Amicis, Intersentia, Antwerpen-Cambridge.

Costa, L., Moreau, V., Thurm, B., Yu, W., Clora, F., Baudry, G., Warmuth, H., Hezel, B., Seydewitz, T., Ranković, A., Kelly, G. and Kropp, J. P.. (2021). The decarbonisation of Europe powered by lifestyle changes. *Environmental Research Letters* 16 044057.

Cox, K.E. (1974). Hydrogen energy: a bibliography with abstracts; cumulative volume [1953 through 1973]. Energy Information Center, University of New Mexico, Albuquerque, NM.

Daly, H.E. ed. (1973, 1980). Economics, Ecology, Ethics. Essays toward a Steady-State Economy. New York, NY: W.H. Freeman and Company.

Danish Energy Agency (2024a). Technology descriptions and projections for long-term energy system planning. Technology Data - Energy transport.

Danish Energy Agency (2024b). Technology descriptions and projections for long-term energy system planning. Technology Data - Energy storage.

De Moor, T. (2023). *Shakeholder society? Social enterprises, citizens and collective action in the community economy.* Rotterdam: Erasmus Research Institute of Management.

Dixit, A.K. and Pindyck, R.S. (1994), *Investment under Uncertainty.* Princeton, NJ: Princeton University Press.

Eich, S. (2022), *The currency of politics. The Political Theory of Money from Aristotle to Keynes,* Oxford: Princeton University Press.

European Commission (2000). Green Paper on greenhouse gas emissions trading within the European Union. COM(2000) 87 final.

European Commission (2003). Directive 2003/87/EC of the European Parliament and of the Council of 13 October 2003 establishing a scheme for greenhouse gas emission allowance trading within the Community and amending Council Directive 96/61/EC, *Official Journal of the EU* L275/32-46.

European Commission (2020). A hydrogen strategy for a climate-neutral Europe. Communication from the Commission to the European Parliament, the Council, the European Economic and Social Committee and the Committee of the Regions. COM (2020) 301 final, Brussels, 8.7.2020.

European Commission (2021). *Communication 'Fit for 55': delivering the EU's 2030 Climate Target on the way to climate neutrality.* COM(2021) 550 final.

Fisher, M. (2009). *Capitalist realism. Is there no alternative?* London:Zero Books.

Friedman, M. (1962). *Capitalism and Freedom.* Chicago, IL: University of Chicago Press.

Fromm, E. (1976). *To Have or To Be?* London: Bloomsbury Academic reprint (2023).

Fuchs, D. (2007). *Business Power in Global Governance,* Boulder, CO: Lynne Rienner Publishers.

Galimova, T., Fasihi, M., Bogdanov, D. and Breyer, C. (2023). Impact of international transportation chains on cost of green e-hydrogen: Global cost of hydrogen and consequences for Germany and Finland. Applied Energy vol.347, 121369. https://doi.org/10.1016/j.apenergy.2023.121369.

Gamson, W. and Modigliani, A. (1989). Media Discourse and Public Opinion on Nuclear Power: A Constructionist Approach, *American Journal of Sociology* 95: 1–37.

Gardiner, M. (2009) Energy requirements for hydrogen gas compression and liquefaction as related to vehicle storage needs. U.S. Department of Energy Hydrogen and Fuel Cells Program Record.

Gardiner, S. M. (2024) The ethics of climate targets, in Brown, D.A., Gwiazdon, K. and Westra, L. eds. (2024) *The Routledge Handbook of Applied Climate Change Ethics.* Abingdon: Routledge. pp.38-51.

Gardiner, S. M. and Weisbach, D. A. (2016) Debating Climate Ethics. Oxford: Oxford University Press.

Gatersleben, B. and Murtagh, N., eds. (2023) Handbook on Pro-Environmental Behaviour Change. Cheltenham: Edward Elgar Publishing.

Girard, R. (1978), *Des choses cachés depuis la fondation du monde*, Paris: Éditions Grasset & Fasquelle.

Goldstein, B. E. (2009). Resilience to surprises through communicative planning. Ecology and Society 14 (2), 33.

Green, D. (2016), *How change happens*. Oxford: Oxford University Press.

Grübler, A. (2010), The costs of the French nuclear scale-up: A case of negative learning by doing, *Energy Policy* 38: 5174–88.

Gupta, S., Tripak, D. A., Burger, N., Gupta, J., Höhne, N., Boncheva, A. I., Kanoan, G. M., Kolstad, C., Kruger, J. A., Michaelowa, A., Murase, S., Pershing, J., Saijo, T. and Sari, A. (2007). Policies, Instruments and Co-operative Arrangements, in: *Climate Change 2007. Mitigation of Climate Change.* Contribution of Working Group III to the Fourth Assessment Report of the Intergovernmental Panel on Climate Change (Metz, B., Davidson, O. R., Bosch, P. R., Dave, R. and Meyer, L. A. (eds.))., Cambridge and New York, NY: Cambridge University Press.

Hager, C. and Haddad, M.A. eds. (2015). *NIMBY is Beautiful. Cases of Local Activism and Environmental Innovation around the World.* New York, NY and Oxford: Berghahn Books.

Hammond, M. (2020). Democratic deliberation for sustainability transformations: between constructiveness and disruption. *Sustainability: Science, Practice and Policy* 16 (1): 220-230.

Hamouchene, H. (2024). Decolonising the Energy Transition in North Africa, in Lang, M., Manahan, M. A., and Bringel, B. (Eds.) (2024). *The Geopolitics of Green Colonialism: Global Justice and Ecosocial Transitions* (1st ed.). London: Pluto Press. pp.52-63.

Hardin, G. (1968). The tragedy of the commons, *Science* 162: 1243-48.

Hardy, J.S. (2014). Linéaments d'une phénoménologie des passions chez Ricœur, *Philosophiques* 41(2) 313-332.

Harremoës, P., Gee, D., MacGarvin, M., Stirling, A., Keys, J., Wynne, B. and Guedes Vaz, S. (2002). *The Precautionary Principle in the 20th Century. Late Lessons from Early Warnings*. London: Earthscan.

Hattingh, J. (2024). *Taking Moral Responsibility for Climate Change by Cities*, in Brown, D.A, Gwiazdon, K. and Westra, L. eds. (2024). The Routledge Handbook of Applied Climate Change Ethics. New York, NY: Routledge. pp.146-157.

Heinberg, R. (2011). *The End of Growth: Adapting to Our New Economic Reality*, Gabriola Island, BC, Canada: New Society Publishers.

Howarth, R.W. and Jacobson, M.Z. (2021). How green is blue hydrogen? Energy Science & Engineering, Modelling and Analysis 00: 1-12.

Hubeau, B. and Cabus, M., eds. (2023). De Tijd Dringt - Time is running out. Berchem: EPO.

Hudson, M. (2023). How could a BRICS+ bank and settlement currency work? *Geopolitical Economy Report*.

IAEA (2008). *Guidance for the Application of an Assessment Methodology for Innovative Nuclear Energy Systems*, INPRO Manual – Overview of the Methodology, International Atomic Energy Agency, Vienna.

Ibana, R.A. (2024) Duties to consider the views of those who will be harmed by climate change, in Brown, D.A, Gwiazdon, K. and Westra, L. eds. (2024). The Routledge Handbook of Applied Climate Change Ethics. New York, NY: Routledge. pp. 29-37.

IEA (2012). *Energy Technology Perspectives 2012. Pathways to a clean energy system*, International Energy Agency, Paris.

IEA (2023). *Global Hydrogen Review 2023*. International Energy Agency, Paris, p.158.

IPCC (2005). *Special Report on Carbon Dioxide Capture and Storage*. Cambridge: Cambridge University Press

IPCC (2012). *Renewable Energy Sources and Climate Change Mitigation*, Special Report. Cambridge: Cambridge University Press.

IPCC (2014). *Climate Change 2014. Mitigation of Climate Change*. WGIII Contribution to the Fifth Assessment Report. Cambridge: Cambridge University Press.

IRENA (2025). *Renewable Power Generation Costs in 2024*. International Renewable Energy Agency, Abu Dhabi.

IRENA and AEA (2022). *Innovation Outlook: Renewable Ammonia*. International Renewable Energy Agency, Abu Dhabi / Ammonia Energy Association, Brooklyn.

Jackson, W. and Jensen, R. (2022). *The Inconvenient Apocalypse*. Notre Dame, IN: University of Notre Dame Press.

Kelton, S. (2020). *The Deficit Myth. Modern Monetary Theory and the Birth of the People's Economy*. New York, NY: PublicAffairs.

Klare, M. (2012), *The Race for What's Left: The Global Scramble for the World's Last Resources*. New York, NY: Metropolitan Books.

Kreidelmeyer, S., Dambeck, H., Kirchner, A. and Wünsch, M. (2020). Kosten und Transformationspfade für strombasierte Energieträger. Prognos AG. Im Auftrag des Bundesministeriums für Wirtschaft und Energie.

Lane, R.E. (2000). *The Loss of Happiness in Market Democracies*. New Haven CT and London: Yale University Press.

Lang, M., Acosta, A. and Martinez, E. (2024). Taking on the Eternal Debts of the South, in Lang, M., Manahan, M.A., Bringel, B., eds. (2024). *The Geopolitics of Green Colonialism. Global Justice and Ecosocial Transitions*. London: Pluto Press. pp.105-117.

Lang, M., Manahan, M.A., Bringel, B., eds. (2024). *The Geopolitics of Green Colonialism. Global Justice and Ecosocial Transitions*. London: Pluto Press.

Latour, B. (2022). *How to inhabit the Earth*. Interviews with Nicolas Truong. Cambridge: Polity Press.

Lehtonen, M. (2022). Building promises of small modular reactors – one conference at a time. *Bulletin of Atomic Scientists*, December 22, 2022.

Lietaer, B. (2001). *The Future of Money*. London: Random House.

Lohmann, L. ed. (2006). *Carbon Trading: A Critical Conversation On Climate Change, Privatization and Power*, Dag Hammarskjöld development dialogue, 48.

Lovins, A.B. (1976). Energy Strategy: The road not taken? *Foreign Affairs* 55 (1): 65-96.

Luyendijk, J. (2015). *Dit kan niet waar zijn: Onder bankiers*. Amsterdam: Uitgeverij Atlas Contact.

Machiavelli, N. (2007). *De Heerser*. Vertaald en toegelicht door Frans Van Dooren. Amsterdam: Athenaeum – Polak & Van Gennep.

Manahan, M.A. (2024). 'Nature-Based Solutions' for a Profit-Based Environmental Governance, in Lang, M., Manahan, M.A., Bringel, B., eds. (2024). *The Geopolitics of Green Colonialism. Global Justice and Ecosocial Transitions*. London: Pluto Press. pp.154-168.

Marcu, A., Vangenechten, D., Alberola, E., Olsen, J., Schleicher, S., Caneill, J-Y. and Cabras, S. (2021). *2021 State of the EU ETS Report*, by ERCST, Wegener Center for Climate & Global Change, BloombergNEF & Ecoact (annual reports, freely accessible from ictsd.org).

Marx, K. (1870), *Het Kapitaal. Een kritische beschouwing over de economie*, Vertaald door Lipschits, I. (1970), Bussum: W. de Haan.

Mazzucato, M. and Collington, R. (2023). *The Big Con*. London: Allen Lane, Penguin Random House.

McCormick, K., Evans, J., Palgan, Y.V. and Frantzeskaki, N. eds. (2023). Sustainable Cities and Communities. Cheltenham: Edward Elgar Publishing.

McFarland, E. (2024). Golden hydrogen - or fool's gold? Bulletin of the Atomic Scientists, March 6, 2024.

McLeod, S. (2023). Maslow's Hierarchy of Needs, https://www.simplypsychology.org/maslow.html.

Meadows, D. H. (1999). *Leverage Points. Places to Intervene in a System.* The Sustainability Institute.

Meadows, D.H., Meadows, D.L, Randers, J. and Behrens, W.W. (1972). *The Limits to Growth*, New York, NY: Universe Books.

Mecklin, J. (2022). The Energy Department's fusion breakthrough: It's not really about generating electricity, *Bulletin of Atomic Scientists*, December 16, 2022.

Meckling, J. (2011). *Carbon Coalitions: Business, Climate Politics, and the Rise of Emissions Trading.* Cambridge, MA: The MIT Press, Cambridge, MA.

Milanovic, B. (2017). *Wereldwijde Ongelijkheid. Welvaart in de 21e eeuw.* Heuten: Spectrum.

Mill, J.S. (1859) On Liberty. Reprinted in Robson, J.M. ed. (1977). Mills Collected Works. Toronto: University of Toronto Press; London: Routledge & Kegan Paul.

Norgaard, K.M. (2011), *Living in Denial. Climate Change, Emotions, and Everyday Life.* Cambrigde, MA: The MIT Press.

Oreskes, N. and Conway, E.M. (2011). Merchants of Doubt. London: Bloomsbury.

Ostrom, E. (1990). *Governing the Commons. The Evolution of Institutions for Collective Action*, Cambridge: Cambridge University Press.

Ostrom, E. (2005). *Understanding Institutional Diversity.* Princeton, NJ: Princeton University Press.

Ostrom, E. (2014). A polycentric approach for coping with climate change. *Annals of Economics and Finance* 15(1): 97-134.

Palm, J. (2023). Energy communities as accelerators of energy transition in cities, in McCormick, K. E. J., Palgan, Y.V. and Frantzeskaki, N. (Eds.) (2023) A Research Agenda for Sustainable Cities and Communities. Cheltenham: Edward Elgar Publishing. Pp 69-80.

Parry, I., Black, S. and Vernon, N. (2021). *Still Not Getting Energy Prices Right: A Global and Country Update of Fossil Fuel Subsidies*, International Monetary Fund, WP/21/236.

Paterson, M. (2021). In Search of Climate Politics. Cambridge: Cambridge University Press.

Pearse, R. and Böhm, S. (2014). Ten reasons why carbon markets will not bring about radical emissions reduction. Carbon Management, 5(4), 325–337.

Phlips, L. (1983). The economics of price discrimination. Cambridge: Cambridge University Press.

Piketty, T. (2022). *A Brief History of Equality. Cambridge*: Belknap Press.

Reynolds, W. and Perkins, H. (1977). *Engineering Thermodynamics.* New York, NY: McGraw Hill.

Rockström, J., Steffen, W., Noone, K., Persson, Å., Chapin III, F.S., Lambin, E. F., Lenton, T.M., Scheffer, M., Folke, C., Schellnhuber, H. J., Nykvist, B., de Wit, C. A., Hughes, T., van der Leeuw, S., Rodhe, H., Sörlin, S., Snyder, P. K., Costanza, R., Svedin, U., Falkenmark, M., Karlberg, L., Corell, R. W., Fabry, V. J., Hansen, J., Walker, B., Liverman, D., Richardson, K., Crutzen, P. and Foley, J. A. (2009). A safe operating space for humanity. Nature 461: 472-75.

Scheer, H. (1993, 2001). *A Solar Manifesto.* London: James & James.

Schleicher-Tappeser, R. (2022). Nanoscience has made electricity directly from sunlight unbeatably cheap. SustainableStrategies.substack.com.

Schneider, M. and Froggatt, A. (2022). *The World Nuclear Industry Status Report 2022.* Paris: A Mycle Schneider Consulting Project.

Schoemaker, P. J. H. (1990). *Strategy, complexity and economic rent,* in *Management Science* 36, 1178-92.

Sehoon, K. (2024). *Companies are buying up cheap carbon offsets – data suggest it may be more about greenwashing than helping the climate.* The Conversation, November 11, 2024.

Service, R.F. (2018). Ammonia – a renewable fuel made from sun, air, and water – could power the globe without carbon. Science (2018). doi:10.1126/science.aau7489.

Shuckburgh, E., ed. (2020). A Blueprint for a Green Future. Cambridge Zero Policy Forum. Centre of Science and Policy. University of Cambridge. www.zero.cam.ac.uk/green-recovery-report.

Sijm, J., Neuhoff, K. and Chen, Y. (2006). CO2 cost pass-through and windfall profits in the power sector, *Climate Policy* 6, 49-72.

Simmons, I. G. (1989). Changing the Face of the Earth. Culture, Environment, History. Oxford: Basil Blackwell.

Spash, C. L. (2017). *Social Ecological Economics*, chapter 1, pp. 3-16, in: Spash, C. L. (ed.), *Routledge Handbook of Ecological Economics*. London and New York, NY: Routledge.

Staffell, I., Scamman, D., Velazquez Abad, A., Balcombe, P., Dodds, P. E., Ekins, P., Shah, N. and Ward, K.R. (2019). The role of hydrogen and fuel cells in the global energy system. Energy & Environmental Science 12 (2019), 463-491.

Steinberger, J. (2024). *The Atlas Network: What we are up against*. Blog at medium.com.

Stern, N. (2006). *Stern Review: The Economics of Climate Change, Executive Summary*. London: HM Treasury.

Stigler, G. (1971). The theory of economic regulation. Bell Journal of Economics and Management Science 2(1): 3-21.

Stirling, A. (2007). A general framework for analysing diversity in science, technology and society. Journal of the Royal Society Interface 4 (15): 707-719.

Teles, F. ed. (2023). Handbook on Local and Regional Governance. Cheltenham: Edward Elgar Publishing.

Thiel, A., Blomquist, W. A. and Garrick, D. E. (2019). *Governing Complexity: Analyzing and Applying Polycentricity*, Cambridge Studies in Economics, Choice, and Society. Cambridge: Cambridge University Press.

Twidell, J. W. and Weir, A. D. (1986). *Renewable Energy Resources*. London and New York, NY: E & F. N. SPON.

UNDP (2007). *Human Development Report 2007/2008, Fighting Climate Change: Human solidarity in a divided world*. United Nations Development Programme.

UNDP (2019). *Human Development Report 2019*, United Nations Development Programme.

UNESCO (2016). *Ethical Principles for Climate Change*. Section 4: Report of COMEST on "Ethical Principles for Climate Change Adaptation and Mitigation" (2015) pp. 76-97.

US National Research Council and National Academy of Engineering (2004). The Hydrogen Economy: Opportunities, Costs, Barriers, and R & D Needs. Executive Summary. Washington, DC: The National Academies Press.

van den Abbeele, E., red. (1985). *Ontmanteling van de groei, leesboek over een andere economie*. Nijmegen: Uitgeverij Markant.

van Liefferinge, G. (2022). *Fuck de Media. Red de Pers*, Berchem: Uitgeverij EPO.

Verbruggen, A. (2008). Renewable and nuclear power: A common future? *Energy Policy* 36(11): 4036-47.

Verbruggen, A. (2009). *Performance evaluation of renewable energy support policies, applied on Flanders' tradable certificates system*. Energy Policy 37: 1385-94.

Verbruggen, A. (2013a). *Revocability and reversibility in societal decision-making*. Ecological Economics 85: 20-37.

Verbruggen, A. (2013b). Belgian nuclear power life extension and fuss about nuclear rents. *Energy Policy* 60: 91-97.

Verbruggen, A. (2015), Backstop Technology: Model Keystone or Energy Systems Transition Guide. *Journal of Natural Resources Policy Research*, 7(2-3): 177-183.

Verbruggen, A. (2021). *Pricing Carbon Emissions. Economic Reality and Utopia*. London: Routledge.

Verbruggen, A. (2022). The geopolitics of trillion US$ oil & gas rents, in *International Journal of Sustainable Energy Planning and Management*, Vol.36: 3-10.

Verbruggen, A. and Al Marchohi, M. (2010). *Views on peak oil and its relation to climate change policy*, in *Energy policy* 38(10): 5572-5581.

Verbruggen, A., Di Nucci, M. R., Fischedick, M., Haas, R., Hvelplund, F., Lauber, V., Lorenzoni, A., Mez, L., Nilsson, L. J., del Rio Gonzalez, P., Schleich, J. and Toke, D. (2015). Europe's electricity regime: restoration or thorough transition. *International Journal of Sustainable Energy Planning and Management* 5: 57-68.

Verbruggen, A., Klemes, J. and Rosen, M. (2016). Assessing Cogeneration Activity in Extraction-Condensing Steam Turbines: Dissolving the Issues by Applied Thermodynamics, in: *Journal of Energy Resources Technology*. Vol. 138 (5), 052005, Transactions of the American Society of Mechanical Engineering.

Verbruggen, A. and Laes, E. (2015). Sustainability assessment of nuclear power: Discourse analysis of IAEA and IPCC. *Environmental Science & Policy* 51: 170-180.Verbruggen, A. and Wealer, B. (2021). *Nuclear Power and Sustainability*, in: Constance, C. (ed.), The Palgrave Handbook of Global Sustainability. Cham: Springer Nature Switzerland AG.

Verbruggen, A., Yermekova, G. and Baigarin, K. (2025). *Dubious promises of hydrogen in a climate constrained world.* Energies 18, 491 (doi.org/10.3390/en18030491).

Verbruggen, A. and Yurchenko, Y. (2017). Positioning nuclear power in the low-carbon electricity transition. *Sustainability* 9(1): 163.

Volberda, H. W., Morgan, R. E., Reinmoeller, P., Hitt, M. A., Ireland, R. D. and Hoskisson, R. E. (2011). *Strategic Management: Competitiveness and Globalization* (Concepts and Cases). Andover: Cengage Learning EMEA.

Voss, J-P. and Simons, A. (2014). Instrument constituencies and the supply side of policy innovation: The social life of emissions trading, *Environmental Politics* 23(5): 735-754.

Wahlund, M. and Palm, J. (2022). The role of energy democracy and energy citizenship for participatory transitions: A comprehensive review. Energy Research & Social Science 87, 102482.

Walsh, L. and Ormond-Skeaping, T. (2022). *The Cost of Delay. Why finance to address Loss and Damage must be agreed at COP27*, Lossanddamagecollaboration.org.

Warwick, N., Griffiths, P., Keeble, J., Archibald, A., Pyle, J. and Shine, K. (2022). Atmospheric implications of increased Hydrogen use.

WCED (1987). *Our Common Future*, World Commission on Environment and Development. Oxford: Oxford University Press.

Wolin, S. (2010). *Democracy Incorporated. Managed Democracy and the Specter of Inverted Totalitarianism*, 5th edition. Princeton, NJ: Princeton University Press.

Yermekova, G. and Baigarin, K. (2023). Nature-based Vision for tackling the Inevitable Environmental Crisis: Water and Energy Resources in Central Asia, REFORM workshop, Technical University of Munich.

Endnotes

Preface and Introduction

[1] Jackson and Jensen (2022) is a recent example, rooted in the Western religious tradition.

[2] Amblard, P. (2017).

[3] Disposition is a person's inherent qualities of mind and character.

[4] See Glossary.

[5] Latour, B. (2022).

[6] The reports of IPCC Working Group I and II are reliable sources of comprehensive and consistent information. Our book covers the domain of IPCC Working Group III, where the information is incomplete and distorted.

[7] Al Jazeera (2024) https://www.aljazeera.com/news/longform/2024/12/27/climate-records-broken-2024.

[8] Lent from IPCC colleague Barry Goldstein, co-author of IPCC (2012).

[9] Wolin, S. (2010) emphasises the difference between mitigative or tactical change versus paradigmatic or strategic change, p.x.

[10] Banks, J. S., Hanushek, E. A., eds. (1997).

[11] UNDP (2007).

[12] Brand and Wissen (2017) call this *Imperial Mode of Living*, essentially being an *Alienating Lifestyle*.

[13] Verbruggen, A. (2013).

[14] Norgaard, K. M. (2011).

[15] The UN Rio Summit in 1992 adopted formally the idea of Sustainable Development and the UNFCCC.

[16] Thiel et al. (2019).

[17] Thiel et al. (2019: 3-5).

[18] Green, D. (2016).

[19] Boström and Lidskog (2024) propose five facets, partly overlapping with the context of figure 2. They skip attention to energy and technology.

[20] Milanovic, B. (2017), pp. 170-181.

[21] Meadows, D. (1999) pp. 17-18.

[22] An example from academia is the demise of independent research; resources (people, funding) are prioritising themes and approaches that can be economically *valorised*. Standards and rules have changed.

[23] The private energy sector has excessively shielded itself with the 'Energy Charter Treaty'.

[24] Bryson et al. (2017), p. 641.

[25] Emissions permit trade was the condition for the US to join the Kyoto Protocol (COP3 in Kyoto, 1997).

[26] Paterson (2021).

[27] This classification follows Piketty (2022) and UNDP (2019) chapter 3, with statistics in terms of inequality in income and in reaping the fruits of growth.

[28] Hager, C., Haddad, M.A., eds. (2015).

[29] Ostrom, E. (2005).

[30] Terms like *complex, wicked, ambiguous*, are avoided when poorly defined and diffusing attention.

[31] Stern, N. (2006) emphasises the need for *drastic and urgent* change, although he defined climate change narrowly as the greatest *market failure* ever seen.

[32] Fisher, M. (2009).

[33] Spash, C.L. (2017), p. 15.

Chapter 1

[1] Verbruggen, A. (2022).

[2] Shuckburgh, E., ed. (2020), p. 3.

[3] IPCC disseminates the mantra, like IPCC WG3 Assessment Report 5, Summary for Policymakers, pp. 12, 14, 20, 26, 27. This is denounced in Schneider, M., Froggatt, A. (2022), Foreword.

[4] An electricity sector-wide technical energy question, also prominent in a doctoral dissertation of 1979 did not receive a correct solution until 35 years later. See Verbruggen A., et al. (2016).

[5] This is entropy; most evident for energy in the form of heat.

[6] A heat pump works like a refrigerator: pumping heat from a cold to a warmer environment.

[7] This book does not provide information on climate and climate change. Workgroups I and II of the IPCC provide all the info for free. Authors, media and politicians use this information.

[8] Some energy uses require little or no technology, such as use of daylight.

[9] Ruggero Schleicher-Tappeser is closely following developments, visit his Sustainable Strategies site. In chapter 2 more info on PV technology follows.

[10] CCS is now advertised in an artificial version with chemical-mechanical energy-intensive processes (IPCC, 2005). After decades of talk and some test cases, artificial CCS is not really applied in the fossil energy sector.

[11] A large natural gas-fired power plant with a gas turbine and steam turbine coupled has a capacity of 300 to 450 MWe. Hydropower plants have a wide span in capacity, from a few tens of kW to thousands of MW.

[12] *"Militaries are huge fossil fuel consumers and have large and complex supply chains, yet only a few States provide disaggregated fuel use data to the UNFCCC. Data is poor, but estimates suggest the world's militaries are responsible for 5.5% of global GHG emissions. This estimate excludes emissions from warfighting itself"*. Source: militaryemissions.org.

[13] For example, Roman aqueducts, or Persian underground canals over dozens of kilometres to deliver water from the mountains to cities.

[14] Costs (and risks) are external if those causing them do not bear them, but pass them on to others, such as fellow citizens, the environment, nature, the future.

[15] Geothermal (heat from the Earth) and tides are two sources not explicitly mentioned here.

[16] Lightning and static electricity are two natural phenomena that can cause fire and

death; they are of no beneficial use to humans.

[17] BP publishes an annual review of commercial energy use.

[18] World Meteorological Organization.

Chapter 2

[1] Simmons, I. G. (1989).

[2] Rockström et al. (2009).

[3] UNEP (United Nations Environment Programme): World Environment Situation Room www.wesr.unep.org.

[4] Jackson, W. & Jensen, R. (2022).

[5] For example, Jean M. Auel.

[6] The Nile Valley with Nubia and Egypt. Mesopotamia, the area between the two streams Euphrates and Tigris. Persia. India. The Mediterranean empires such as Greece, Carthage and Rome. The Maya and Inca in Central and South America. The Asian empires Myanmar with Bagan, Cambodia with Angkor Wat, Vietnam with Cham, Indonesia with Borobudur, ... and more.

[7] Concerning the exact time period, information sources differ.

[8] The eagle was the symbol of Roman military power. In 105 BC, Gaius Marius assigned an Aquila to every legion. With the Edict of Milan (313 AD), the Christian cross became the prominent symbol in the Roman Empire.

[9] Gunpowder was a mixture of saltpetre, sulphur and charcoal.

[10] Reynolds, W. & Perkins, H. (1977).

[11] Schneider, M. & Froggatt, A. (2022).

[12] Various sources assign different percentages to the GHG emissions by energy. UNEP states 65 percent. WRI (World Resources Institute, wri.org) 76 percent. IEA beyond 80 percent. Differences depend mainly on demarcations between direct and indirect use of fossil fuels, and classifications of industrial activities.

[13] Scheer (1993), chapter 1.

[14] Similar to colonisation and conversion of subjugated peoples being sold as divine missions.

[15] Boulding's article is reprinted in Daly ed. (1973, 1980), next to many other seminal articles by, e.g., Ehrlich & Ehrlich, Hardin, Georgescu-Roegen, Schumacher, Mishan, ...

[16] This section is fully based on publications by Ruggero Schleicher-Tappeser, available on the site Sustainable Strategies (in German and English), for example the November 2023 papers "Energy transition: Which technologies matter" and "Why photovoltaics is becoming unbeatably inexpensive".

[17] A nanometre is 10-9 metre, or 1 metre consists of 1 billion nanometres.

[18] *Economies of density* are lost when two or more wires deliver electricity in the same street.

[19] Large industrial plants may install an electric power plant on site, mostly as a fossil-fired Combined Heat & Power (CHP) unit valorising the heat flows, otherwise discarded to the environment. Petroleum refineries, chemical plants, food processing plants, etc. benefit from CHP plants.

[20] Stigler, G. (1971) received the Nobel prize for economics in 1982.

[21] Verbruggen, A. (2021), pp. 114–116.

[22] Stadtwerke is the German name; they mostly covered several public services: electricity, district heat, water, ... The profits from these activities were mostly used to finance other services, such as local public transport.

[23] Directive 96/92/EC of the European Parliament and of the Council of 19 December 1996 concerning common rules for the internal market in electricity. Document 31996L0092.

[24] *Unbundling* was the term then used.

[25] Such opportunities are a positive result of re-regulating the electricity sector to a more transparent, open activity.

[26] Hager, C. (2015) is used as the main information source.

[27] The EUR was a unit created by and for banks only, in 1999 becoming the euro (€), launched as a currency in 2002.

[28] Verbruggen, A. (2021), chapter 5, pp. 60-72.

[29] Verbruggen, A. (2009).

[30] This lesson is not new. The Greek philosopher Aristotle already stated, "Treat equal things equally, unequal things unequally". Verbruggen, A. (2021), chapter 2, pp. 17-30 contains a scholarly treatment of the aspect of diversity. More practically, consider the incredible diversity of the real economy in all sectors, where markets are *segmented* (split into parts), most goods show much variety with each having its own price.

[31] In Denmark, the NGO INFORSE (°1992) developed a domestic centre for renewable energy, and a world-wide network of 145 NGOs in 60 countries. See the site inforse.org.

[32] Scheer, H. (1993, 2001).

[33] The lobby group chose the name MAGRITTE, a known Belgian surrealist painter, with a museum in Brussels sponsored by ENGIE. Perhaps psychologists and marketers can interpret this choice of name.

[34] Verbruggen, A., et al. (2015); Verbruggen, A. (2021), p.70–71.

[35] This battle revealed how the giant energy companies managed to hijack the then leading academic journal on energy policy (Energy Policy, Elsevier). Independent editor Nicky France, who had built Energy Policy into a pluralistic, diverse platform, was replaced by M. Jefferson (Shell) and L. Greening (US energy industry). See 'Transversal Issues' on the site avielverbruggen.be.

Chapter 3

[1] *Atomic* energy is the most correct name, better than *nuclear* energy. Historically, atomic was the standard name, still clear for organisations, such as: International Atomic Energy Agency (IAEA), the European EURATOM, the Bulletin of the Atomic Scientists. The general term nuclear (like in nuclear city, nuclear task) obscures the actual link to atomic weapons. *Discursive power* hides content with misleading words.

[2] Triptych *Renewable Energy, Nuclear Power, Carbon Capture & Storage*, or: RE, NP,

CCS.

[3] Bradford, P. (2012).

[4] Oreskes, N., Conway, E.M. (2011).

[5] This history section is taken from Verbruggen, A. & Wealer, B. (2021). There you find more references, not mentioned in this chapter.

[6] Enrico Fermi was an Italian atomic physicist, Nobel Prize winner in physics in 1938, who fled to the US because of fascism (his wife was Jewish). He played an important role in the Manhattan project.

[7] A breeder reactor produces more fuel than it consumes. The doubling time is the duration to double the initial amount of fuel, and is between 8 and 20 years depending on the type of breeder reactor.

[8] India obtained its own atomic weapons in 1974, Pakistan in 1998, and North Korea in 2006.

[9] The structure represents an iron atom (a Uranium atom would not have provided a usable building); attention was drawn to the "atom", before the spin doctors replaced it with "nucleus".

[10] Verbruggen, A. (2015).

[11] Surprisingly, the site now houses an amusement park.

[12] The capacity factor was 7 percent.

[13] Mecklin, J. (2022).

[14] Comments on the Fukushima catastrophe are available in Dutch 'Seven Opinion Pieces on Atomic Energy'. The hydrogen explosions and frivolous handling of risks are also covered, see avielverbruggen.be.

[15] In 1900, Planck identified quanta in electromagnetic radiation; in 1926–28, Heisenberg and Schrödinger developed quantum theory; Hahn and Meitner discovered atomic nuclear fission.

[16] The Bulletin of the Atomic Scientists, freely available at thebulletin.org.

[17] World Nuclear Industry Status Report, freely available at worldnuclearreport.org.

[18] Fraudster may sound harsh, but knowingly or negligently spreading misinformation is a criminal act. This certainly applies to war propaganda, see pioneer Joseph Goebbels during the Nazi regime. Atomic propaganda is equally reckless and risky.

[19] NPT = Non-Proliferation Treaty, or Treaty for the Non-Proliferation of nuclear weapons.

[20] IAEA (2008).

[21] WCED (1987).

[22] Verbruggen, A., Laes, E. (2015).

[23] All major reinsurance multinationals (like Swiss, Mannheim, Lloyds, ...) refuse to insure atomic power plants for major accidents. The risk specialists assess the atomic risks as too high, and refuse to receive insurance premiums in US$ millions in return for indemnity for atomic power generation. But ordinary citizens are labelled stupid and backward by the atomic lobby when they too refuse to bear the risks. Rejecting atomic power risks is just doing what the top specialists in risk assessment and evaluation do.

[24] The IPCC WG3 reports of 2014 (AR5), 2018 (SR 1.5°C), 2022 (AR6) are freely accessible at ipcc.ch; Verbruggen, A. (2021), pp. 106–111.

[25] Principles Governing IPCC Work, Section 4.3.3, freely accessible via ipcc.ch.

[26] This was verified with the critical authors.

[27] I have the evidence at hand, because on my thorough comments the responsible IPCC staff did not reply.

[28] In the diversity of IPCC authorships, there are CLA (Coordinating Lead Author), LA (Lead Author), and CA (Contributing Author). The last ones are not submitted to the full screening process, but can sneak in, so-to-speak, via lobbying the CLAs.

[29] Verbruggen, A. (2021), p.108.

[30] This 'success' has never been as great as proclaimed, see Grübler, A. (2010). France is the European country with major problems in electricity supply today, due to ageing atomic power plants and towering bills looming for decommissioning and caring for high-level atomic waste.

[31] IEA (2012).

[32] Lehtonen, M. (2022).

[33] In November 2023, the Nuscale 'Carbon Free Power Project' in Idaho, US is stopped. Nuscale's CEO, John Hopkins argued the decision with tribal wisdom of Sioux Indians: *When you are riding a dead horse, the best strategy is to dismount.*

[34] Gamson, W. & Modigliani, A. (1989); Fuchs, D. (2007).

[35] Complex is a buzz word used too often, and mostly inappropriately, as a stopgap on thinking things through. Use the word only when the basic conditions are present to call a situation or system truly complex.

[36] Gamson, W. & Modigliani, A. (1989).

[37] A profitability analysis takes only money flows of an investor into account. This is a component of a comprehensive cost-benefit analysis which also considers non-monetary effects, such as impacts on nature and ecosystems, health impacts, impacts on future generations, etc.

[38] Electricity is a phenomenon that needs an outlet (useful use) immediately after its creation (generation, production). If the instantaneous possible outlet is 5000 MW, and nuclear power provides 3000 MW and renewable (wind, light) provides 4500 MW, then there is a surplus of 2500 MW, or an outright conflict as to which of the two inflexible suppliers has to step out. Computer models do not see those conflicts if they work with only annual totals of electricity produced.

[39] Verbruggen, A. (2008); Verbruggen, A. & Yurchenko, Y. (2017).

[40] Helen Caldicott is the woman who described this without pardon.

[41] This joke is reserved for fusion reactors. These use massive amounts of electricity to try to obtain heat. If engineers are (ever) going to figure out how to capture that (any) heat, they want to turn it into electricity at an efficiency of ? (see the low efficiencies of atomic power plants today). An expensive, sardonic joke this is for sure.

[42] A wind turbine has a similar core: the blades capture wind that turns a turbine shaft, and from the rotation the alternator extracts electricity. There are no extra flabs: wind comes from nature, and the unused wind simply flows on into nature.

[43] In the heyday of atomic power (1980–81), 4 reactors of 915MWe each started up in TRICASTIN (France) for gas diffusion enrichment for nuclear fuel in the megalomaniacal atomic programme envisaged. Belgium's 12.5% share, is now with ENGIE and EDF who

have seized Belgian electricity generation. More detail in Verbruggen, A. (2013b), table 1.

44 Flabs only refer to the installations and activities related to the *fuel cycle and cooling water* (or air) flows brought to the turbine and as waste flows afterwards. Sunlight and wind flows have no flabs in generating electricity. For knowledge on renewable energy, see Twidell, J.W. & Weir, A.D. (1986).

45 Track price trends year by year in IRENA reports, freely accessible at irena.org

Chapter 4

1 Chapter based on Verbruggen, A., Yermekova, G., Baigarin, K. (2025).

2 Distinguishing hydrogen as energy commodity or as chemical substance is crucial in assessing its future role.

3 Staffel et al. (2019); IRENA and AEA (2022); IEA (2023).

4 Shuckburgh ed. (2020); Cebon, D., Ainalis, D. (2021); Howarth and Jacobson (2021).

5 Bossel et al. (2004), p.107.

6 IPCC (2012).

7 Bumiller, E., Nagourney, A. (2006) New York Times February 1, Bush: 'America is addicted to oil'; Wolin (2010) p. 133.

8 Cox (1974).

9 Bundesministerium für Forschung und Technologie (1975) Einsatzmöglichkeiten neuer Energiesysteme. Teil III: Wasserstoff.

10 Christina Lu (2023) Green Hydrogen is not a Silver Bullet. Foreign Policy.

11 The White House. President George W. Bush. Office of the Press Secretary June 25, 2003.

12 US National Research Council and National Academy of Engineering (2004). All text of this section is literally copied from this report, except the Bush statements.

13 Weekly Compilation of Presidential Documents. Monday, February 3, 2003. Vol. 39, No. 5, p. 111. Washington, D.C.: Government Printing Office. Twenty-one years later, the availability of hydrogen cars is minimal in 2024.

14 This fascinating property is the narrow prop of utopian tales about an imagined hydrogen energy economy, typical for delusive truths.

15 European Commission (2020).

16 Hydrogen Insight 28 November 2023.

17 Hydrogen Insight 17 September 2024, p.18.

18 European Commission – Press release. Commission approves €998 million Dutch State aid scheme to support hydrogen production. Brussels, 29 July 2024.

19 Hamouchene, H. (2024).

20 Lang, M. et al. (2024).

21 McFarland, E. Golden hydrogen – or fool's gold? Bulletin of the Atomic Scientists. March 6, 2024.

22 Radnichenko R. V. (2018) General power engineering: hydrogen in power engineering. Yurait Publishing House, p.150.

23 Damu, Z. (2021) Possibilities of hydrogen application in Kazakhstan economy.

24 Rhodes, R. (2011) Explosive lessons in Hydrogen Safety, NASA.

[25] Long-suppressed-hydrogen-explosion-risk-report-and-video-released-after-ruling-from-UK-commissioner
[26] IEA (2023).
[27] UNIDO, IRENA, IDOS (2023). Green hydrogen for sustainable industrial development. A policy toolkit for developing countries, p. 73.
[28] Warwick, N., et al. (2022).
[29] Bossel et al. (2004).
[30] Kreidelmeyer, S. et al. (2020), p. 23.
[31] Madsen, H.T. (2022) Water treatment for green hydrogen: what you need to know. Hydrogen Tech World.
[32] Kreidelmeyer et al. (2020), pp. 28-29.
[33] Howarth, R.W., Jacobson, M.Z. (2021).
[34] Danish Energy Agency (2024a), fig.11, p. 118.
[35] Danish Energy Agency (2024a), p. 116.
[36] Gardiner, M. (2009).
[37] Service, R.F. (2018).
[38] Bossel et al. (2004), pp. 97-100.
[39] Danish Energy Agency (2024b), p. 113.
[40] Cebon, D., Ainalis, D. (2021).
[41] Bossel et al. (2004), p. 107.
[42] Kreidelmeyer et al. (2020), pp. 22-23.
[43] Danish Energy Agency (2024a), pp. 95-146.
[44] Danish Energy Agency (2024b), pp. 73-92.
[45] IRENA and AEA (2022), p. 22.
[46] Bertagni et al. (2023), fig.4, pp. 4-5.
[47] UNECE (2023) Nitrogen still a major threat to ecosystems in large parts of Europe.
[48] Rockström, J. et al. (2009).
[49] Bertagni et al. (2023), p. 3.
[50] Bertagni et al. (2023), pp. 2-3.
[51] Bertagni et al. (2023), fig.1, p. 2.
[52] IRENA and AEA (2022).
[53] IRENA and AEA (2022), pp. 10-12.
[54] IRENA and AEA (2022), p. 20.
[55] IRENA and AEA (2022), p. 65.
[56] Howarth and Jacobson (2021).
[57] Kreidelmeyer et al. (2020).
[58] Cebon, D., Ainalis, D. (2021).
[59] Galimova, T., et al. (2023).
[60] Bertagni et al. (2023), p. 3.
[61] IRENA and AEA (2022), p. 11.
[62] Svevind (2023) Introduction to Green Hydrogen. Hyrasia One.
[63] Kazakhstan Electric Power industry Key Factors.
[64] Yermekova, G., Baigarin, K. (2023).
[65] Yara (2024) Hydrogen on hydropower plant at Herøya, Norway.
[66] Verbruggen, A. et al. (2015).

Chapter 5

[1] The energy industry includes owners of oil & gas wells, fossil fuel and electricity corporates, and traders on the exchange platforms who also obtain billions of US dollars through speculative transactions. How the super profits are shared among these agents is not known in detail.

[2] Verbruggen, A. (2022).

[3] London School of Economics (LSE) and University College London (UCL).

[4] The Guardian published results electronically on 21 July 2022, and on 22 July in front page print.

[5] The research is valorised in Walsh, L. and Ormond-Skeaping, T. (2022). An international team of researchers associated with the International Institute for Applied Systems Analysis (IIASA) has continued to work on the results to dissect the super profits of oil & gas multinationals.

[6] Machiavelli, N. (2007).

[7] Morelli, A. (2022). 10 principles of war propaganda. DeWereldMorgen.

[8] Collon, M. (2022). The war began back in 2015 when Kiev bombed regions in the east of Ukraine. DeWereldMorgen.

[9] Wolin, S. (2010).

[10] The full analysis is available in Verbruggen, A. (2022).

[11] More regulations and obligations exist to eliminate or capture pollutants other than CO_2, such as sulphur and nitrogen causing sulfuric acid and nitric acid, nitrogen oxides as elements causing ozone in the environment under the influence of light, hydrocarbon compounds from incomplete combustion such as dioxins, or carcinogenic poly-aromatics. Environmental reports provide information in this regard.

[12] BP (2021).

[13] World Bank percentage figures are used as an illustration in Verbruggen, A. (2021), p. 98, fig 7.3.

[14] Gabriel Mbaga Obiang Lima (president OPEC), Al Jazeera, 1 Feb 2023.

[15] Walsh, L., Ormond-Skeaping, T. (2022).

[16] For the year 2021, the Oil & Gas rents based on World Bank data, is approximately US$1,790 billion in price level 2021. For the year 2022, the International Energy Agency (IEA) estimates it at US$3,750 billion, presumably in price level of 2022, without explaining the method of calculation. Some caution is needed, because of the rising inflation after 2020.

[17] Amounts and prices are always given in purchasing power terms of the year 2020. To avoid confusion, nominal historical prices have not been listed.

[18] Meadows, D. et al. (1972).

[19] WCED (1987).

[20] Friedman, M. (1962).

[21] Democratic societies use the institution of the 'free market' to organise economic activities under the supervision of democratic administrators. Hubeau, B., Cabus, M., eds. (2023), pp. 162-165.

[22] US President Reagan said *"Government is not a solution to problems; government itself is the problem"*. This seems correct vis-à-vis himself as president: these kinds of movie actors are (part of) the problem.

[23] Wolin, S. (2010), p.xi, pp. 8-9, and ch.4.
[24] Adriaensens, D., Iraq: "the biggest corruption scandal in history" (29/1/2021), Iraq: failing state, made in the USA (7/12/2022), DeWereldMorgen.
[25] Only Bernie Sanders and Paul Rand voted against.
[26] Grégoire Lalieu (Investig'Action) informs on the meaning of sanctions, and the creation of a People's Tribunal on sanctions: A creeping killer: economic sanctions could be worse than an atomic bomb, DeWereldMorgen.
[27] See Vanoost, L., Find culprit gas leak Nord Stream - ask logical question: who benefits? DeWereldMorgen (28 September 2022). Vanoost proposes three factors to unravelling international conflicts: "motive, opportunity, and capacity" of the parties involved. The motive factor is also present in Roman criminal law: "*Is fecit cui prodest*" or "*He did it, who benefited*".
[28] On 8 February 2023, Seymour Hersh posts a blog detailing the attack on the North Stream pipelines by the US with support from Norway. Hersh is the investigative journalist who uncovered My Lai (Vietnam 1969) and the Abu Ghraib scandal (Iraq 2004). As before, his 2023 revelations are again relegated to the damned corner by US and Western politicians and mass media. These interests later ballooned thainto a pro-Ukrainian group allegedly carrying out this attack (perhaps when NATO was on holiday to the southern hemisphere for a while?).
[29] Heinberg, R. (2011).
[30] Klare, M. (2012).
[31] Verbruggen, A., Al Marchohi, M. (2010).
[32] BP (2021).
[33] Reserves are a subset of resources.
[34] Think of the bathtub or sink here for a moment: the drain is clogged (the atmosphere can no longer absorb stray greenhouse gases); the tap can supply enough oil & gas, but should be turned off.
[35] For example, Amartya Sen, David Bromley. Apart from these and like-minded economists, I found only few publications on rents in the standard economics literature, except Schoemaker, P.J.H (1990).
[36] Volberda, H.W. et al. (2011).
[37] SIPRI (Stockholm International Peace Research Institute).
[38] Wolin, S. (2010), p. 41.
[39] In 2023, military spending as a percent of GDP, was 37 percent in Ukraine, 8.2 percent in Algeria, 7.1 percent in Saudi Arabia, 5.4 percent in Oman (SIPRI data).

Chapter 6

[1] Hager, C. (2015).
[2] *Masterminding* (Verbruggen, A. (2021)) is a sophisticated form of influencing and steering from a distance, mainly through the deployment of discursive power (Fuchs, D. (2007)). Influential corporates determining energy and climate policy is masterminding, an update of the captured regulation phenomenon described by Stigler (1971), laureate of the 1982 Nobel Prize in economics.

[3] The CDM = Clean Development *Mechanism* was a "Kyoto-twist" of the Clean Development *Fund* requested by India for the developing countries. The emission permits were CER = Certified Emission Rights.

[4] Wara, M. (2007).

[5] Lohmann, L. ed. (2006).

[6] For example: Milton Friedman at Chicago University.

[7] See the essay 'On Liberty' by John Stuart Mill (1806-1873), whosework and wisdom are still relevant today.

[8] It is like banning knives because they also may be used in wounding and murdering others.

[9] Fisher, M. (2009).

[10] See first paragraph of the Preface.

[11] Lang, M. et al. (2024).

[12] Lang, M., Acosta, A, Martinez, E. (2024), p. 108 mention US$2.5 billion for the Philippines atomic plant.

[13] *May 1968* is the name of these movements, which in reality took place over a longer period, in many countries in different ways.

[14] Maurice Strong (Canada), tirelessly active for the environment, co-organiser of the UN Conference on the Environment (Stockholm, 1972). On development, UNCTAD was a framework in which the global South put inequality on the agenda, as was the UN Conference on Monetary Reform (Arusha initiative, 1980). In 1970, the "Treaty against the Proliferation of Nuclear Weapons" (NPT) came into force.

[15] Fisher, M. (2009) dissects this development from a cultural point of view, entirely different from the techno-economic analysis in this book. However, the findings are similar, as is the political intensity of his disenchantment of neoliberalism, making his analysis invigorating rather than depressing.

[16] Verbruggen, A. (2021), pp. 97-100.

[17] WCED (1987).

[18] WCED (1987), p. 51.

[19] The Murdoch media empire as an example.

[20] Spash, C.L. (2017), p. 15.

[21] Latour, B. (2023), pp. 49-50.

[22] Fisher, M. (2009).

[23] Wolin, S. (2010).

[24] UNDP (2019), chapter 3.

[25] Or: $(5\%_{12}) \times 27 = 112.5$.

[26] Hattingh, J. (2024), pp. 148, 154.

[27] Fisher, M. (2009).

[28] Steinberger, J. (2024).

[29] Wolin, S. (2010) p. 268.

[30] Also called an "Ethical Living Minimum Income". This income provides a decent living, covering housing, food, education, mobility, etc. Half of the world's population lacks such an income.

[31] Eich, S. (2022), p. xvii.

[32] Marx, K. called this intermediate token the 'general equivalent'.

[33] To support bartering, communities have also established the institution of 'market', with sellers (supply), buyers (demand), and a public regulator to monitor fair practices. A market is free whether or not participating in it is a free choice without barriers or coercion.

[34] Aristotle's Politica (para 1265) criticises Plato's Laws.

[35] The worst brutal power was that of European colonialism over the rest of the world. The shiploads of looted gold and silver expanded the circulation of money in Europe.

[36] Lang, M. et al. eds (2024).

[37] Lang, M., Acosta, A., Martinez, E. (2024), p. 107.

[38] Marx, K. (1870).

[39] In a historical building is painted on the wall: Money is an adequate servant, yet a perfidious master.

[40] Lietaer, B. (2001) answers the question What is Money? Money is an Agreement, within a community to use something as a Medium of Exchange.

[41] Compliance with the 'gold standard' has been highly variable throughout history. For example, the Roman imperial silver coins had a silver content above 95 percent in the period 31BC- AD100. Afterwards, the content went down to 35 percent in AD 250.

[42] Eich (2022), p.219.

[43] Russia was the other main victor defeating German Nazism, but with more than 20 million casualties and large territories economically and materially devastated, its international capabilities were limited.

[44] Hudson, M. (2023).

[45] Sealed in Belgium by a *Protocol on Productivity* (1954): to produce a bigger economic cake together, while maintaining a balanced distribution of the cake between the parties.

[46] The United Nations Development Programme provides appropriate information about (unequal) development.

[47] Hudson, M. (2023).

[48] Miel Dullaert in DeWereldMorgen: War in Ukraine: Europe falls to its knees (20 March 2023), and BRICS countries want to de-dollarise world trade (30 May 2023).

[49] See the example of the International Atomic Energy Agency [chapter 3].

[50] South-North conference in Arusha, in the year 1980.

[51] Eich (2022), p.191.

[52] K. Marx saw the bank for the poor established by Proudhon in 1848 as a confusion of cause (social power) and effect (the circulation of money).

[53] Eich (2020), p. 195.

[54] Recall Reagan's 1980 statement that "government is the problem", and therefore not an agent to defend the public interest.

[55] TARP (Troubled Asset Relief Program) with a starting fund of US$700 billion, quickly followed by thousands of billions of dollars from the Federal Reserve to purchase the 'troubled assets' of banks and corporations.

[56] Hudson, M. (2023).

[57] Lang, M., Acosta, A., Martinez, E. (2024), p. 105.
[58] Verbruggen, A. (2021), chapter 2.
[59] Walsh, L. & Ormond-Skeaping, T. (2022).
[60] Euro countries also to the ECB, European Central Bank in Frankfurt am Main, Germany.
[61] Kelton, S. (2020).
[62] Lietaer, B. (2001) was a pioneer in explaining how money systems work. He was an authority in the study and development of local currency systems. He died in 2019, but his work is still alive and relevant.
[63] Verbanck, E. Government spending and public debt. DeWereldMorgen 12 April 2023.
[64] Not just the basic goods of food, clothing, housing, transport, but increasingly the goods and services for education, schooling, cultural development, sports practice, etc. Humans do not live to work, but work to live.
[65] Nobel laureate Elinor Ostrom's life's work revolves around developing institutions for the self-governance of community assets. At the heart of her proposals is the balance of individual expenditures against revenues, or in a broader scope: costs against benefits, by all the individual participants in a self-government alliance. Achieving the correct economic-financial balance for each participant is crucial for establishing sustainable arrangements and institutions, allowing self-governance of community assets to work.

Chapter 7

[1] Bernanke, head of the US federal reserve.
[2] With new technologies, the control has been automised on most important public transport lines.
[3] Cited in Daly, H. (1973, 1980), pp. 331-332.
[4] Fisher, M. (2009) p. 29.
[5] Verbruggen, A. (2021), pp. 165-172 Annex B: Cost-benefit analysis in the context of climate change.
[6] Matheson & Howard (1968), p. 11: a decision is an irrevocable allocation of resources, in the sense that it would take additional resources, perhaps prohibitive in amount, to change the allocation.
[7] Cline, W.R. (1992).
[8] Harremoës et al. (2002).
[9] Stirling, A. (2007).
[10] Goldstein, B.E. (2009).
[11] Production factors are energy, materials, labour, services from outside the factory, investment capital and financial services.
[12] Becker, G.S. (1971), p. 3.
[13] Phlips, L. (1983), p. 1, p. 7.
[14] Volberda et al. (2011).
[15] It is *advocacy* because none of the proposed instruments is really working.
[16] Verbruggen, A. (2021), pp. 17-30: chapter 2.

[17] Boiteux, M. (1956).
[18] Permanent means 50 times per second in a 50Hz system, or 3000 times per minute. Practical pricing periods cover 15 minutes or maximum 1 hour.
[19] Verbruggen, A. (2021), annex E, pp. 190-198.
[20] Verbruggen (2021), annex E explains the difference in a mathematical and graphical way.
[21] Organising a trade in daylight is also a void idea.
[22] Sijm, J. et al (2006).
[23] Verbruggen, A. (2009).
[24] Verbruggen, A. (2009).
[25] EPEX (European Power Exchange) is an electricity trading platform, to which a number of European countries are affiliated.
[26] This is: the short-term marginal cost is always equal to the long-term marginal cost.
[27] Parry, I, et al. (2021).

Chapter 8

[1] Stern, N. (2006) receiving wide press coverage.
[2] Verbruggen, A. (2021).
[3] The ECs' name given is *allowance* for the *permit* of 1 ton CO_2 or CO_2-eq emission. Permit refers to *licensed pollution*. ECs' ETS adds property rights for polluters on permits tenable for years, bankable and tradable.
[4] Shell could gain more than €500 million speculation profits via the ETS, assessed by research journalists Luuk Sengers and Evert de Vos (De Groene Amsterdammer, 14 February 2024).
[5] Reynebeau, M. (De Standaard, 14 Dec. 2022) mentions 12,498 registered lobbyist units, with 49,059 staff.
[6] Corporate Europe Observatory (CEO); 'Follow the Money' (NGO of the Netherlands).
[7] In EU policy, comitology is officialised. Committees of EC officials and stakeholders hold regular consultations. The most powerful and richest stakeholders exert greatest influence.
[8] Masterminding: creating a special something, and orchestrating its operation.
[9] The methods estimate future positive and negative cash flows of proposed investments, and balance them, taking into account the year in which the cash flows occur, and the uncertainty about the flows themselves. Dixit, A.K. & Pindyck, R.S. (1994).
[10] The belief is also widespread in Working Group 3 of the IPCC. E.g., Gupta, S. & Tripak, D.A. et al. (2007), pp. 745-807.
[11] The EU Commission's proposal was for a tax (levy) on energy/CO_2 emissions from companies. In 1990: 1 EUR/t of emissions, add 1 EUR/t each subsequent year, up to a maximum of 10 EUR/t. For your information: EUR was replaced by Euro from 1 January 1999; Euro coins and notes arrived from 1 January 2002.
[12] Volberda et al. (2011).
[13] Meckling, J. (2011).

[14] Emissions trading is an abbreviation of emissions permit trading, e.g., Emissions Trading Scheme, System.

[15] Newspeak is a fictional language in George Orwell's book *1984*. It is a language created and controlled by the totalitarian state as a tool to restrict freedom of thought and concepts that threaten the regime (such as freedom, self-expression, individuality and peace). Source: Wikipedia.

[16] The UN Framework Convention on Climate Change (UNFCCC), art. 3.1.

[17] See internet information on Al Gore's speech and also comments on it.

[18] In March 2001, the Bush administration withdrew the US from the Kyoto Protocol, leaving the world saddled with emissions trading, and a crippled climate policy.

[19] Verbruggen, A. (2021), chapter 4, pp. 48-59.

[20] Observed prices at the permit exchanges are not the result of scarcity but of speculation.

[21] European Commission (2000).

[22] Some member states organised a modest exercise with auctioning a small amount of licences.

[23] In Latin: contradictio in terminis.

[24] European Commission (2003).

[25] Voss, J-P. & Simons, A. (2014).

[26] Mazzucato, M. & Collington, R. (2023).

[27] Verbruggen, A. (2021), chapter 6, pp. 73-85.

[28] Patents for *supercritical* coal boilers were filed, increasing the efficiency of the latest coal-fired plants by a few %-points, to around 46-48%. These innovations are *lost spending on the moribund.*

[29] Arcelor Mittal, so far earning money from the ETS, is now receiving subsidies from the Belgian and Flemish governments for investing in technology to reduce emissions.

[30] Pearse, R., Böhm, S. (2014).

[31] For example: Friends of the Earth, Transnational Institute. CEO (Corporate Europe Observatory) is also highly critical.

[32] IRENA.org.

[33] Sijm et al. (2006).

[34] Electricity companies are familiar with speculative operations, as they also carry them out in purchasing fuels for their thermal power plants.

[35] Marcu et al. (2021).

[36] The 'Market Stability Reserve' is an administrative range of surplus permits in stock, providing hints for speculation on the exchange platforms.

[37] The BlueNext platform in Paris was closed in 2010 due to market fraud of 10-20 billion euros (Verbruggen, A. (2021), p. 116). After Brexit, ICE London serves the UK emissions trading in £.

[38] EMBER-energy.org publishes graphs of the posted permit prices.

[39] In phase 3, the annual averages were: 751 million permits auctioned to power generators, and 825 million awarded free to the overall industry, with the share given to power generators decreasing over time.

[40] Cornelis, L. (2019) offers an innovative questioning from law & legislation; Luyendijk, J. (2015) provides a journalistic look from the inside.

[41] European Commission (2021).

[42] Carbon Border Adjustment Mechanism (CBAM) will ensure that imported products will also pay a carbon price at the border in the sectors covered (EC website).

[43] Headlines in a Belgian newspaper: *EU also does non-European companies pay for CO2* (De Standaard, 14 Dec.2022). Misleading EU *also does ... pay*, because European companies don't pay; they get free permits.

[44] Cornerstone of Green Deal *also makes citizens pay* for emissions (De Standaard, 19 Dec.2022). Facts are: industry does not pay, the full bill lands with citizens.

[45] The EU state aid review in 2014 favoured large-scale wind farms and photovoltaic fields at the expense of small-scale projects. Also, the 'Fit for 55' Communication mentions offshore wind, but no word on citizen or cooperative projects. Verbruggen, A. (2021), pp. 70-71.

[46] European Commission. SWD (2021) 601 final, PART 2/4, Annex 3, pp. 103-104.

[47] Ackerman, B.A. & Stewart, R.B. (1988).

[48] This hint is assigned to soccer star Johan Cruijff (the Netherlands).

Chapter 9

[1] Girard, R. (1978). Dutch edition in 1990: What was hidden from the beginning of time ... Kok Agora-DNB, Pelckmans.

[2] On 16 February 2019, Wim Vandenkeybus and Ultima Vez presented the dance theatre *Trap Town* at deSingel (Antwerp). The text mentioned is in the play's notes.

[3] Fisher, M. (2009).

[4] Official statistics state around 6%, triple 2%, by including the 66 percent energy losses of the plants. Obtaining all services with renewable electricity will drastically cut primary energy use. IPCC (2012), Annex II.

[5] WCED (1987).

[6] WCED (1987), p .8.

[7] WCED (1987), pp .43, 44, 55-57.

[8] WCED (1987), pp .43, 48, 49, 51.

[9] WCED (1987), pp .9, 46, 65.

[10] The focus is now more on the 17 SDG – Sustainable Development Goals, not considered as a good alternative by some development experts, e.g., Green, D. (2016), pp. 145-147.

[11] See the *Communication* of the Fit-for-55 package [chapter 8, section 8.7].

[12] Fisher, M. (2009), p. 19.

[13] It is recommended to consider also P for Peace, and for Participation.

[14] In marketing is also referred to 4Ps: 'Product, Place, Promotion, Price'. Suppose the first P of Product is dropped. Does the remaining 3P make any sense?

[15] Title mentions 'fuels'; bio feedstock may partially replace fossil hydrocarbon.

[16] Reuters, 14 June 2022.

[17] In German *Energiewende*.

[18] The exercise of power has four successive stages to move or paralyse individuals: (1) inform/convince; (2) entice/bribe; (3) oblige/coerce; (4) remove/eliminate [chapter 10].

[19] The term *commercial energy* points to its distinction from natural energy such as daylight, wind currents that ventilate, and from *somatic energy* of the human body [chapter 1].

[20] EBES (Sociétés Réunies d'Energie du Bassin de l'Escaut) was a major private producer of electricity in Belgium, alongside INTERCOM and UNERG. In 1990, they merged to form ELECTRABEL, now part of ENGIE (France).

[21] From the 1920s-70s, the cartoon character 'Reddy Kilowatt' introduced people to this then-new phenomenon.

[22] Monopoly-oligopoly giant electricity producers want to shield their 'market' as much as possible.

[23] The Belgian private sector organised its own regulatory system in 1955. Verbruggen, A. (2021), pp. 114-15.

[24] This is ⅓ of the total annual GHG emissions, being 53.79 billion tons CO_2-eq. in 2022.

[25] Brand, U., Wissen, M. (2017).

[26] Lovins, A.B. (1976).

[27] Verbruggen, A. (2021), pp. 97-100.

[28] This is the *rebound effect*. Boulanger, P-M., et al. (2013).

[29] Ingrid Robeyns uses the term 'limitarism', with interesting suggestions about the 'what' and 'why', but less explicit in addressing the 'how' and 'who' questions. Interview, The Correspondent (April 2023).

[30] WCED (1987), p. 44.

[31] Stay Grounded is an action group working for fewer planes, fewer and smaller airports, etc.

[32] Data from S. Gössling, Lund University (Sweden).

[33] Costa, L., et al. (2021).

[34] van den Abbeele, E., ed. (1985), and Barlow, N. et al. eds. (2022).

[35] Daly, H. (1973, 1980).

[36] WCED (1987), p .51.

[37] It could also be named *Omega degrowth*, Ω reflecting the end after up & down.

[38] Jackson, W. & Jensen, R. (2022).

[39] In 2024, the cost of PV power from utility installations was 4.3 US$ ct. per kWh.

[40] IRENA (2025), p.15.

[41] Capacity factor = (kWh annual production of an installation)/ (maximum possible annual production being the capacity in kW * 8760 hours (= hours in a standard year)).

[42] A wink to the token of Extinction Rebellion.

[43] See Ruggero Schleicher-Tappeser (2022) for the advances in battery technology.

[44] 'Road pricing' means payments determine priority in using roads, substitute for 'first come, first served' in road queues.

[45] At the turn of the century, deep renovation was problematic. Good materials and techniques were lacking, and administrative regulations hampered demo projects. Anno 2025, the situation is the opposite.

[46] Schleicher-Tappeser, R. (2022).

[47] Verbruggen, A. (2021), ch. 8, pp. 151-154.

[48] IEA (2024) Integrating Solar and Wind. Global experience and emerging challenges.

Chapter 10

[1] Böhm, S., Sullivan, S. eds. (2021) offer various contributions from the social sciences.

[2] Girard, R. (1978), Achterhuis, H. (1988), Van Bladel, L. (1989).

[3] Hardy, J.S. (2014).

[4] Fisher, M. (2009).

[5] Latour, B. (2024).

[6] The information on Maslow's contribution is based on McLeod, S. (2023), and on a Feb. 24, 2020 paper by Elizabeth Hopper: https://www.thoughtco.com/maslows-hierarchy-of-needs-4582571.

[7] This income provides a decent living, with basic amenities in terms of housing, food, education, mobility, etc. Half the world's population does not have this necessary income.

[8] See Preface, figure 2, factor Ideas.

[9] This means: the have-be dualities are distributed like a normal Bell-shaped density function. One tip of the Bell-shape covers the extreme '100% to be' minority, the other tip the extreme '100% to have' minority. Between the opposite tips, the Bell's body holds the vast majority of more equilibrated 'to be/to have' blends.

[10] During a protracted dockers' strike in 1973, I observed close by the prominence of dignity and solidarity, the emergence of natural leaders, the shortfall in conceptual frames and in forward dynamic vision and planning.

[11] Fromm (1976), p. 138.

[12] Fromm (1976), final ch.9, pp. 151-175, quote p. 151.

[13] Bamberg, S. (2023), p. 387.

[14] Based on Fromm (1976), pp. 154, 157.

[15] Fromm (1976), p. 158.

[16] Fromm (1976), p. 161.

[17] Fromm (1976), pp. 166, 168, 169.

[18] Wolin, S. (2010), p. 26.

[19] Wolin, S. (2010), p. 30.

[20] Wolin, S. (2010), chapter 3, pp. 41-68.

[21] Wolin, S. (2010), p. 10.

[22] Wolin, S. (2010), p. 48.

[23] Wolin, S. (2010), p. 49.

[24] Wolin, S. (2010), p. 78.

[25] Wolin, S. (2010), p. 7.

[26] Wolin, S. (2010), pp. 289-292.

[27] My underscores.

[28] McCormick, K. et al. (2023).

[29] Lang, M. et al. (2024).

[30] Paterson, M. (2021).

[31] Stern, N. (2006).

[32] Norgaard, K. (2011).

[33] Paterson, M. (2021), p.27; his terminology is purification versus complexity; he substitutes *and* for *versus*.

[34] Palm, J. (2023).

[35] Ajl, M. (2021).

[36] Lang, M. et al. (2024).

[37] Steinberger, J. (2024) The Atlas Network: What we are up against. https://jksteinberger.medium.com/what-we-are-up-against-2290ba8c4b5.

[38] Avelino, F. (2021).

[39] Green, D. (2016), pp. 28-46.

[40] Wolin, S. (2010), pp. 222-224.

[41] Verbruggen, A. (2021), pp. 122-127.

[42] Could it be that stock-stakeholders rule transition arenas? in Brunnengräber, A. and Di Nucci, M., ed. (2014), pp. 119-131.

[43] van Liefferinge, G. (2022).

[44] E.g., Shireen Abu Akleh, Palestinian journalist murdered on 11 May 2022 by Israeli occupation forces. This murder is part of the Zionist genocide on the Palestinians. Israel is a chosen ally of the EU - including you?

[45] The proverb *"Even if the lie flies fast, the truth will always catch up with it"* is not appeasing: the lie causes a lot of damage in the meantime, and when the harm is done, the truth comes too late.

[46] De Moor, T. (2023).

[47] Cornelis, L. (2019).

[48] Hammond, M. (2020).

[49] Gatersleben, B., Murtagh, N., eds. (2023).

[50] Hillel refers to self-care in his famous quote: *If I am not for myself, who will be for me? If I am only for myself, what am I? And if not now, when?*

[51] Hardin (1968) proposed to use transient goodwill for installing *mutual coercion, mutually agreed upon.*

[52] Gardiner, S.M., Weisbach, D.A. (2016) evaluate self-interest from an ethical perspective.

[53] Fromm (1976), p. 60.

[54] This behaviour is called 'free riding'. The 'prisoners' dilemma' describes the choice of individuals to cooperate or not. Cooperation ultimately produces the best outcomes for the parties involved.

[55] Often stated as unlimited power exercised by one person, as in Hobbes' Leviathan.

[56] Thiel, A. et al. (2019).

[57] Teles, F. ed. (2023), pp. 3, 27.

[58] Bouckaert, G. (2023) Effective local governance, in Teles, F. ed. (2023), pp. 26-38.

[59] Marxists may see this as successful appropriation of the most essential means of production by the people.

[60] Wahlund, M., Palm, J. (2022).
[61] Ostrom, E. (1990, 2005, 2014).
[62] Elinor Ostrom systematised the methodology for 'Institutional Analysis and Development'.
[63] Hardin, G. (1968).
[64] Ostrom, E. (1990), pp. 42-45.
[65] Can you personally imagine, walking in a nature reserve you point out to other hikers the rules mentioned at the entrance to the reserve, such as keeping their dog on a leash.
[66] Brown, D.A., Gwiazdon, K. and, Westra, L. eds. (2024), p. 1.
[67] Ibana, R.A. (2024), p. 31.
[68] Hattingh, J. (2024), p. 148.
[69] Hattingh, J. (2024), p. 154.
[70] Gardiner, S.M. (2024), pp. 38, 40.
[71] Gardiner, S.M. (2024), pp. 45-47.
[72] UNESCO (2016), pp. 76-97.
[73] UNESCO (2016), pp .80.
[74] UNESCO (2016), pp .83-85.
[75] UNESCO (2016), pp. 86-87.
[76] UNESCO (2016), p. 92.
[77] UNESCO (2016), p. 95.

Transformation viewpoints

[1] For example: legal and regulatory perspectives would be very welcome.
[2] Volberda, H.W. et al. (2011).
[3] Amblard, P. (2017) Saint Jean, L'Apocalypse, Illustrée par La Tapisserie d'Angers, commentée par Paule Amblard. Editions Diane de Selliers, Paris.
[4] Bourdieu, J, Heilbron, J. eds. (2024) discuss Pierre Bourdieu's contributions on reflexivity by social scientists.
[5] Lang, M. et al., eds. (2024).
[6] Brand, U., Wissen, M. (2017).
[7] Norgaard, K. (2011).
[8] IPCC Working Group I and II reports (www.ipcc.ch); Rockström et al. (2009); daily media, like Al Jazeera.
[9] Fromm, E. (1976).
[10] Amblard, P. (2017). Her recital of the biblical text, with the tapestry of Angers (France) as direction, is remarkable. She opens the wealth of the original text, and clarifies the enrichments on the tapestries. For example, prolific displays of Pythagoras' bivium Y-symbol, reminding that a person is continuously confronted by the choice between good and evil.
[11] 1% of the world's population, or about 80 million people.
[12] About 10% of the world's population, which includes politicians, officials of international bureaucracies and national governments, service providers to the superrich and their excessive lifestyle, including private jets, superyachts, mansions, ... up to space tourism.

[13] Pre-historic climate events and collapses are of little relevance to today's Anthropocene.

[14] Preface, figure 1.

[15] Chapter 6, section 6.2.

[16] Chapter 5.

[17] Wolin, S. (2010).

[18] Wolin, S. (2010), p. 96.

[19] In the past, successful movements for profound change relied on experiences and insights articulated in a coherent whole (Fromm, E. (1976), Ch.7 Religion, Character and Society, pp.115-144). Three monotheistic religions provide notable examples: Torah, Bible, Koran.

[20] Meadows, D. (1999), p. 18.

[21] Fromm, E. (1976), p. 118-19.

[22] Meadows, D. (1999) pp. 17-18 argues that new systems arise out of the mindset or paradigm, being the real influential leverage point.

[23] Kuhn, T. (1962).

[24] Verbruggen, A. (2021), chapter 2.

[25] Chapters 1 and 2, figures 3 and 5.

[26] Electric driven vehicles are exemplary. Chapter 9, figure 17 summarises the substitution.

[27] 18bn is half of the 36bn energy-related CO_2 emissions per year, 3/4 of all GHG emissions.

[28] Chapter 3 shows the source and sink flabs for the atomic plants.

[29] The technology is of the family of technologies that made mobile phones cheap super-devices.

[30] Mill, J.S. (1859) On Liberty.

[31] Wolin, S. (2010), pp. 9-10.

[32] Chapters 3 and 4.

[33] Wolin, S. (2010).

[34] Verbruggen, A. (2021), chapter 8.

[35] Lietaer, B. (2001).

[36] Bernanke, B. (2009), then head of the US Federal Reserve.

[37] Kelton, S. (2020).

[38] Fischer, M. (2009), p.2 states *It is easier to imagine the end of the world than it is to imagine the end of capitalism*, referring to Frederic Jameson and Slavoj Žižek.

[39] Wolin, S. (2010), p. 290.

[40] The French names are: Avoir, Pouvoir, Valoir, Savoir.

[41] Arusha South-North Conference (1980): chapter 10, section 1.

[42] Clear examples are elections in the US, from the president to a majority of Senate and House members.

[43] Fischer, M. (2009), p. 2.

[44] Fischer, M. (2009), p. 81.

[45] See chapter 10, section 4 against Wolin's pessimism.

[46] Daly, H. (1973, 1980).

[47] UNESCO (2016), pp. 87-88.

[48] Latour, B. (2022).

[49] Daly, H.E., ed. (1973, 1980).

[50] WCED (1987), p. 51.

[51] UNESCO (2016) and the World Commission on the Ethics of Scientific Knowledge and Technology COMEST.

[52] Brown, D.A., Gwiazdon, K., Westra, L. eds (2024).

[53] UNESCO (2016), p. 85.

[54] Gardiner, S.M. (2024), pp. 38, 40.

[55] UNESCO (2016), pp. 83-93.

[56] Universal Declaration of Human Rights.

[57] Ibana, R.A. (2024), p. 31.

[58] Hattingh, J. (2024).

[59] Gardiner, S.M. (2024), p. 47

[60] The Universal Declaration of Human Rights (1948) art.25.

[61] UNESCO (2016), p. 83.

[62] Verbruggen, A. (2013).

[63] Zarathustra identified these four indispensable elements.

[64] Girard, R. (1978).

[65] Jackson, W., Jensen, J. (2022), pp. 43-44.

[66] Manahan, M.A. (2024).

[67] UNESCO (2016), pp. 89-90.

[68] UNESCO (2016), p. 92.

[69] UNESCO (2016), Principle #10, pp. 91-93.

[70] The Universal Declaration of Human Rights (1948), preamble.

[71] Norgaard, K.M. (2011).

[72] Meadows, D. (1999), p. 18.

[73] Thomas Kuhn's recommendations as summarised by Donella Meadows (1999), p. 18.

[74] Fromm, E. (1976).

[75] Ostrom (1990, 2005); Teles, F. ed. (2023), Thiel, A. et al. Eds (2019).

[76] Hager, C. (2015) is used as the main information source.

[77] UNESCO (2016), pp. 86-87.

[78] Ostrom, E. (1990), Ostrom, E. (2005).

[79] Elinor Ostrom systematised the methodology for 'Institutional Analysis and Development'.

[80] Teles, F. ed. (2023), pp. 3, 27.

[81] Bouckaert, G. (2023) Effective local governance, in Teles, F. ed. (2023), pp. 26-38.

[82] See chapter 10, section 10.7.

[83] Wolin, S. (2010).

[84] Wolin, S. (2010), p. 48.

[85] Lane, R.E. (2000).

[86] UNESCO (2016), p. 89.

[87] Chapter 10, section 5.

[88] Angers (West of Paris) houses the Middle-aged Apocalypse tapestries in the city's impressive castle. The 1950s Le Chant du Monde tapestries of Jean Lurçat are exposed in the 12th century St. John hospital. Most of the Apocalypse tapestries show the exile St. John as an outside observer of the revealed stories.

www.ingramcontent.com/pod-product-compliance
Lightning Source LLC
Chambersburg PA
CBHW040141270326
41928CB00023B/3289